樋口大輔

I made it to the World Cup! Compared with last year, when I had no idea about what my future held, the difference is like heaven and earth. Indeed, you never know what to expect in life. That's why it's fun, isn't it? Now I know I could not have come this far alone. This has been possible because I have friends who scold, encourage and help me as I go. I pick up my pen every day hoping that Shô will become a friend like that to you.

- Daisuke Higuchi

Daisuke Higuchi's manga career began in 1992 when the artist was honored with third prize in the 43rd Osamu Tezuka Award. In that same year, Higuchi debuted as creator of a romantic action story titled **Itaru**. In 1998, **Weekly Shonen Jump** began serializing **Whistle!** Higuchi's realistic soccer manga became an instant hit with readers and eventually inspired an anime series, debuting on Japanese TV in May of 2002. The artist is currently working on a yet-to-be-published new series.

WHISTLE!
VOL. 2: ON YOUR MARKS

The SHONEN JUMP Manga Edition

STORY AND ART BY
DAISUKE HIGUCHI

English Adaptation/Marv Wolfman
Translation/Naomi Kokubo
Touch-Up Art & Lettering/Mark Griffin
Cover, Graphics & Layout/Sean Lee
Editor/Eric Searleman

Editor in Chief, Books/Alvin Lu
Editor in Chief, Magazines/Marc Weidenbaum
VP of Publishing Licensing/Rika Inouye
VP of Sales/Gonzalo Ferreyra
Sr. VP of Marketing/Liza Coppola
Publisher/Hyoe Narita

Printed in the U.S.A.

Published by VIZ Media, LLC
P.O. Box 77010 • San Francisco, CA 94107

SHONEN JUMP Manga Edition
10 9 8 7 6 5 4 3 2
First printing, October 2004
Second printing, August 2007

www.viz.com

THE WORLD'S
MOST POPULAR MANGA

www.shonenjump.com

PARENTAL ADVISORY
WHISTLE! is rated A and is
suitable for readers of all ages.
ratings.viz.com

WHISTLE!

Vol. 2

On Your Marks

Story and Art by Daisuke Higuchi

SHŌ KAZAMATSURI

Josui Junior High

● **Soccer Team Forward**

KŌ KAZAMATSURI

YŪKO KATORI

TATSUYA MIZUNO

Josui Junior High

● **Soccer Team Middle Fielder**

C H A R A C T E R S

KATSURŌ SHIBUSAWA

Musashinomori

Soccer Team
 Famous Goal
 Keeper

SEIJI FUJISHIRO

Musashinomori

Soccer Team
Ace Striker

SHIGEKI SATŌ

Josui Junior High

Soccer Team
 Temporary Goal
 Keeper

*N*OT WILLING TO GIVE UP HIS DREAM, SHŌ KAZAMATSURI, A SUBSTITUTE PLAYER AT MUSASHINOMORI (A SCHOOL KNOWN FOR ITS EXCELLENT SOCCER TEAM), TRANSFERS TO JOSUI JUNIOR HIGH, IN ORDER TO PLAY SOCCER.

BUT ON THE FIRST DAY AT HIS NEW SCHOOL, SHŌ IS DISGRACED IN FRONT OF EVERYONE...THUS HUMILIATING HIM INTO STARTING INTENSE PRACTICE SESSIONS ON HIS OWN.

AT THE SAME TIME, TATSUYA, WHO HAS BEEN DIS-SATISFIED WITH THE CONDITION OF THE SOCCER TEAM, EXPLODES WITH ANGER. AFTER THE LOWER-CLASS STUDENT TEAM WINS AGAINST THE UPPER-CLASS STUDENT TEAM IN A MINI-GAME, THE SOCCER TEAM IS TRANSFORMED, WITH TATSUYA AND SHŌ AS ITS DRIVING FORCES. RESENTING TATSUYA, THE UPPER-CLASS STUDENTS QUIT THE TEAM, LEAVING THEM REDUCED TO ONLY SEVEN PLAYERS, AND...?!

S T O R Y

WHISTLE!

Vol. 2
On Your Marks

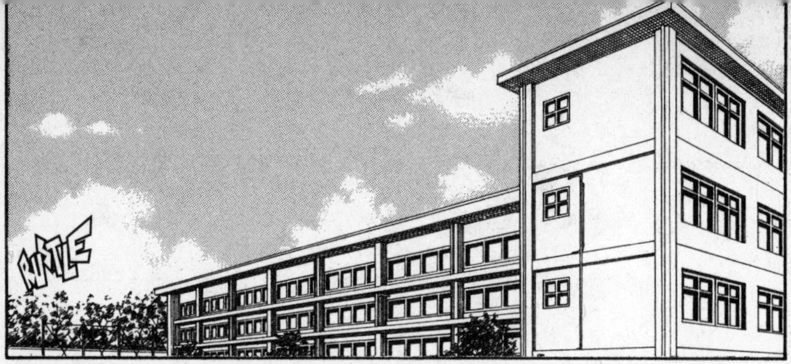
RUSTLE

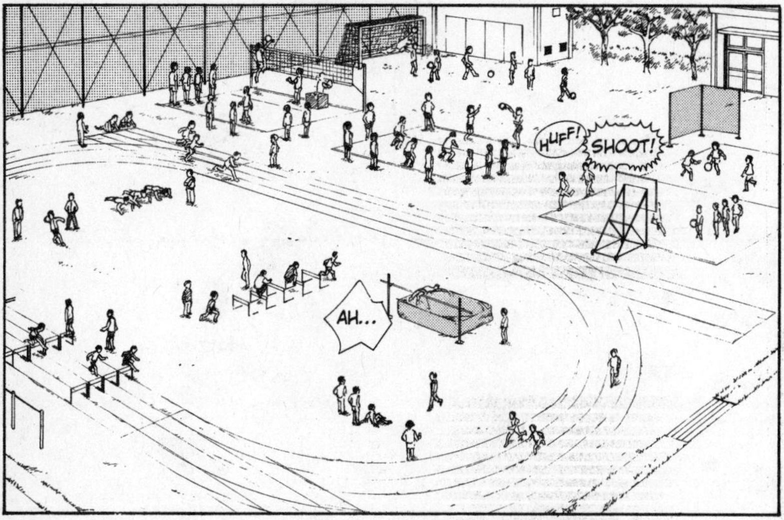
SHOOT!
HUFF!
AH...

STAGE.8 THE TASTE OF ODEN

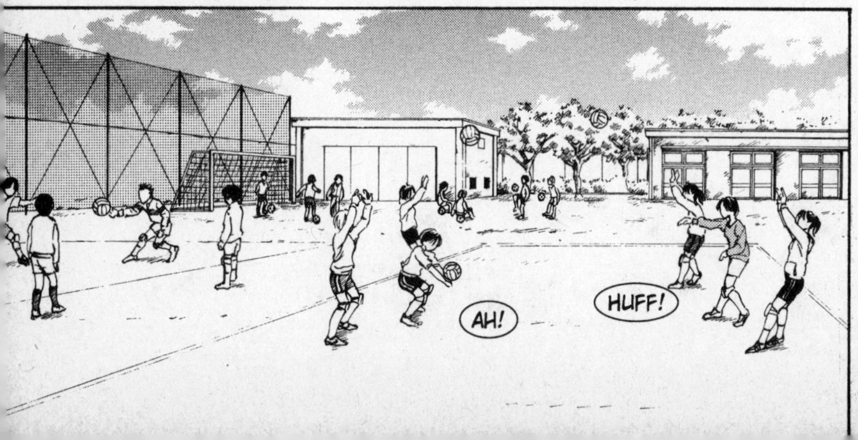
HUFF!
AH!

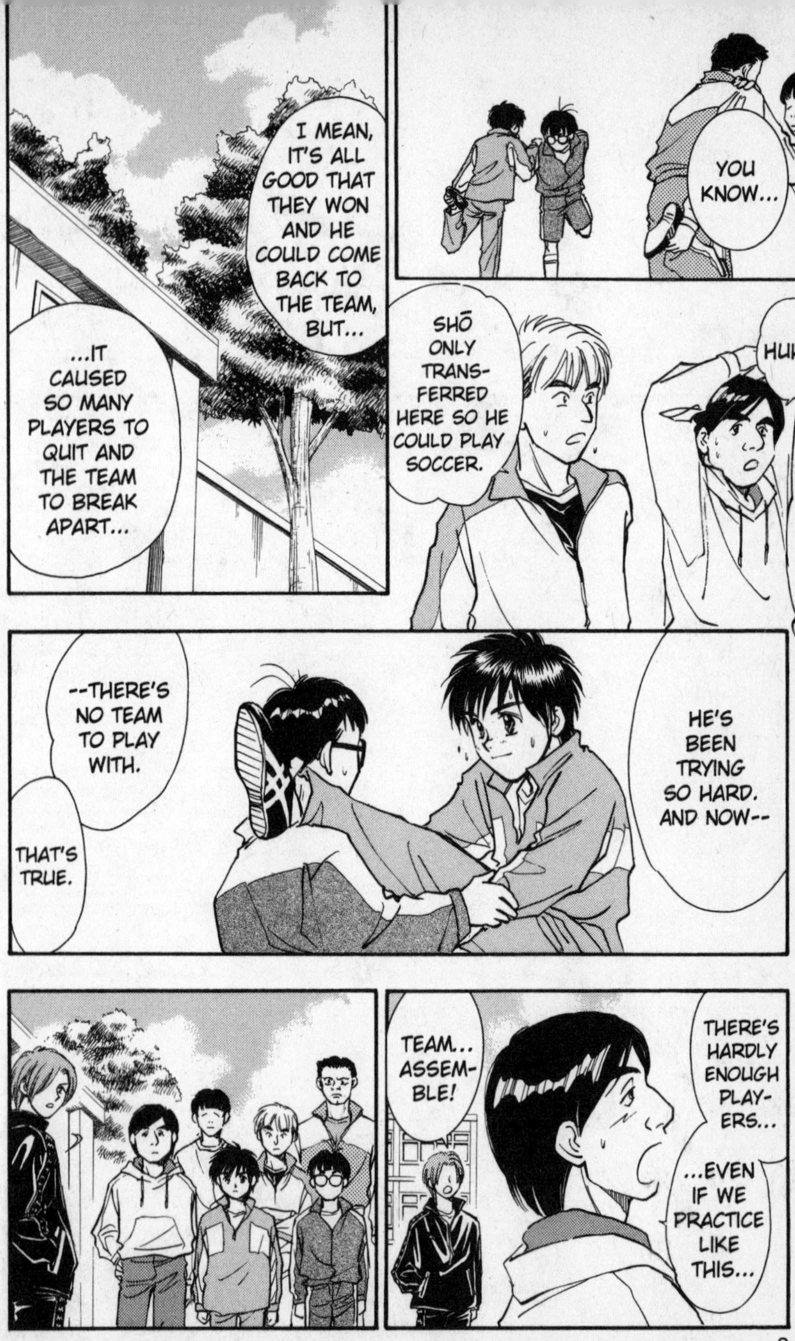
YOU KNOW...
HUH?
SHŌ ONLY TRANSFERRED HERE SO HE COULD PLAY SOCCER.
I MEAN, IT'S ALL GOOD THAT THEY WON AND HE COULD COME BACK TO THE TEAM, BUT...
...IT CAUSED SO MANY PLAYERS TO QUIT AND THE TEAM TO BREAK APART...
HE'S BEEN TRYING SO HARD. AND NOW--
--THERE'S NO TEAM TO PLAY WITH.
THAT'S TRUE.
THERE'S HARDLY ENOUGH PLAYERS...
...EVEN IF WE PRACTICE LIKE THIS...
TEAM... ASSEMBLE!

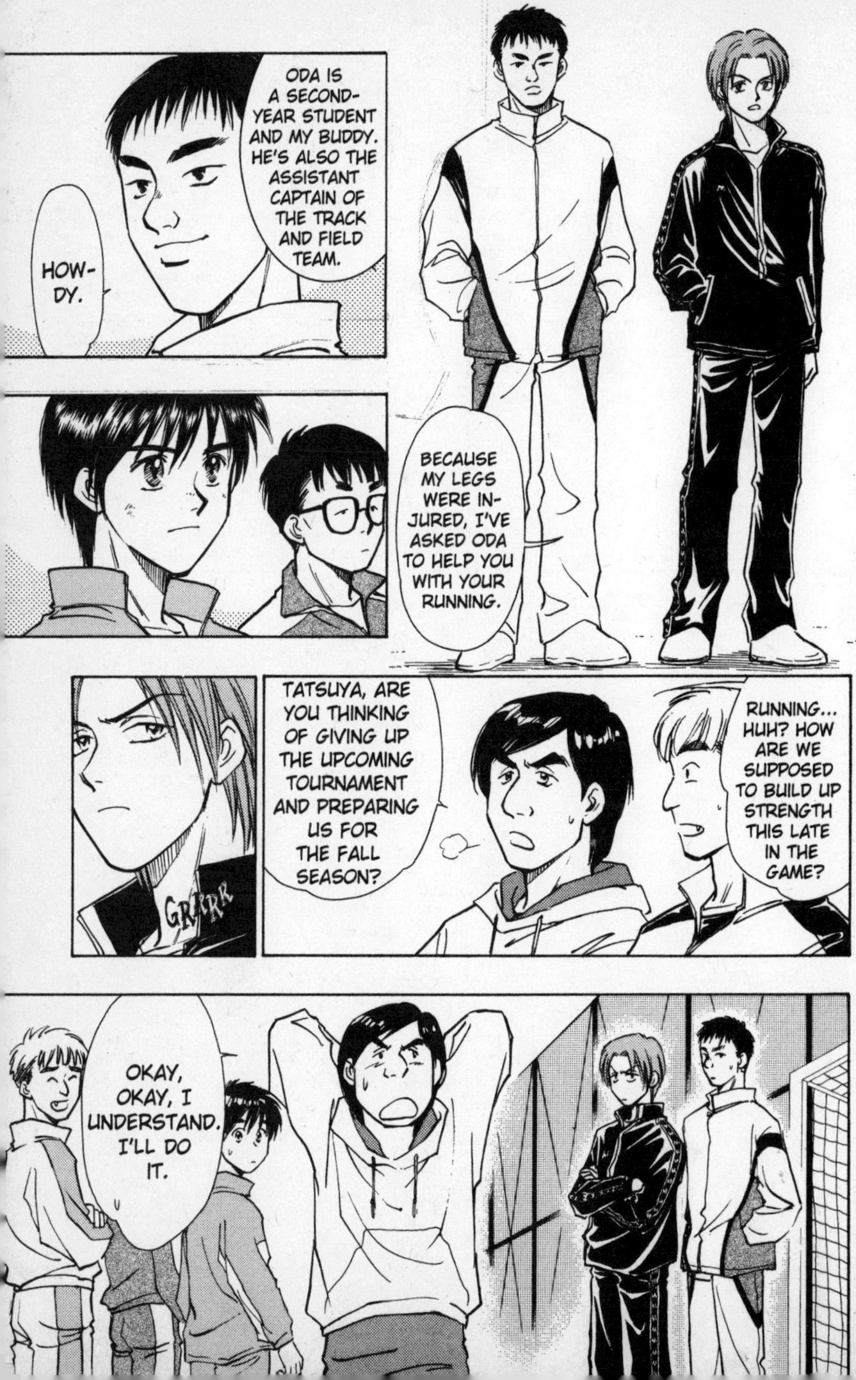
ODA IS A SECOND-YEAR STUDENT AND MY BUDDY. HE'S ALSO THE ASSISTANT CAPTAIN OF THE TRACK AND FIELD TEAM.
HOW-DY.
BECAUSE MY LEGS WERE IN-JURED, I'VE ASKED ODA TO HELP YOU WITH YOUR RUNNING.
GRRRR
TATSUYA, ARE YOU THINKING OF GIVING UP THE UPCOMING TOURNAMENT AND PREPARING US FOR THE FALL SEASON?
RUNNING... HUH? HOW ARE WE SUPPOSED TO BUILD UP STRENGTH THIS LATE IN THE GAME?
OKAY, OKAY, I UNDERSTAND. I'LL DO IT.

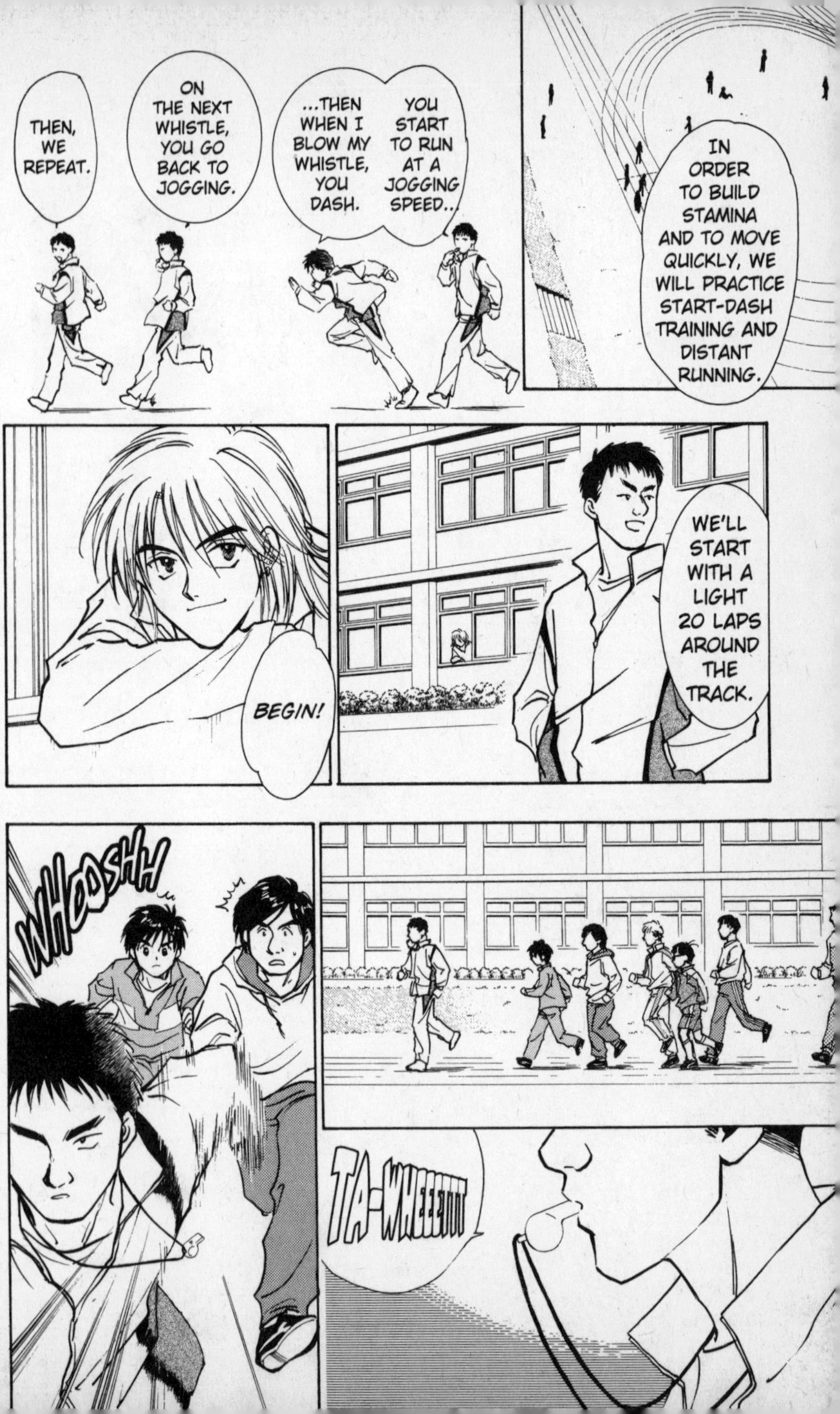
IN ORDER TO BUILD STAMINA AND TO MOVE QUICKLY, WE WILL PRACTICE START-DASH TRAINING AND DISTANT RUNNING.
YOU START TO RUN AT A JOGGING SPEED...
...THEN WHEN I BLOW MY WHISTLE, YOU DASH.
ON THE NEXT WHISTLE, YOU GO BACK TO JOGGING.
THEN, WE REPEAT.
WE'LL START WITH A LIGHT 20 LAPS AROUND THE TRACK.
BEGIN!
TA-WHEEEETTT
WHOOSHH

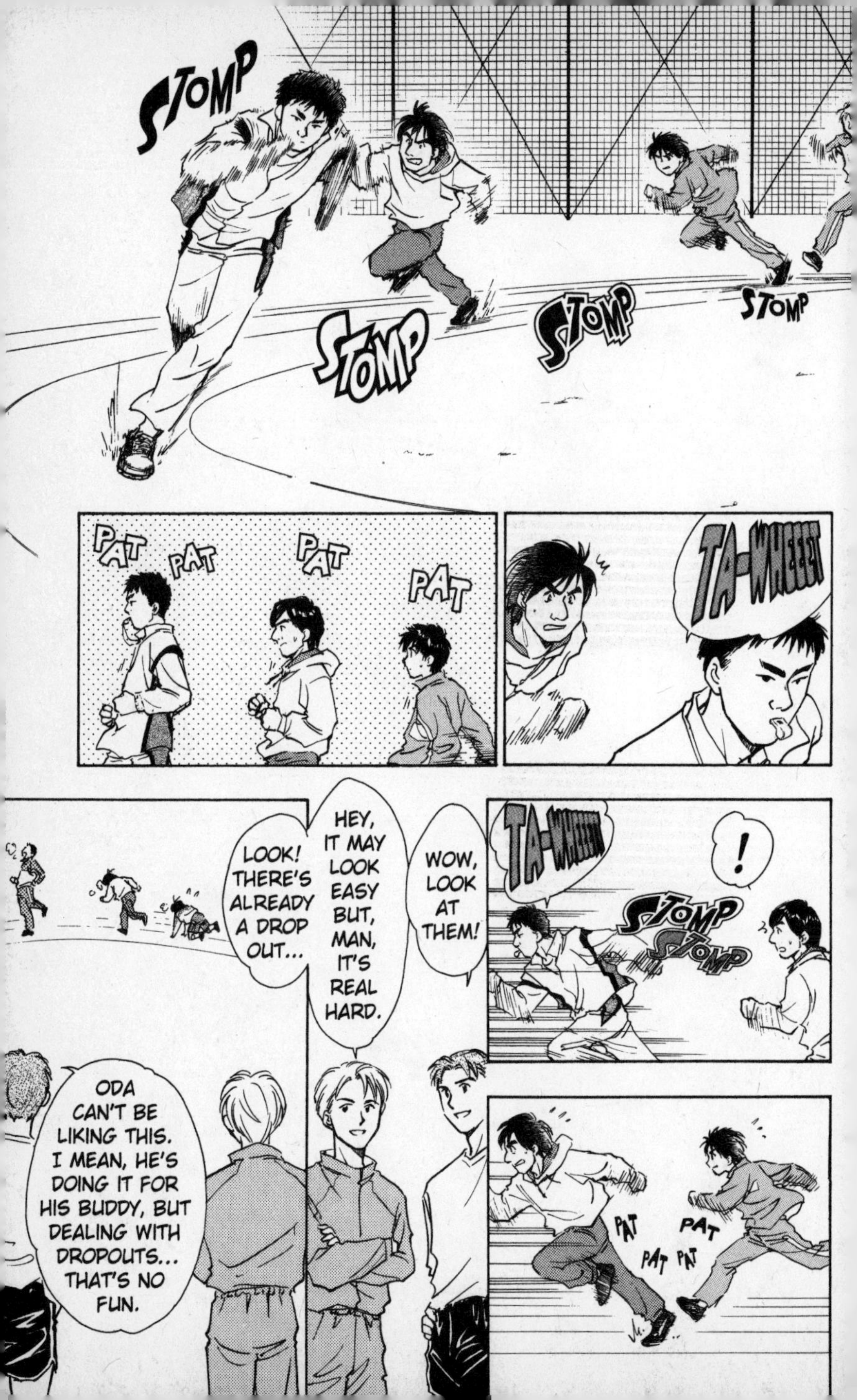
STOMP
STOMP
STOMP
STOMP
TA-WHEEEET
PAT
PAT
PAT
PAT
TA-WHEEEET
!
STOMP
STOMP
WOW, LOOK AT THEM!
HEY, IT MAY LOOK EASY BUT, MAN, IT'S REAL HARD.
LOOK! THERE'S ALREADY A DROP OUT...
PAT
PAT
PAT
PAT
ODA CAN'T BE LIKING THIS. I MEAN, HE'S DOING IT FOR HIS BUDDY, BUT DEALING WITH DROPOUTS... THAT'S NO FUN.

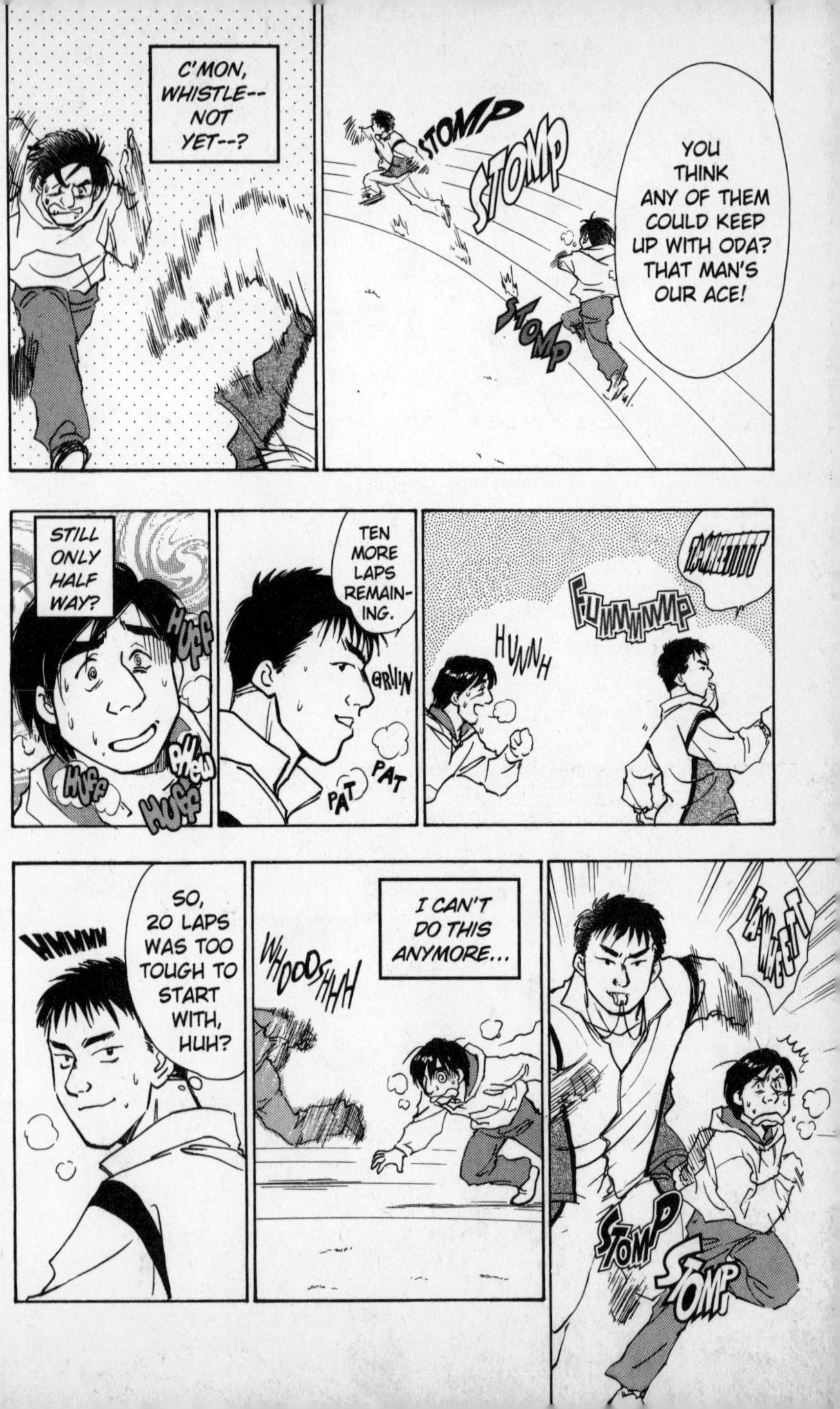
C'MON, WHISTLE-- NOT YET--?
STOMP
STOMP
STOMP
YOU THINK ANY OF THEM COULD KEEP UP WITH ODA? THAT MAN'S OUR ACE!
STILL ONLY HALF WAY?
HUFF
PHEW
HUFF
HUFF
TEN MORE LAPS REMAIN-ING.
GRIN
PAT
PAT
HUNNH
SO, 20 LAPS WAS TOO TOUGH TO START WITH, HUH?
HMMMM
I CAN'T DO THIS ANYMORE...
WHOOOSHHH
STOMP
STOMP

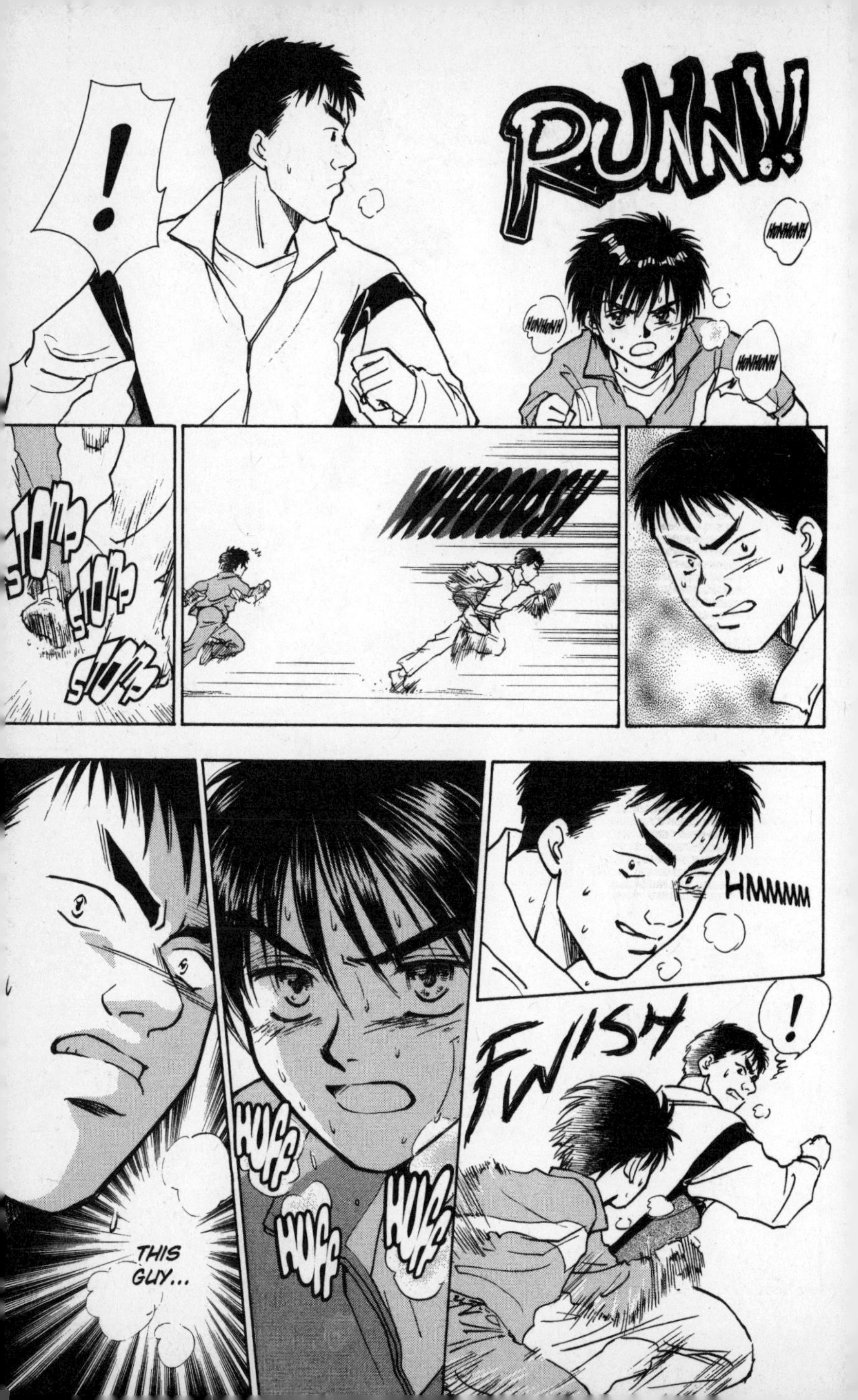
RUNN!!
HONHONH
HONHONH
HONHONH
!
WHOOOSH
STOMP
STOMP
STOMP
HMMMMM
!
FWISH
HUFF
HUFF
HUFF
THIS GUY...

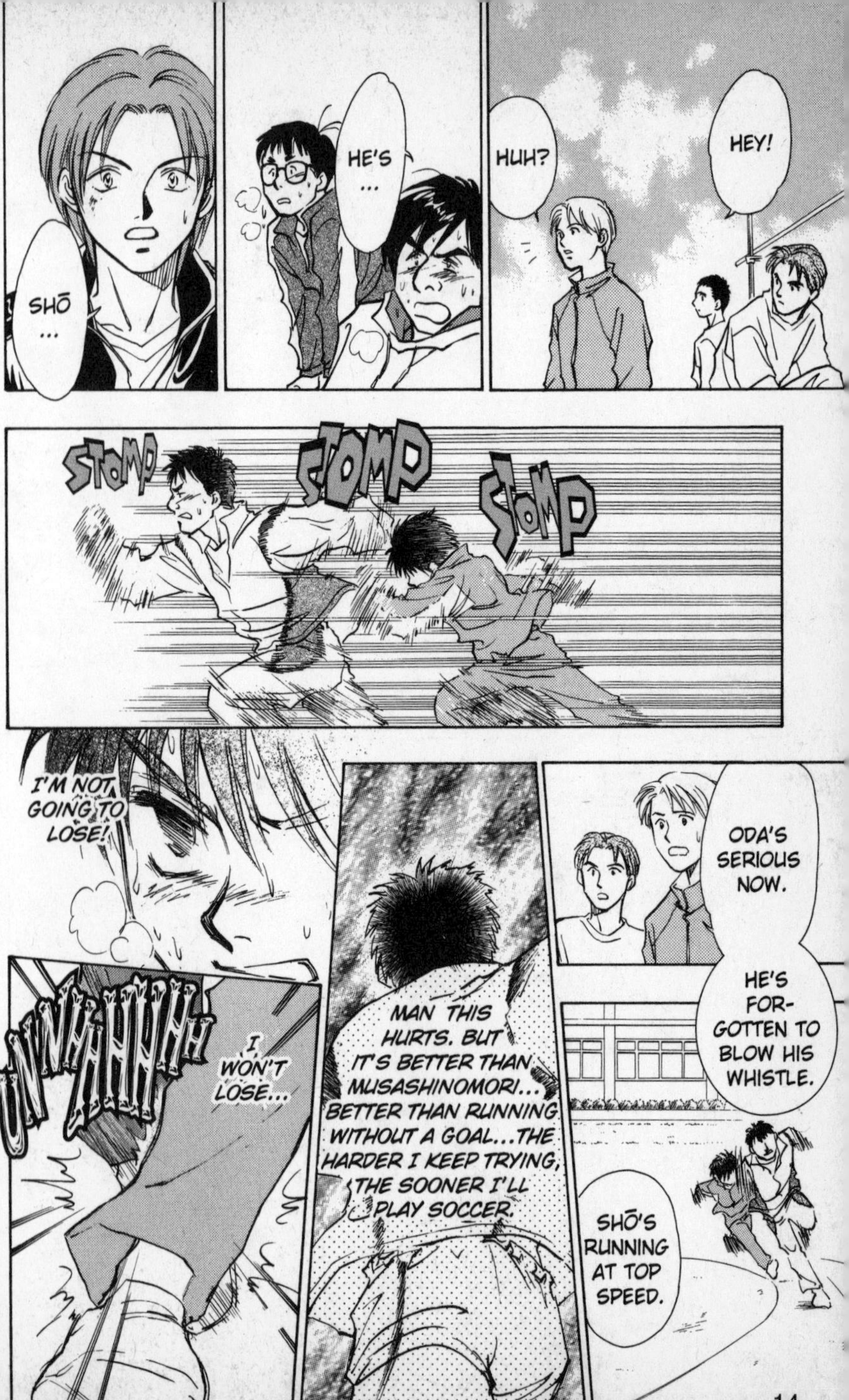
HEY!
HUH?
HE'S ...
SHŌ ...
STOMP
STOMP
STOMP
ODA'S SERIOUS NOW.
HE'S FOR-GOTTEN TO BLOW HIS WHISTLE.
SHŌ'S RUNNING AT TOP SPEED.
MAN THIS HURTS. BUT IT'S BETTER THAN MUSASHINOMORI... BETTER THAN RUNNING WITHOUT A GOAL...THE HARDER I KEEP TRYING, THE SOONER I'LL PLAY SOCCER.
I'M NOT GOING TO LOSE!
UNNAHHHHH
I, WON'T LOSE...

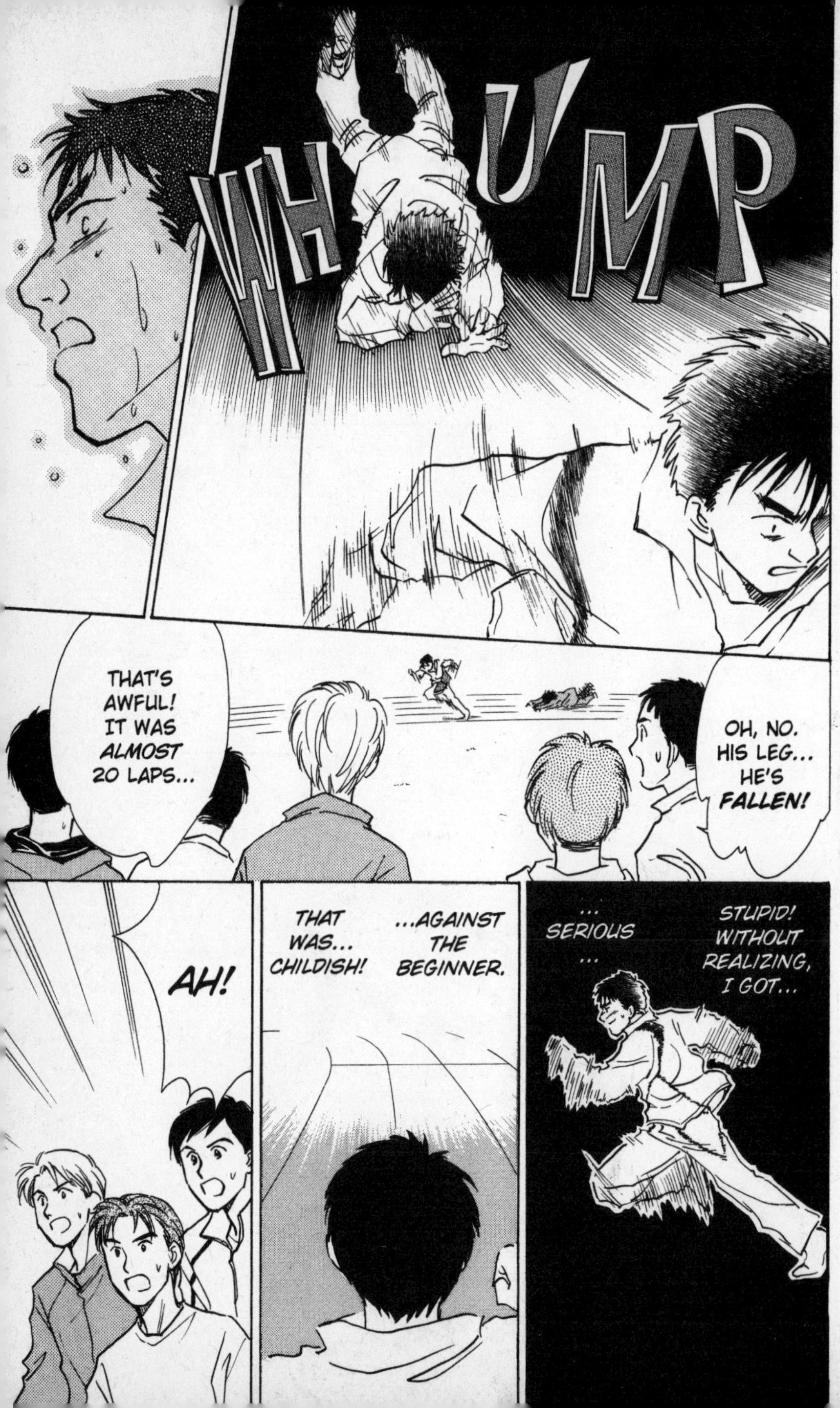
WHUMP
THAT'S AWFUL! IT WAS ALMOST 20 LAPS...
OH, NO. HIS LEG... HE'S FALLEN!
AH!
THAT WAS... CHILDISH!
...AGAINST THE BEGINNER.
STUPID! WITHOUT REALIZING, I GOT...
... SERIOUS ...

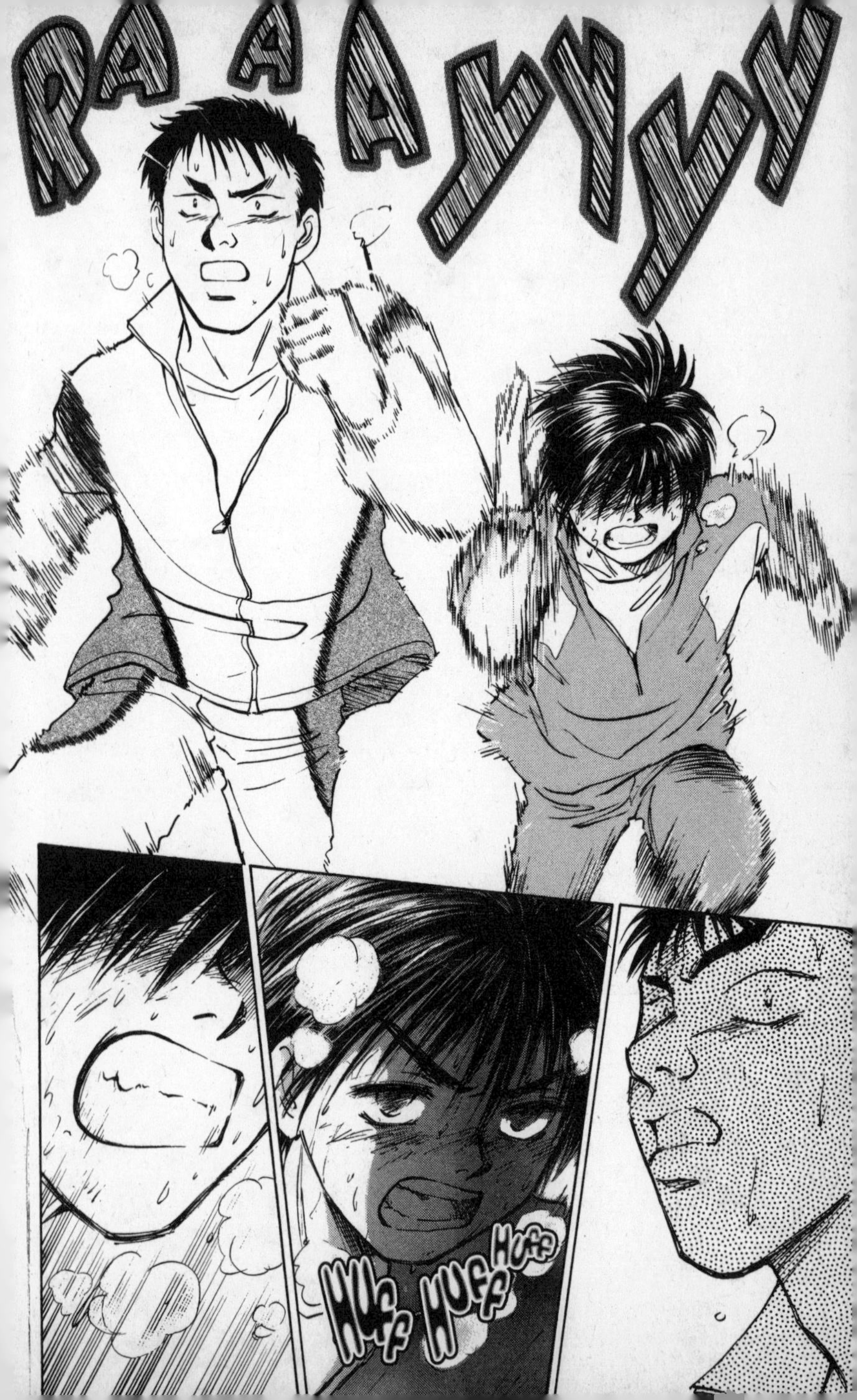
RAAAYYYY
HUFF HUFF HUFF

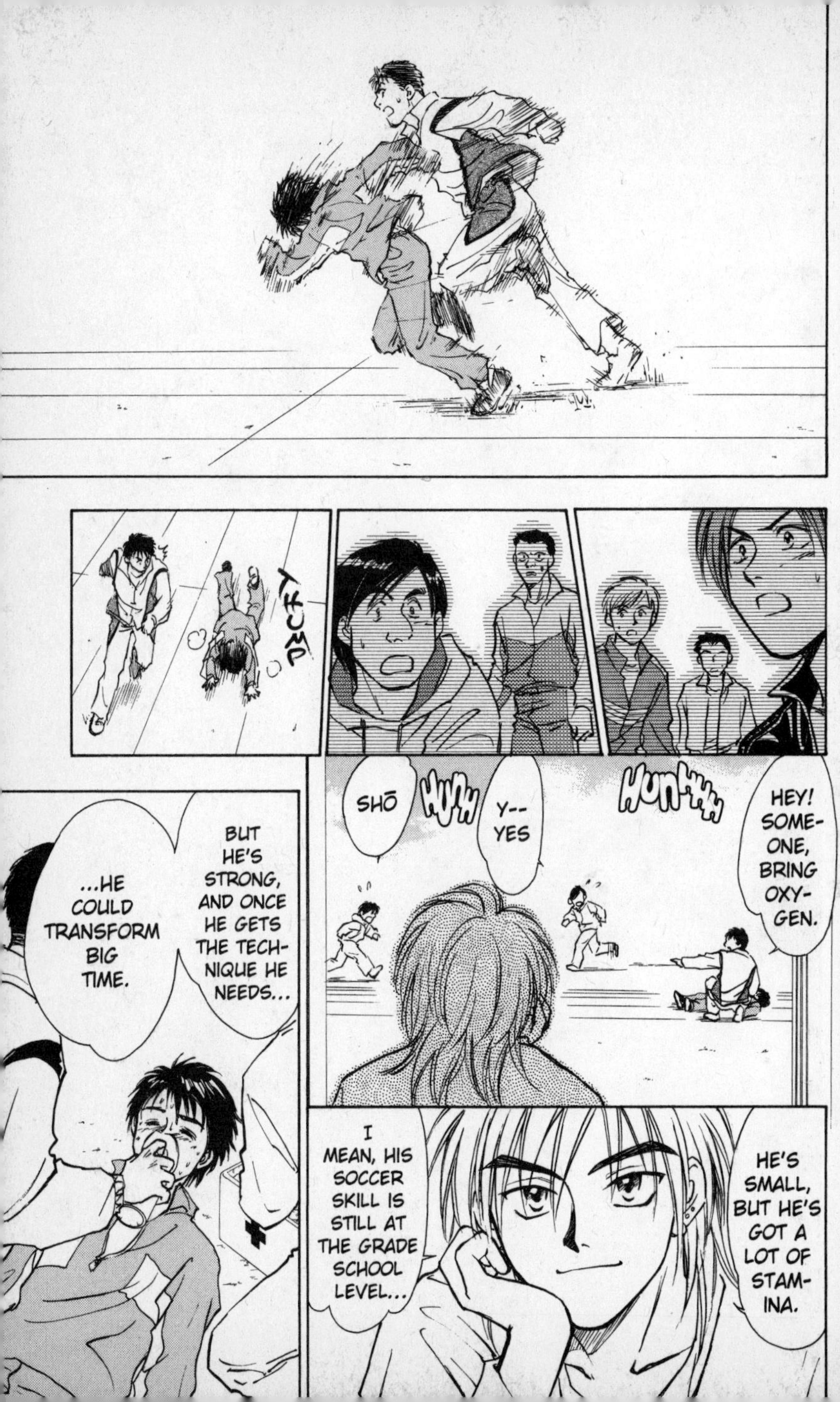
THUMP
HEY! SOME-ONE, BRING OXY-GEN.
HUNHHH
Y--YES
HUNH
SHŌ
HE'S SMALL, BUT HE'S GOT A LOT OF STAM-INA.
I MEAN, HIS SOCCER SKILL IS STILL AT THE GRADE SCHOOL LEVEL...
BUT HE'S STRONG, AND ONCE HE GETS THE TECH-NIQUE HE NEEDS...
...HE COULD TRANSFORM BIG TIME.

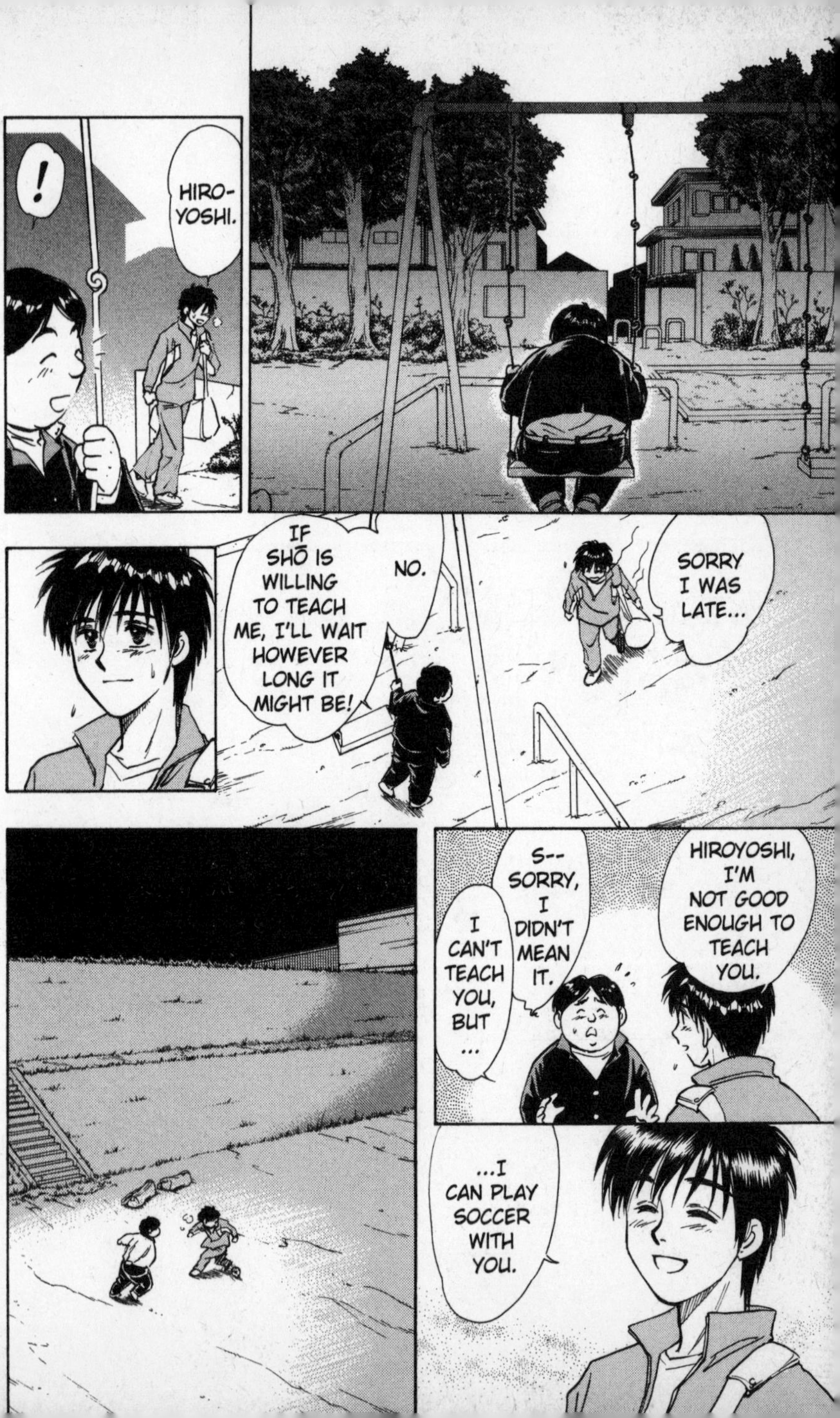
!
HIRO-YOSHI.
SORRY I WAS LATE...
NO.
IF SHŌ IS WILLING TO TEACH ME, I'LL WAIT HOWEVER LONG IT MIGHT BE!
HIROYOSHI, I'M NOT GOOD ENOUGH TO TEACH YOU.
S-- SORRY, I DIDN'T MEAN IT.
I CAN'T TEACH YOU, BUT ...
...I CAN PLAY SOCCER WITH YOU.

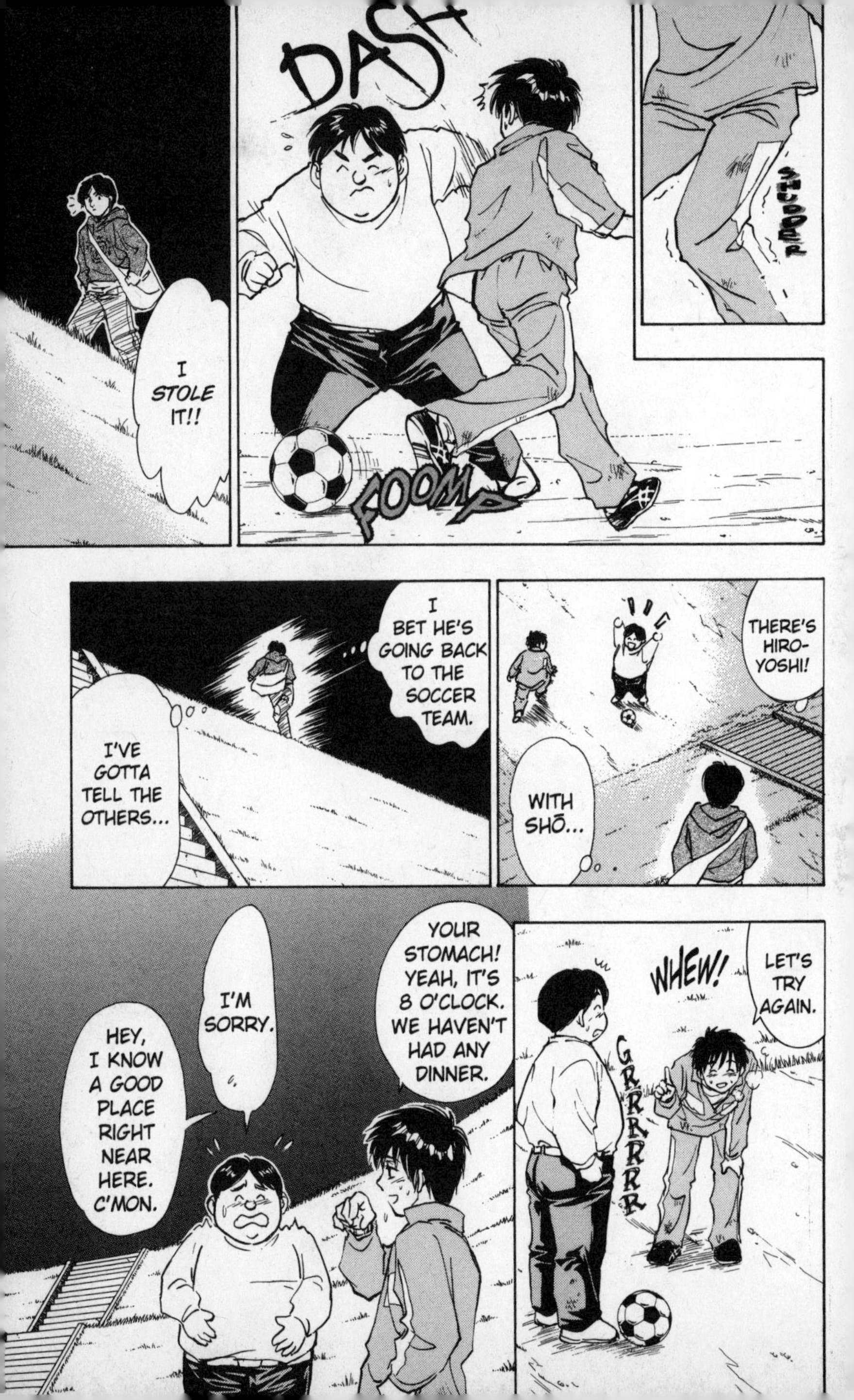
SHUDDER
DASH
FOOMP
I STOLE IT!!
THERE'S HIRO-YOSHI!
WITH SHŌ...
I BET HE'S GOING BACK TO THE SOCCER TEAM.
I'VE GOTTA TELL THE OTHERS...
LET'S TRY AGAIN.
WHEW!
GRRRRRRR
YOUR STOMACH! YEAH, IT'S 8 O'CLOCK. WE HAVEN'T HAD ANY DINNER.
I'M SORRY.
HEY, I KNOW A GOOD PLACE RIGHT NEAR HERE. C'MON.

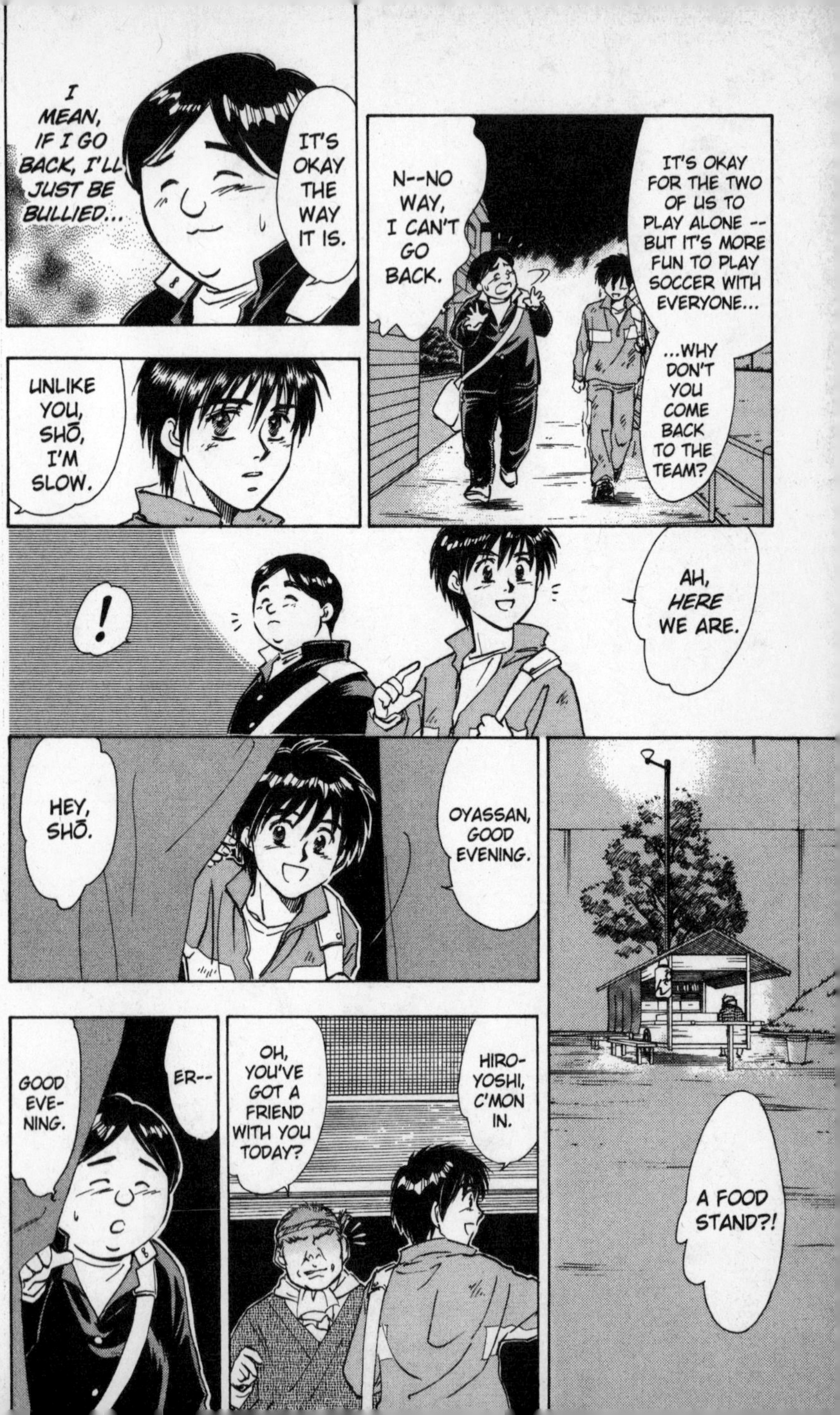
IT'S OKAY FOR THE TWO OF US TO PLAY ALONE -- BUT IT'S MORE FUN TO PLAY SOCCER WITH EVERYONE...
...WHY DON'T YOU COME BACK TO THE TEAM?
N--NO WAY, I CAN'T GO BACK.
IT'S OKAY THE WAY IT IS.
I MEAN, IF I GO BACK, I'LL JUST BE BULLIED...
UNLIKE YOU, SHŌ, I'M SLOW.
AH, *HERE* WE ARE.
!
A FOOD STAND?!
OYASSAN, GOOD EVENING.
HEY, SHŌ.
HIRO-YOSHI, C'MON IN.
OH, YOU'VE GOT A FRIEND WITH YOU TODAY?
ER--
GOOD EVE-NING.

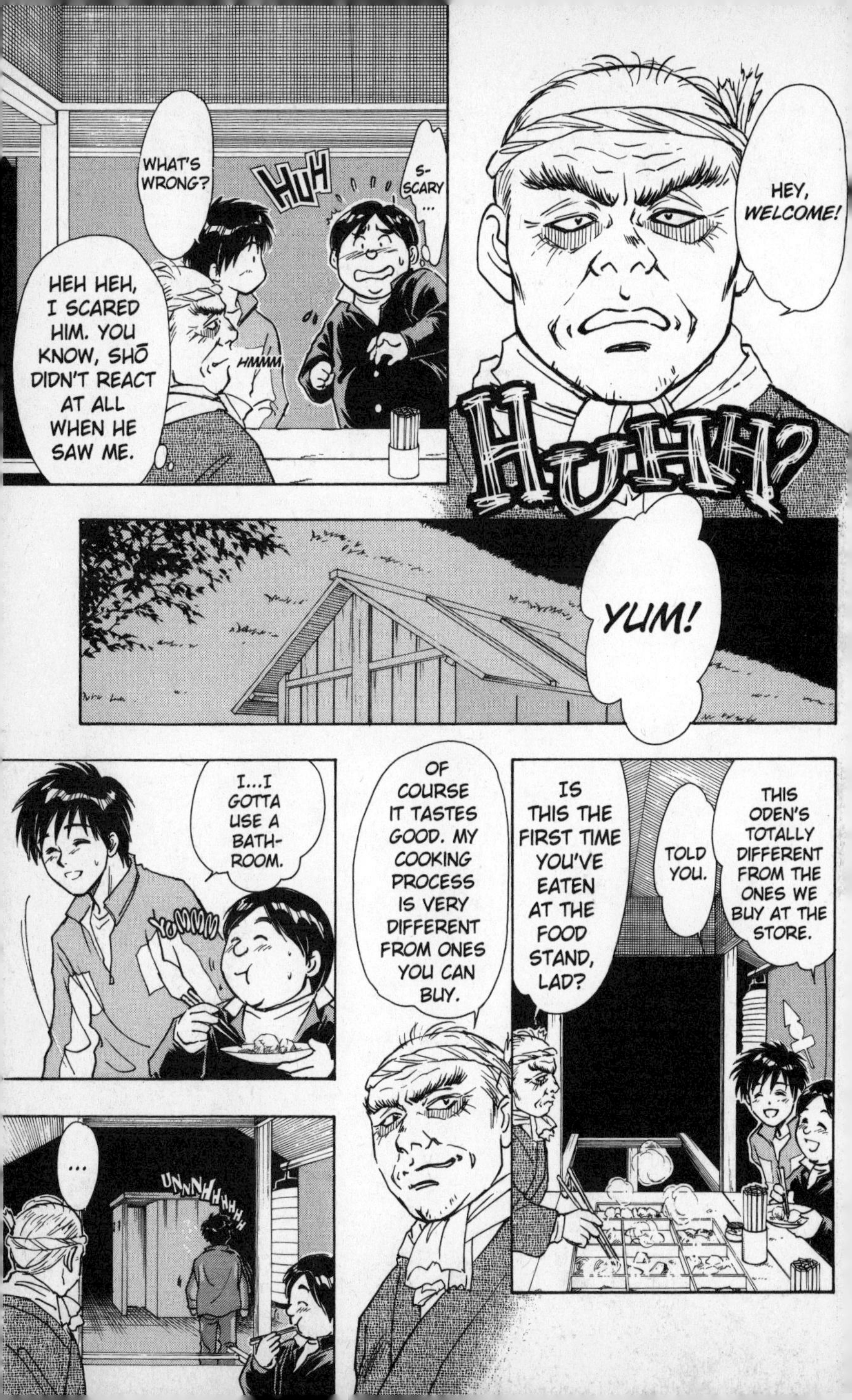
HEY, WELCOME!
HUHH?
S-SCARY...
HUH
WHAT'S WRONG?
HEH HEH, I SCARED HIM. YOU KNOW, SHŌ DIDN'T REACT AT ALL WHEN HE SAW ME.
HMMM
YUM!
THIS ODEN'S TOTALLY DIFFERENT FROM THE ONES WE BUY AT THE STORE.
TOLD YOU.
IS THIS THE FIRST TIME YOU'VE EATEN AT THE FOOD STAND, LAD?
OF COURSE IT TASTES GOOD. MY COOKING PROCESS IS VERY DIFFERENT FROM ONES YOU CAN BUY.
I...I GOTTA USE A BATH-ROOM.
...
UNNNHHHHHH

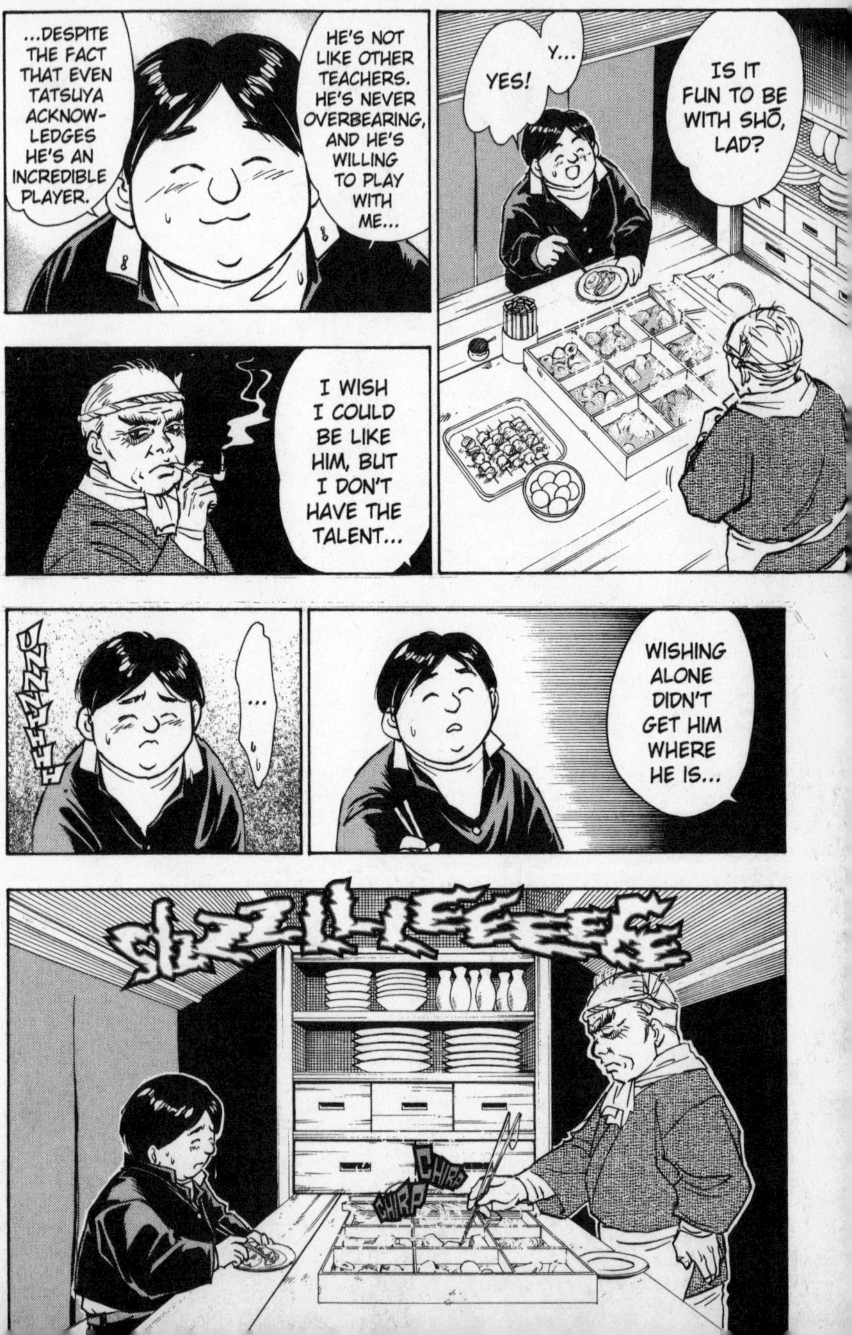
IS IT FUN TO BE WITH SHŌ, LAD?
Y... YES!
HE'S NOT LIKE OTHER TEACHERS. HE'S NEVER OVERBEARING, AND HE'S WILLING TO PLAY WITH ME...
...DESPITE THE FACT THAT EVEN TATSUYA ACKNOW-LEDGES HE'S AN INCREDIBLE PLAYER.
I WISH I COULD BE LIKE HIM, BUT I DON'T HAVE THE TALENT...
WISHING ALONE DIDN'T GET HIM WHERE HE IS...
...
SIZZLEEEE
CHIRP
CHIRP

READ THIS WAY

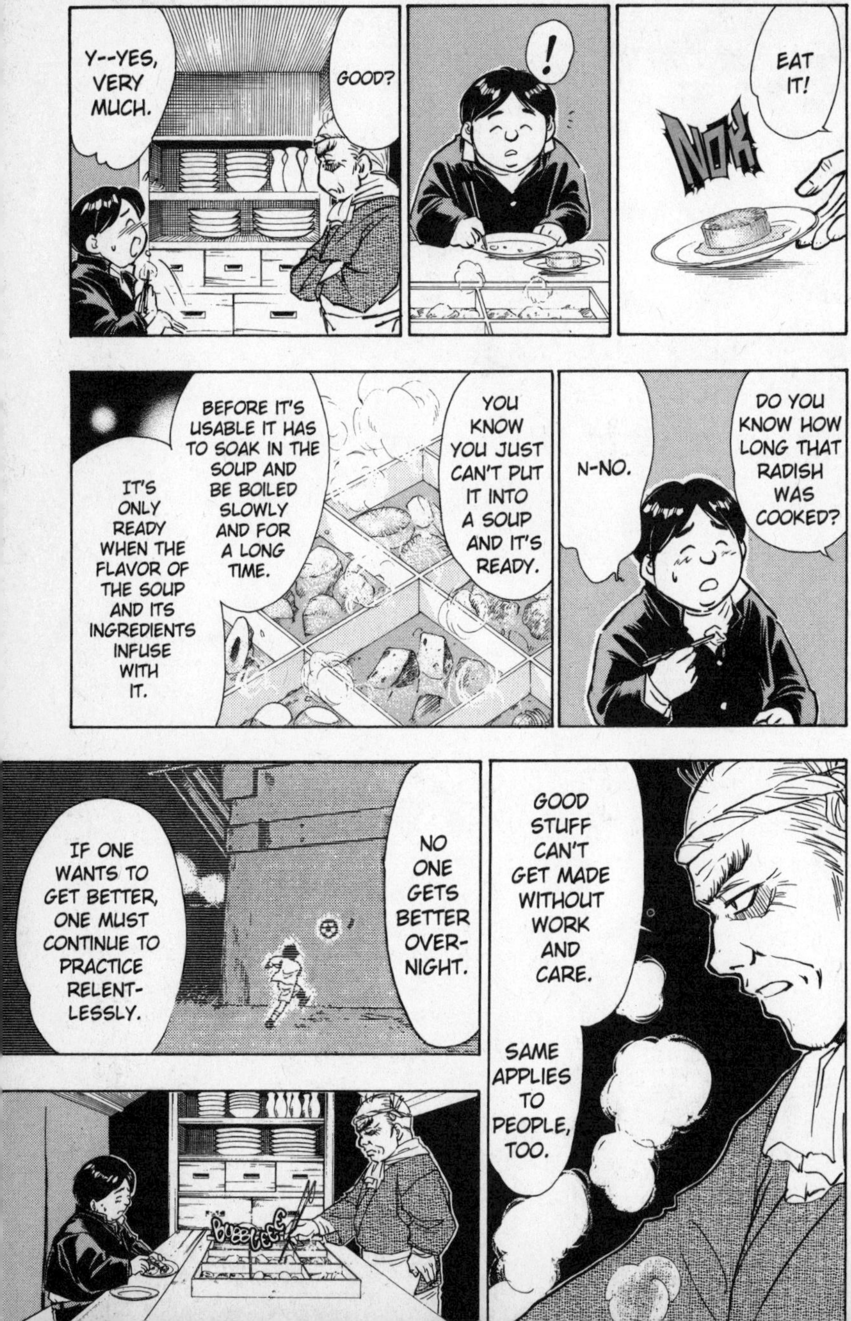
EAT IT!
NOK
!
GOOD?
Y--YES, VERY MUCH.
DO YOU KNOW HOW LONG THAT RADISH WAS COOKED?
N-NO.
YOU KNOW YOU JUST CAN'T PUT IT INTO A SOUP AND IT'S READY.
BEFORE IT'S USABLE IT HAS TO SOAK IN THE SOUP AND BE BOILED SLOWLY AND FOR A LONG TIME.
IT'S ONLY READY WHEN THE FLAVOR OF THE SOUP AND ITS INGREDIENTS INFUSE WITH IT.
GOOD STUFF CAN'T GET MADE WITHOUT WORK AND CARE.
SAME APPLIES TO PEOPLE, TOO.
NO ONE GETS BETTER OVER-NIGHT.
IF ONE WANTS TO GET BETTER, ONE MUST CONTINUE TO PRACTICE RELENT-LESSLY.
BUBBLEEE

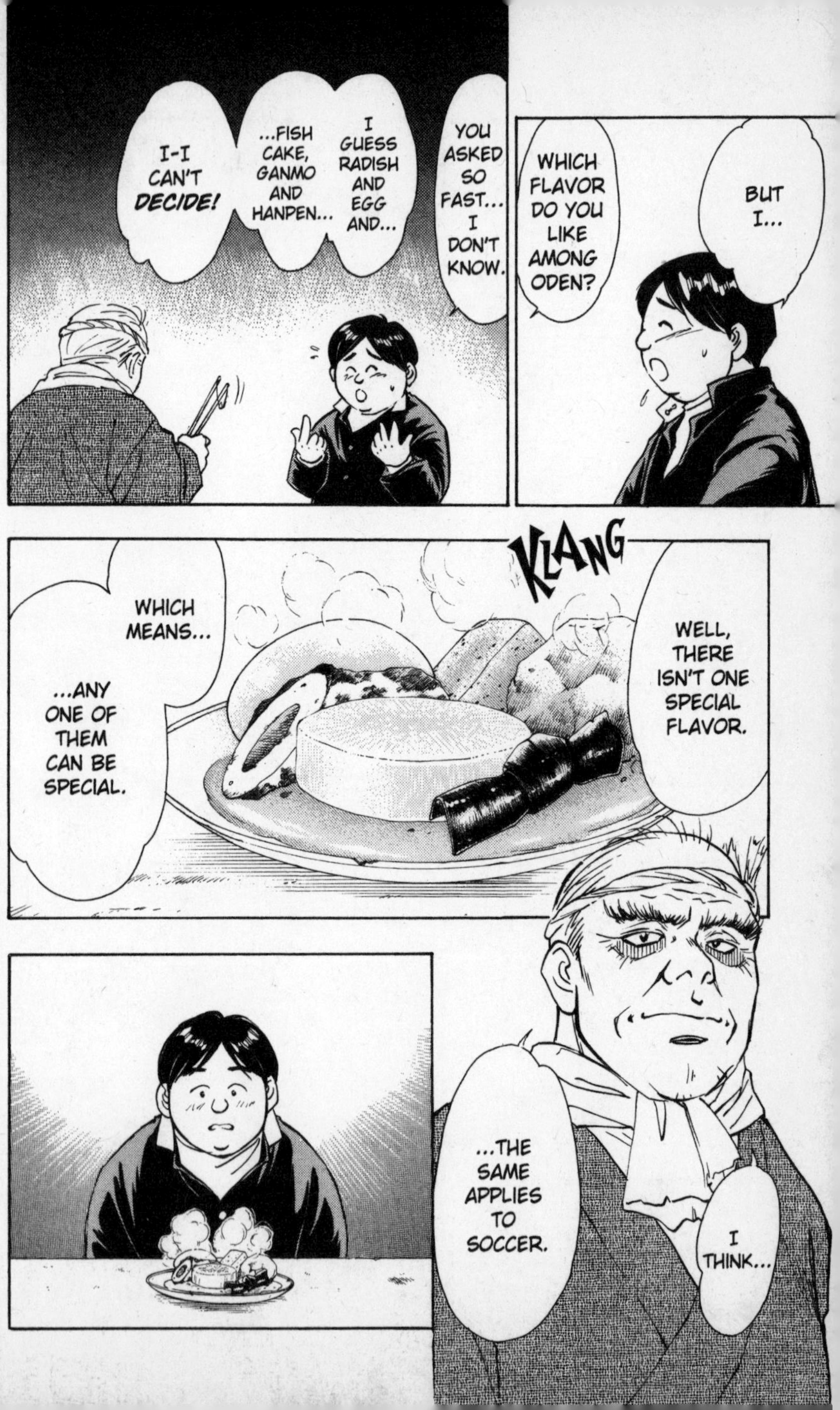
BUT I...
WHICH FLAVOR DO YOU LIKE AMONG ODEN?
YOU ASKED SO FAST... I DON'T KNOW.
I GUESS RADISH AND EGG AND...
...FISH CAKE, GANMO AND HANPEN...
I-I CAN'T *DECIDE!*
KLANG
WELL, THERE ISN'T ONE SPECIAL FLAVOR.
WHICH MEANS...
...ANY ONE OF THEM CAN BE SPECIAL.
I THINK...
...THE SAME APPLIES TO SOCCER.

READ THIS WAY

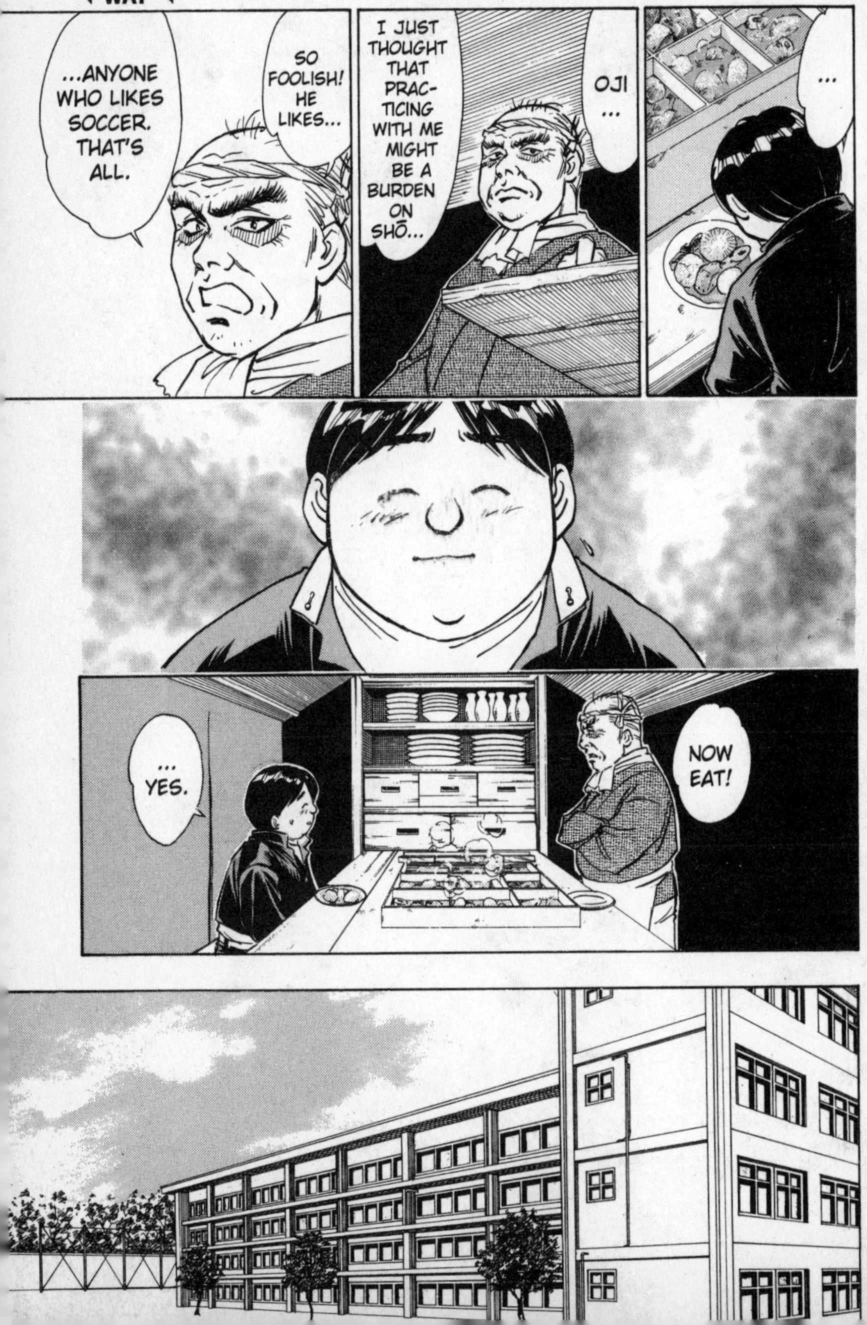
...
OJI ...
I JUST THOUGHT THAT PRAC-TICING WITH ME MIGHT BE A BURDEN ON SHŌ...
SO FOOLISH! HE LIKES...
...ANYONE WHO LIKES SOCCER. THAT'S ALL.
NOW EAT!
... YES.

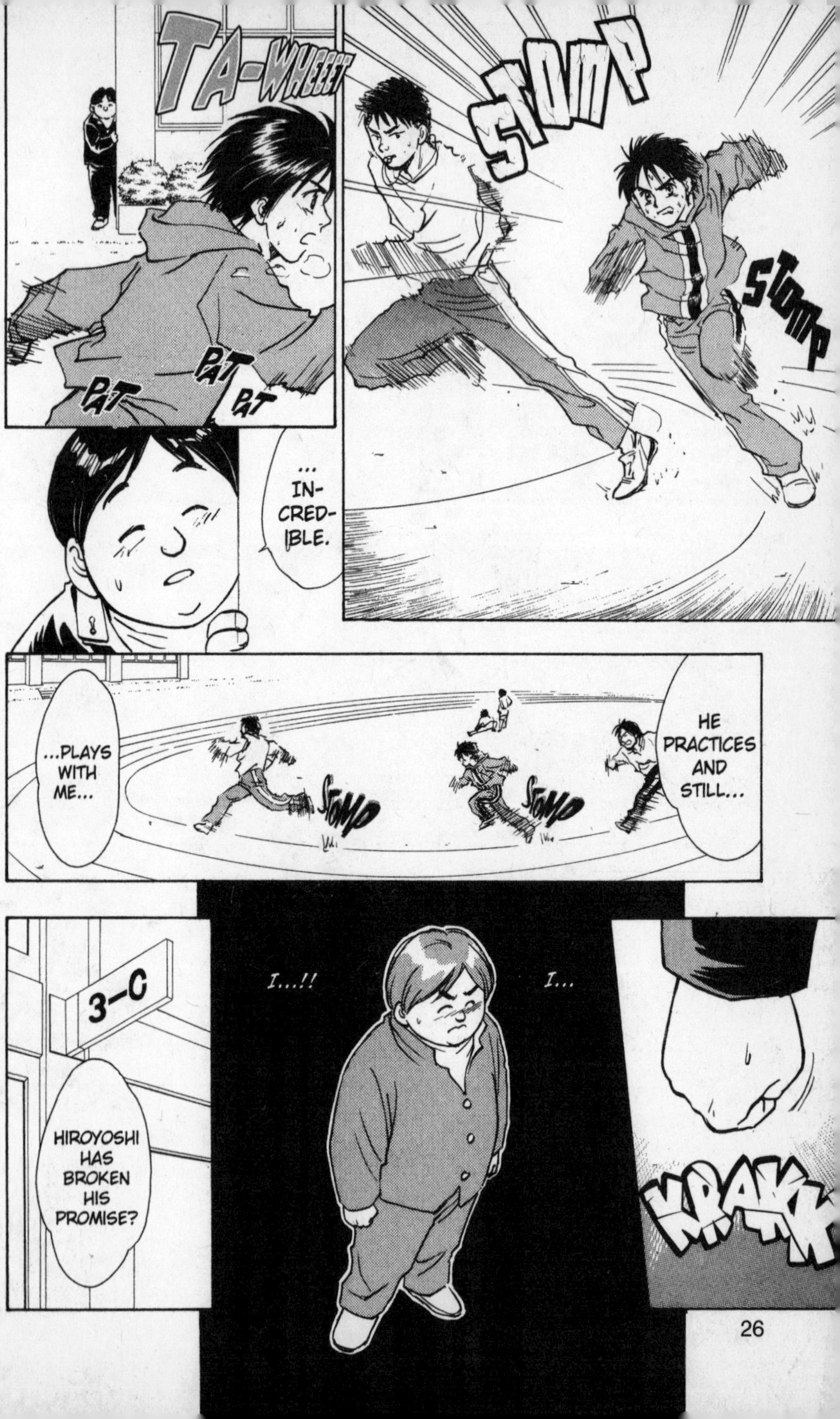
STOMP
STOMP
TA-WHEEEE
PAT
PAT
PAT
... IN-CRED-IBLE.
HE PRACTICES AND STILL...
...PLAYS WITH ME...
STOMP
STOMP
KRAKK
I...
I...!!
3-C
HIROYOSHI HAS BROKEN HIS PROMISE?

READ THIS WAY

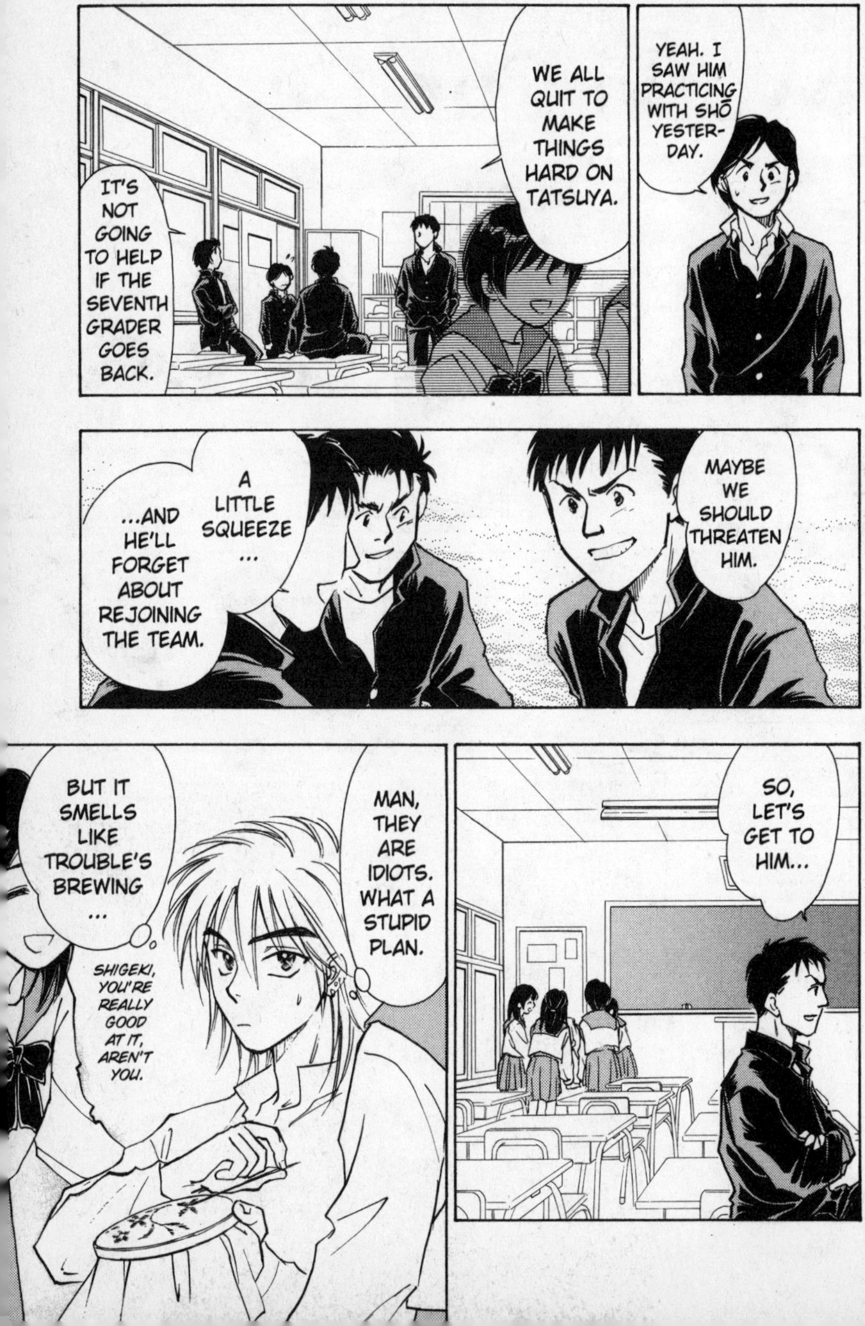
YEAH. I SAW HIM PRACTICING WITH SHŌ YESTER-DAY.
WE ALL QUIT TO MAKE THINGS HARD ON TATSUYA.
IT'S NOT GOING TO HELP IF THE SEVENTH GRADER GOES BACK.
MAYBE WE SHOULD THREATEN HIM.
A LITTLE SQUEEZE ...
...AND HE'LL FORGET ABOUT REJOINING THE TEAM.
SO, LET'S GET TO HIM...
MAN, THEY ARE IDIOTS. WHAT A STUPID PLAN.
BUT IT SMELLS LIKE TROUBLE'S BREWING ...
SHIGEKI, YOU'RE REALLY GOOD AT IT, AREN'T YOU.

World Cup Report

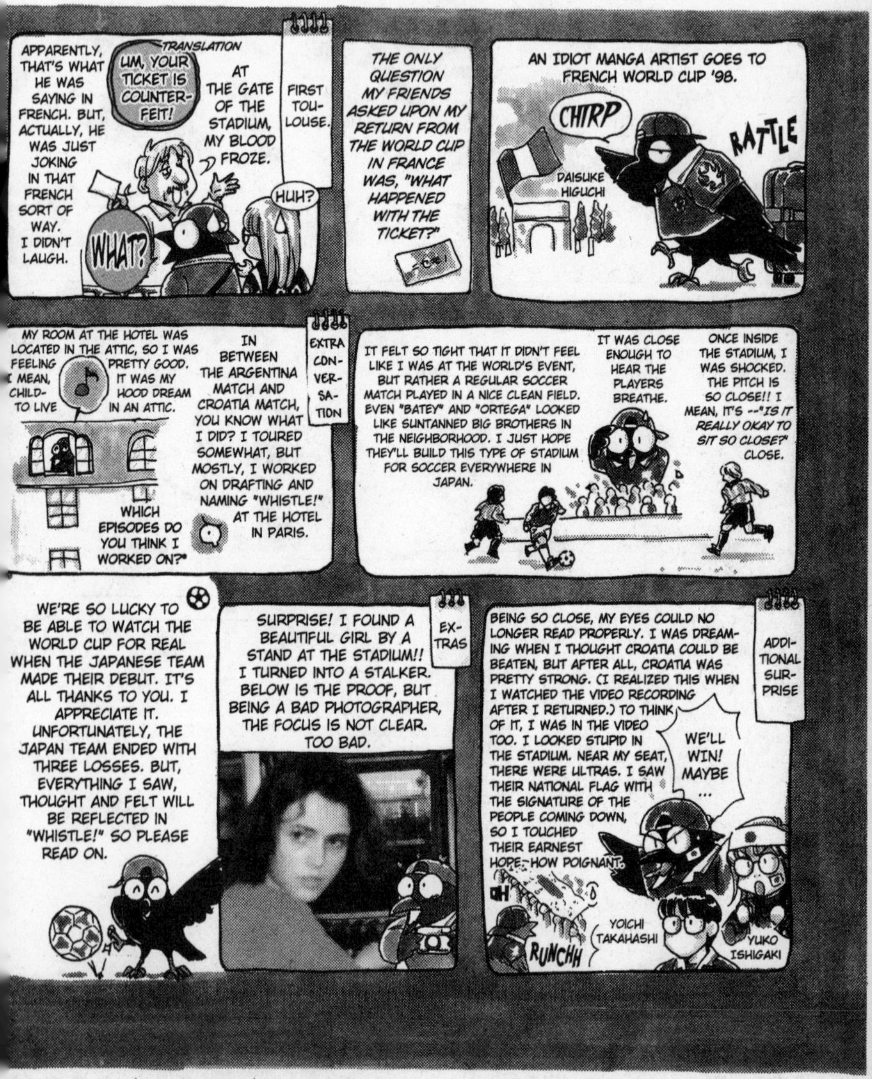
AN IDIOT MANGA ARTIST GOES TO FRENCH WORLD CUP '98.
CHIRP
RATTLE
DAISUKE HIGUCHI
THE ONLY QUESTION MY FRIENDS ASKED UPON MY RETURN FROM THE WORLD CUP IN FRANCE WAS, "WHAT HAPPENED WITH THE TICKET?"
FIRST TOULOUSE.
AT THE GATE OF THE STADIUM, MY BLOOD FROZE.
TRANSLATION
UM, YOUR TICKET IS COUNTERFEIT!
HUH?
WHAT?
APPARENTLY, THAT'S WHAT HE WAS SAYING IN FRENCH. BUT, ACTUALLY, HE WAS JUST JOKING IN THAT FRENCH SORT OF WAY. I DIDN'T LAUGH.
ONCE INSIDE THE STADIUM, I WAS SHOCKED. THE PITCH IS SO CLOSE!! I MEAN, IT'S --"IS IT REALLY OKAY TO SIT SO CLOSE?" CLOSE.
IT WAS CLOSE ENOUGH TO HEAR THE PLAYERS BREATHE.
IT FELT SO TIGHT THAT IT DIDN'T FEEL LIKE I WAS AT THE WORLD'S EVENT, BUT RATHER A REGULAR SOCCER MATCH PLAYED IN A NICE CLEAN FIELD. EVEN "BATEY" AND "ORTEGA" LOOKED LIKE SUNTANNED BIG BROTHERS IN THE NEIGHBORHOOD. I JUST HOPE THEY'LL BUILD THIS TYPE OF STADIUM FOR SOCCER EVERYWHERE IN JAPAN.
EXTRA CONVERSATION
IN BETWEEN THE ARGENTINA MATCH AND CROATIA MATCH, YOU KNOW WHAT I DID? I TOURED SOMEWHAT, BUT MOSTLY, I WORKED ON DRAFTING AND NAMING "WHISTLE!" AT THE HOTEL IN PARIS.
WHICH EPISODES DO YOU THINK I WORKED ON?*
MY ROOM AT THE HOTEL WAS LOCATED IN THE ATTIC, SO I WAS FEELING PRETTY GOOD.
I MEAN, IT WAS MY CHILDHOOD DREAM TO LIVE IN AN ATTIC.
ADDITIONAL SURPRISE
BEING SO CLOSE, MY EYES COULD NO LONGER READ PROPERLY. I WAS DREAMING WHEN I THOUGHT CROATIA COULD BE BEATEN, BUT AFTER ALL, CROATIA WAS PRETTY STRONG. (I REALIZED THIS WHEN I WATCHED THE VIDEO RECORDING AFTER I RETURNED.) TO THINK OF IT, I WAS IN THE VIDEO TOO. I LOOKED STUPID IN THE STADIUM. NEAR MY SEAT, THERE WERE ULTRAS. I SAW THEIR NATIONAL FLAG WITH THE SIGNATURE OF THE PEOPLE COMING DOWN, SO I TOUCHED THEIR EARNEST HOPE. HOW POIGNANT.
WE'LL WIN! MAYBE ...
OH
RUNCHH
YOICHI TAKAHASHI
YUKO ISHIGAKI
EXTRAS
SURPRISE! I FOUND A BEAUTIFUL GIRL BY A STAND AT THE STADIUM!! I TURNED INTO A STALKER. BELOW IS THE PROOF, BUT BEING A BAD PHOTOGRAPHER, THE FOCUS IS NOT CLEAR. TOO BAD.
WE'RE SO LUCKY TO BE ABLE TO WATCH THE WORLD CUP FOR REAL WHEN THE JAPANESE TEAM MADE THEIR DEBUT. IT'S ALL THANKS TO YOU. I APPRECIATE IT. UNFORTUNATELY, THE JAPAN TEAM ENDED WITH THREE LOSSES. BUT, EVERYTHING I SAW, THOUGHT AND FELT WILL BE REFLECTED IN "WHISTLE!" SO PLEASE READ ON.

***A: Episode 19 and 20.**

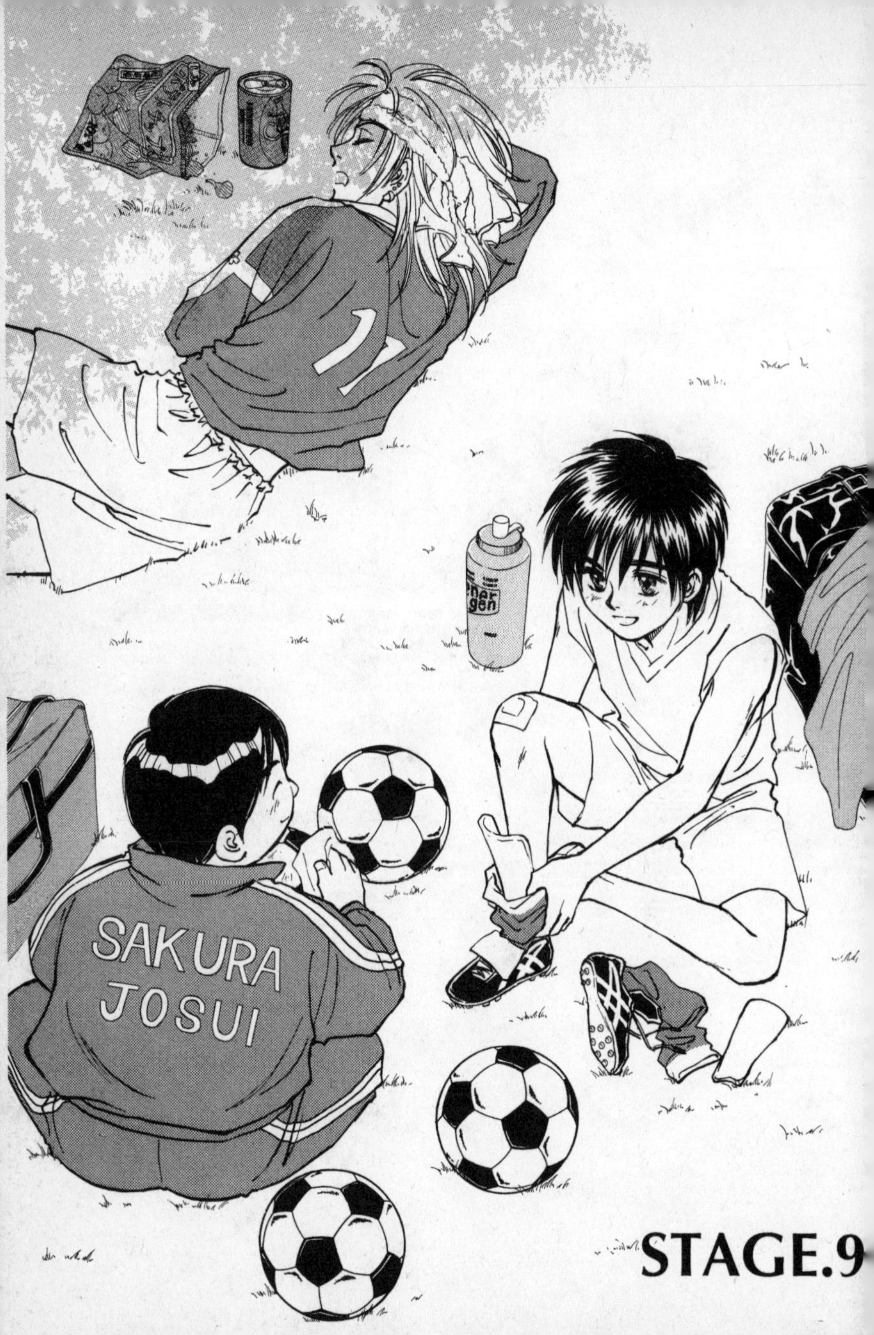
SAKURA
JOSUI

STAGE.9
STRAIGHT THOUGHTS

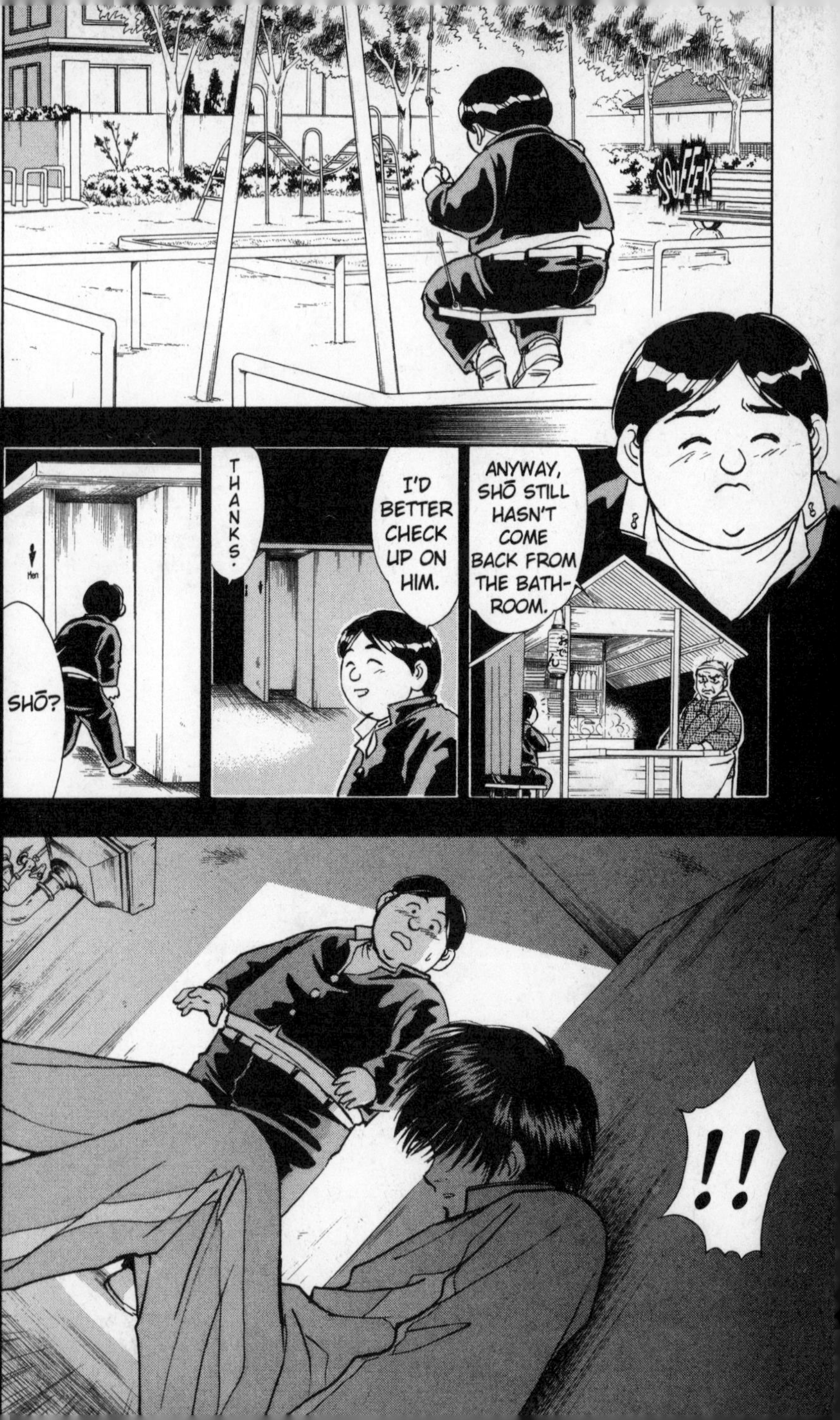
SQUEEK
ANYWAY, SHŌ STILL HASN'T COME BACK FROM THE BATH-ROOM.
I'D BETTER CHECK UP ON HIM.
THANKS.
Men
SHŌ?
!!

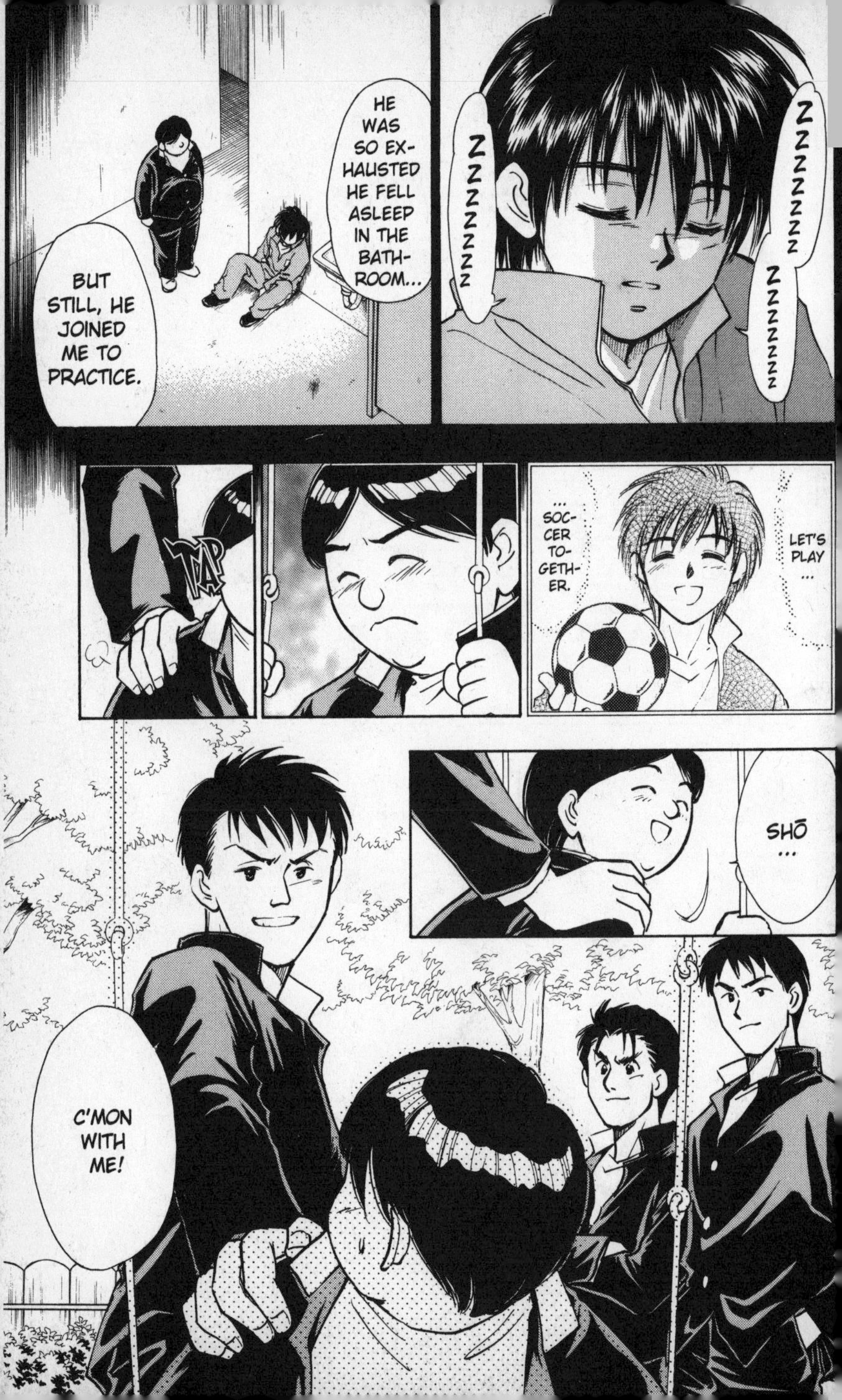
ZZZZZZZ
ZZZZZZZ
ZZZZZZZ
HE WAS SO EX-HAUSTED HE FELL ASLEEP IN THE BATH-ROOM...
BUT STILL, HE JOINED ME TO PRACTICE.
LET'S PLAY ...
... SOC-CER TO-GETH-ER.
TAP
SHŌ ...
C'MON WITH ME!

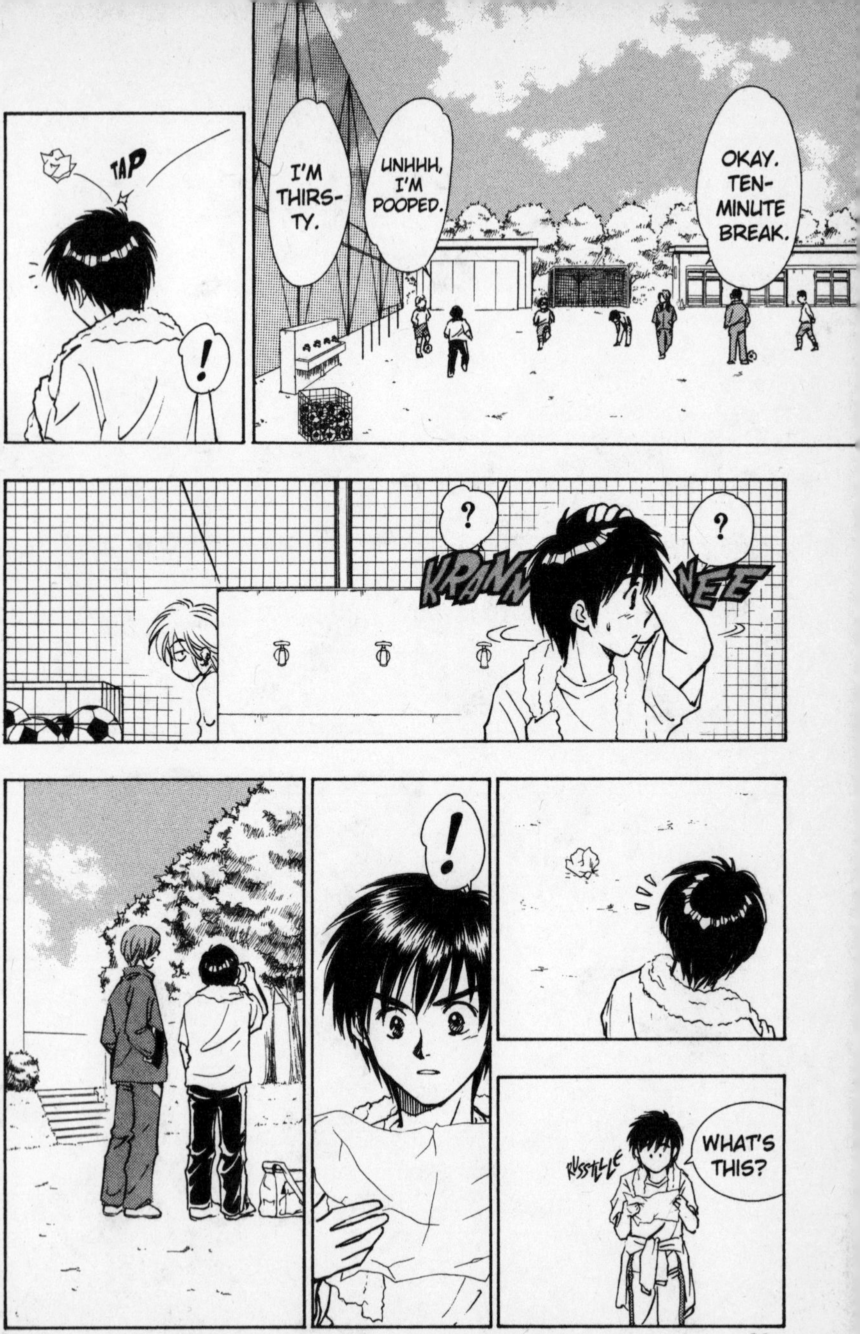
OKAY. TEN-MINUTE BREAK.
UNHHH, I'M POOPED.
I'M THIRS-TY.
TAP
!
?
KRANNNEE
?
!
RUSSTLLE
WHAT'S THIS?

READ THIS WAY

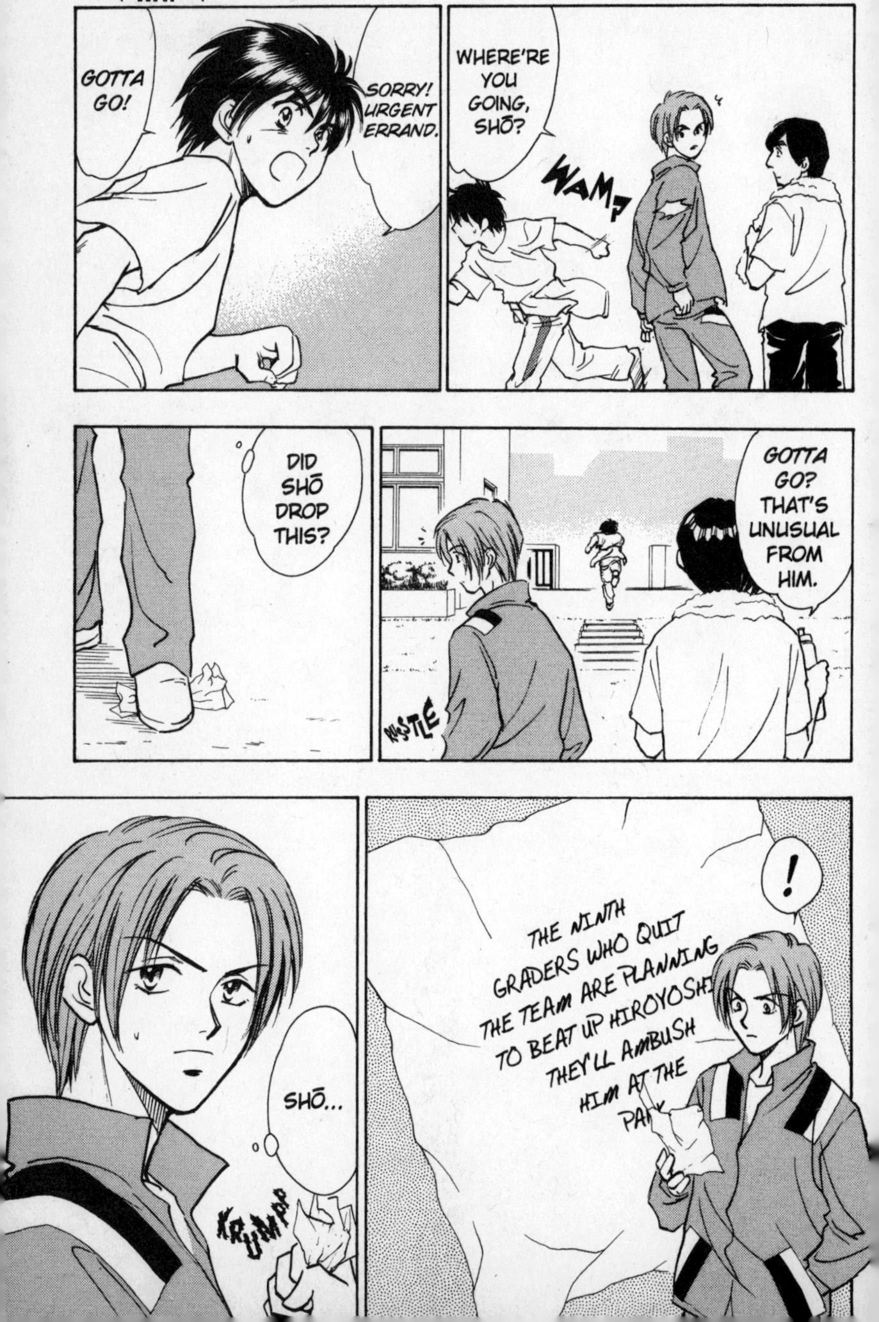
WHERE'RE YOU GOING, SHŌ?
WAM
SORRY! URGENT ERRAND.
GOTTA GO!
GOTTA GO? THAT'S UNUSUAL FROM HIM.
RUSTLE
DID SHŌ DROP THIS?
!
THE NINTH GRADERS WHO QUIT THE TEAM ARE PLANNING TO BEAT UP HIROYOSHI
THEY'LL AMBUSH HIM AT THE PA
SHŌ...
KRUMPP

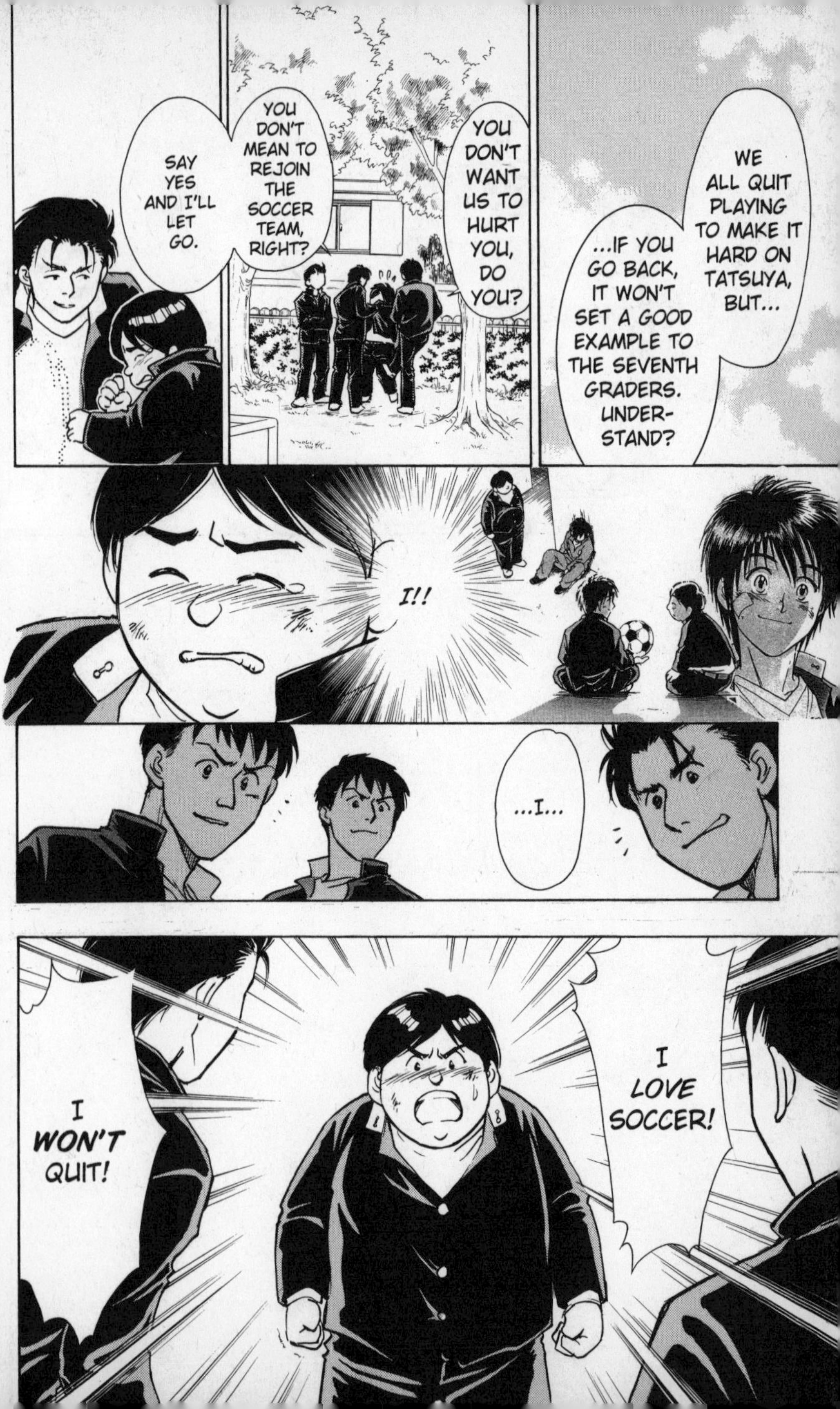
WE ALL QUIT PLAYING TO MAKE IT HARD ON TATSUYA, BUT...
...IF YOU GO BACK, IT WON'T SET A GOOD EXAMPLE TO THE SEVENTH GRADERS. UNDER-STAND?
YOU DON'T WANT US TO HURT YOU, DO YOU?
YOU DON'T MEAN TO REJOIN THE SOCCER TEAM, RIGHT?
SAY YES AND I'LL LET GO.
I!!
...I...
I LOVE SOCCER!
I WON'T QUIT!

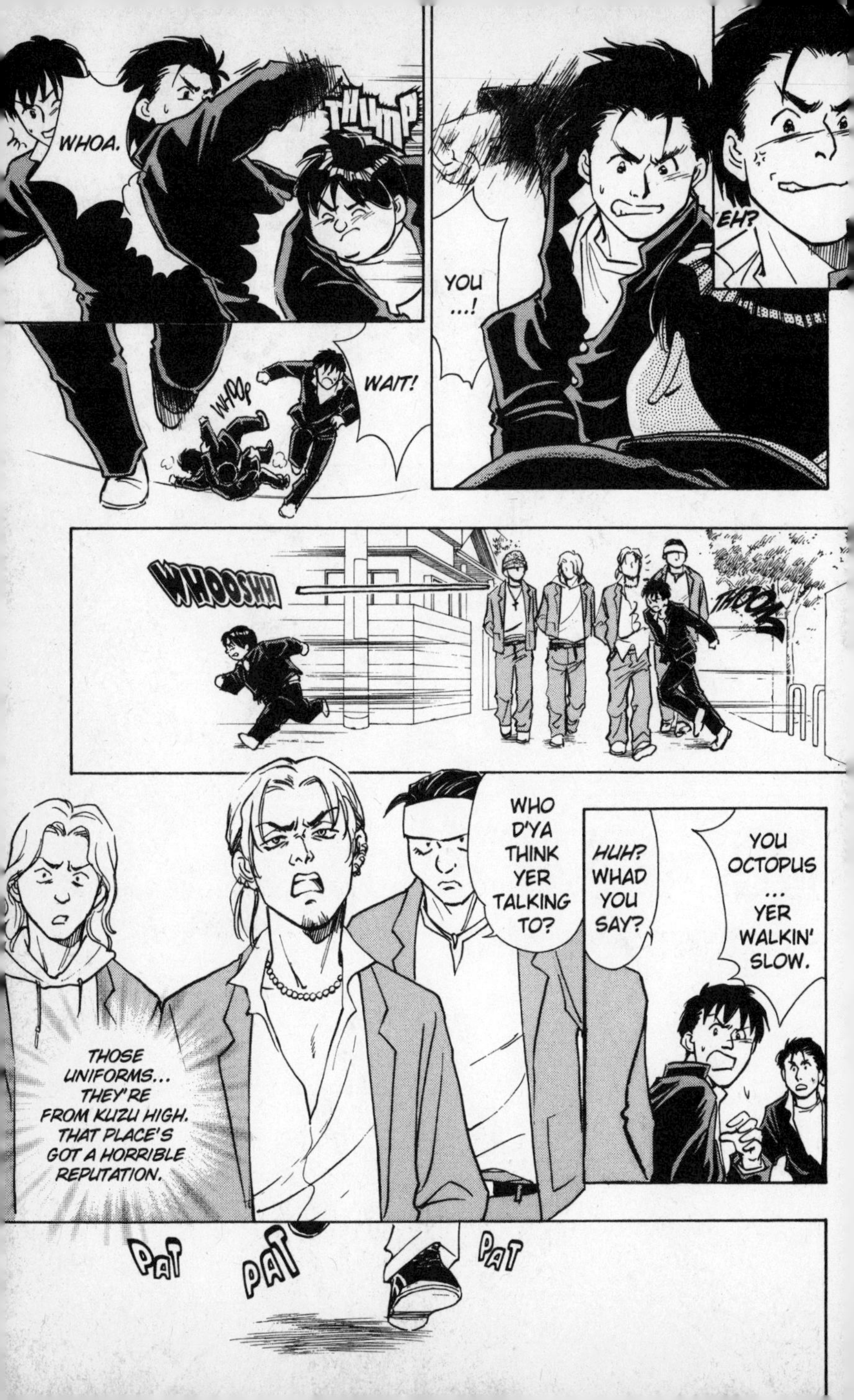
EH?
YOU ...!
THUMP
WHOA.
WAIT!
WHOOP
THOOM
WHOOSHH
YOU OCTOPUS ... YER WALKIN' SLOW.
HUH? WHAD YOU SAY?
WHO D'YA THINK YER TALKING TO?
THOSE UNIFORMS... THEY'RE FROM KUZU HIGH. THAT PLACE'S GOT A HORRIBLE REPUTATION.
PAT
PAT
PAT

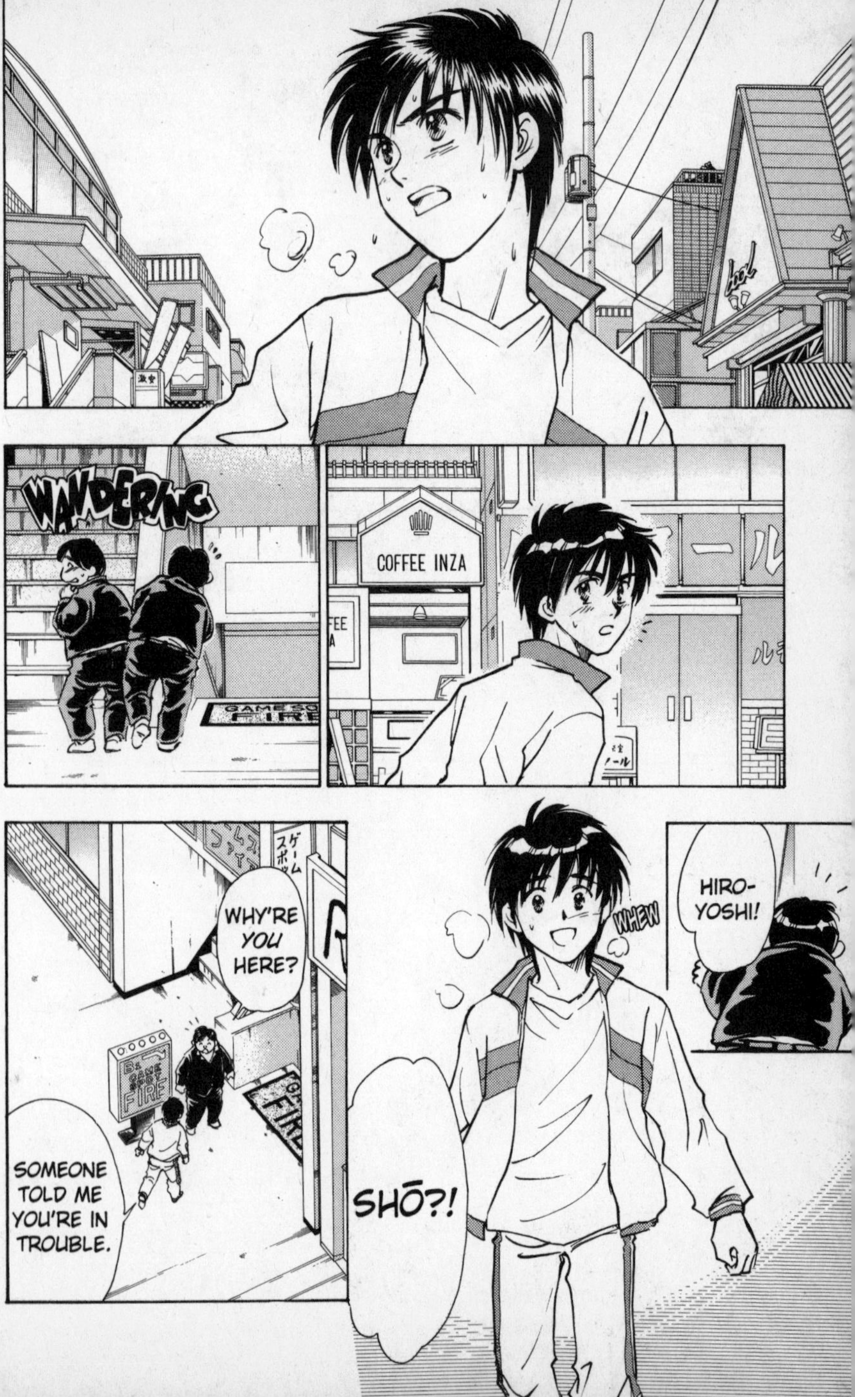
COFFEE INZA
WANDERING
HIRO-YOSHI!
WHEW
SHŌ?!
WHY'RE YOU HERE?
SOMEONE TOLD ME YOU'RE IN TROUBLE.

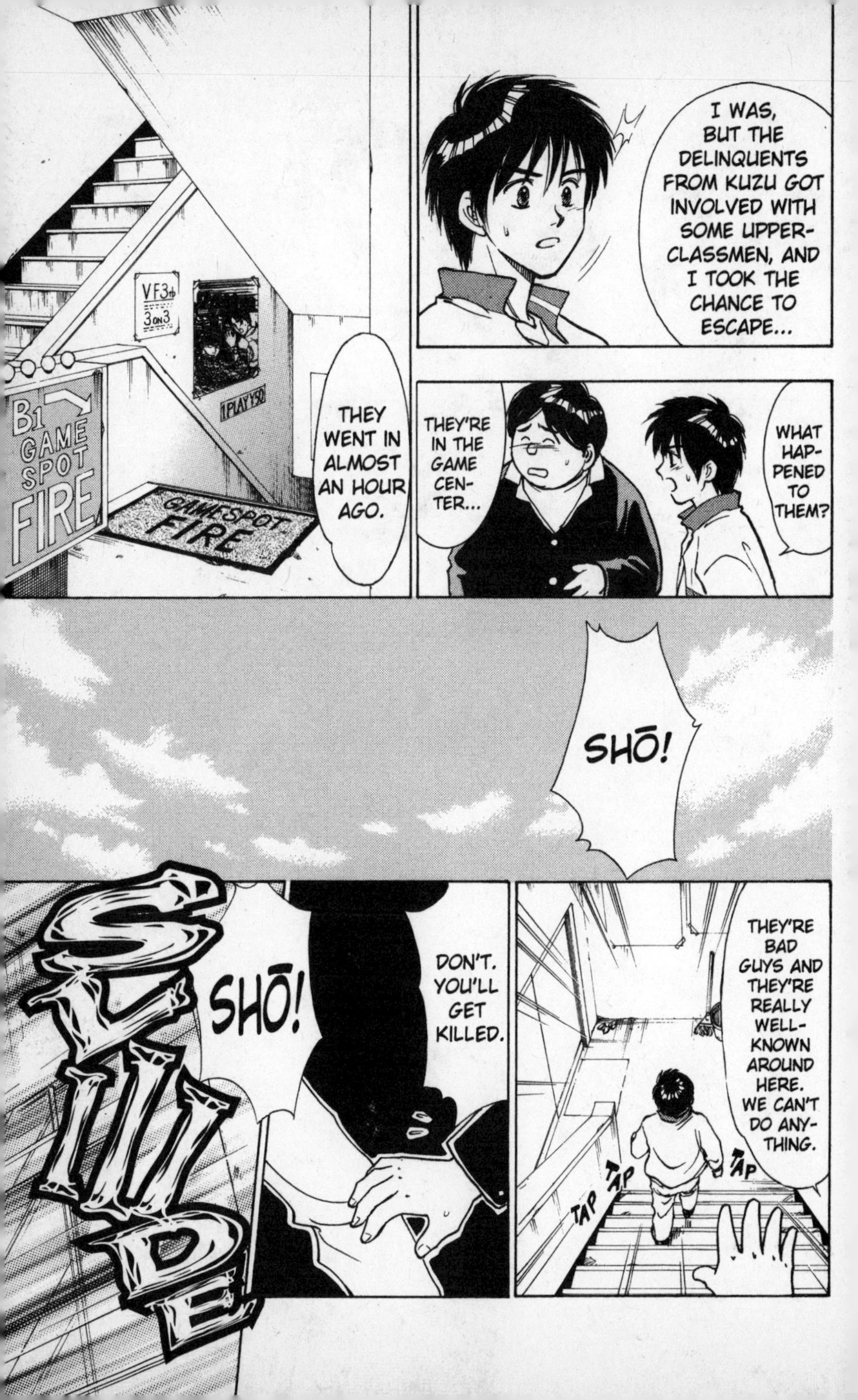

I WAS, BUT THE DELINQUENTS FROM KUZU GOT INVOLVED WITH SOME UPPER-CLASSMEN, AND I TOOK THE CHANCE TO ESCAPE...
WHAT HAP-PENED TO THEM?
THEY'RE IN THE GAME CEN-TER...
THEY WENT IN ALMOST AN HOUR AGO.
VF3rd
3on3
1PLAY ¥50
B1
GAME SPOT FIRE
GAMESPOT FIRE
SHŌ!
THEY'RE BAD GUYS AND THEY'RE REALLY WELL-KNOWN AROUND HERE. WE CAN'T DO ANY-THING.
TAP TAP TAP TAP
DON'T. YOU'LL GET KILLED.
SHŌ!
SLIDE

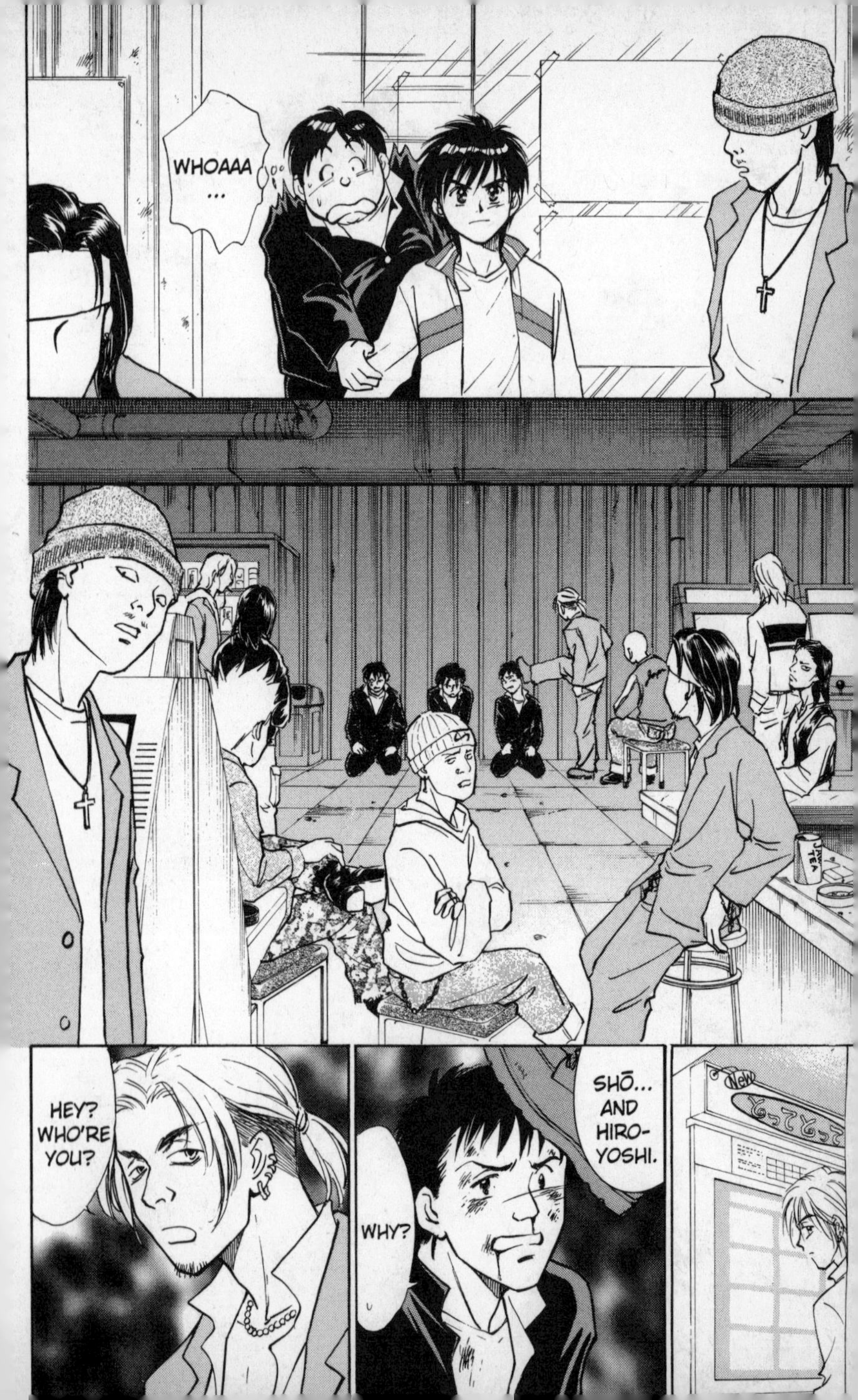
WHOAAA ...
JAVA TEA
SHŌ... AND HIRO-YOSHI.
HEY? WHO'RE YOU?
WHY?
New

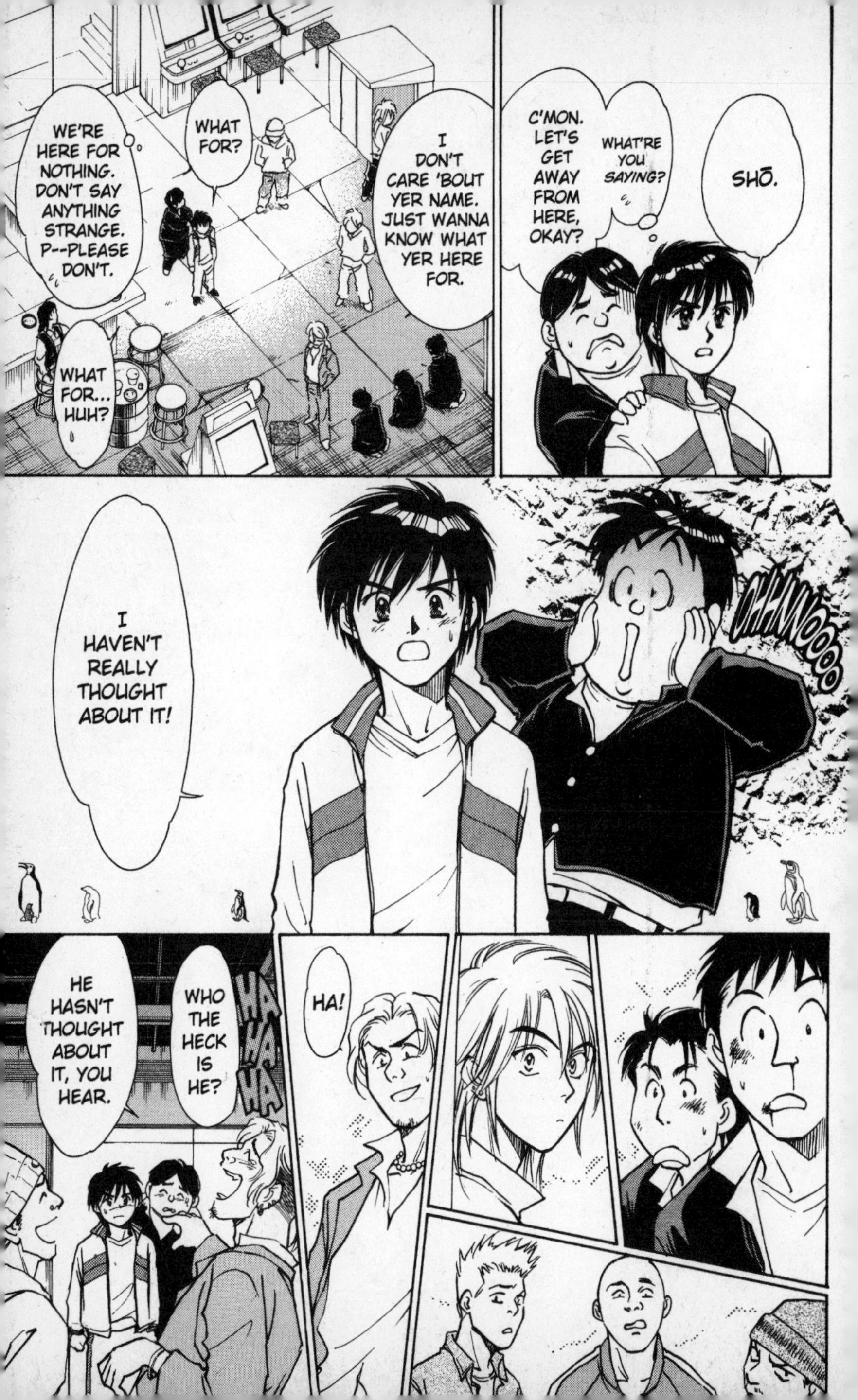
SHŌ.
WHAT'RE YOU SAYING?
C'MON. LET'S GET AWAY FROM HERE, OKAY?
I DON'T CARE 'BOUT YER NAME. JUST WANNA KNOW WHAT YER HERE FOR.
WHAT FOR?
WE'RE HERE FOR NOTHING. DON'T SAY ANYTHING STRANGE. P--PLEASE DON'T.
WHAT FOR... HUH?
OHHNOOOOO
I HAVEN'T REALLY THOUGHT ABOUT IT!
HA!
WHO THE HECK IS HE?
HA HA HA HA
HE HASN'T THOUGHT ABOUT IT, YOU HEAR.

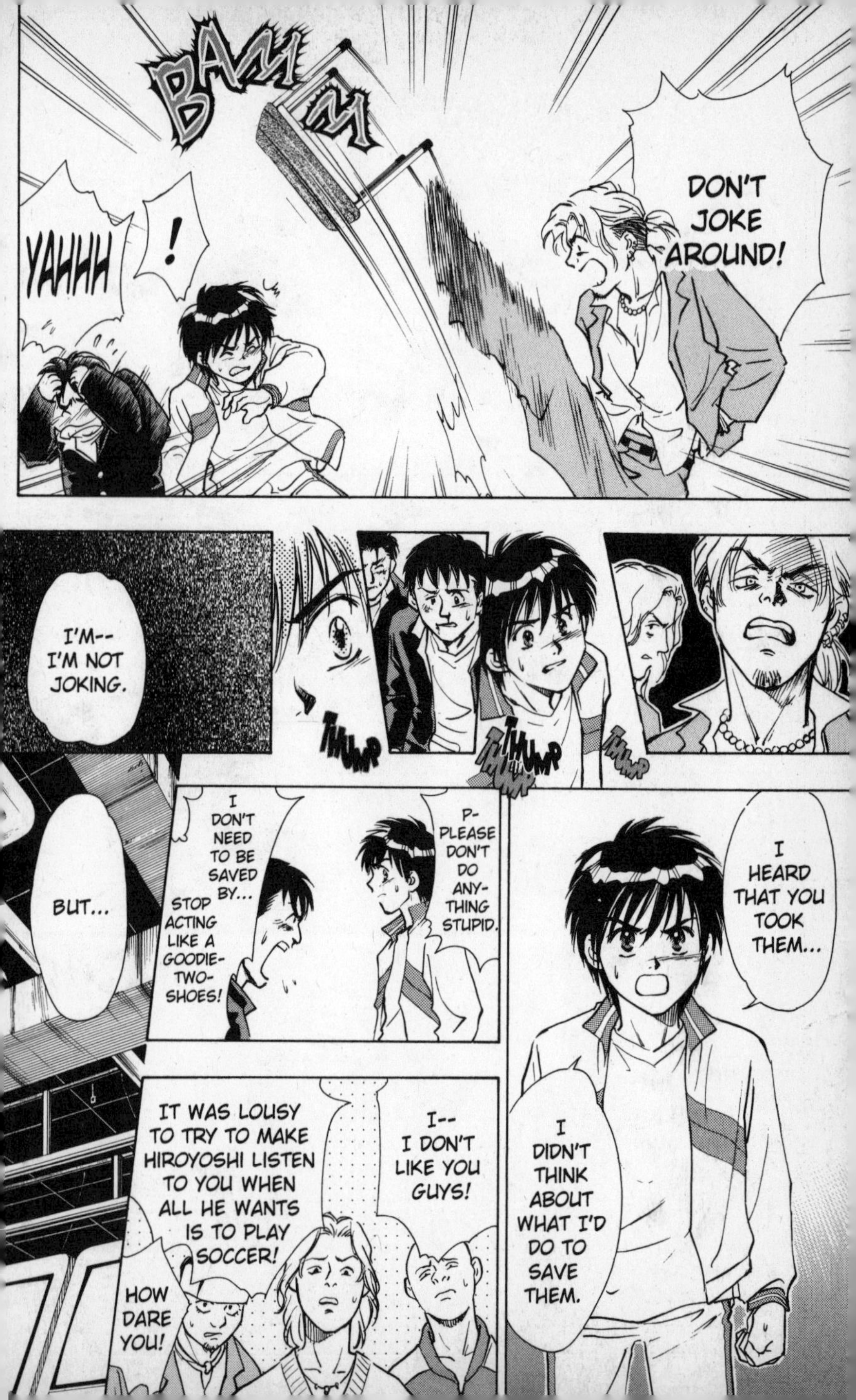
BAMM
DON'T JOKE AROUND!
!
YAHHH
THUMP
THUMP
THUMP
THUMP
I'M-- I'M NOT JOKING.
I HEARD THAT YOU TOOK THEM...
P-PLEASE DON'T DO ANYTHING STUPID.
I DON'T NEED TO BE SAVED BY...
STOP ACTING LIKE A GOODIE-TWO-SHOES!
BUT...
I DIDN'T THINK ABOUT WHAT I'D DO TO SAVE THEM.
I-- I DON'T LIKE YOU GUYS!
IT WAS LOUSY TO TRY TO MAKE HIROYOSHI LISTEN TO YOU WHEN ALL HE WANTS IS TO PLAY SOCCER!
HOW DARE YOU!

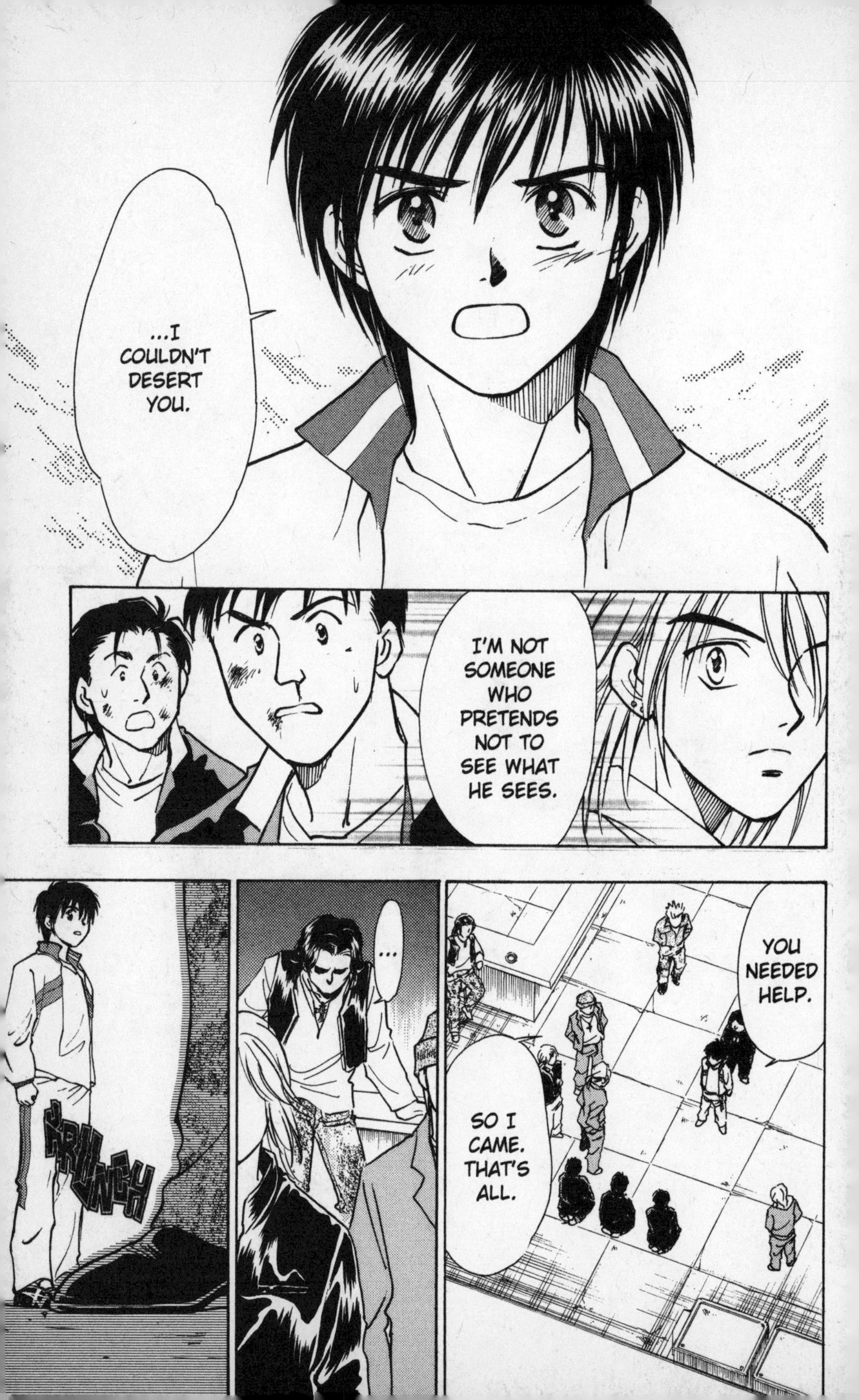
...I COULDN'T DESERT YOU.
I'M NOT SOMEONE WHO PRETENDS NOT TO SEE WHAT HE SEES.
YOU NEEDED HELP.
SO I CAME. THAT'S ALL.
...
KRUNCH

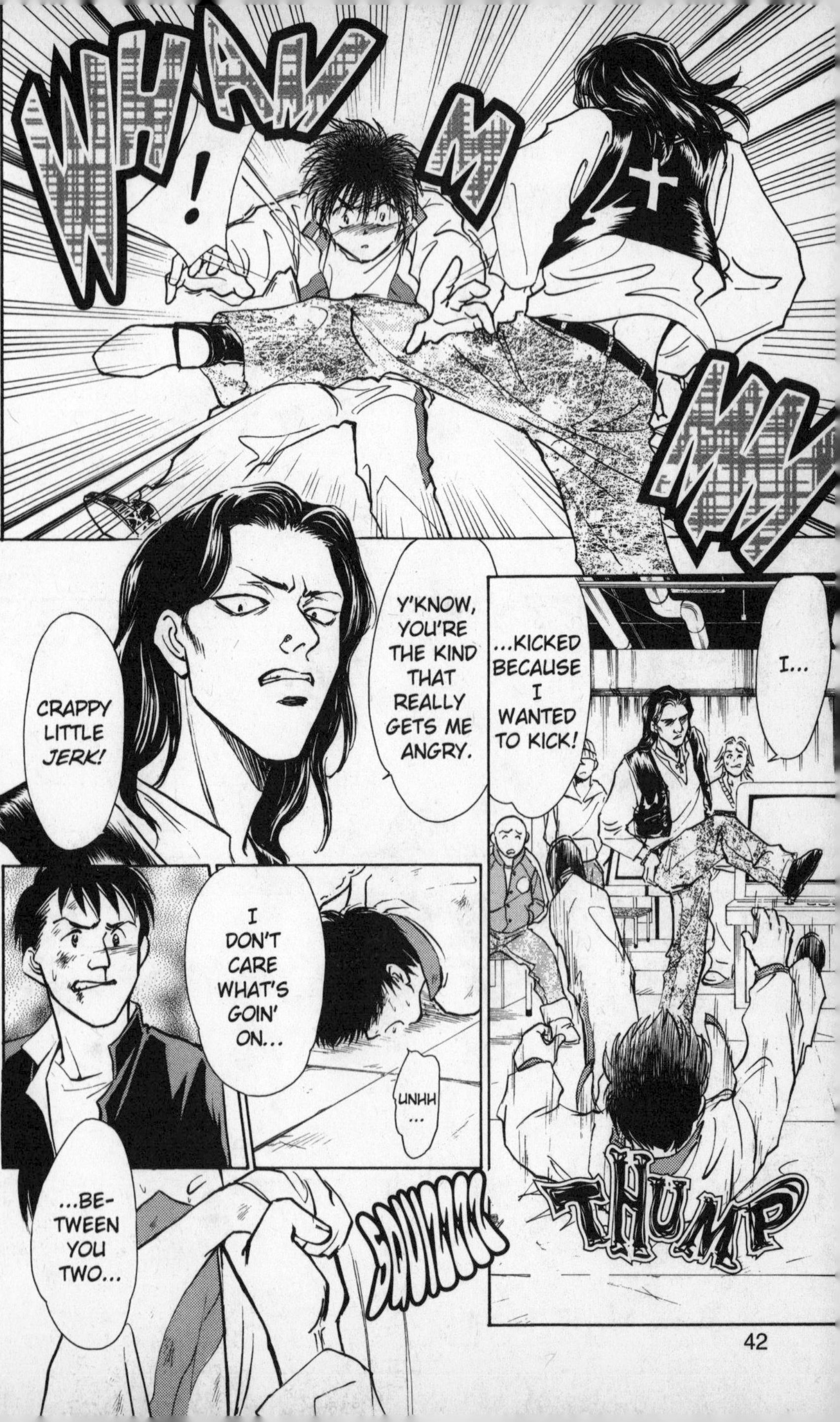
WHAMMMM
!
I...
...KICKED BECAUSE I WANTED TO KICK!
THUMP
Y'KNOW, YOU'RE THE KIND THAT REALLY GETS ME ANGRY.
CRAPPY LITTLE JERK!
I DON'T CARE WHAT'S GOIN' ON...
UNHH ...
...BE-TWEEN YOU TWO...

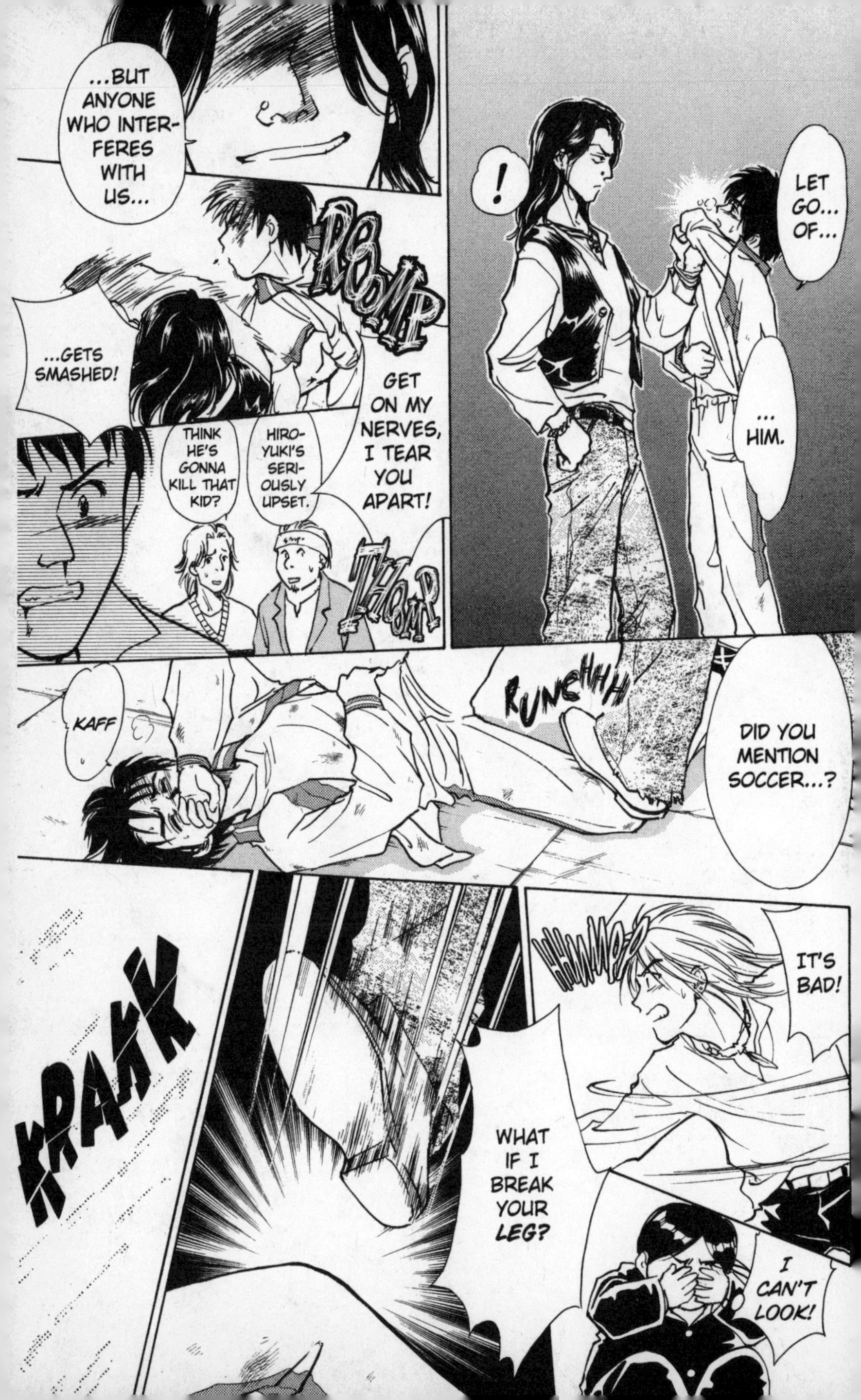
...BUT ANYONE WHO INTER-FERES WITH US...
ROOMP
...GETS SMASHED!
GET ON MY NERVES, I TEAR YOU APART!
THINK HE'S GONNA KILL THAT KID?
HIRO-YUKI'S SERI-OUSLY UPSET.
THOMP
!
LET GO... OF...
... HIM.
KAFF
RUNCHHH
DID YOU MENTION SOCCER...?
KRAKK
WHAT IF I BREAK YOUR LEG?
IT'S BAD!
I CAN'T LOOK!

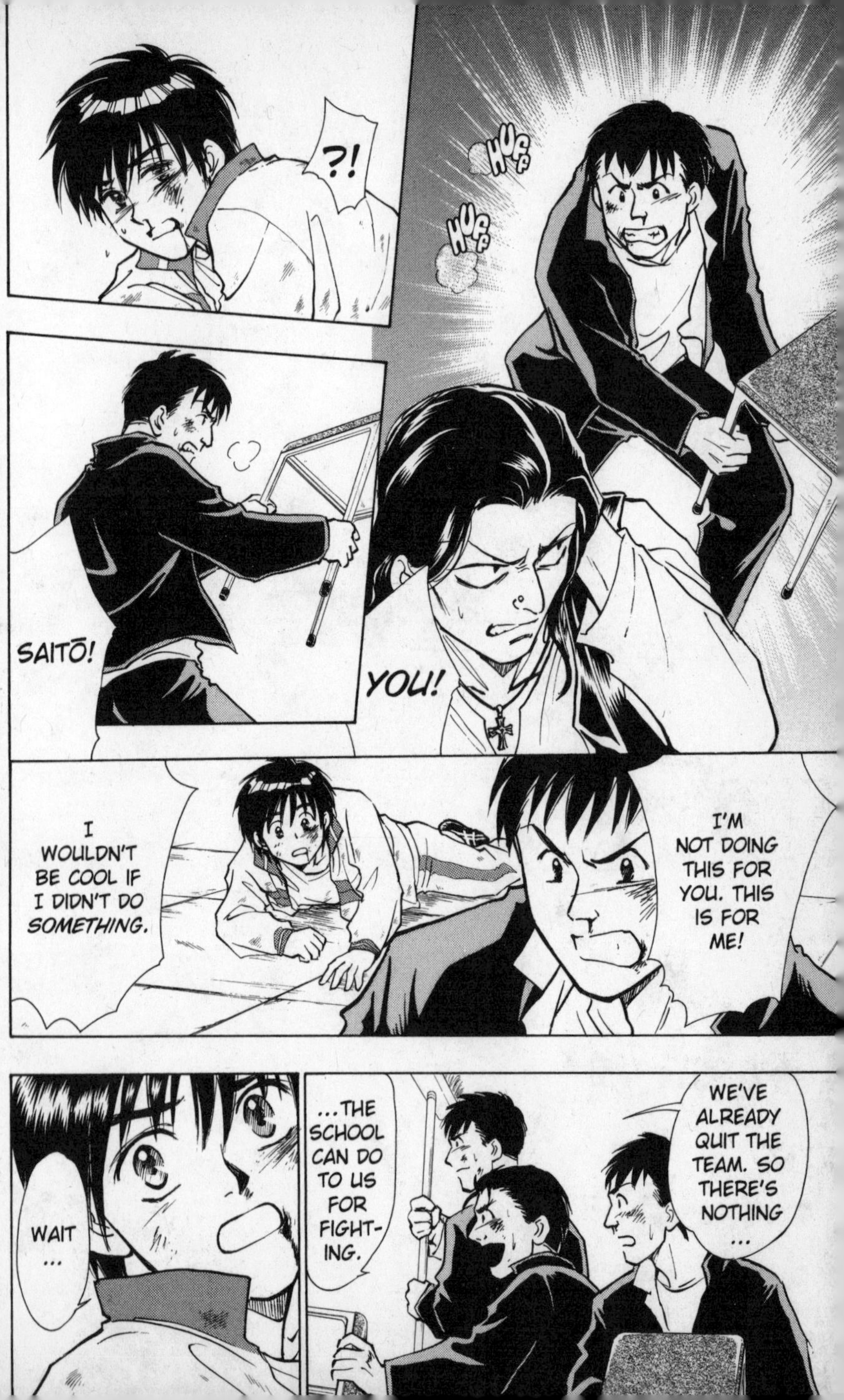
HUFF
HUFF
?!
YOU!
SAITŌ!
I'M NOT DOING THIS FOR YOU. THIS IS FOR ME!
I WOULDN'T BE COOL IF I DIDN'T DO SOMETHING.
WE'VE ALREADY QUIT THE TEAM. SO THERE'S NOTHING ...
...THE SCHOOL CAN DO TO US FOR FIGHTING.
WAIT ...

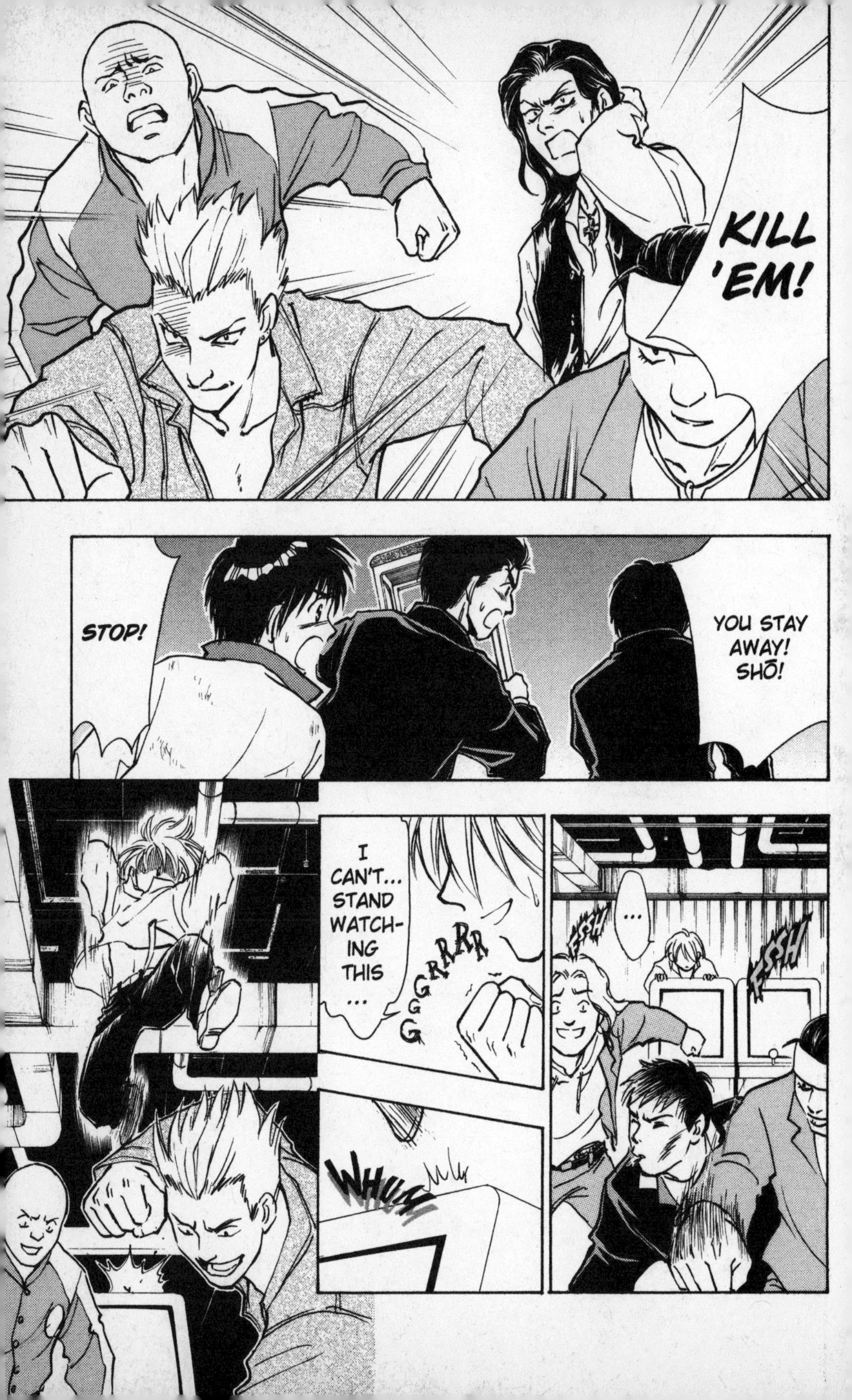
KILL 'EM!
YOU STAY AWAY! SHŌ!
STOP!
...
FSSH
FSSH
I CAN'T... STAND WATCHING THIS...
GGGRRRR
WHUM

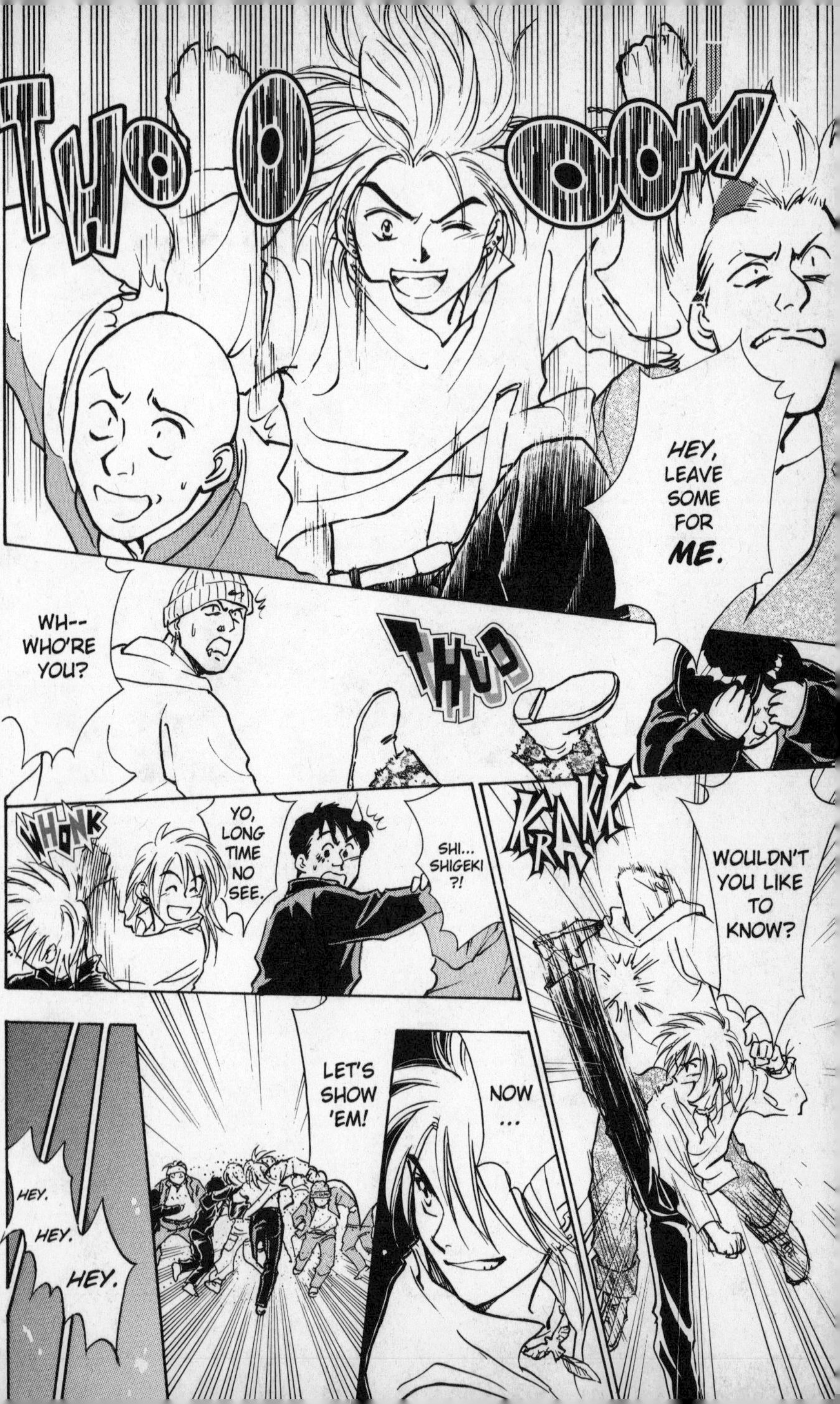

THOOOOOM
HEY, LEAVE SOME FOR ME.
THUD
WH-- WHO'RE YOU?
KRAKK
WOULDN'T YOU LIKE TO KNOW?
WHONK
YO, LONG TIME NO SEE.
SHI... SHIGEKI ?!
NOW ...
LET'S SHOW 'EM!
HEY.
HEY.
HEY.

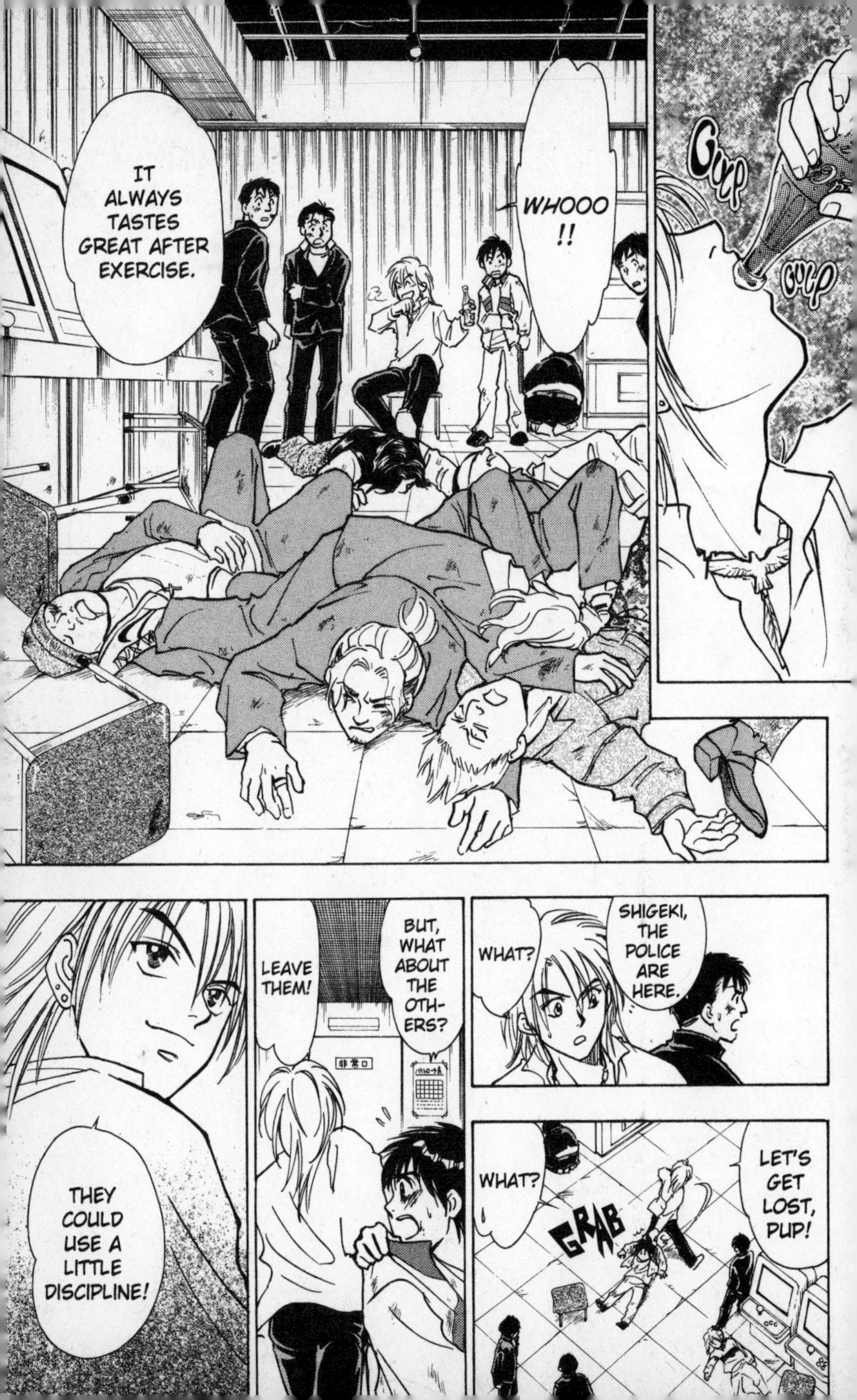
GULP
GULP
WHOOO!!
IT ALWAYS TASTES GREAT AFTER EXERCISE.
SHIGEKI, THE POLICE ARE HERE.
WHAT?
LET'S GET LOST, PUP!
WHAT?
GRAB
BUT, WHAT ABOUT THE OTHERS?
LEAVE THEM!
THEY COULD USE A LITTLE DISCIPLINE!

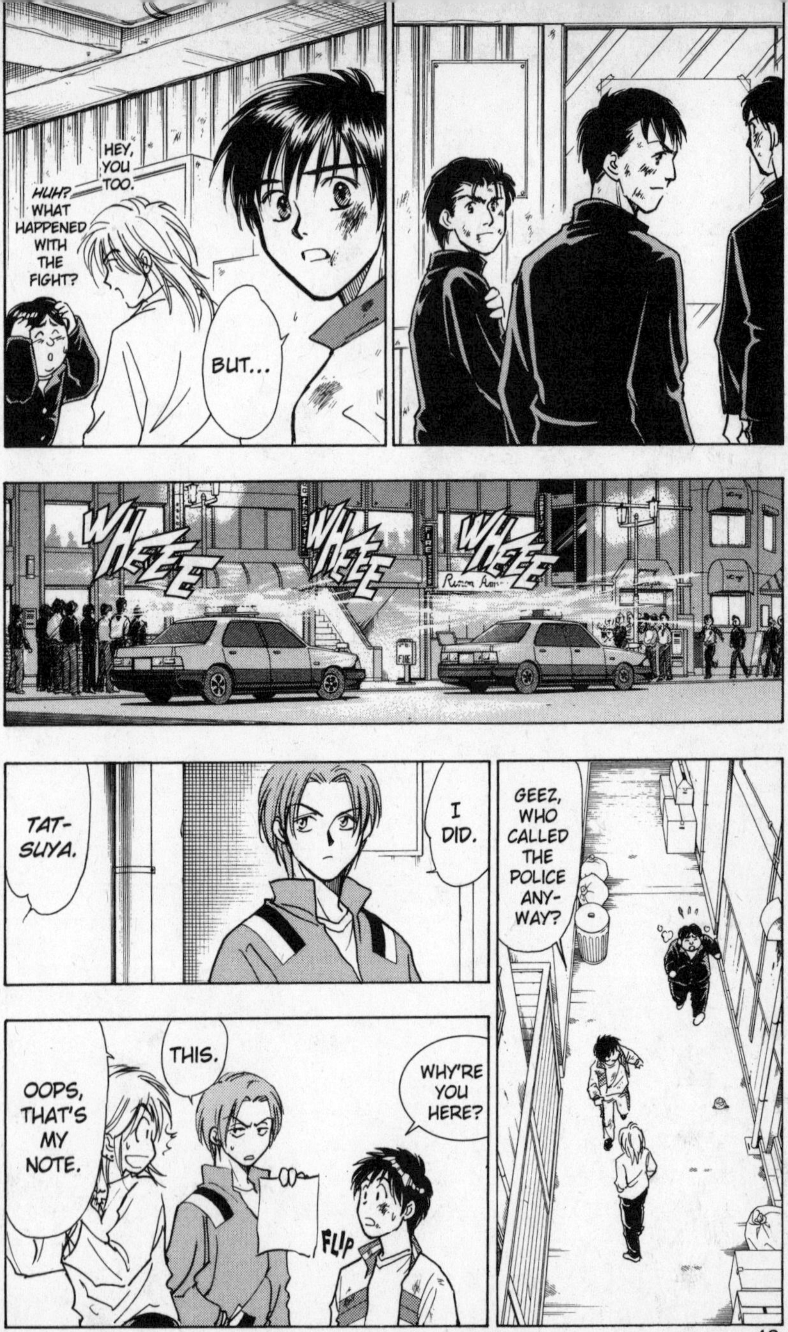
BUT...
HEY, YOU TOO.
HUH? WHAT HAPPENED WITH THE FIGHT?
WHEEE
WHEEE
WHEEE
FIRE
GEEZ, WHO CALLED THE POLICE ANYWAY?
I DID.
TAT-SUYA.
WHY'RE YOU HERE?
THIS.
FLIP
OOPS, THAT'S MY NOTE.

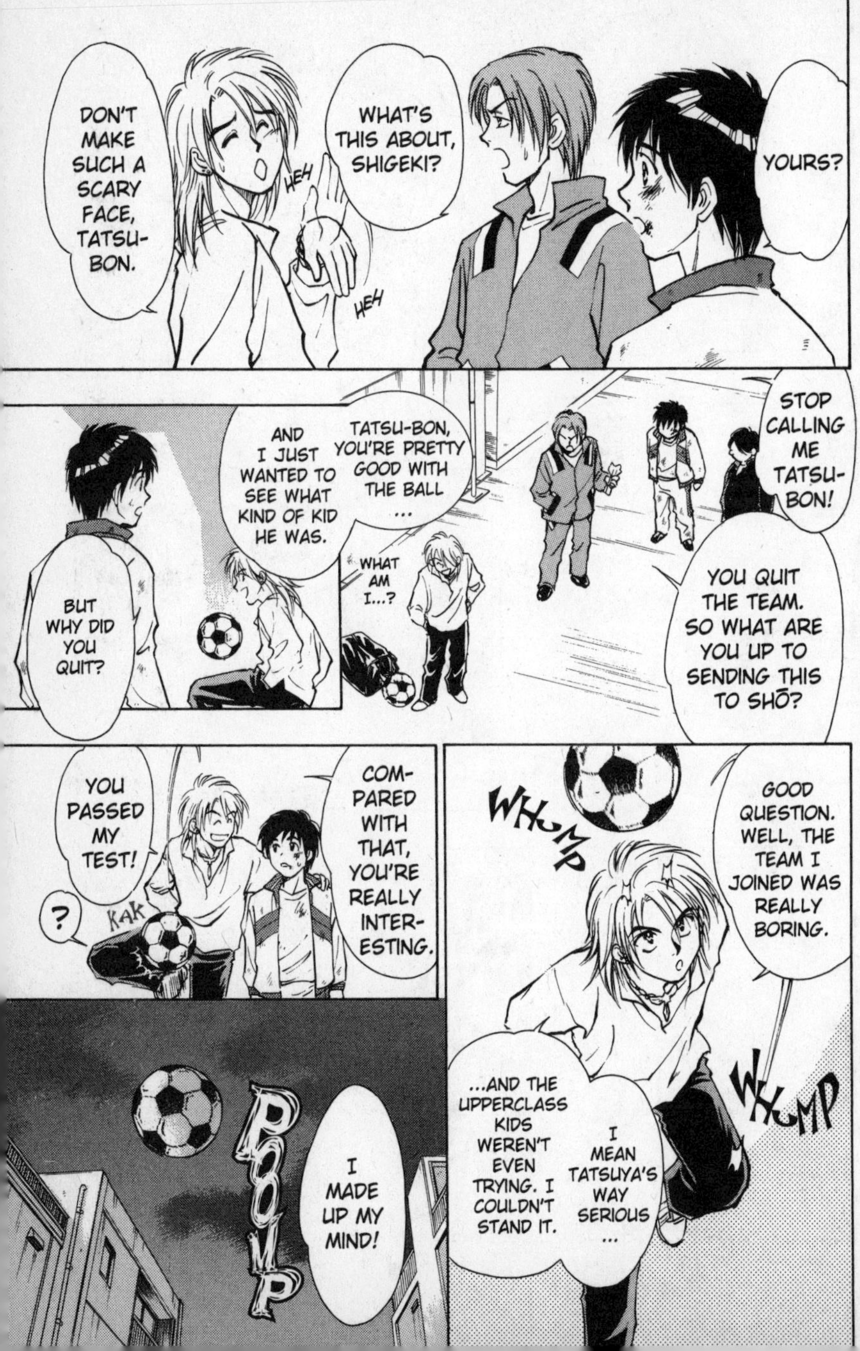
YOURS?
WHAT'S THIS ABOUT, SHIGEKI?
DON'T MAKE SUCH A SCARY FACE, TATSU-BON.
HEH HEH
STOP CALLING ME TATSU-BON!
YOU QUIT THE TEAM. SO WHAT ARE YOU UP TO SENDING THIS TO SHŌ?
WHAT AM I...?
TATSU-BON, YOU'RE PRETTY GOOD WITH THE BALL ...
AND I JUST WANTED TO SEE WHAT KIND OF KID HE WAS.
BUT WHY DID YOU QUIT?
GOOD QUESTION. WELL, THE TEAM I JOINED WAS REALLY BORING.
WHUMP
I MEAN TATSUYA'S WAY SERIOUS ...
...AND THE UPPERCLASS KIDS WEREN'T EVEN TRYING. I COULDN'T STAND IT.
WHUMP
COM-PARED WITH THAT, YOU'RE REALLY INTER-ESTING.
YOU PASSED MY TEST!
?
KAK
I MADE UP MY MIND!
POOMP

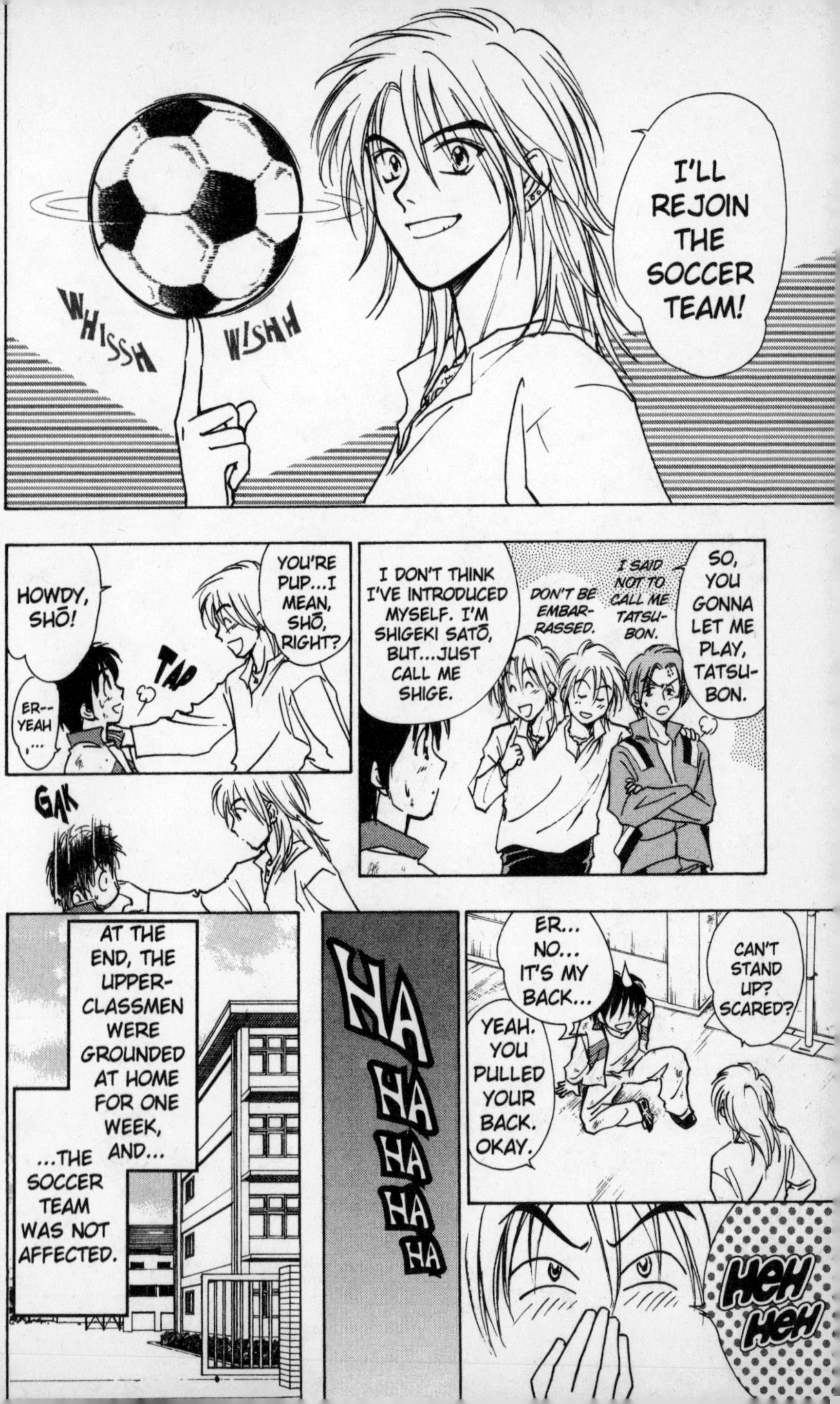
WHISSH
WISHH
I'LL REJOIN THE SOCCER TEAM!
SO, YOU GONNA LET ME PLAY, TATSU-BON.
I SAID NOT TO CALL ME TATSU-BON.
DON'T BE EMBAR-RASSED.
I DON'T THINK I'VE INTRODUCED MYSELF. I'M SHIGEKI SATŌ, BUT...JUST CALL ME SHIGE.
YOU'RE PUP...I MEAN, SHŌ, RIGHT?
HOWDY, SHŌ!
TAP
ER--YEAH,...
GAK
CAN'T STAND UP? SCARED?
ER... NO... IT'S MY BACK...
YEAH. YOU PULLED YOUR BACK. OKAY.
HEH HEH
HA HA HA HA HA HA
AT THE END, THE UPPER-CLASSMEN WERE GROUNDED AT HOME FOR ONE WEEK, AND...
...THE SOCCER TEAM WAS NOT AFFECTED.

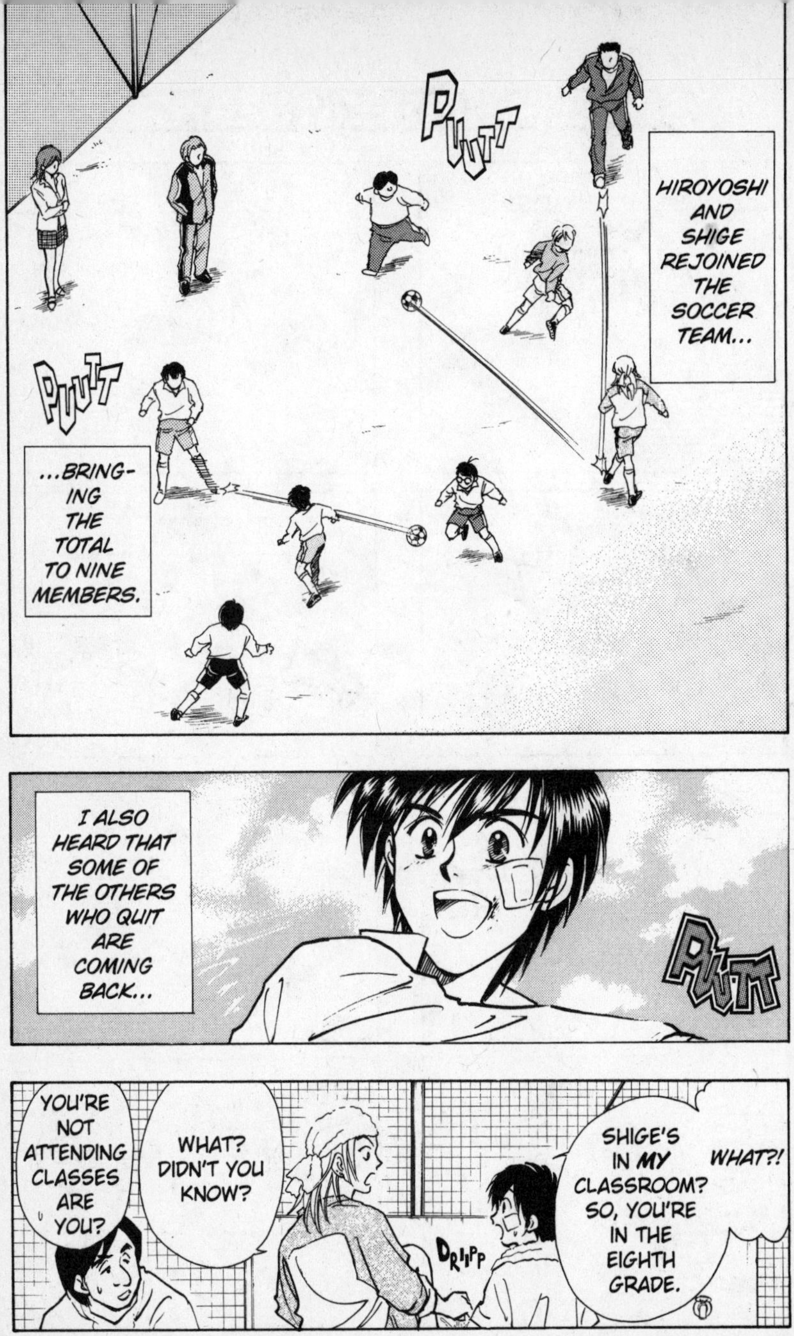
PUUTT
HIROYOSHI AND SHIGE REJOINED THE SOCCER TEAM...
PUUTT
...BRING-ING THE TOTAL TO NINE MEMBERS.
I ALSO HEARD THAT SOME OF THE OTHERS WHO QUIT ARE COMING BACK...
PATT
YOU'RE NOT ATTENDING CLASSES ARE YOU?
WHAT? DIDN'T YOU KNOW?
DRIIPP
SHIGE'S IN *MY* CLASSROOM? SO, YOU'RE IN THE EIGHTH GRADE.
WHAT?!

SMALL WHISTLE! THEATRE!!

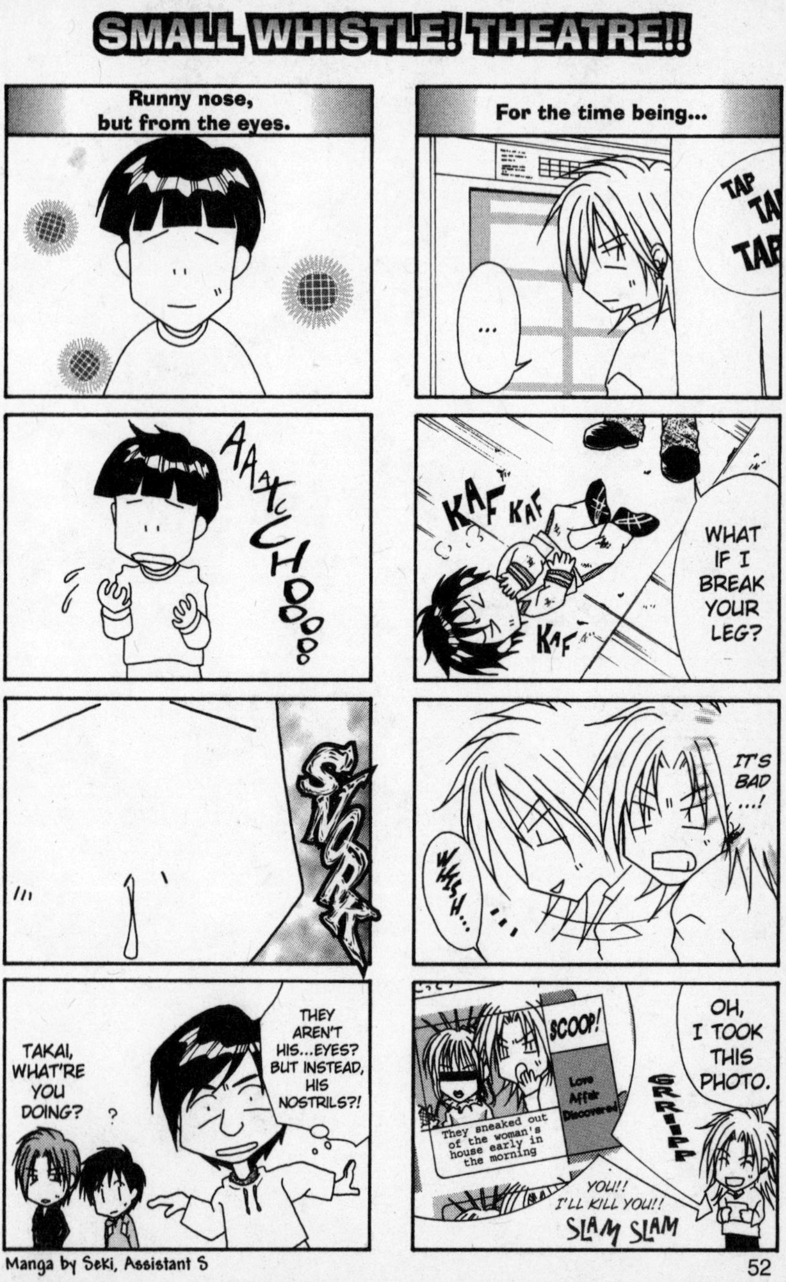
For the time being...
...
TAP TAP TAP
KAF KAF
KAF
WHAT IF I BREAK YOUR LEG?
IT'S BAD ...!
WHISH...
OH, I TOOK THIS PHOTO.
SCOOP!
Love Affair Discovered
They sneaked out of the woman's house early in the morning
GRRIPP
YOU!! I'LL KILL YOU!!
SLAM SLAM
Runny nose, but from the eyes.
AAAATCHOOOOO
SNORK
THEY AREN'T HIS...EYES? BUT INSTEAD, HIS NOSTRILS?!
TAKAI, WHAT'RE YOU DOING?
?

Manga by Seki, Assistant S

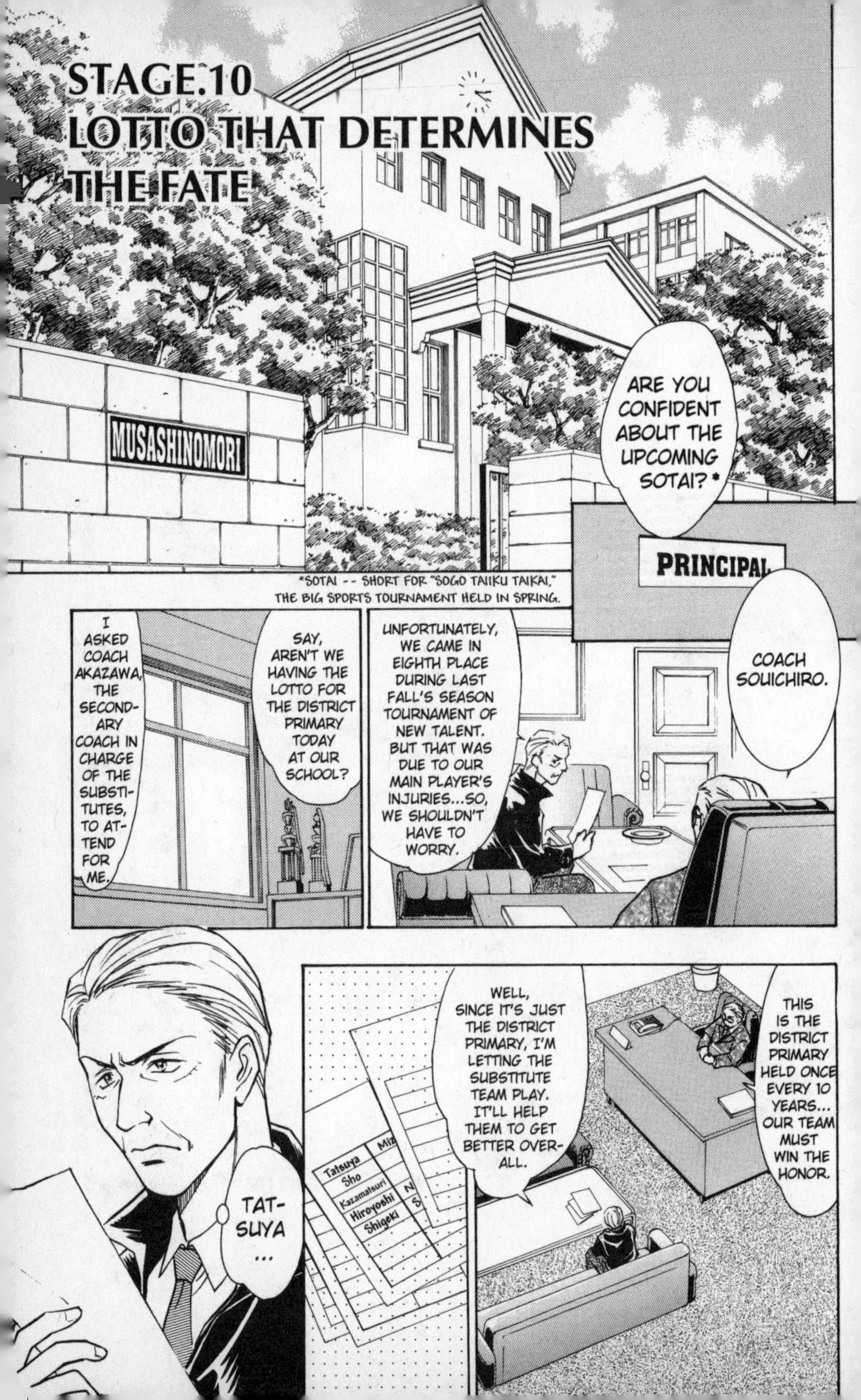
STAGE.10
LOTTO THAT DETERMINES THE FATE
MUSASHINOMORI
ARE YOU CONFIDENT ABOUT THE UPCOMING SOTAI? *
PRINCIPAL
*SOTAI -- SHORT FOR "SOGO TAIIKU TAIKAI," THE BIG SPORTS TOURNAMENT HELD IN SPRING.
COACH SOUICHIRO.
UNFORTUNATELY, WE CAME IN EIGHTH PLACE DURING LAST FALL'S SEASON TOURNAMENT OF NEW TALENT. BUT THAT WAS DUE TO OUR MAIN PLAYER'S INJURIES...SO, WE SHOULDN'T HAVE TO WORRY.
SAY, AREN'T WE HAVING THE LOTTO FOR THE DISTRICT PRIMARY TODAY AT OUR SCHOOL?
I ASKED COACH AKAZAWA, THE SECONDARY COACH IN CHARGE OF THE SUBSTITUTES, TO ATTEND FOR ME.
THIS IS THE DISTRICT PRIMARY HELD ONCE EVERY 10 YEARS... OUR TEAM MUST WIN THE HONOR.
WELL, SINCE IT'S JUST THE DISTRICT PRIMARY, I'M LETTING THE SUBSTITUTE TEAM PLAY. IT'LL HELP THEM TO GET BETTER OVERALL.
Tatsuya
Sho
Kazamatsuri
Hiroyoshi
Shigeki
TATSUYA ...

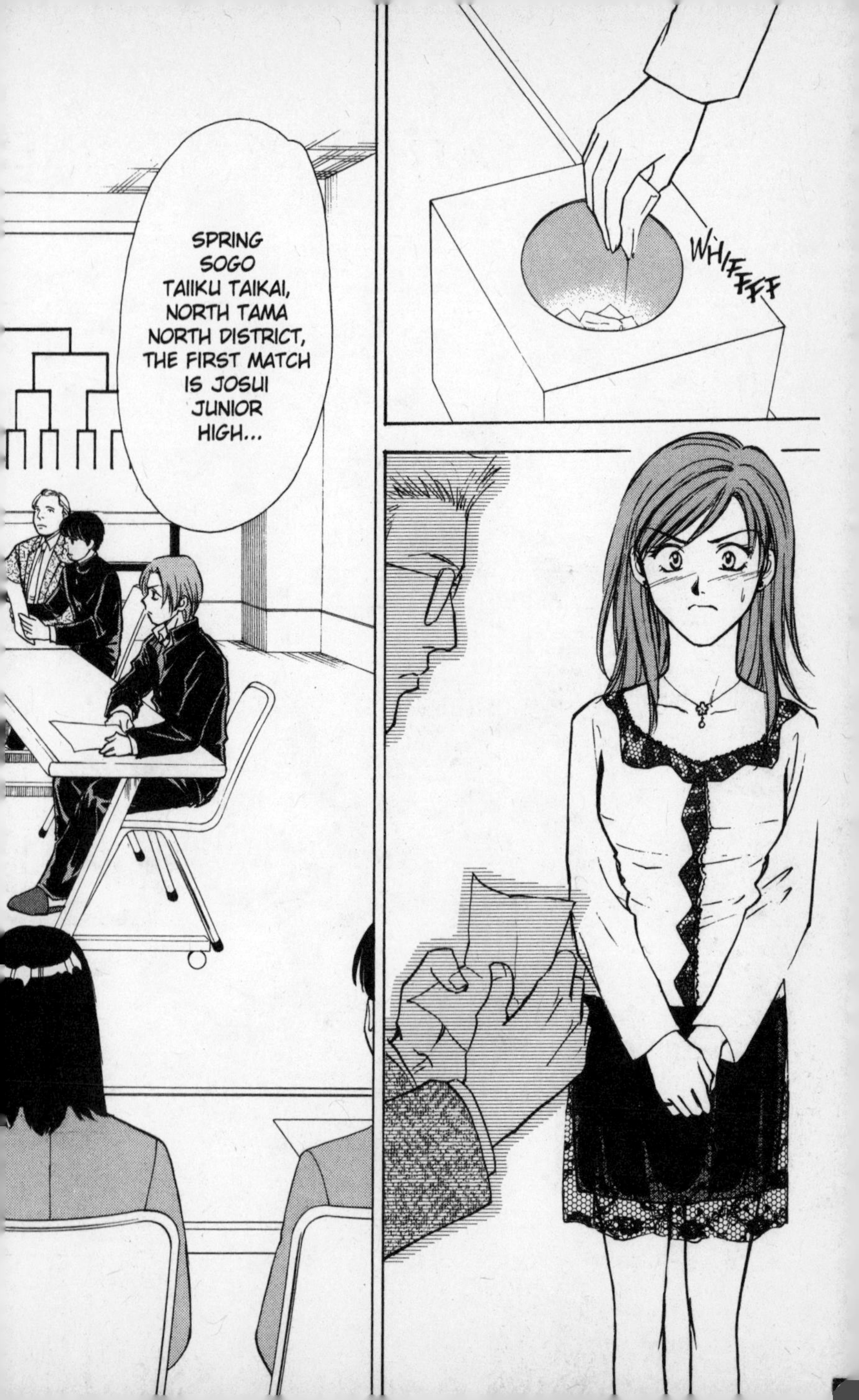

WHIFFFF
SPRING SOGO TAIIKU TAIKAI, NORTH TAMA NORTH DISTRICT, THE FIRST MATCH IS JOSUI JUNIOR HIGH...

STAGE.10 LOTTO THAT DETERMINES THE FATE

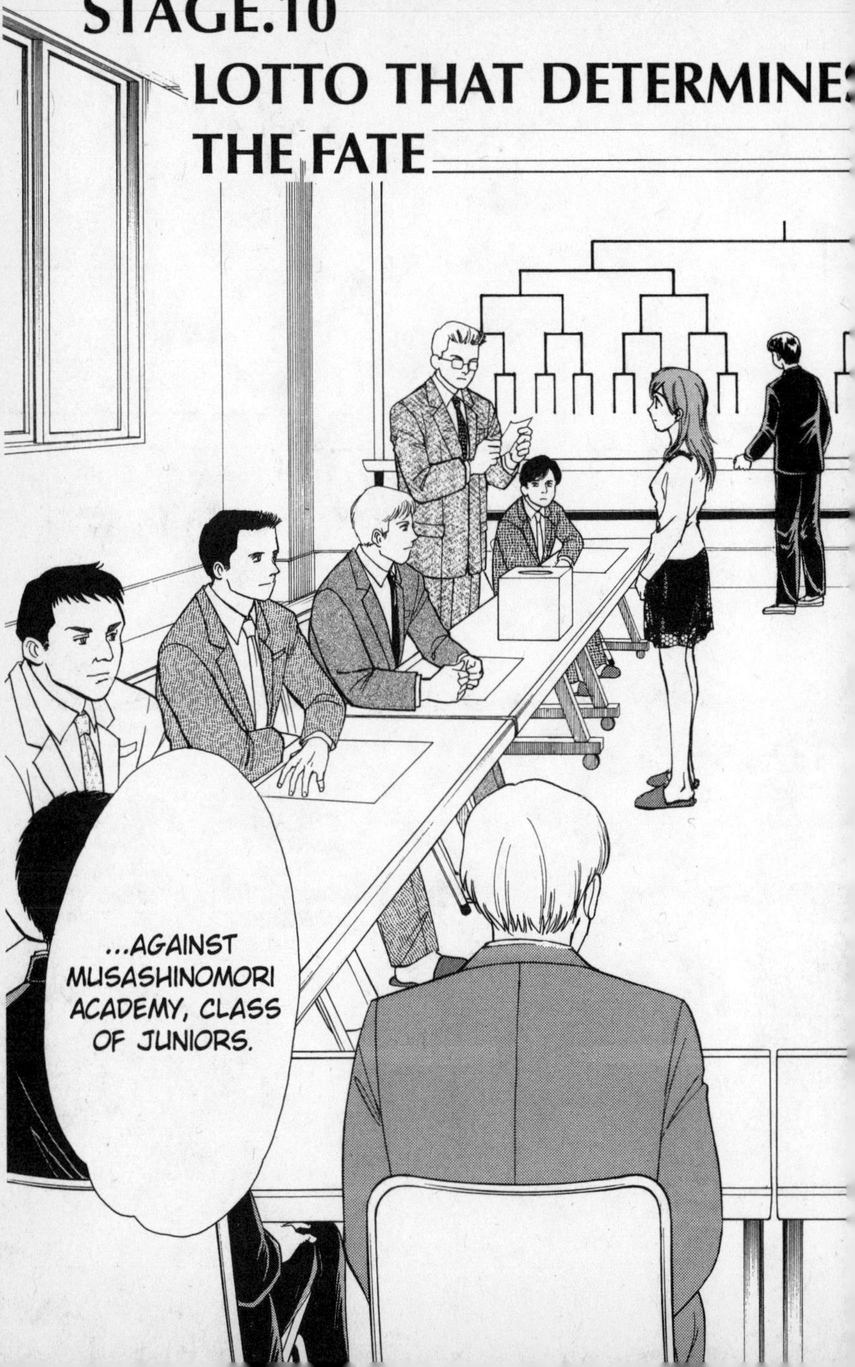
...AGAINST MUSASHINOMORI ACADEMY, CLASS OF JUNIORS.

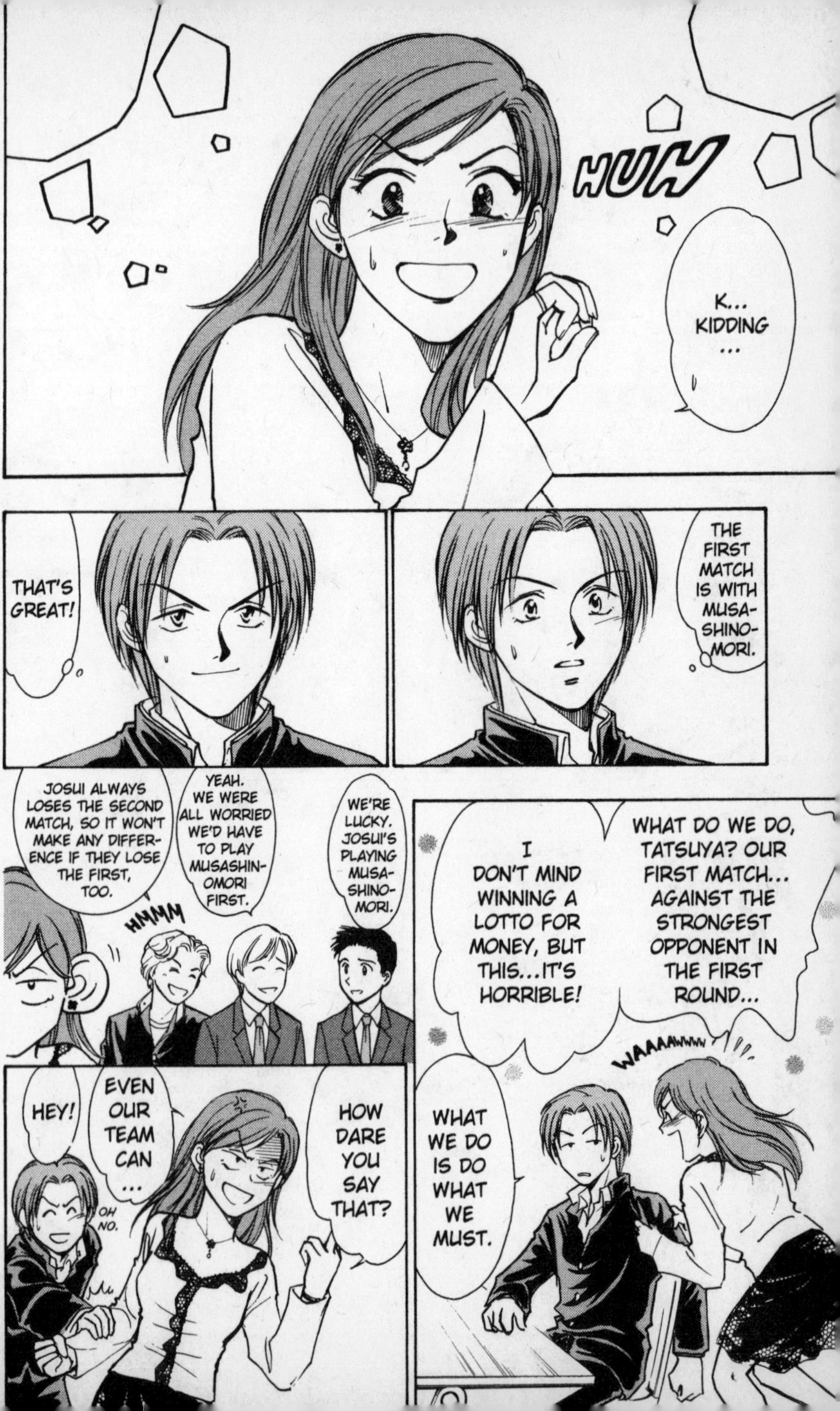
HUH
K... KIDDING...
THE FIRST MATCH IS WITH MUSA-SHINO-MORI.
THAT'S GREAT!
WHAT DO WE DO, TATSUYA? OUR FIRST MATCH... AGAINST THE STRONGEST OPPONENT IN THE FIRST ROUND...
I DON'T MIND WINNING A LOTTO FOR MONEY, BUT THIS...IT'S HORRIBLE!
WAAAAWWWW
WHAT WE DO IS DO WHAT WE MUST.
WE'RE LUCKY. JOSUI'S PLAYING MUSA-SHINO-MORI.
YEAH. WE WERE ALL WORRIED WE'D HAVE TO PLAY MUSASHINO-OMORI FIRST.
JOSUI ALWAYS LOSES THE SECOND MATCH, SO IT WON'T MAKE ANY DIFFER-ENCE IF THEY LOSE THE FIRST, TOO.
HMMM
HOW DARE YOU SAY THAT?
EVEN OUR TEAM CAN...
HEY!
OH NO.

READ THIS WAY

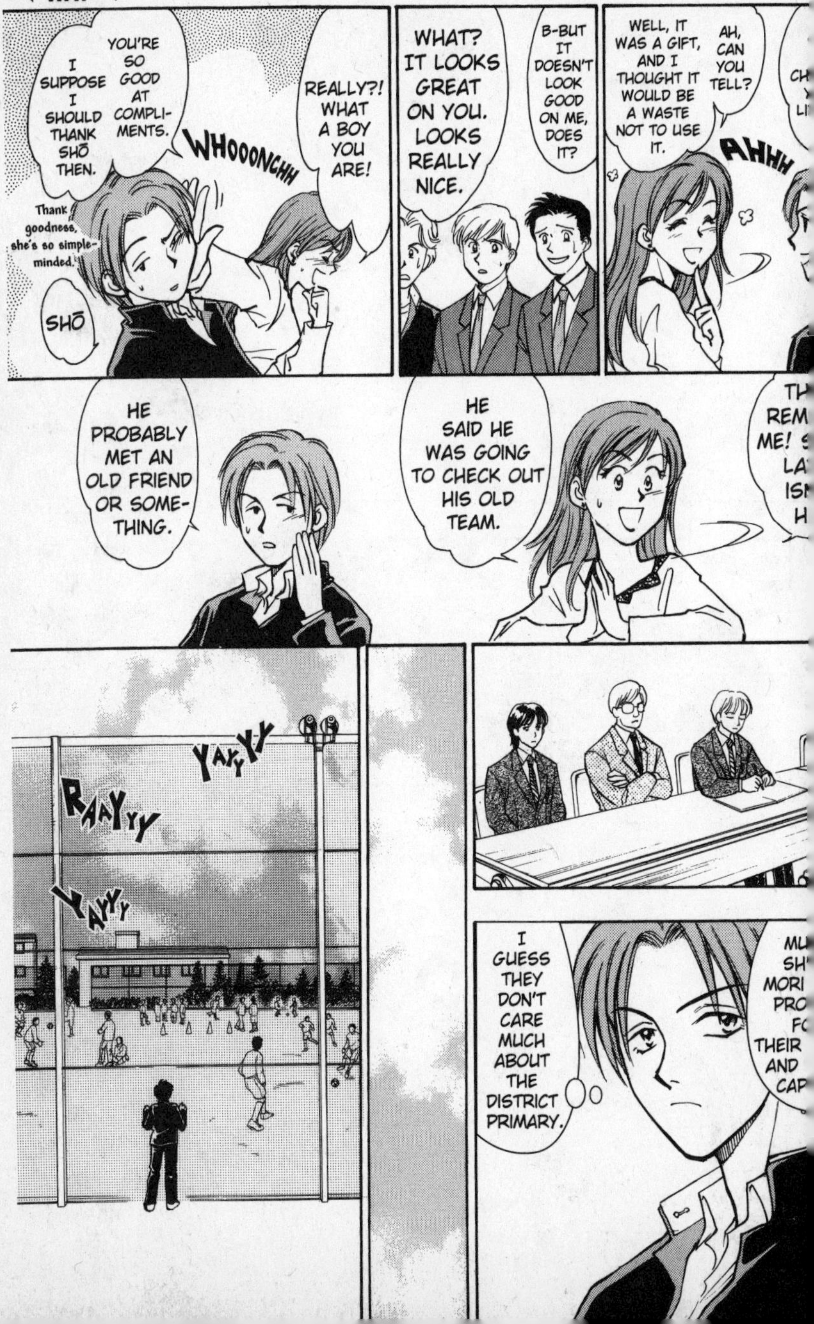
AH, CAN YOU TELL?
WELL, IT WAS A GIFT, AND I THOUGHT IT WOULD BE A WASTE NOT TO USE IT.
AHHH
B-BUT IT DOESN'T LOOK GOOD ON ME, DOES IT?
WHAT? IT LOOKS GREAT ON YOU. LOOKS REALLY NICE.
REALLY?! WHAT A BOY YOU ARE!
WHOOONCHH
YOU'RE SO GOOD AT COMPLIMENTS.
I SUPPOSE I SHOULD THANK SHŌ THEN.
Thank goodness, she's so simple-minded.
SHŌ
HE SAID HE WAS GOING TO CHECK OUT HIS OLD TEAM.
HE PROBABLY MET AN OLD FRIEND OR SOMETHING.
I GUESS THEY DON'T CARE MUCH ABOUT THE DISTRICT PRIMARY.
YAYYY
RAAYYY
YAYYY

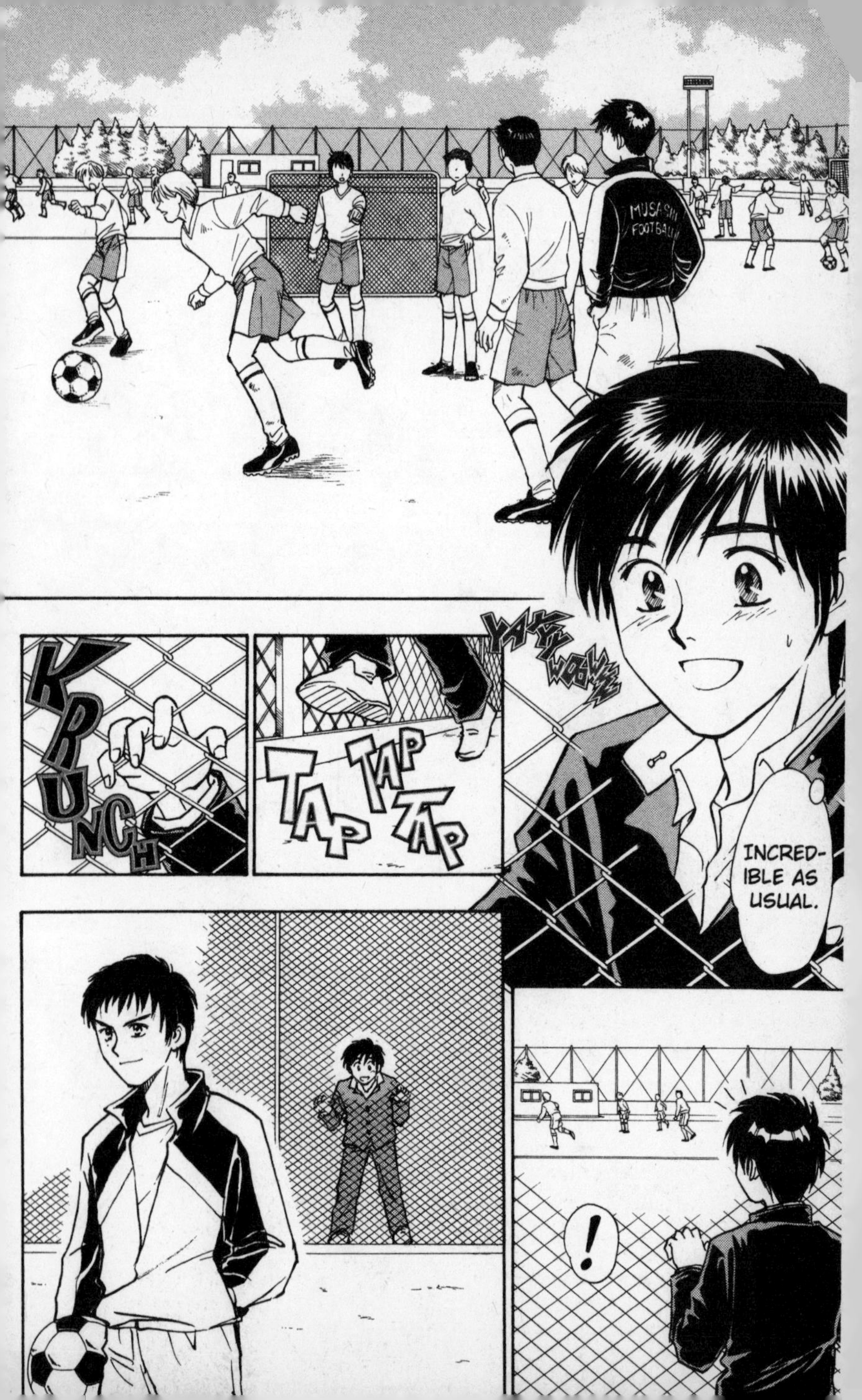
MUSASHI FOOTBALL
INCRED-IBLE AS USUAL.
TAP TAP TAP TAP
KRUNCH
!

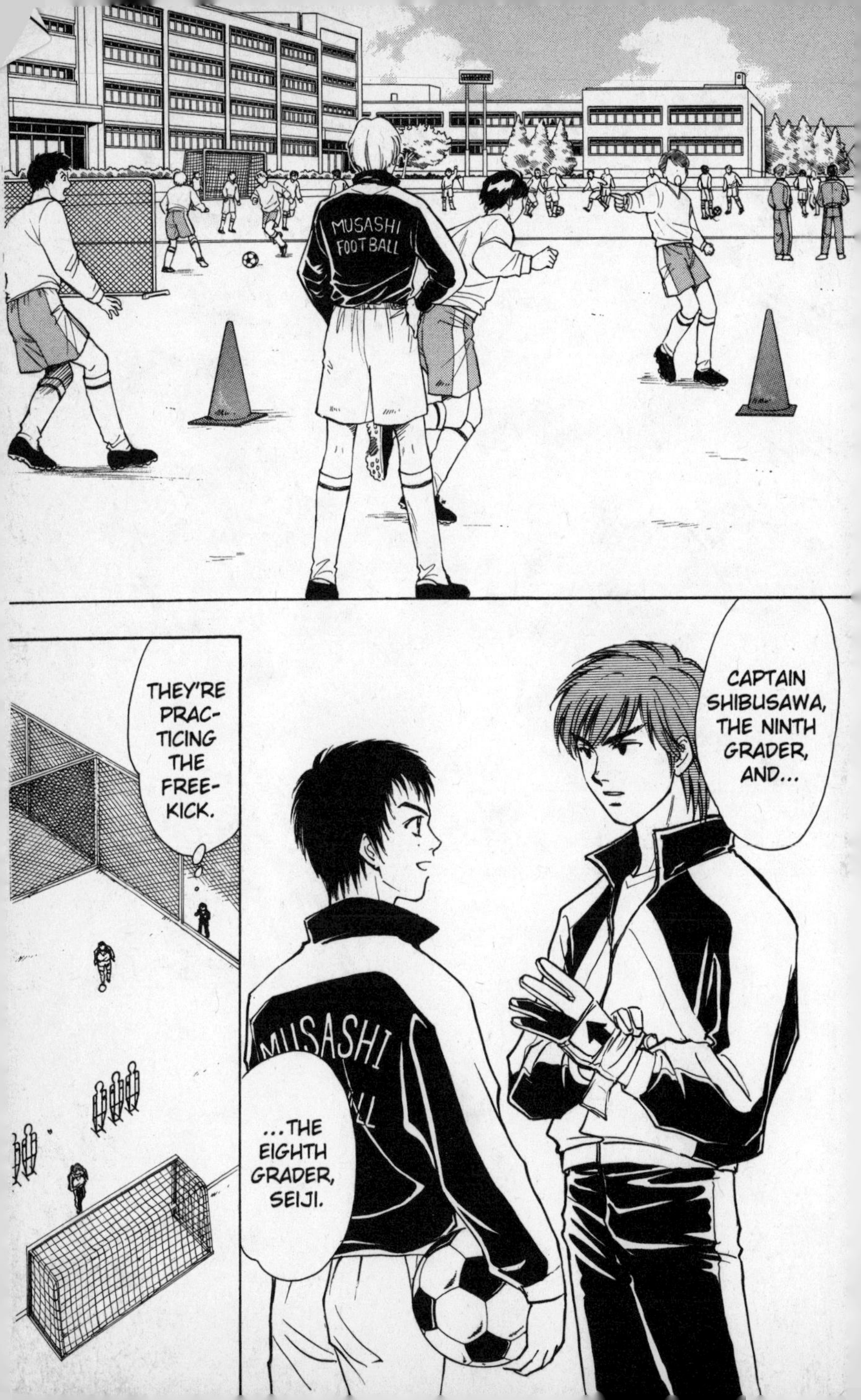
MUSASHI FOOTBALL
CAPTAIN SHIBUSAWA, THE NINTH GRADER, AND...
...THE EIGHTH GRADER, SEIJI.
MUSASHI
THEY'RE PRACTICING THE FREE-KICK.

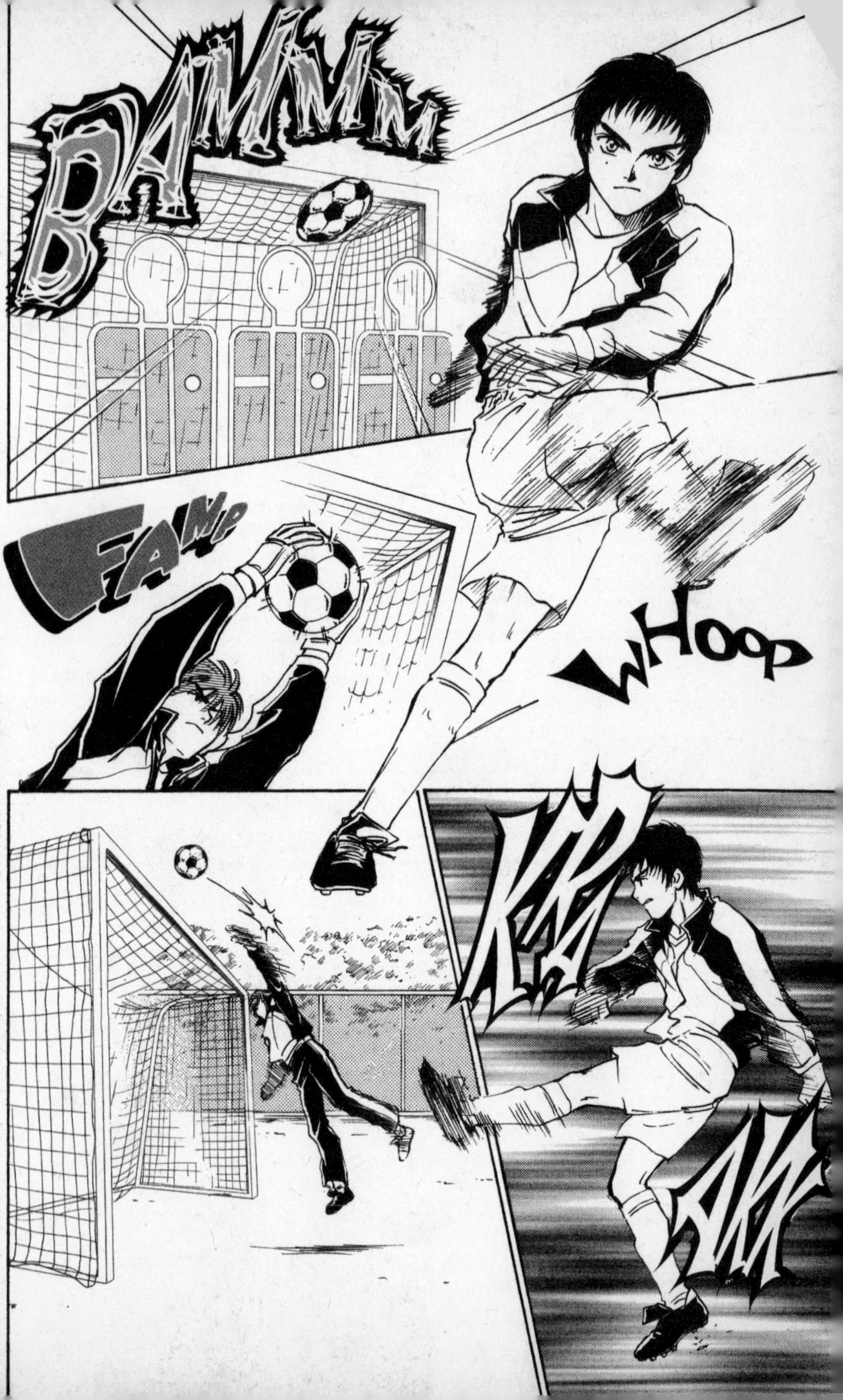
BAMMM
FAMP
WHOOP
KAKAKAK

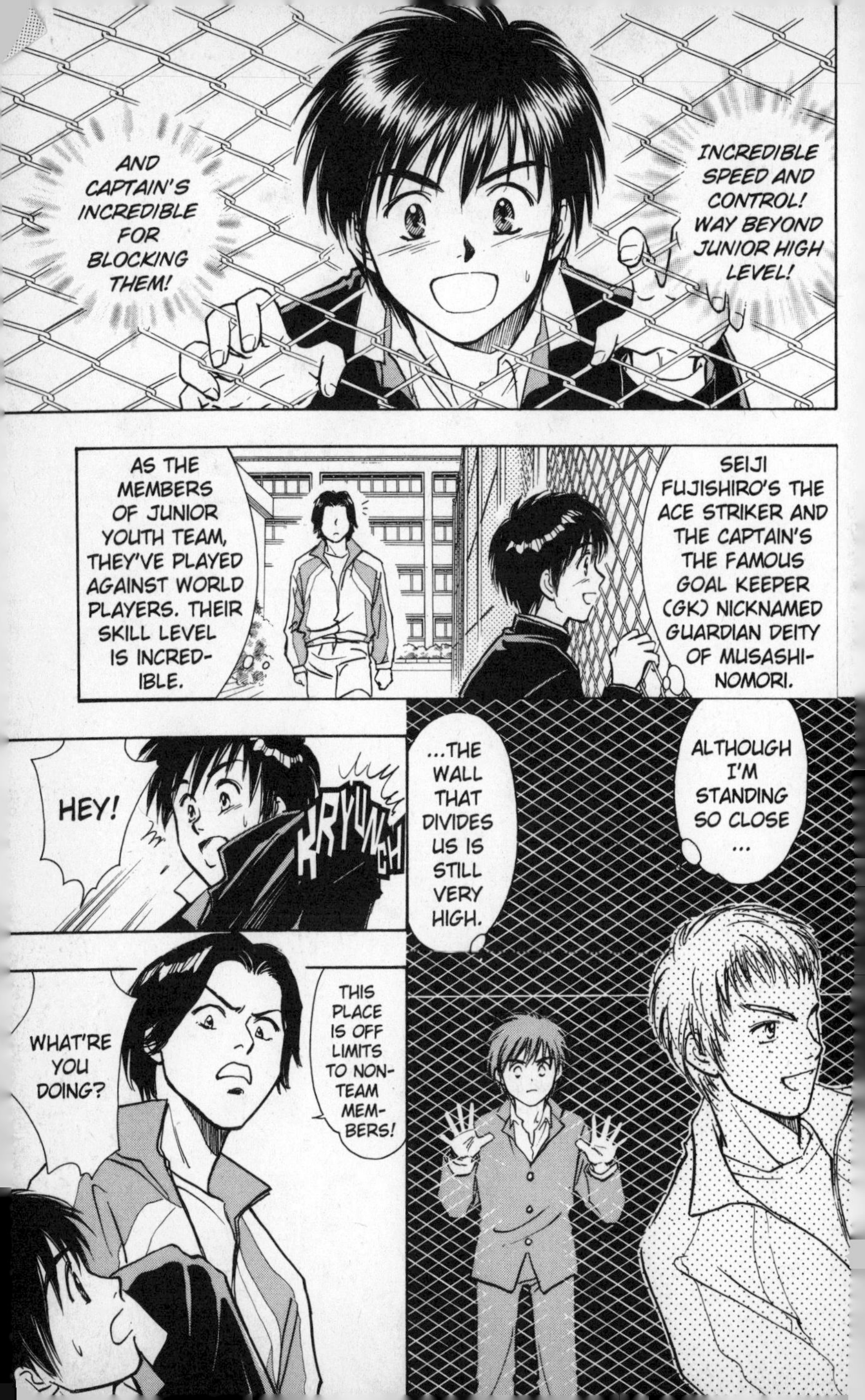
INCREDIBLE SPEED AND CONTROL! WAY BEYOND JUNIOR HIGH LEVEL!
AND CAPTAIN'S INCREDIBLE FOR BLOCKING THEM!
SEIJI FUJISHIRO'S THE ACE STRIKER AND THE CAPTAIN'S THE FAMOUS GOAL KEEPER (GK) NICKNAMED GUARDIAN DEITY OF MUSASHI-NOMORI.
AS THE MEMBERS OF JUNIOR YOUTH TEAM, THEY'VE PLAYED AGAINST WORLD PLAYERS. THEIR SKILL LEVEL IS INCRED-IBLE.
ALTHOUGH I'M STANDING SO CLOSE ...
...THE WALL THAT DIVIDES US IS STILL VERY HIGH.
HEY!
KRYUNCH
THIS PLACE IS OFF LIMITS TO NON-TEAM MEM-BERS!
WHAT'RE YOU DOING?

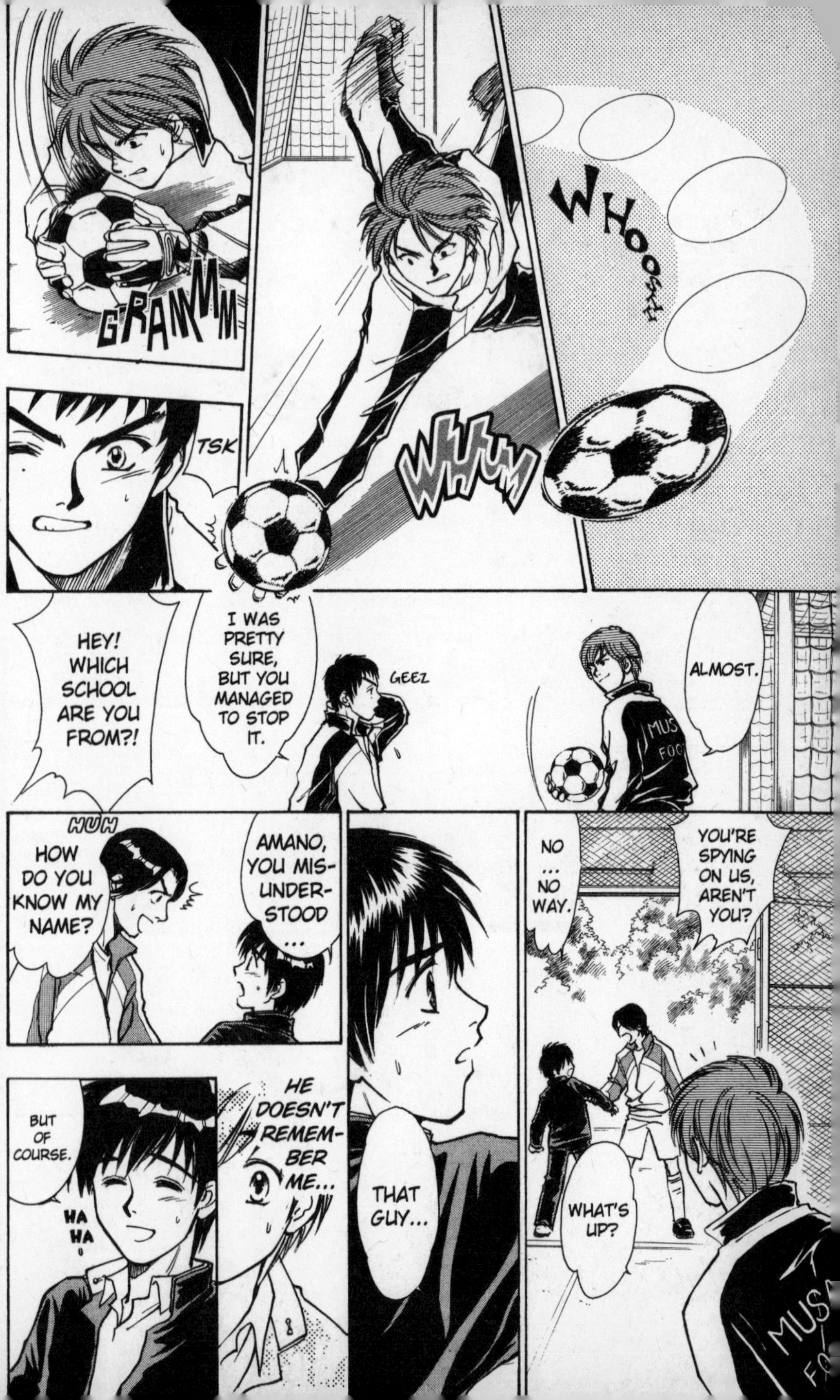
GRAMMM
WHOOSH
TSK
WHUM
HEY! WHICH SCHOOL ARE YOU FROM?!
I WAS PRETTY SURE, BUT YOU MANAGED TO STOP IT.
GEEZ
ALMOST.
MUS FOO
HUH
HOW DO YOU KNOW MY NAME?
AMANO, YOU MIS-UNDER-STOOD ...
NO ... NO WAY.
YOU'RE SPYING ON US, AREN'T YOU?
BUT OF COURSE.
HA HA
HE DOESN'T REMEM-BER ME...
THAT GUY...
WHAT'S UP?
MUSA FO

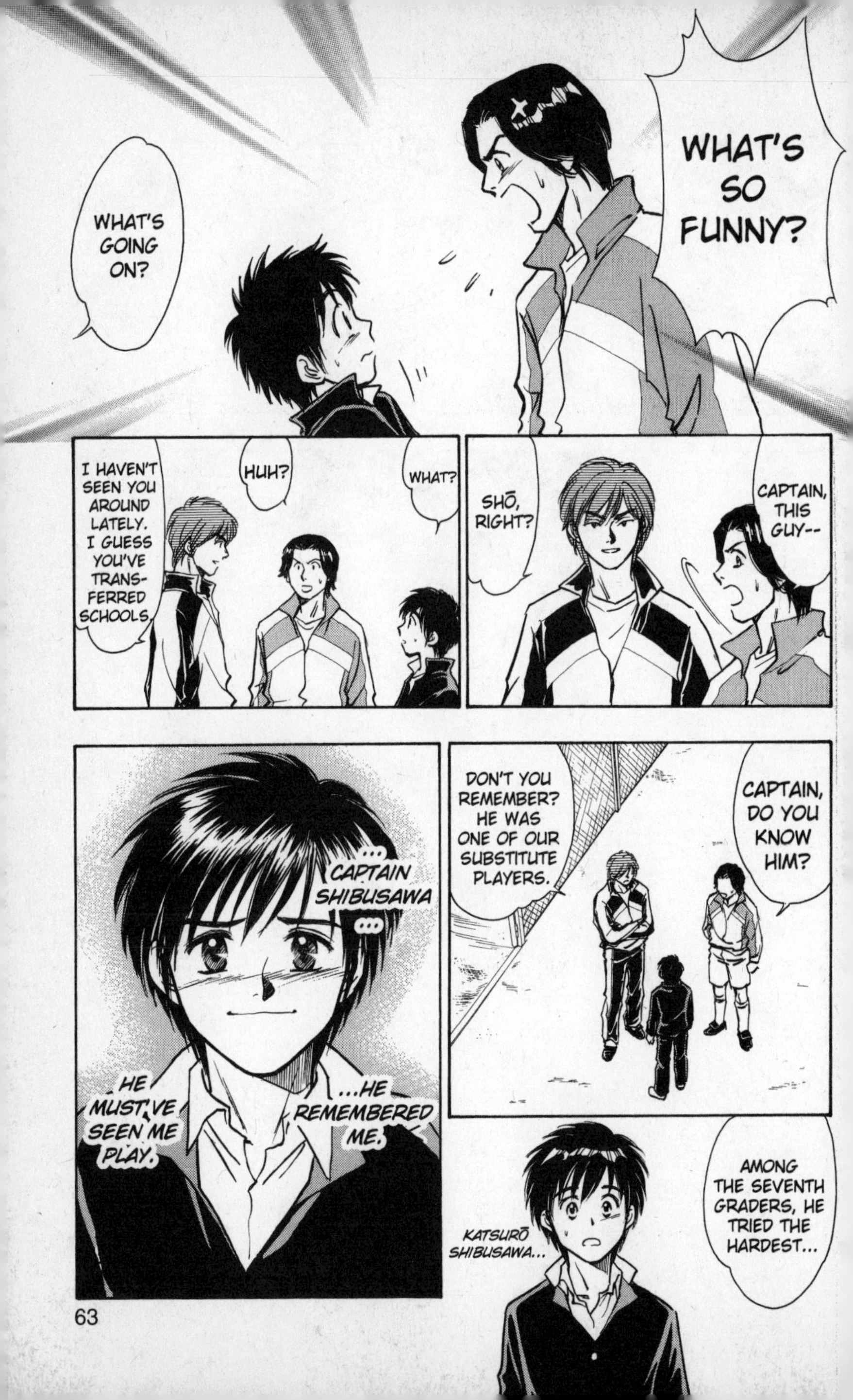
WHAT'S SO FUNNY?
WHAT'S GOING ON?
CAPTAIN, THIS GUY--
SHŌ, RIGHT?
WHAT?
HUH?
I HAVEN'T SEEN YOU AROUND LATELY. I GUESS YOU'VE TRANS-FERRED SCHOOLS.
CAPTAIN, DO YOU KNOW HIM?
DON'T YOU REMEMBER? HE WAS ONE OF OUR SUBSTITUTE PLAYERS.
AMONG THE SEVENTH GRADERS, HE TRIED THE HARDEST...
KATSURŌ SHIBUSAWA...
...CAPTAIN SHIBUSAWA...
...HE REMEMBERED ME.
HE MUST'VE SEEN ME PLAY.

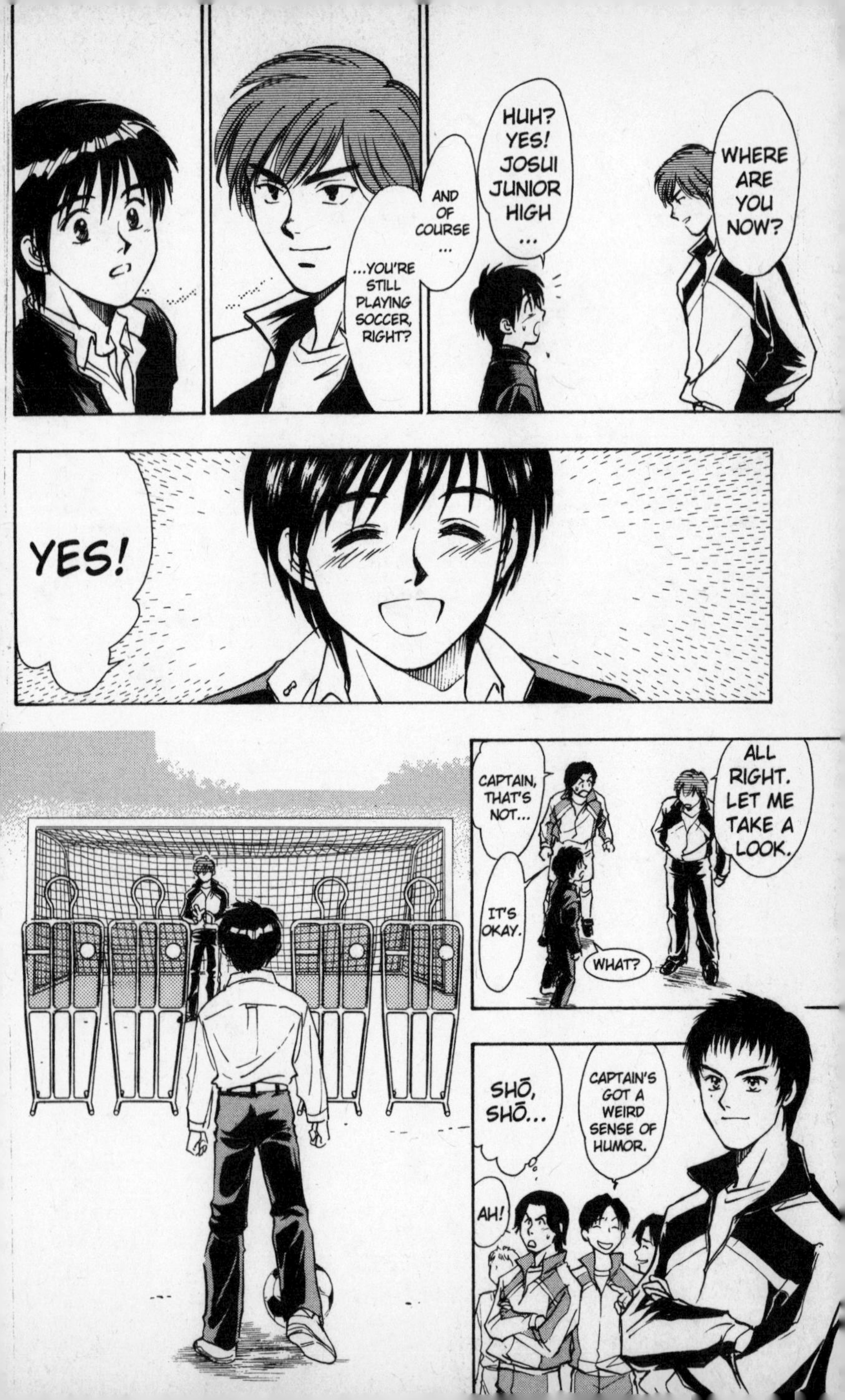
WHERE ARE YOU NOW?
HUH? YES! JOSUI JUNIOR HIGH ...
AND OF COURSE ...
...YOU'RE STILL PLAYING SOCCER, RIGHT?
YES!
ALL RIGHT. LET ME TAKE A LOOK.
CAPTAIN, THAT'S NOT...
IT'S OKAY.
WHAT?
CAPTAIN'S GOT A WEIRD SENSE OF HUMOR.
SHŌ, SHŌ...
AH!

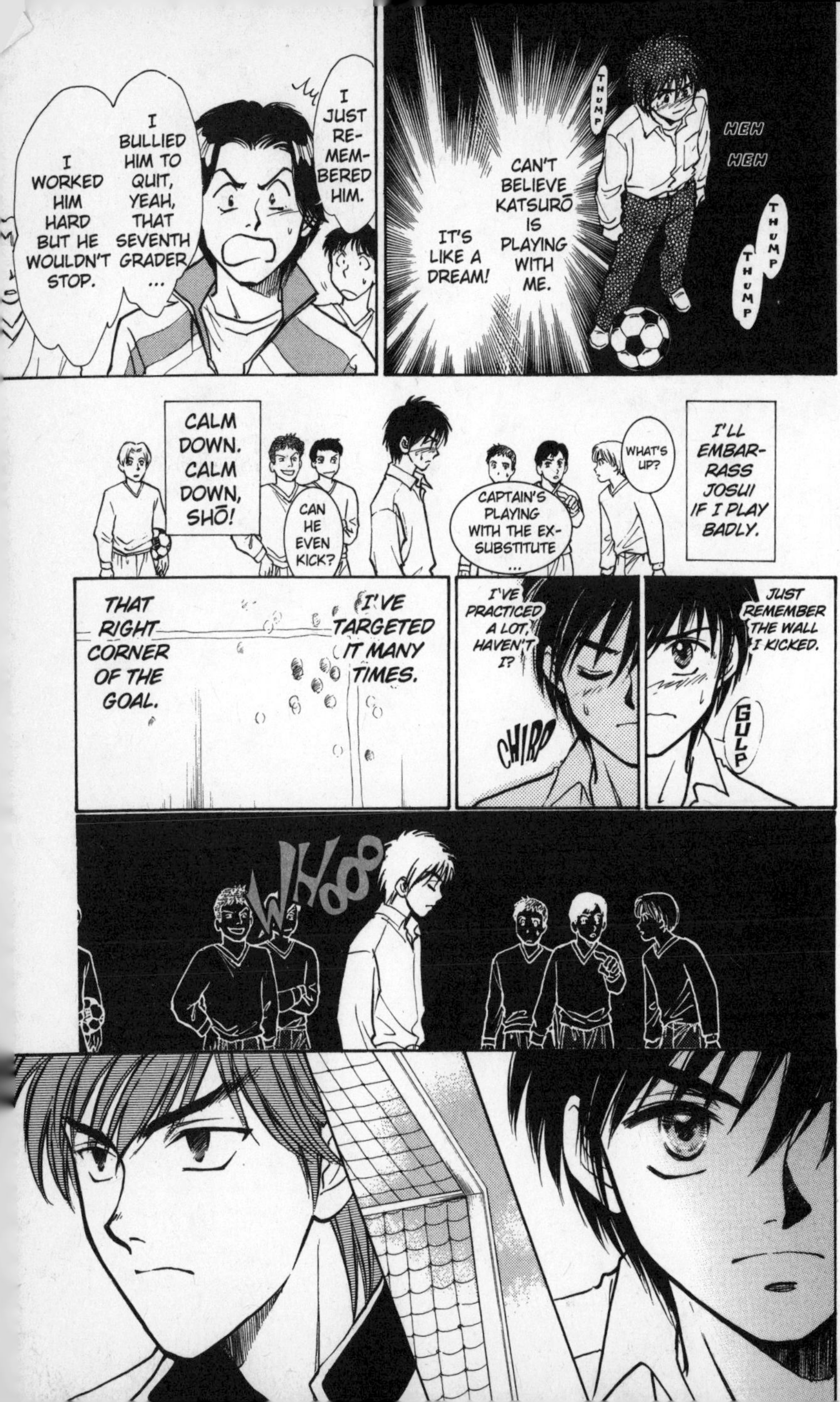
THUMP
CAN'T BELIEVE KATSURŌ IS PLAYING WITH ME.
IT'S LIKE A DREAM!
HEH HEH
THUMP
THUMP
I JUST RE-MEM-BERED HIM.
I BULLIED HIM TO QUIT, YEAH, THAT SEVENTH GRADER ...
I WORKED HIM HARD BUT HE WOULDN'T STOP.
I'LL EMBAR-RASS JOSUI IF I PLAY BADLY.
WHAT'S UP?
CAPTAIN'S PLAYING WITH THE EX-SUBSTITUTE ...
CAN HE EVEN KICK?
CALM DOWN. CALM DOWN, SHŌ!
JUST REMEMBER THE WALL I KICKED.
GULP
I'VE PRACTICED A LOT, HAVEN'T I?
CHIRP
I'VE TARGETED IT MANY TIMES.
THAT RIGHT CORNER OF THE GOAL.
WHOOP

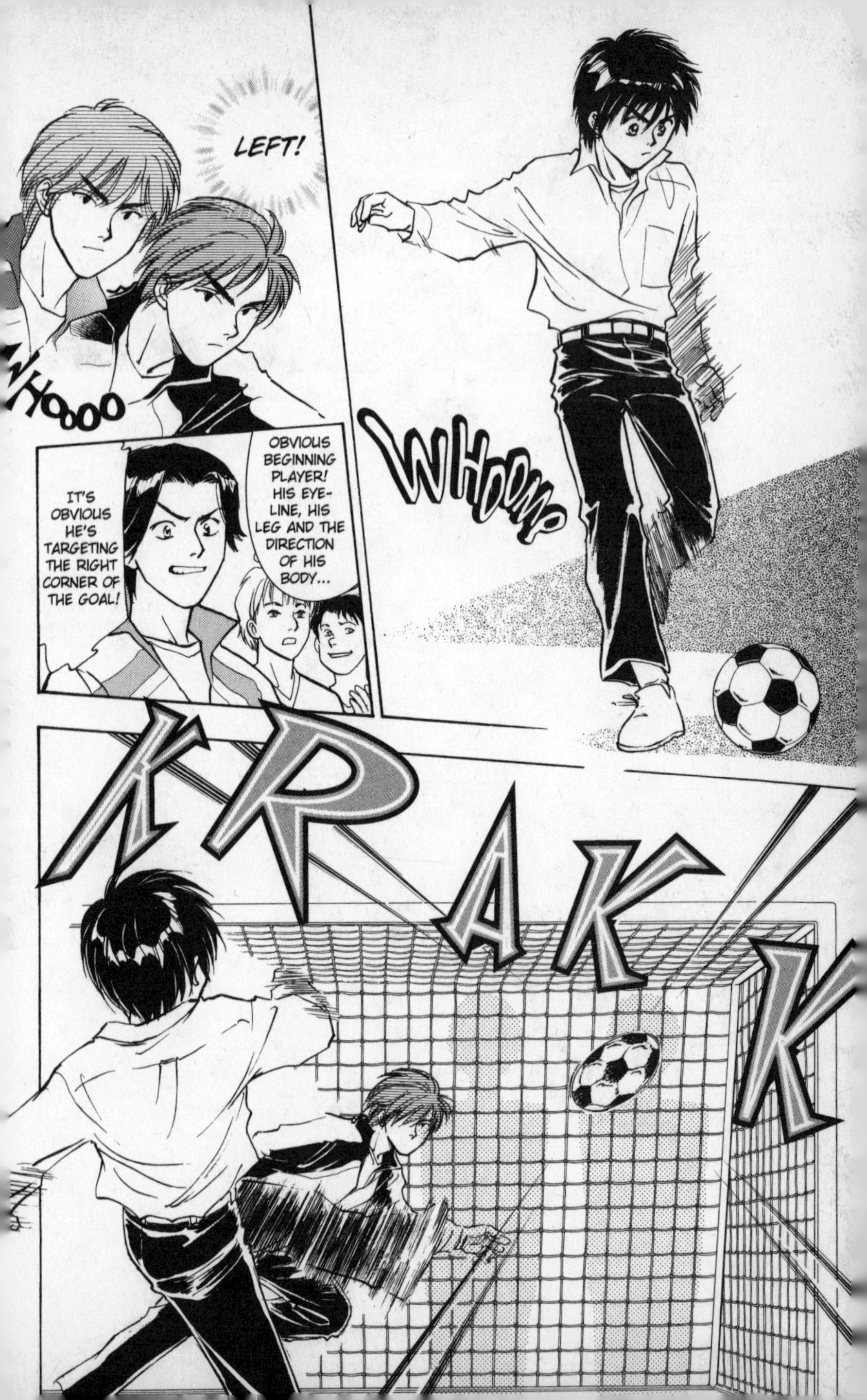
WHOOMP
LEFT!
WHOOOO
OBVIOUS BEGINNING PLAYER! HIS EYE-LINE, HIS LEG AND THE DIRECTION OF HIS BODY...
IT'S OBVIOUS HE'S TARGETING THE RIGHT CORNER OF THE GOAL!
KRAKK

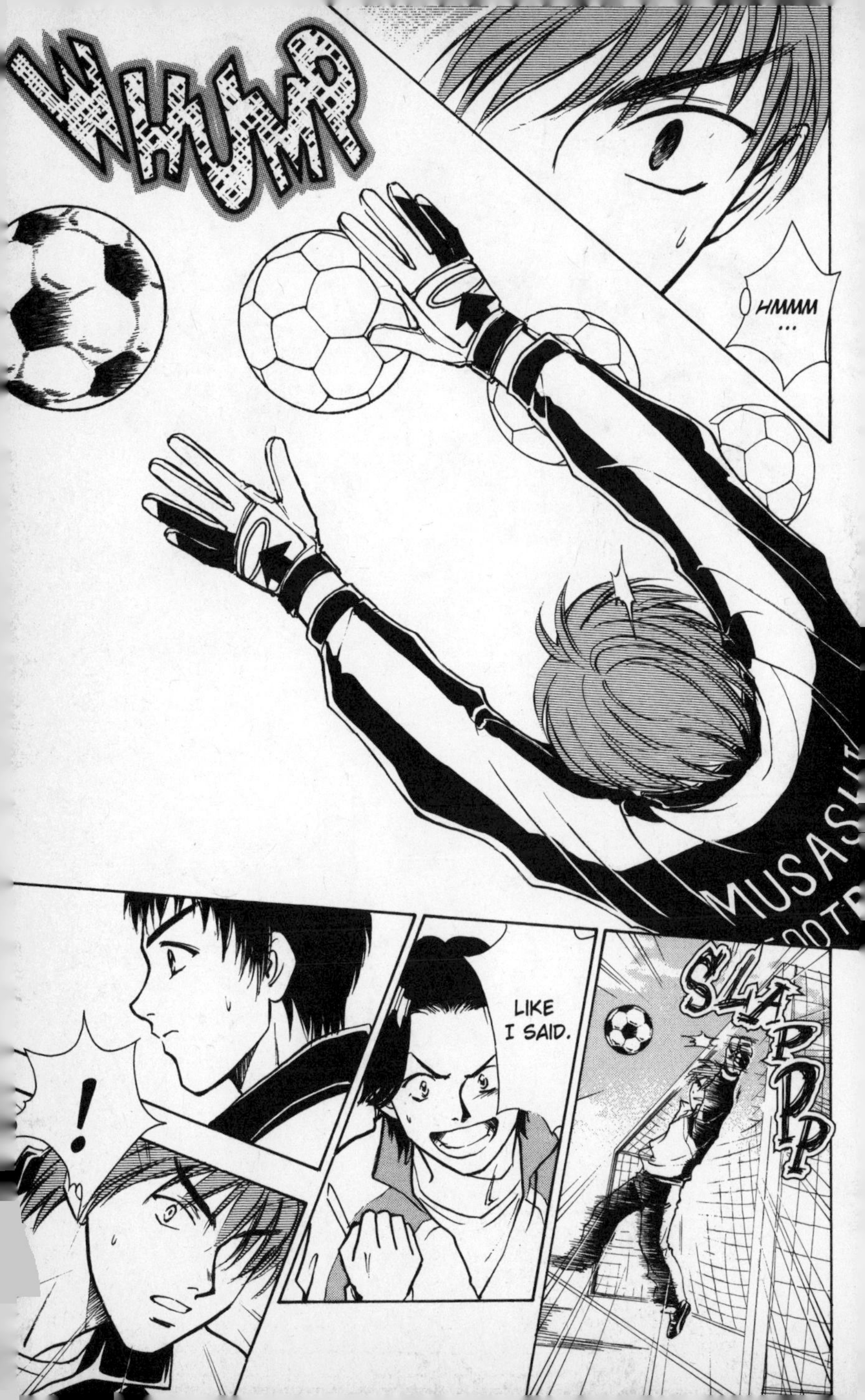
WHUMP
HMMM ...
MUSASH
SLAPPP
LIKE I SAID.
!

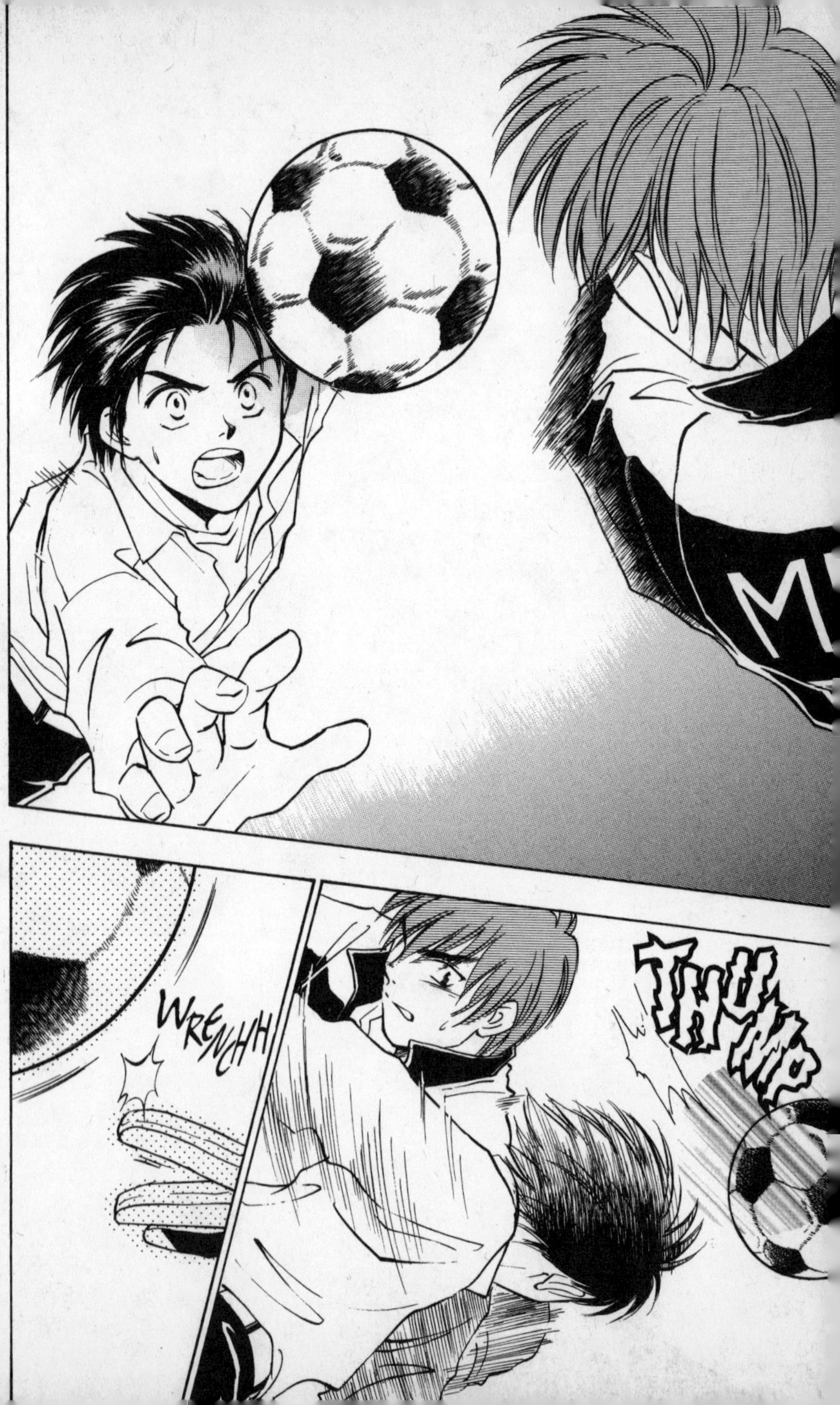
THUMP
WRENCHH

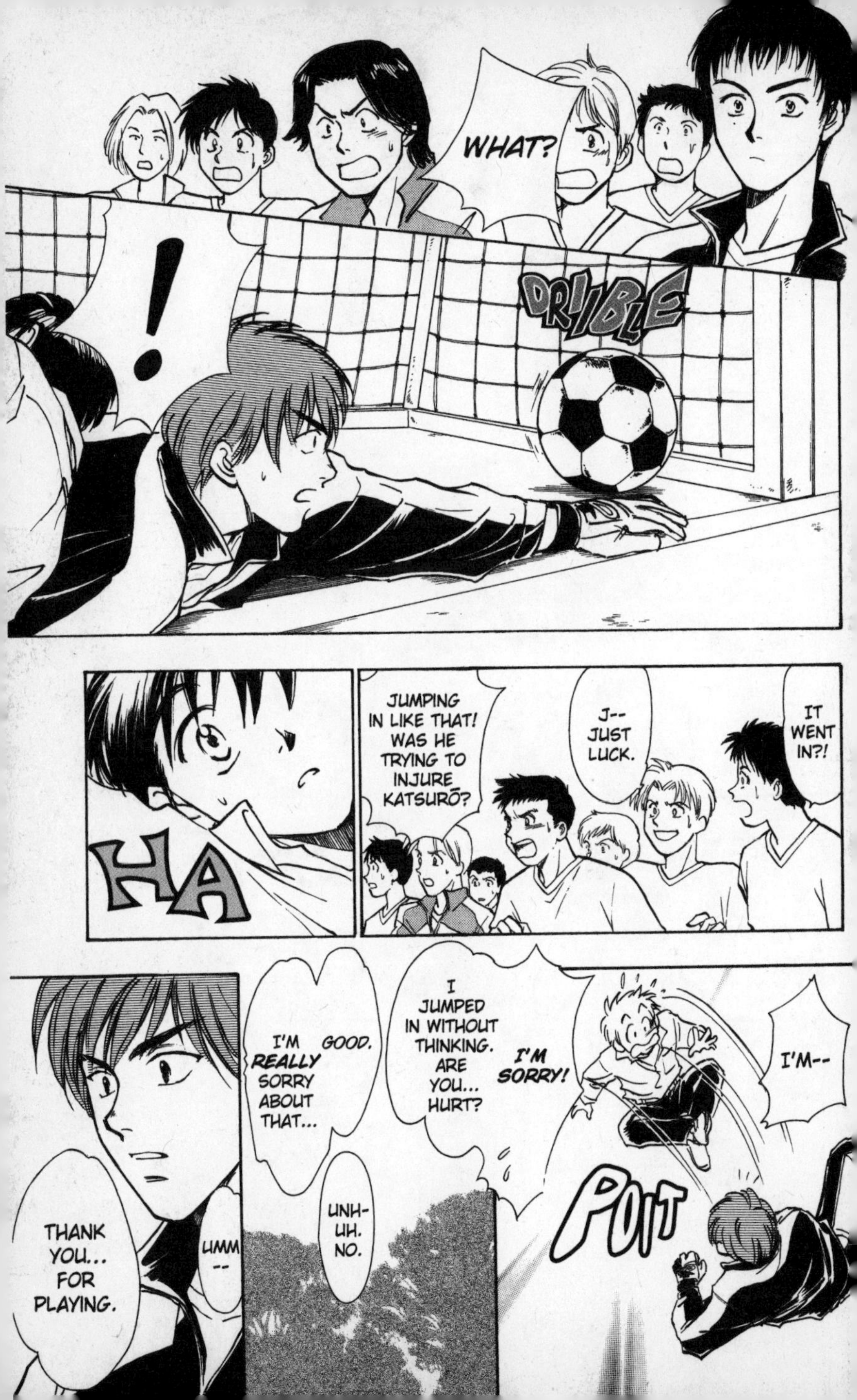
WHAT?
!
DRIBLE
IT WENT IN?!
J-- JUST LUCK.
JUMPING IN LIKE THAT! WAS HE TRYING TO INJURE KATSURŌ?
HA
I'M--
POIT
I'M SORRY!
I JUMPED IN WITHOUT THINKING. ARE YOU... HURT?
GOOD. I'M REALLY SORRY ABOUT THAT...
UNH-UH. NO.
UMM--
THANK YOU... FOR PLAYING.

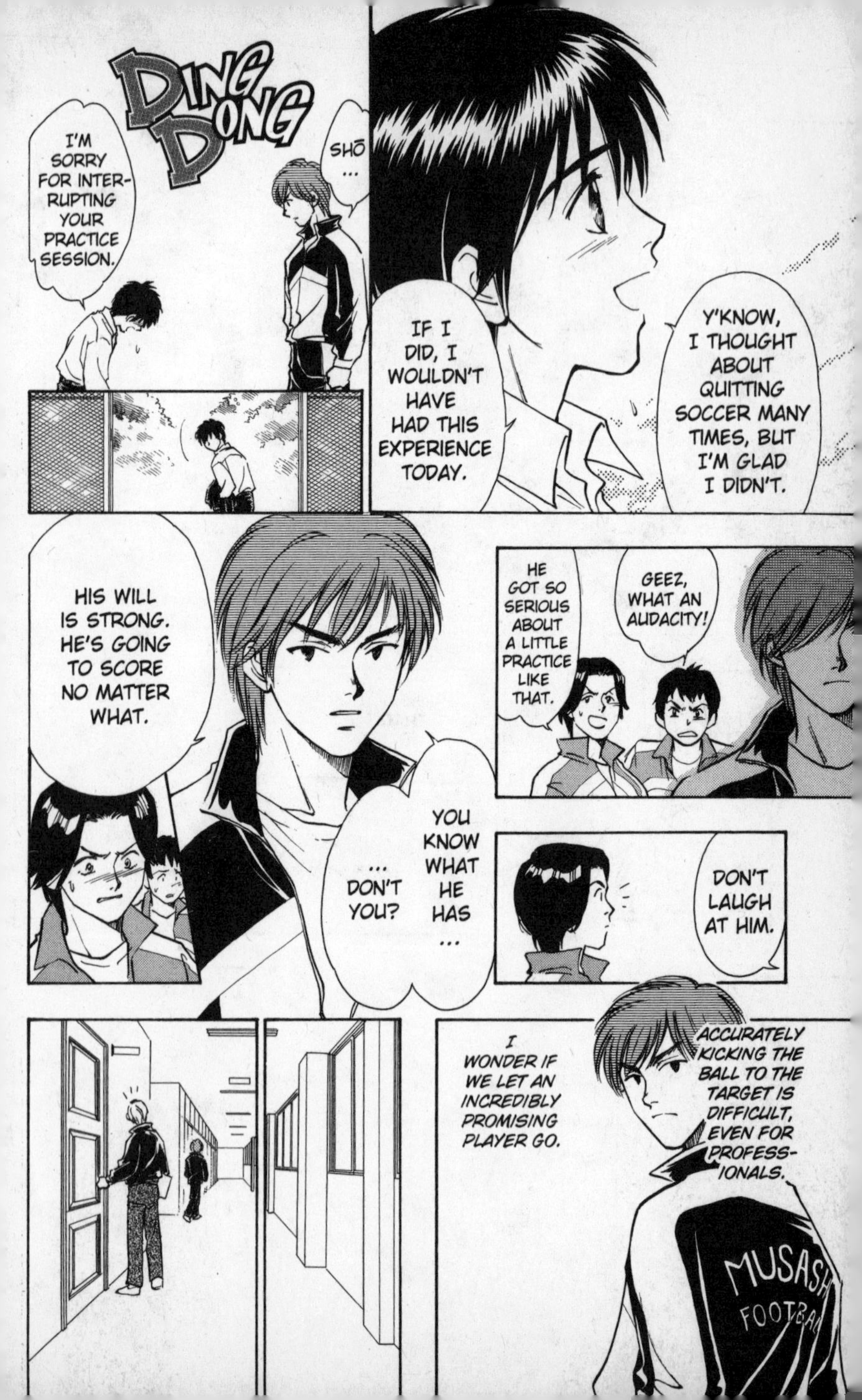
DING DONG
I'M SORRY FOR INTER-RUPTING YOUR PRACTICE SESSION.
SHŌ ...
Y'KNOW, I THOUGHT ABOUT QUITTING SOCCER MANY TIMES, BUT I'M GLAD I DIDN'T.
IF I DID, I WOULDN'T HAVE HAD THIS EXPERIENCE TODAY.
HE GOT SO SERIOUS ABOUT A LITTLE PRACTICE LIKE THAT.
GEEZ, WHAT AN AUDACITY!
DON'T LAUGH AT HIM.
YOU KNOW WHAT HE HAS ... ... DON'T YOU?
HIS WILL IS STRONG. HE'S GOING TO SCORE NO MATTER WHAT.
ACCURATELY KICKING THE BALL TO THE TARGET IS DIFFICULT, EVEN FOR PROFESS-IONALS.
I WONDER IF WE LET AN INCREDIBLY PROMISING PLAYER GO.
MUSASHI FOOTBA

READ THIS WAY

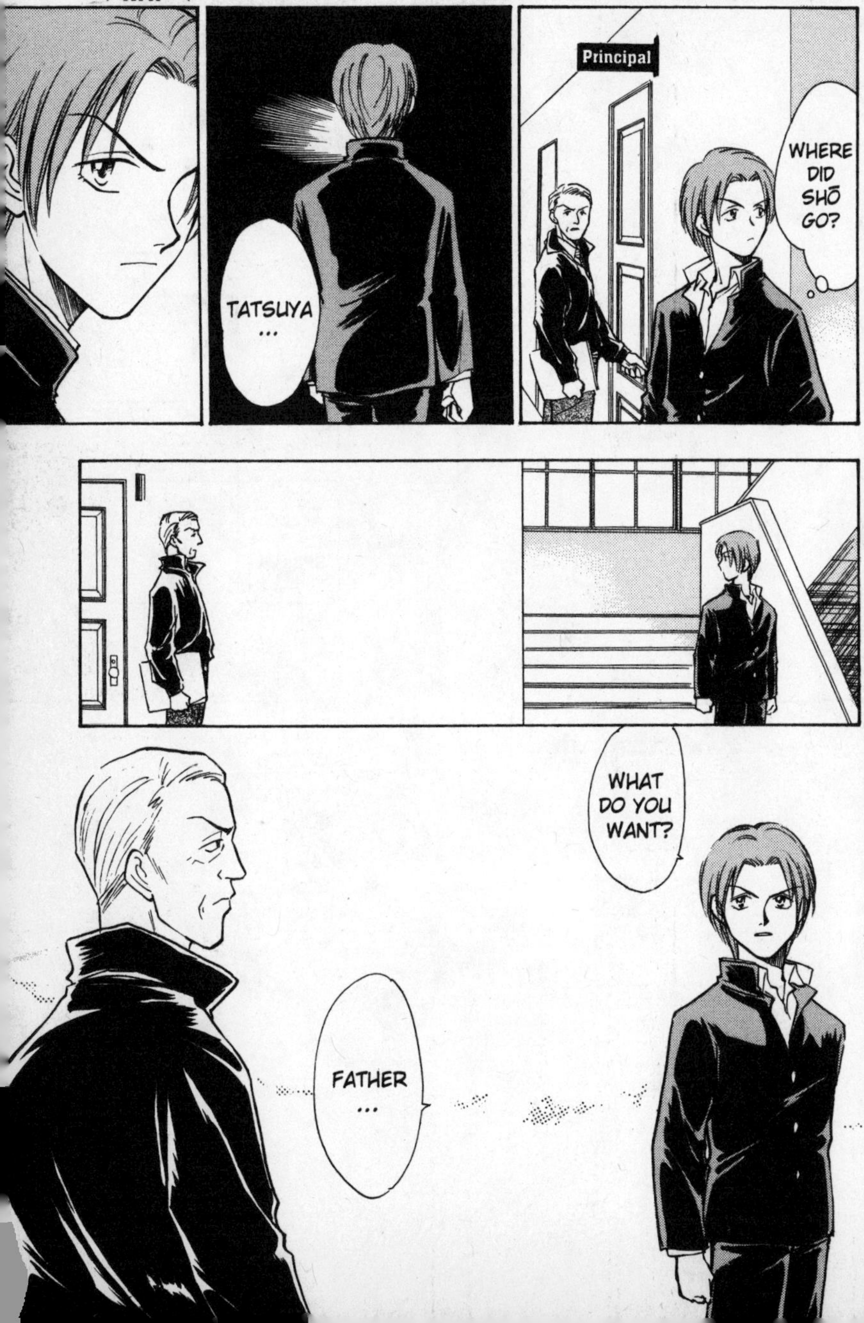
Principal
WHERE DID SHŌ GO?
TATSUYA ...
WHAT DO YOU WANT?
FATHER ...

DAISUKE NOTE

◎ SINCE IT WAS VERY POPULAR, HERE ARE THE PROFILES OF THE MAIN CHARACTERS.

SIGEKI SATŌ

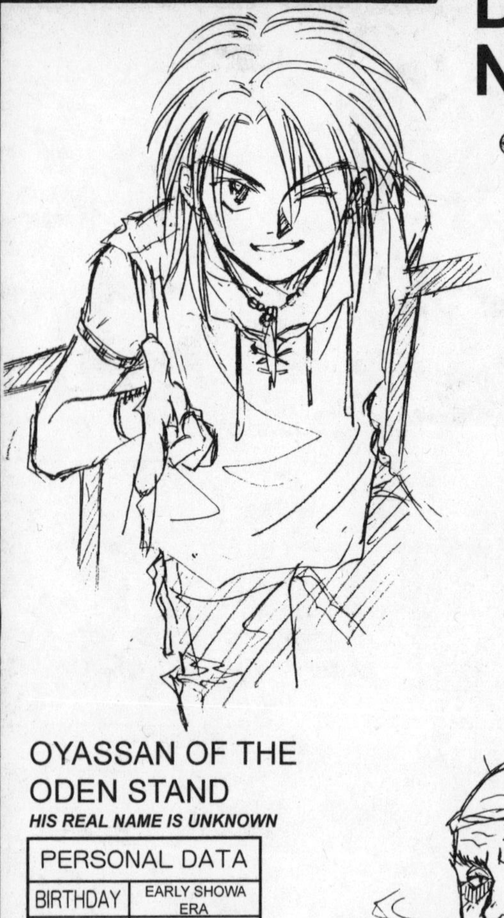

PERSONAL DATA	
BIRTHDAY	1983. 7. 8
SIZE	171cm 58kg
BLOOD TYPE	B
FAVORITE FOOD	MONJA YAKI PANCAKE, COKE
WHAT HE DISLIKES	DOCTORS
HOBBY & SPECIAL SKILLS	HANDICRAFTS, HELPING OUT PEOPLE IN NEED

OYASSAN OF THE ODEN STAND

HIS REAL NAME IS UNKNOWN

PERSONAL DATA	
BIRTHDAY	EARLY SHOWA ERA
SIZE	144cm 60kg
BLOOD TYPE	B
FAVORITE FOOD	SILVER RICE AND BETTARA ZUKE
WHAT HE DISLIKES	FROGS
HOBBY & SPECIAL SKILLS	MAKING TEMPLES AND CASTLES USING THE EMPTY CIGARETTE BOXES. COOKING ODEN

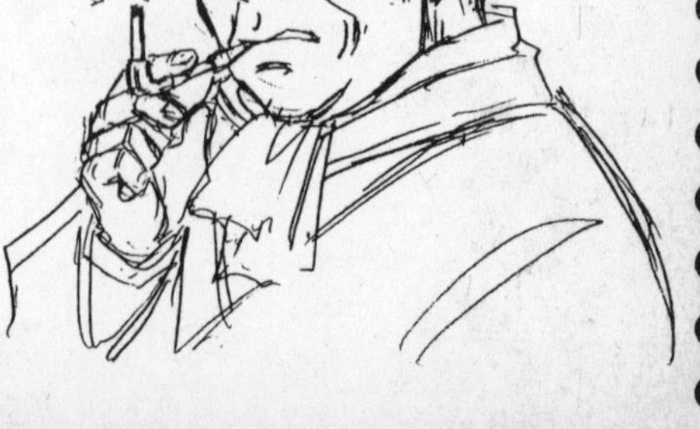

STAGE.11 THE REASON WHY HE MUST WIN

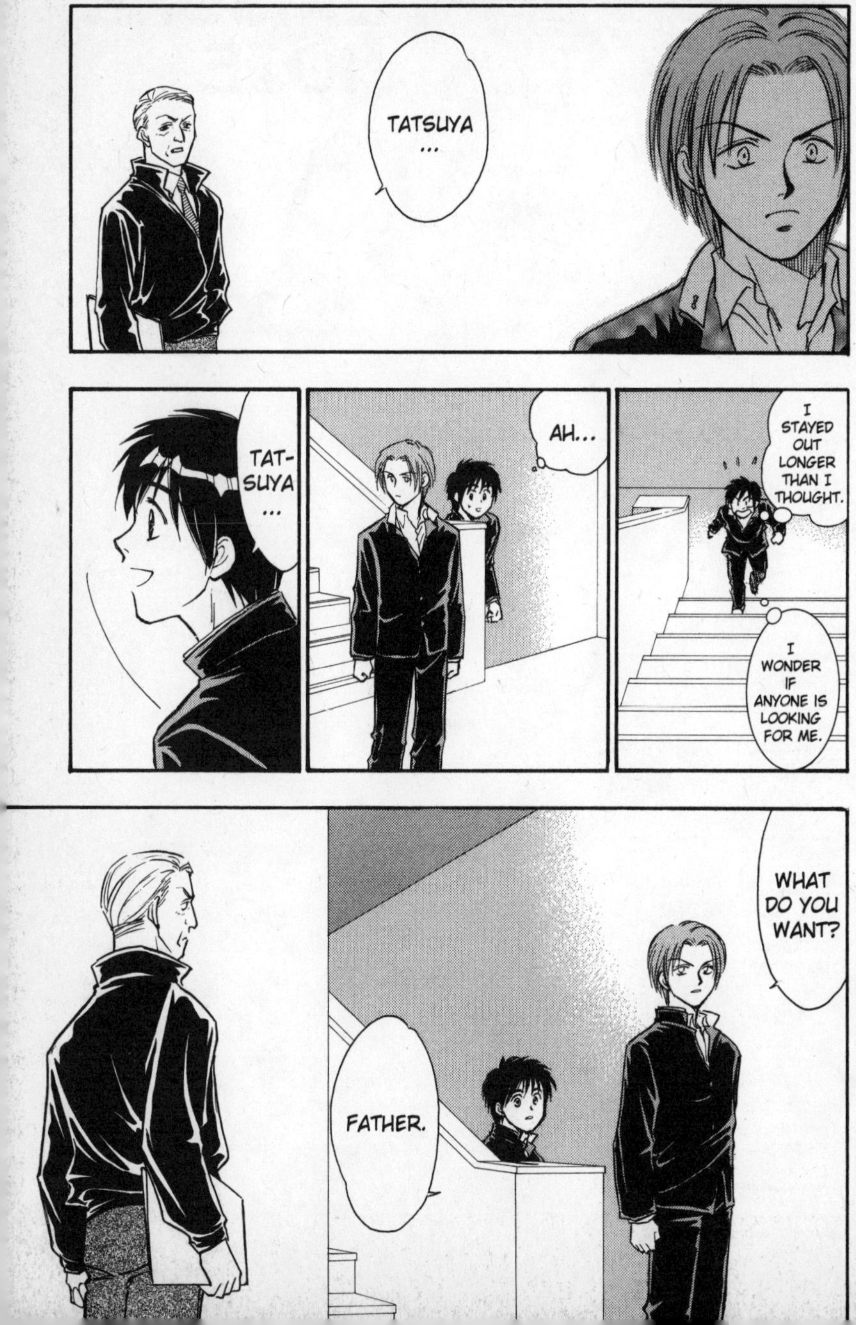

TATSUYA ...
I STAYED OUT LONGER THAN I THOUGHT.
I WONDER IF ANYONE IS LOOKING FOR ME.
AH...
TAT-SUYA ...
WHAT DO YOU WANT?
FATHER.

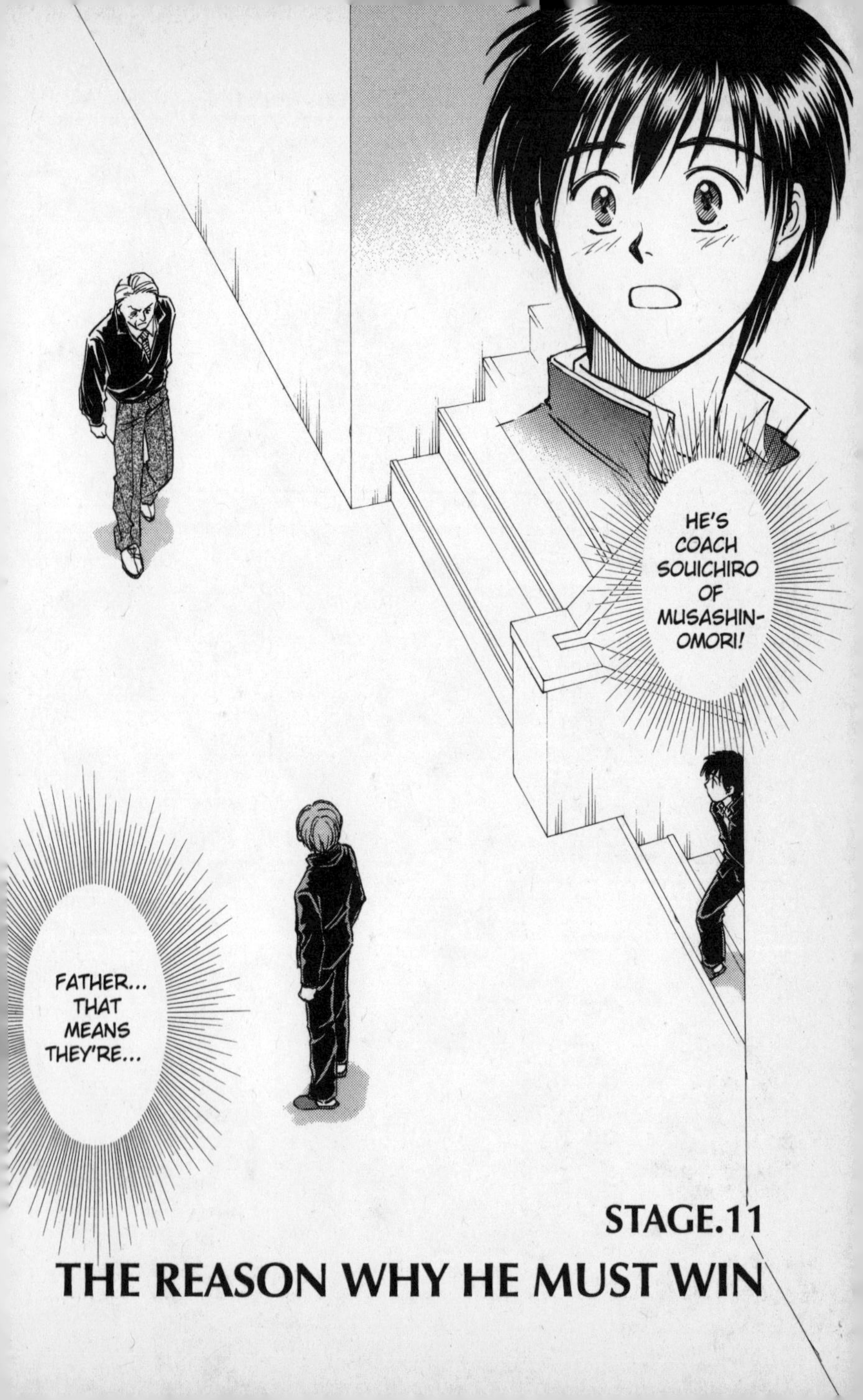

HE'S COACH SOUICHIRO OF MUSASHINO-OMORI!
FATHER... THAT MEANS THEY'RE...

STAGE.11
THE REASON WHY HE MUST WIN

READ THIS WAY

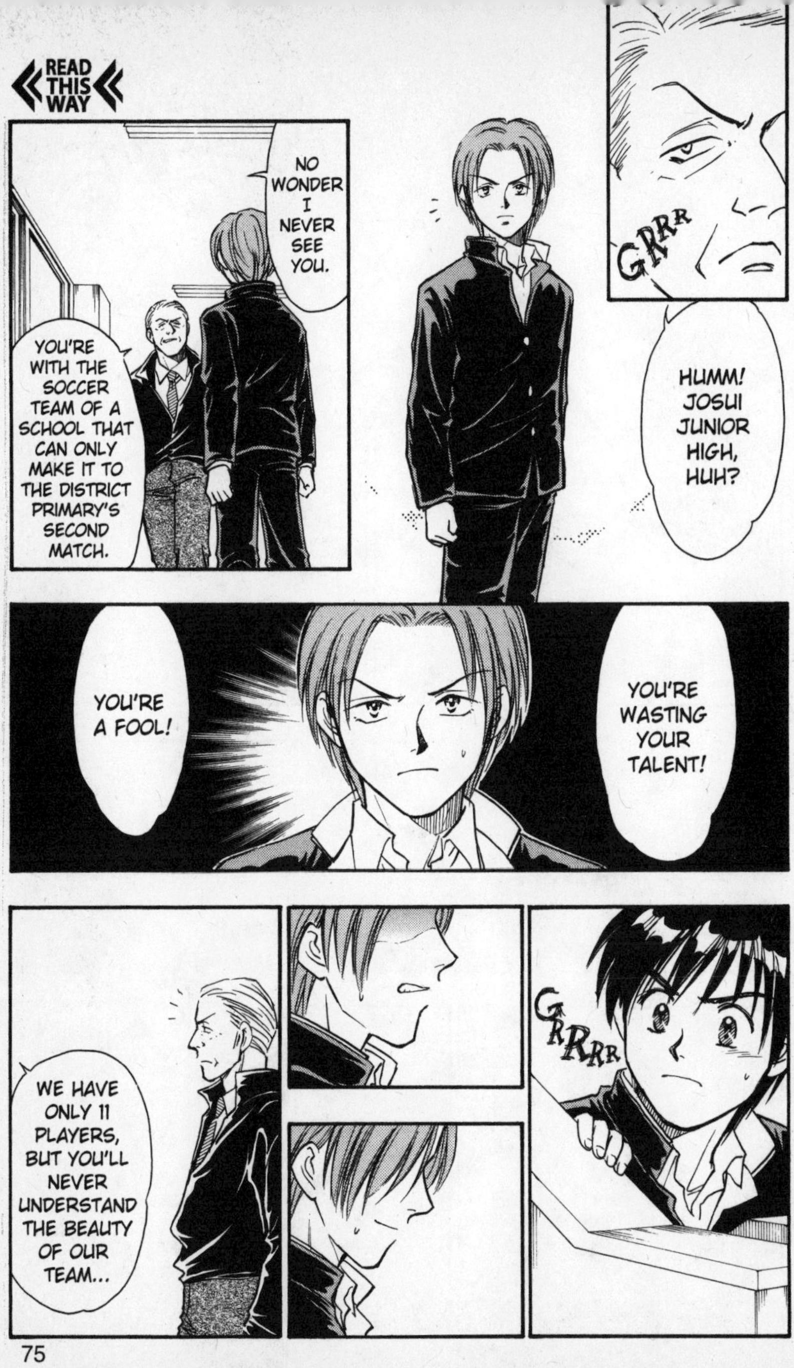

GRRR
HUMM! JOSUI JUNIOR HIGH, HUH?
NO WONDER I NEVER SEE YOU.
YOU'RE WITH THE SOCCER TEAM OF A SCHOOL THAT CAN ONLY MAKE IT TO THE DISTRICT PRIMARY'S SECOND MATCH.
YOU'RE WASTING YOUR TALENT!
YOU'RE A FOOL!
GRRRRR
WE HAVE ONLY 11 PLAYERS, BUT YOU'LL NEVER UNDERSTAND THE BEAUTY OF OUR TEAM...

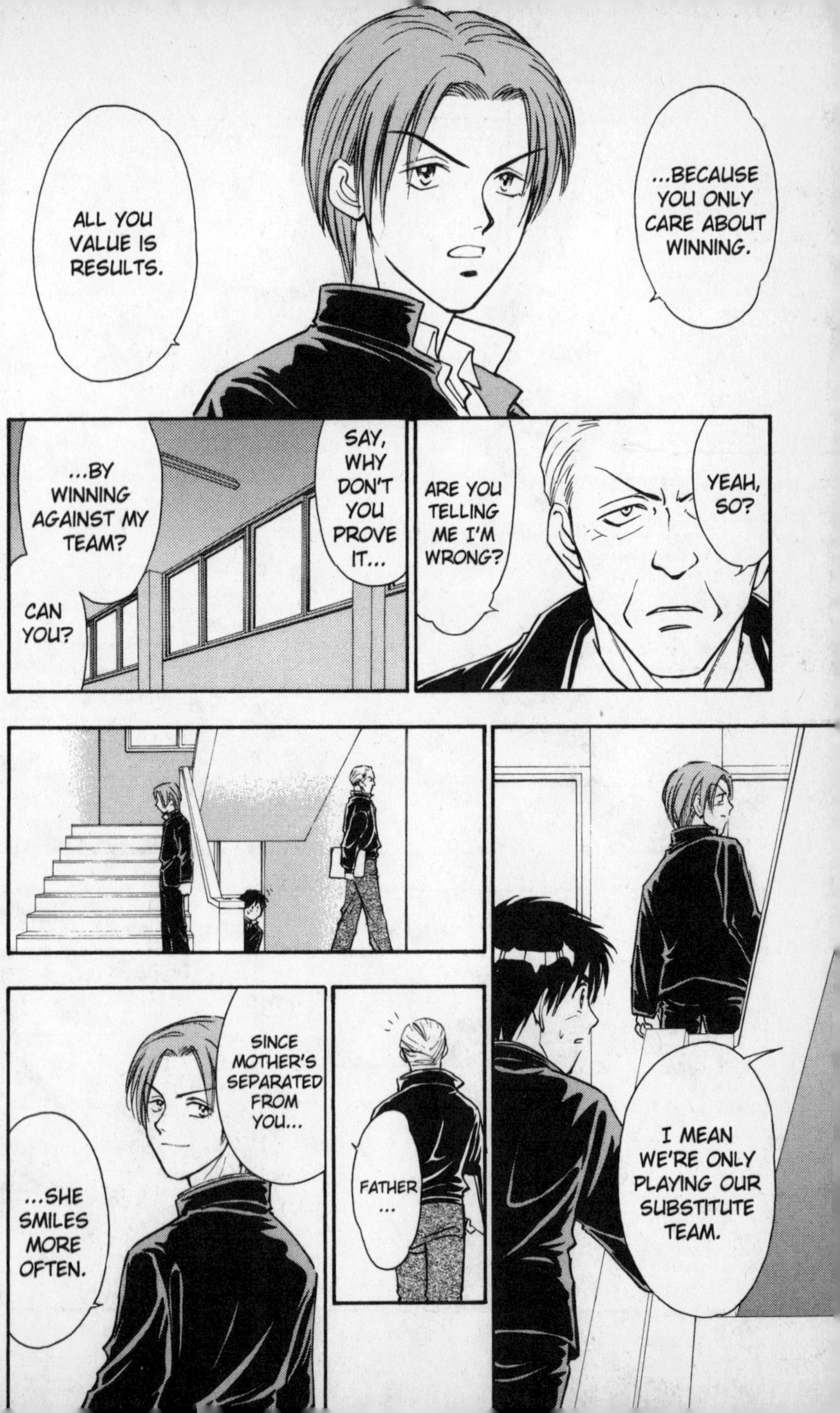
...BECAUSE YOU ONLY CARE ABOUT WINNING.
ALL YOU VALUE IS RESULTS.
YEAH, SO?
ARE YOU TELLING ME I'M WRONG?
SAY, WHY DON'T YOU PROVE IT...
...BY WINNING AGAINST MY TEAM?
CAN YOU?
I MEAN WE'RE ONLY PLAYING OUR SUBSTITUTE TEAM.
FATHER ...
SINCE MOTHER'S SEPARATED FROM YOU...
...SHE SMILES MORE OFTEN.

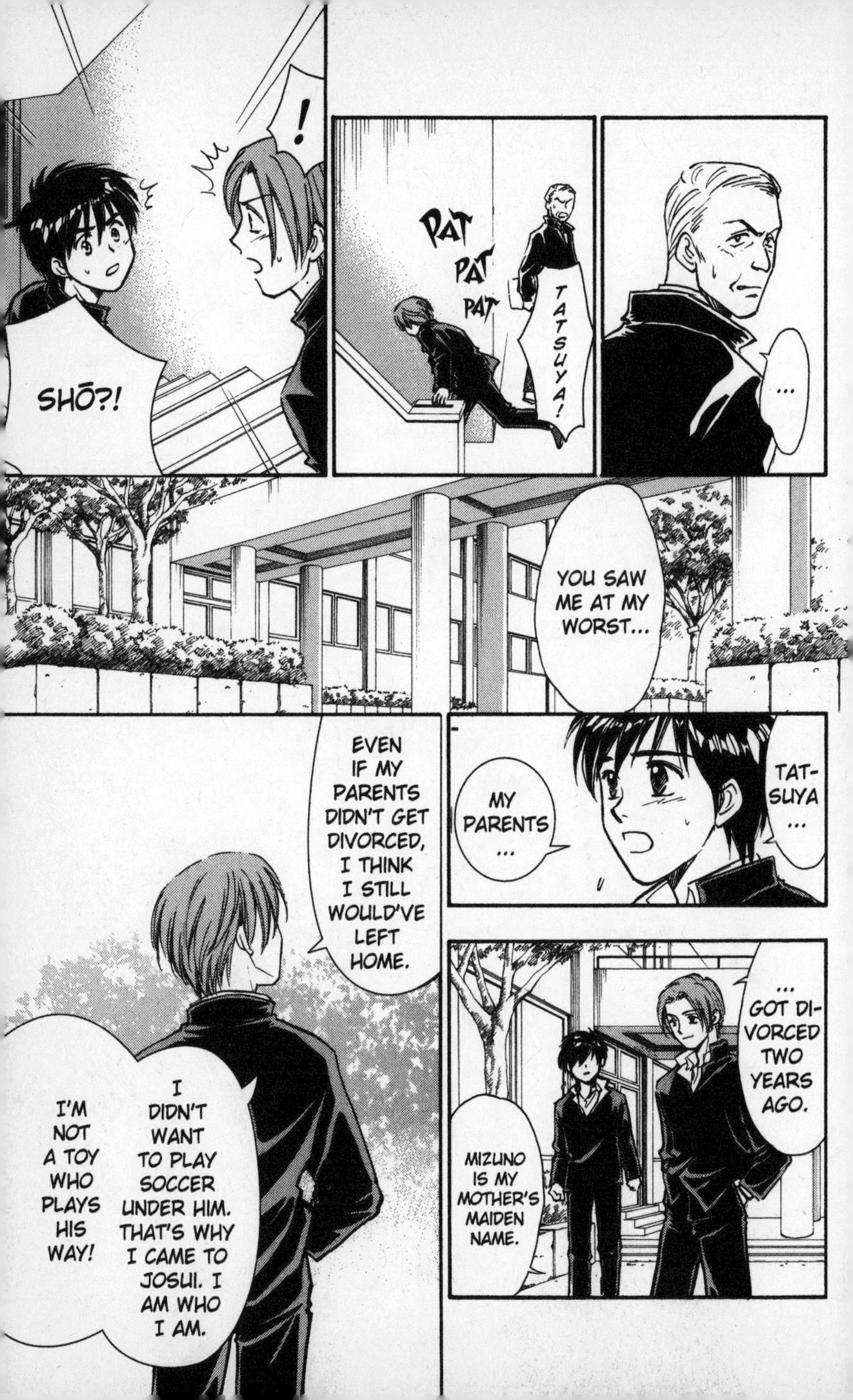
...
PAT PAT PAT
TATSUYA!
!
SHŌ?!
YOU SAW ME AT MY WORST...
TAT-SUYA...
MY PARENTS...
...GOT DI-VORCED TWO YEARS AGO.
MIZUNO IS MY MOTHER'S MAIDEN NAME.
EVEN IF MY PARENTS DIDN'T GET DIVORCED, I THINK I STILL WOULD'VE LEFT HOME.
I DIDN'T WANT TO PLAY SOCCER UNDER HIM. THAT'S WHY I CAME TO JOSUI. I AM WHO I AM.
I'M NOT A TOY WHO PLAYS HIS WAY!

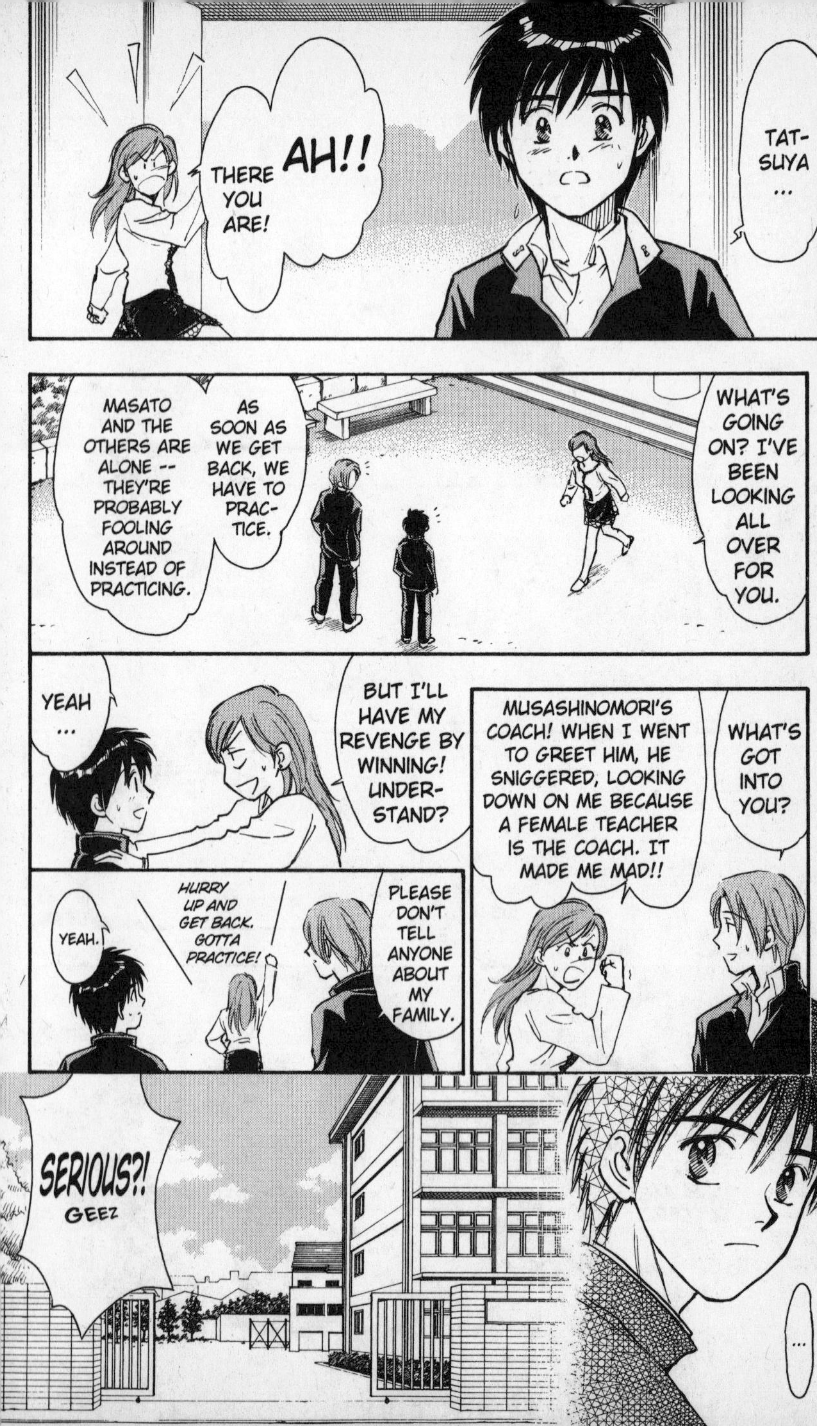
TAT-SUYA ...
AH!!
THERE YOU ARE!
WHAT'S GOING ON? I'VE BEEN LOOKING ALL OVER FOR YOU.
AS SOON AS WE GET BACK, WE HAVE TO PRAC-TICE.
MASATO AND THE OTHERS ARE ALONE -- THEY'RE PROBABLY FOOLING AROUND INSTEAD OF PRACTICING.
WHAT'S GOT INTO YOU?
MUSASHINOMORI'S COACH! WHEN I WENT TO GREET HIM, HE SNIGGERED, LOOKING DOWN ON ME BECAUSE A FEMALE TEACHER IS THE COACH. IT MADE ME MAD!!
BUT I'LL HAVE MY REVENGE BY WINNING! UNDER-STAND?
YEAH ...
PLEASE DON'T TELL ANYONE ABOUT MY FAMILY.
HURRY UP AND GET BACK. GOTTA PRACTICE!
YEAH.
...
SERIOUS?!
GEEZ

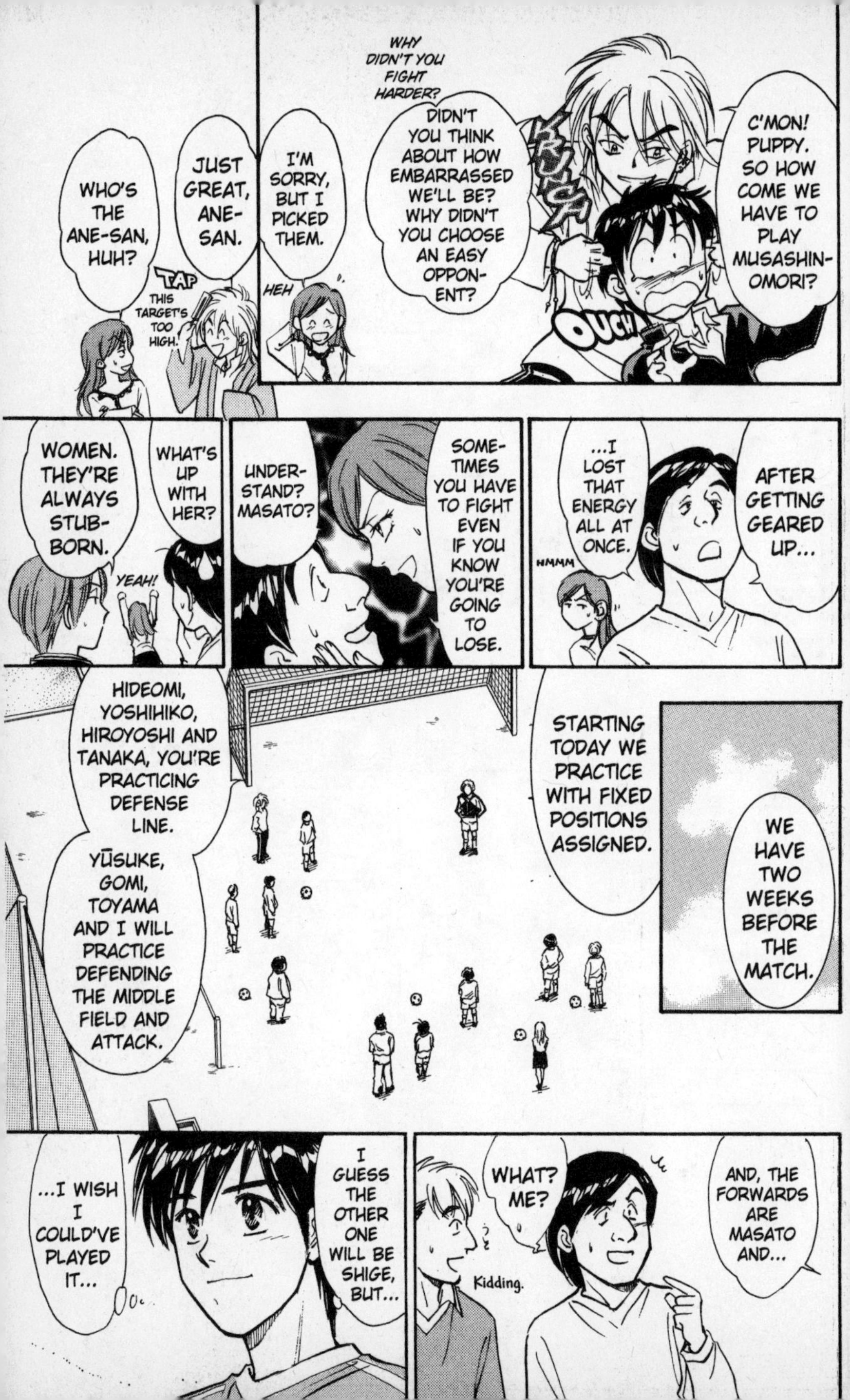
C'MON! PUPPY. SO HOW COME WE HAVE TO PLAY MUSASHINOMORI?
OUCH
DIDN'T YOU THINK ABOUT HOW EMBARRASSED WE'LL BE? WHY DIDN'T YOU CHOOSE AN EASY OPPONENT?
WHY DIDN'T YOU FIGHT HARDER?
I'M SORRY, BUT I PICKED THEM.
HEH
JUST GREAT, ANE-SAN.
TAP
THIS TARGET'S TOO HIGH.
WHO'S THE ANE-SAN, HUH?
AFTER GETTING GEARED UP...
...I LOST THAT ENERGY ALL AT ONCE.
HMMM
SOMETIMES YOU HAVE TO FIGHT EVEN IF YOU KNOW YOU'RE GOING TO LOSE.
UNDERSTAND? MASATO?
WHAT'S UP WITH HER?
WOMEN. THEY'RE ALWAYS STUBBORN.
YEAH!
WE HAVE TWO WEEKS BEFORE THE MATCH.
STARTING TODAY WE PRACTICE WITH FIXED POSITIONS ASSIGNED.
HIDEOMI, YOSHIHIKO, HIROYOSHI AND TANAKA, YOU'RE PRACTICING DEFENSE LINE.
YŪSUKE, GOMI, TOYAMA AND I WILL PRACTICE DEFENDING THE MIDDLE FIELD AND ATTACK.
AND, THE FORWARDS ARE MASATO AND...
WHAT? ME?
Kidding.
I GUESS THE OTHER ONE WILL BE SHIGE, BUT...
...I WISH I COULD'VE PLAYED IT...

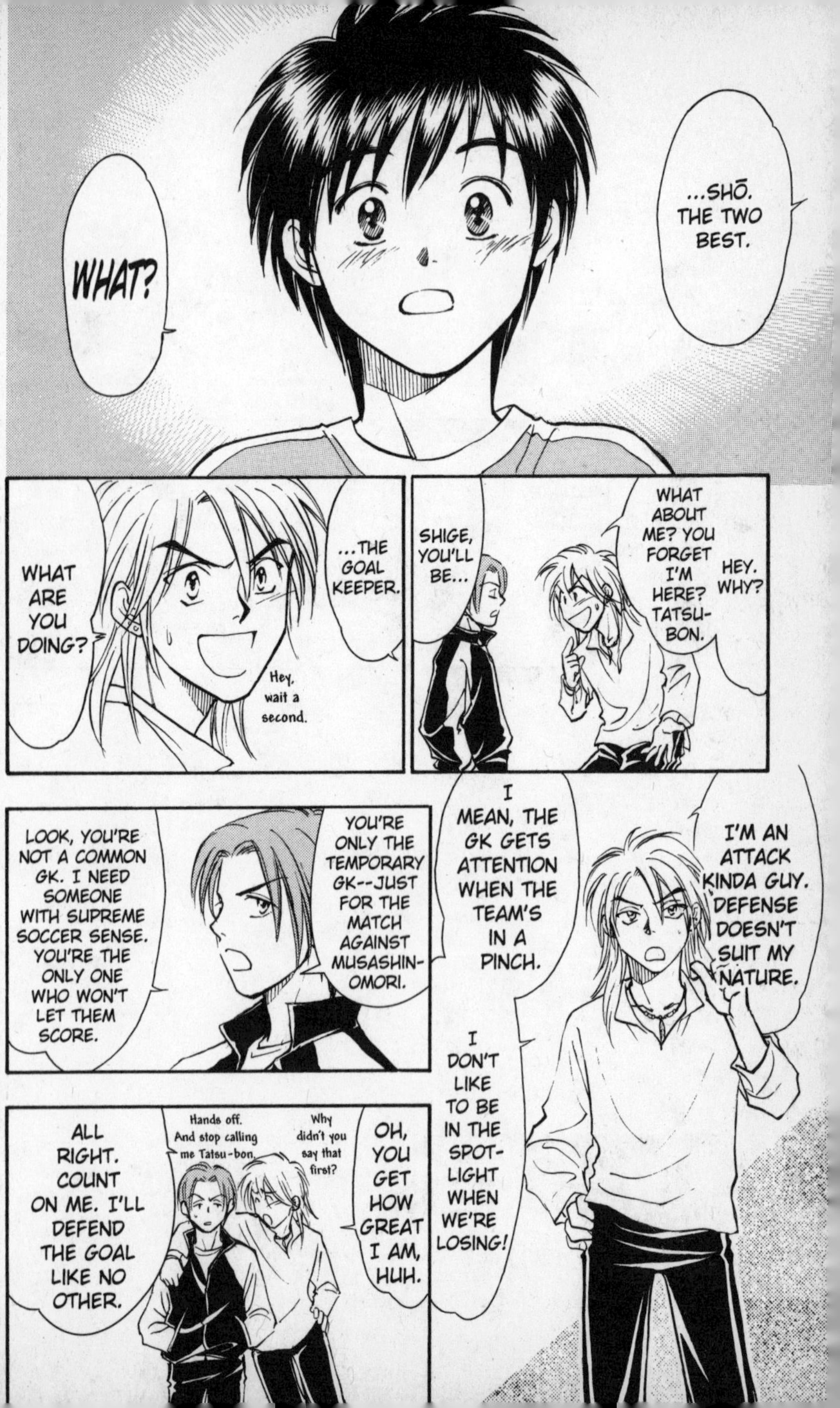
...SHŌ. THE TWO BEST.
WHAT?
WHAT ABOUT ME? YOU FORGET I'M HERE? TATSU-BON.
HEY. WHY?
SHIGE, YOU'LL BE...
...THE GOAL KEEPER.
Hey, wait a second.
WHAT ARE YOU DOING?
I'M AN ATTACK KINDA GUY. DEFENSE DOESN'T SUIT MY NATURE.
I MEAN, THE GK GETS ATTENTION WHEN THE TEAM'S IN A PINCH.
I DON'T LIKE TO BE IN THE SPOTLIGHT WHEN WE'RE LOSING!
YOU'RE ONLY THE TEMPORARY GK--JUST FOR THE MATCH AGAINST MUSASHINOMORI.
LOOK, YOU'RE NOT A COMMON GK. I NEED SOMEONE WITH SUPREME SOCCER SENSE. YOU'RE THE ONLY ONE WHO WON'T LET THEM SCORE.
OH, YOU GET HOW GREAT I AM, HUH.
Why didn't you say that first?
Hands off. And stop calling me Tatsu-bon.
ALL RIGHT. COUNT ON ME. I'LL DEFEND THE GOAL LIKE NO OTHER.

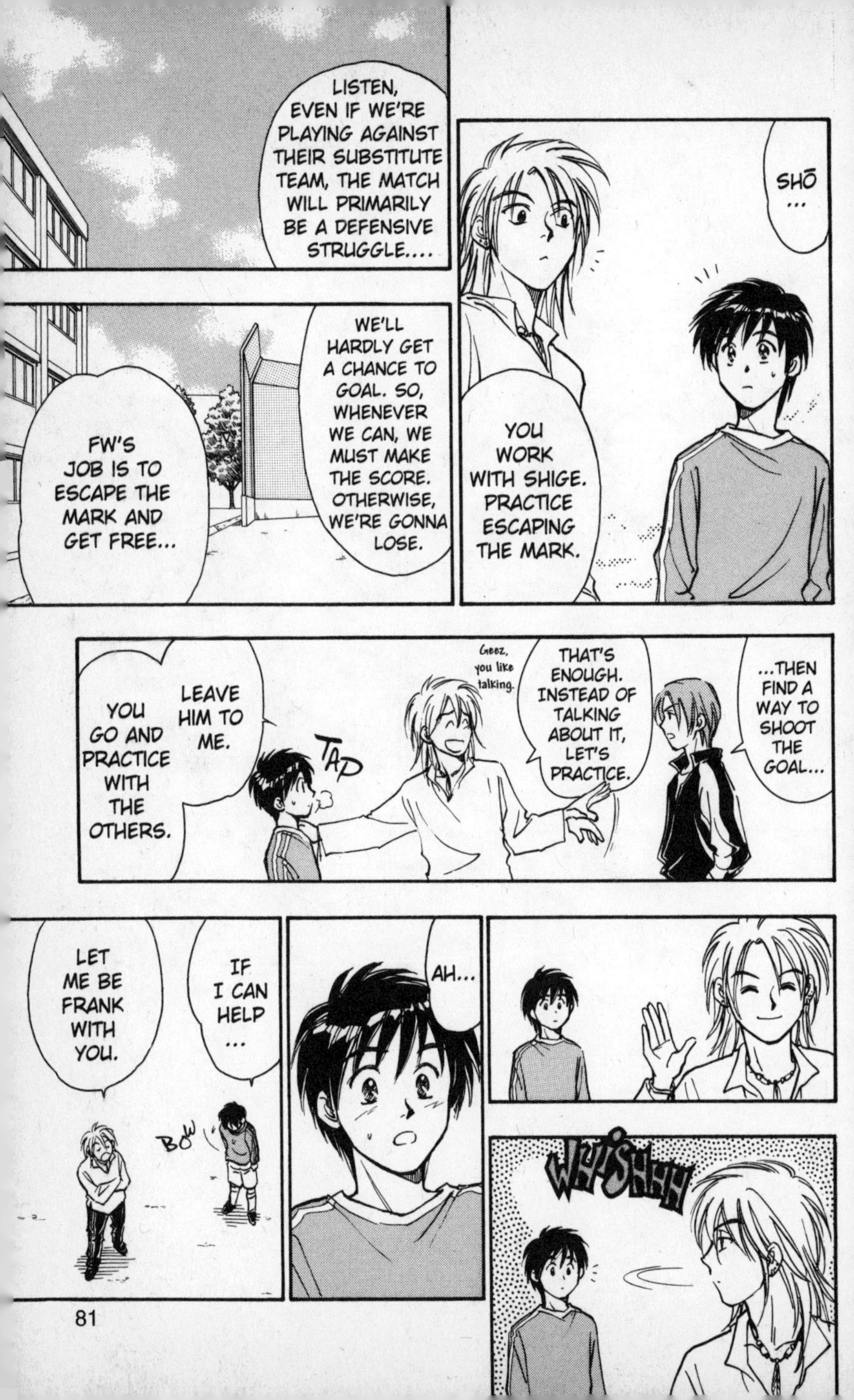
SHŌ...
YOU WORK WITH SHIGE. PRACTICE ESCAPING THE MARK.
LISTEN, EVEN IF WE'RE PLAYING AGAINST THEIR SUBSTITUTE TEAM, THE MATCH WILL PRIMARILY BE A DEFENSIVE STRUGGLE....
WE'LL HARDLY GET A CHANCE TO GOAL. SO, WHENEVER WE CAN, WE MUST MAKE THE SCORE. OTHERWISE, WE'RE GONNA LOSE.
FW'S JOB IS TO ESCAPE THE MARK AND GET FREE...
...THEN FIND A WAY TO SHOOT THE GOAL...
THAT'S ENOUGH. INSTEAD OF TALKING ABOUT IT, LET'S PRACTICE.
Geez, you like talking.
TAP
LEAVE HIM TO ME.
YOU GO AND PRACTICE WITH THE OTHERS.
WHISHHH
AH...
IF I CAN HELP...
BOW
LET ME BE FRANK WITH YOU.

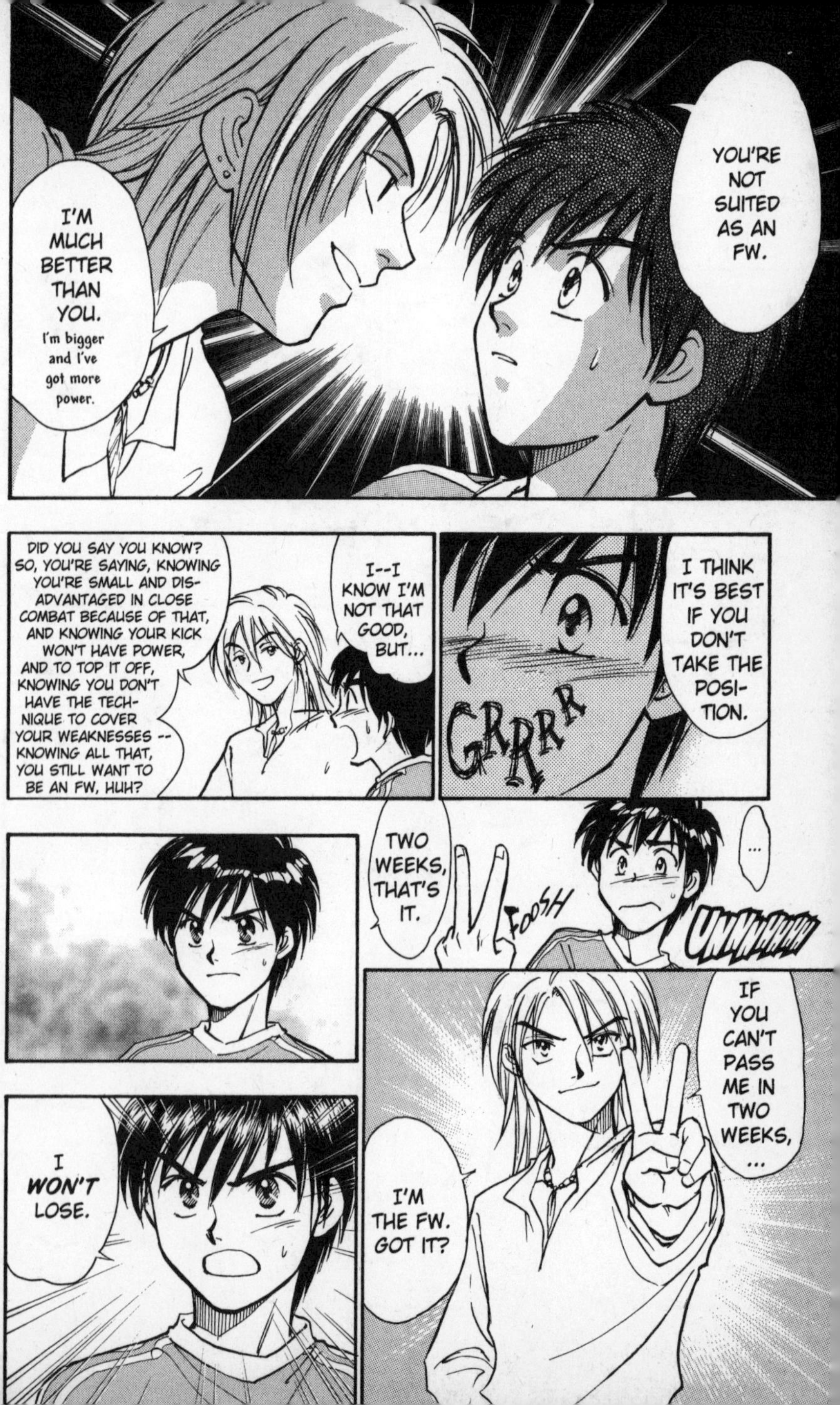

YOU'RE NOT SUITED AS AN FW.
I'M MUCH BETTER THAN YOU.
I'm bigger and I've got more power.
I THINK IT'S BEST IF YOU DON'T TAKE THE POSI-TION.
GRRRR
I--I KNOW I'M NOT THAT GOOD, BUT...
DID YOU SAY YOU KNOW? SO, YOU'RE SAYING, KNOWING YOU'RE SMALL AND DIS-ADVANTAGED IN CLOSE COMBAT BECAUSE OF THAT, AND KNOWING YOUR KICK WON'T HAVE POWER, AND TO TOP IT OFF, KNOWING YOU DON'T HAVE THE TECH-NIQUE TO COVER YOUR WEAKNESSES -- KNOWING ALL THAT, YOU STILL WANT TO BE AN FW, HUH?
...
UNNHHHH
TWO WEEKS, THAT'S IT.
FOOSH
IF YOU CAN'T PASS ME IN TWO WEEKS, ...
I'M THE FW. GOT IT?
I WON'T LOSE.

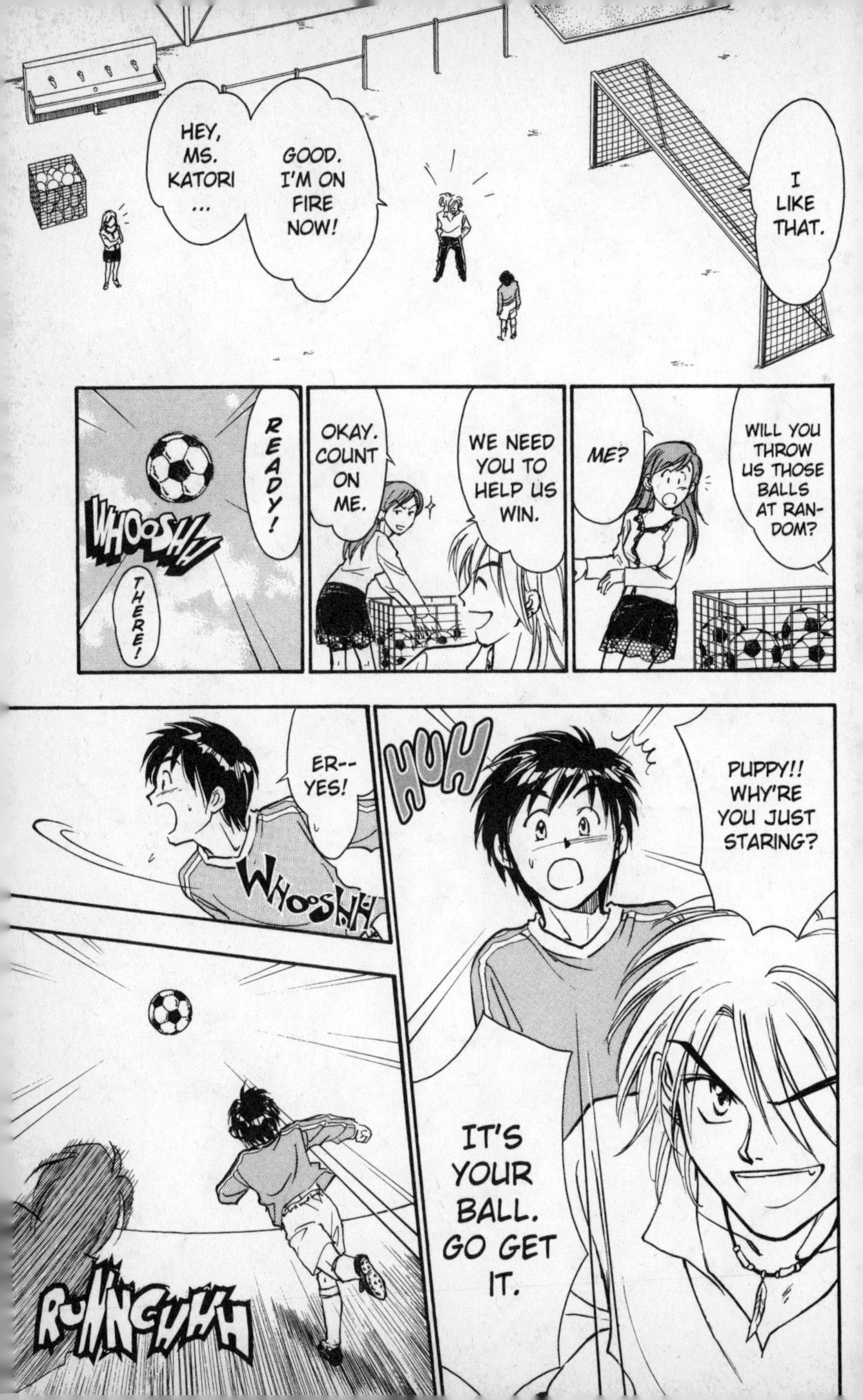
I LIKE THAT.
GOOD. I'M ON FIRE NOW!
HEY, MS. KATORI ...
WILL YOU THROW US THOSE BALLS AT RANDOM?
ME?
WE NEED YOU TO HELP US WIN.
OKAY. COUNT ON ME.
READY!
WHOOSH
THERE!
PUPPY!! WHY'RE YOU JUST STARING?
HUH
ER-- YES!
IT'S YOUR BALL. GO GET IT.

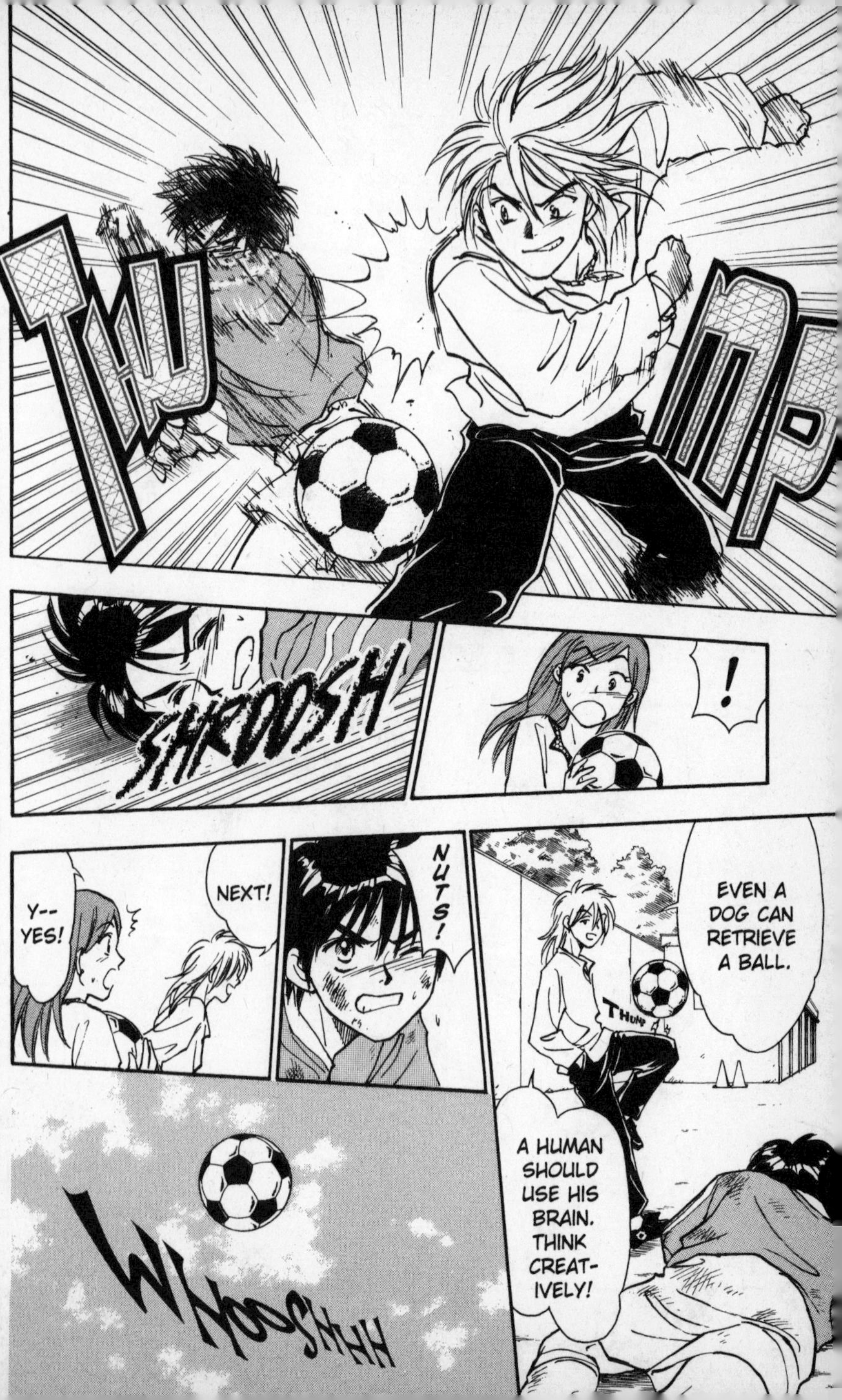
THUMP
SHROOSH
!
EVEN A DOG CAN RETRIEVE A BALL.
THUMP
A HUMAN SHOULD USE HIS BRAIN. THINK CREAT-IVELY!
NUTS!
NEXT!
Y-- YES!
WHOOSHHH

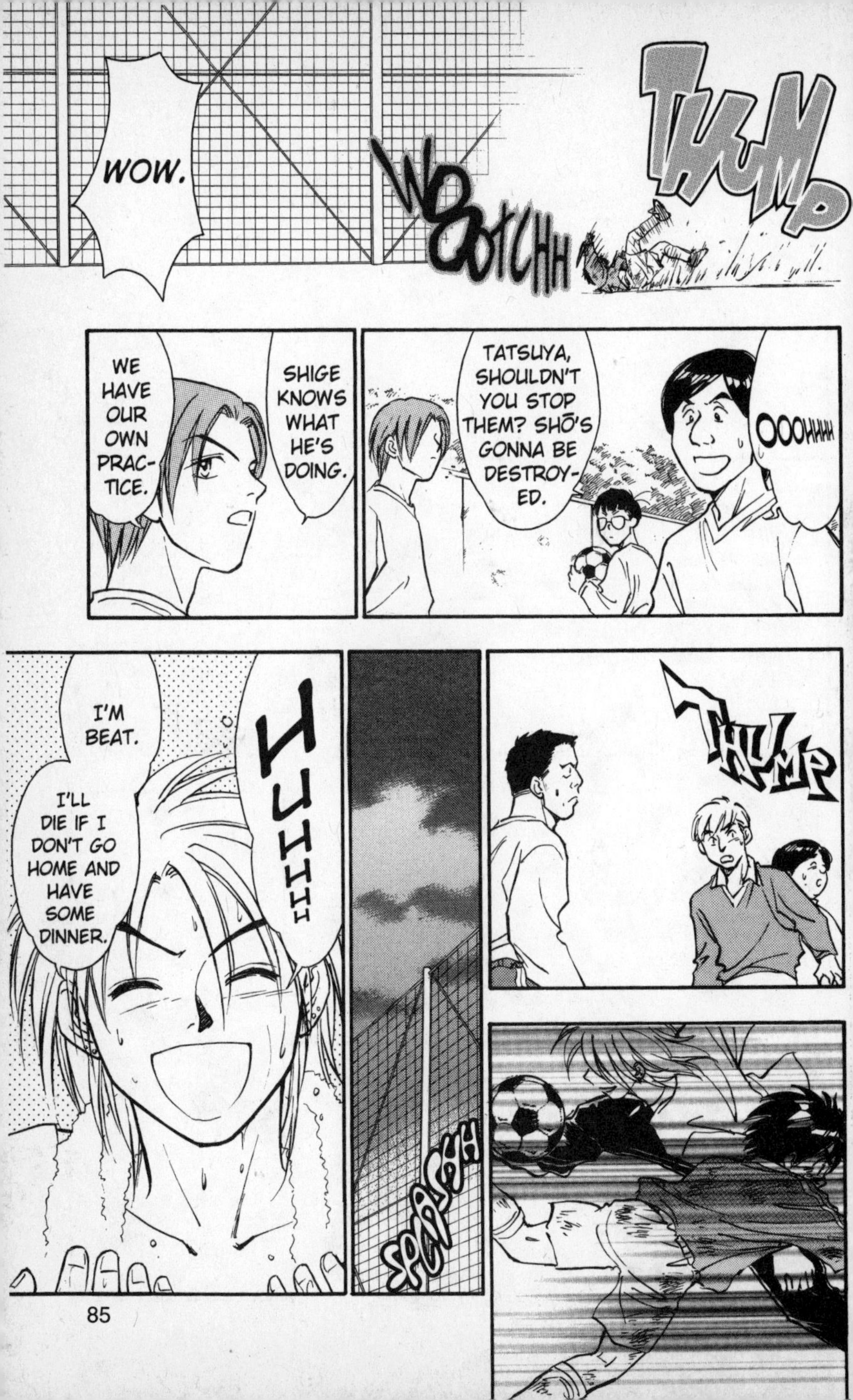
THUMP
WOOTCHHH
WOW.
OOOHHHH
TATSUYA, SHOULDN'T YOU STOP THEM? SHŌ'S GONNA BE DESTROY-ED.
SHIGE KNOWS WHAT HE'S DOING.
WE HAVE OUR OWN PRAC-TICE.
THUMP
SPLASH
HUHHHH
I'M BEAT.
I'LL DIE IF I DON'T GO HOME AND HAVE SOME DINNER.

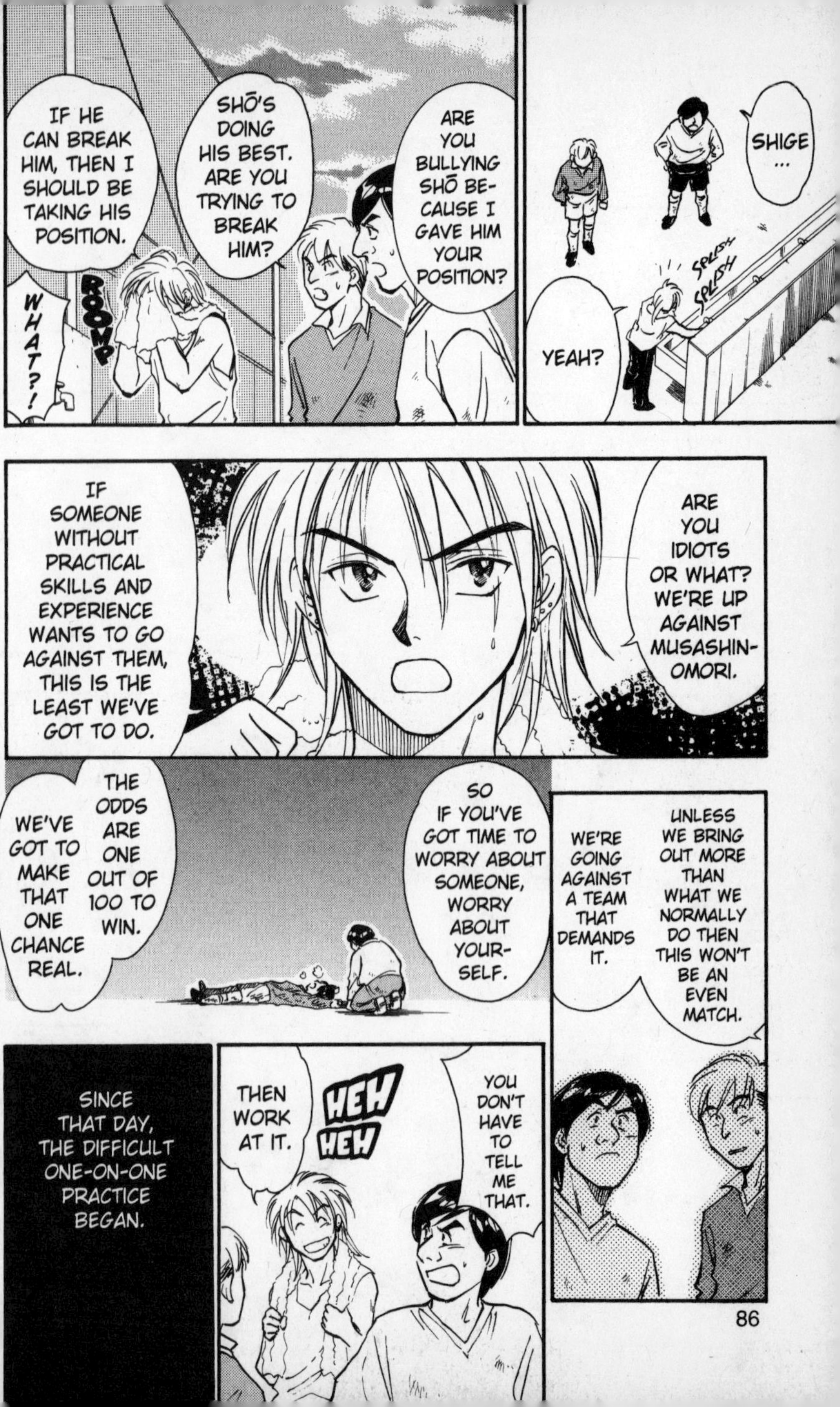
SHIGE ...
SPLISH SPLISH
YEAH?
ARE YOU BULLYING SHŌ BECAUSE I GAVE HIM YOUR POSITION?
SHŌ'S DOING HIS BEST. ARE YOU TRYING TO BREAK HIM?
IF HE CAN BREAK HIM, THEN I SHOULD BE TAKING HIS POSITION.
ROOMP
WHAT?!
ARE YOU IDIOTS OR WHAT? WE'RE UP AGAINST MUSASHINOMORI.
IF SOMEONE WITHOUT PRACTICAL SKILLS AND EXPERIENCE WANTS TO GO AGAINST THEM, THIS IS THE LEAST WE'VE GOT TO DO.
UNLESS WE BRING OUT MORE THAN WHAT WE NORMALLY DO THEN THIS WON'T BE AN EVEN MATCH.
WE'RE GOING AGAINST A TEAM THAT DEMANDS IT.
SO IF YOU'VE GOT TIME TO WORRY ABOUT SOMEONE, WORRY ABOUT YOURSELF.
THE ODDS ARE ONE OUT OF 100 TO WIN.
WE'VE GOT TO MAKE THAT ONE CHANCE REAL.
YOU DON'T HAVE TO TELL ME THAT.
HEH HEH
THEN WORK AT IT.
SINCE THAT DAY, THE DIFFICULT ONE-ON-ONE PRACTICE BEGAN.

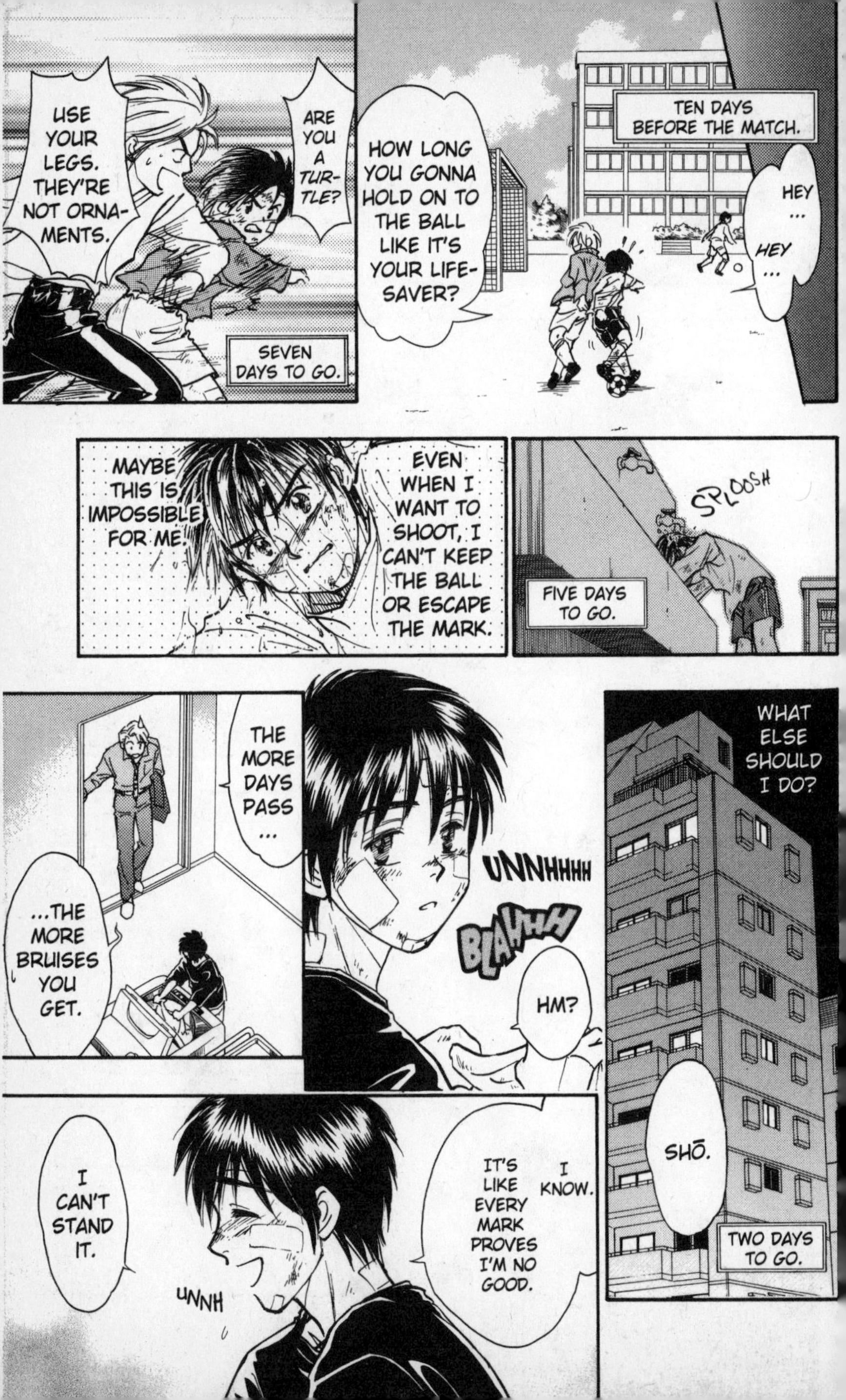
TEN DAYS BEFORE THE MATCH.
HEY ... HEY ...
HOW LONG YOU GONNA HOLD ON TO THE BALL LIKE IT'S YOUR LIFE-SAVER?
ARE YOU A TUR-TLE?
USE YOUR LEGS. THEY'RE NOT ORNA-MENTS.
SEVEN DAYS TO GO.
SPLOOSH
FIVE DAYS TO GO.
EVEN WHEN I WANT TO SHOOT, I CAN'T KEEP THE BALL OR ESCAPE THE MARK.
MAYBE THIS IS IMPOSSIBLE FOR ME.
WHAT ELSE SHOULD I DO?
SHŌ.
TWO DAYS TO GO.
UNNHHHH
BLAHHH
HM?
THE MORE DAYS PASS ...
...THE MORE BRUISES YOU GET.
I KNOW.
IT'S LIKE EVERY MARK PROVES I'M NO GOOD.
UNNH
I CAN'T STAND IT.

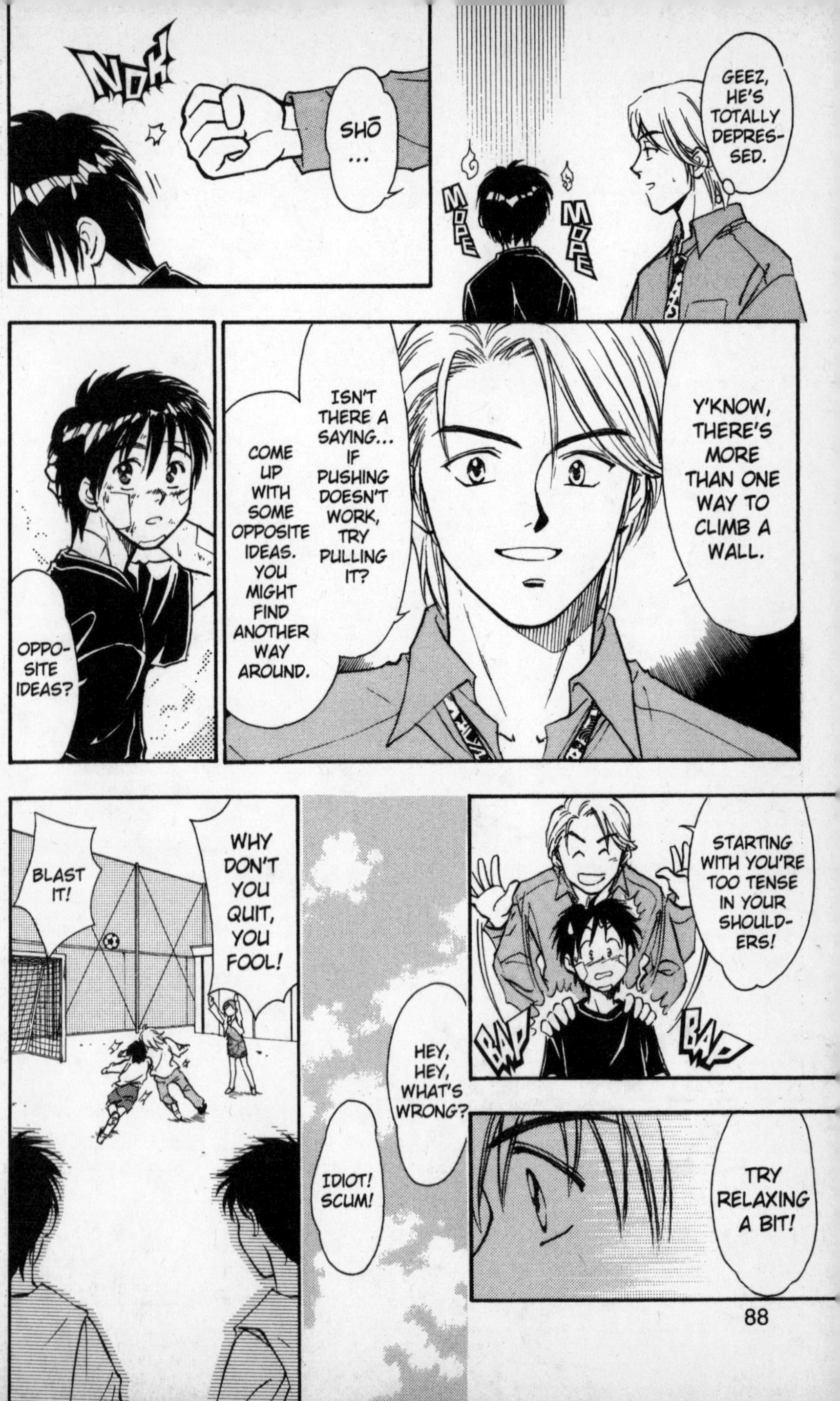
GEEZ, HE'S TOTALLY DEPRES-SED.
MOPE
MOPE
SHŌ ...
NOK
Y'KNOW, THERE'S MORE THAN ONE WAY TO CLIMB A WALL.
ISN'T THERE A SAYING... IF PUSHING DOESN'T WORK, TRY PULLING IT?
COME UP WITH SOME OPPOSITE IDEAS. YOU MIGHT FIND ANOTHER WAY AROUND.
OPPO-SITE IDEAS?
STARTING WITH YOU'RE TOO TENSE IN YOUR SHOULD-ERS!
BAP
BAP
TRY RELAXING A BIT!
HEY, HEY, WHAT'S WRONG?
IDIOT! SCUM!
WHY DON'T YOU QUIT, YOU FOOL!
BLAST IT!

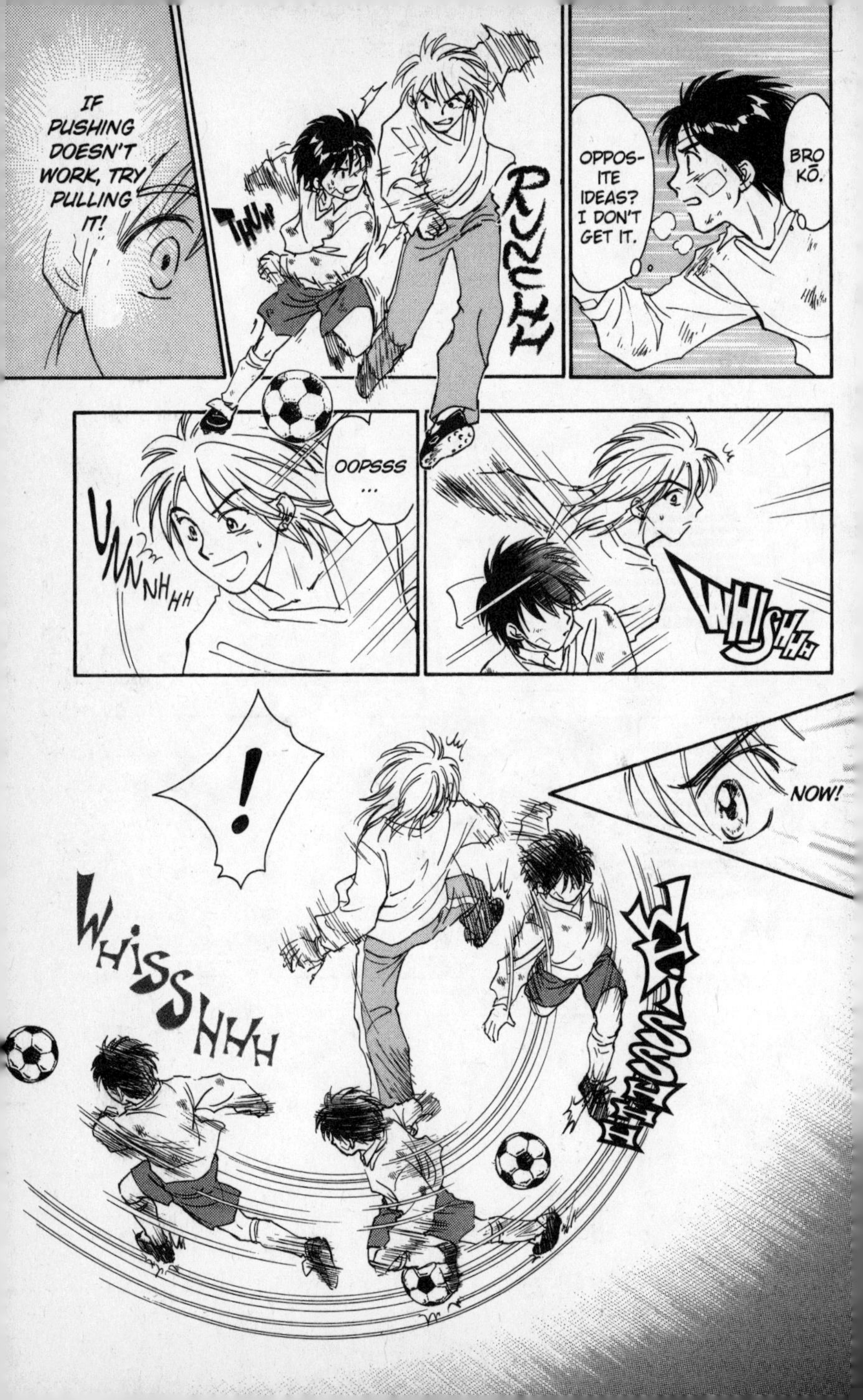
BRO KŌ.
OPPOSITE IDEAS? I DON'T GET IT.
IF PUSHING DOESN'T WORK, TRY PULLING IT!
WHISHHH
OOPSSS ...
UNNNNHHH
NOW!
!
WHISSHHH

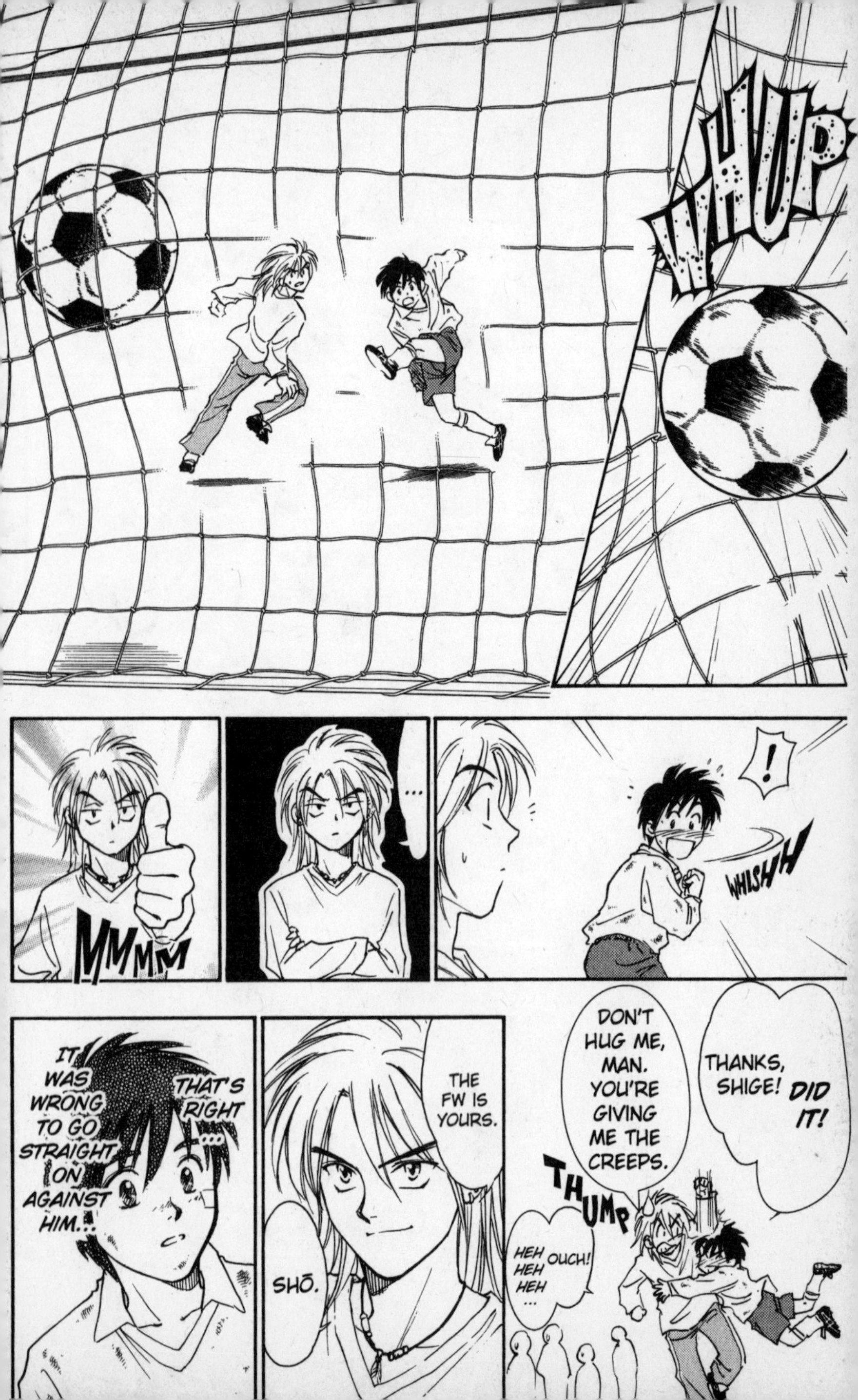

WHUP
MMMM
...
!
WHISHH
DID IT!
THANKS, SHIGE!
DON'T HUG ME, MAN. YOU'RE GIVING ME THE CREEPS.
THUMP
OUCH!
HEH HEH HEH ...
THE FW IS YOURS.
SHŌ.
THAT'S RIGHT ...
IT WAS WRONG TO GO STRAIGHT ON AGAINST HIM...

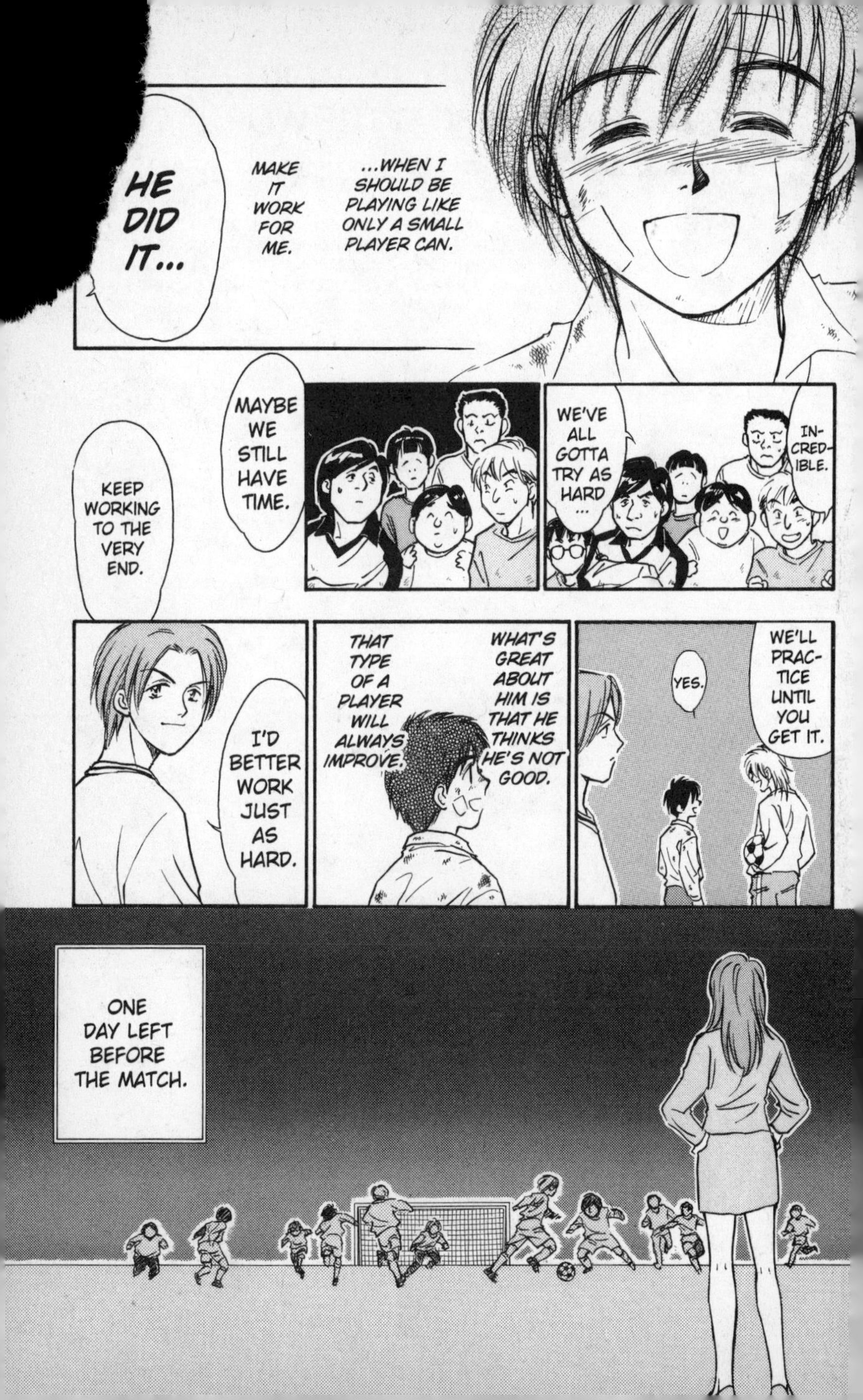
...WHEN I SHOULD BE PLAYING LIKE ONLY A SMALL PLAYER CAN.
MAKE IT WORK FOR ME.
HE DID IT...
INCREDIBLE.
WE'VE ALL GOTTA TRY AS HARD...
MAYBE WE STILL HAVE TIME.
KEEP WORKING TO THE VERY END.
WE'LL PRACTICE UNTIL YOU GET IT.
YES.
WHAT'S GREAT ABOUT HIM IS THAT HE THINKS HE'S NOT GOOD.
THAT TYPE OF A PLAYER WILL ALWAYS IMPROVE.
I'D BETTER WORK JUST AS HARD.
ONE DAY LEFT BEFORE THE MATCH.

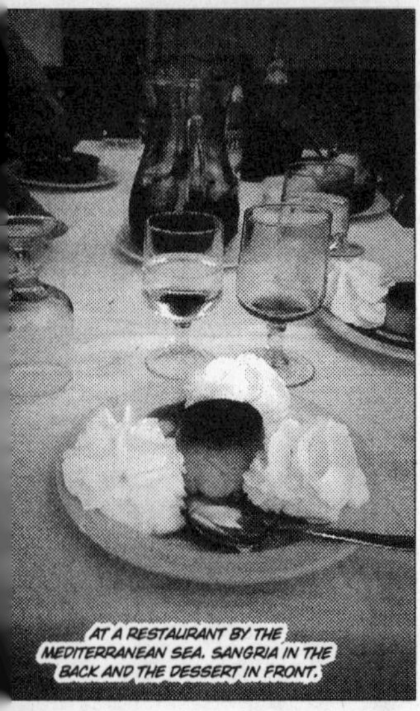

AT A RESTAURANT BY THE MEDITERRANEAN SEA. SANGRIA IN THE BACK AND THE DESSERT IN FRONT.

FOOD (CULTURE) JOUR
FROM THE WORLD C

I WON'T WRITE ABOUT THE GAME, BECAUSE I AN ADDITIONAL 100 YEARS BEFORE I CAN DO IT WI SO, PLEASE EXCUSE ME. BESIDES, HOW THE JAPA 11 PLAYED AT THE WORLD CUP HAS ALREADY BEEN DISCUSSED AND EVALUATED IN DEPTH. SO THERE'S NO POINT FOR ME TO DO THAT. AFTER ALL, I AM A MANGA ARTIST. SO I BELIEVE I SHOULD EXPRESS WHAT I THOUGHT AND FELT IN THE MANGA ITSELF. I IMAGINED THAT THE JOSUI VS. MUSASHINOMORI MATCH WAS WHAT THE JAPAN VS. ARGENTINA MATCH MIGHT BE LIKE. DURING THE FIRST DEBUT AT THE FRENCH WORLD CUP '98, THE JAPAN TEAM LOST THREE MATCHES. BUT, WHAT'S IMPORTANT IS WHAT ONE DOES AFTER ONE LOSES. I BELIEVE THE JAPAN TEAM WILL BECOME MUCH STRONGER AND SHOW THEIR BRAVE FACES AT SYDNEY 2000.

AS FOR THE THE FOOD JOURNAL: DURING THE FIRST HALF OF THE TRIP, I STAYED IN BARCELONA, SPAIN, AND THE LATTER HALF IN PARIS. SPAIN IS A YUMMY COUNTRY. I DIDN'T MISS JAPANESE FOOD AT ALL. FACING THE MEDITERRANEAN SEA, THEY HAVE ABUNDANT SEAFOOD. PAELLA WAS INCREDIBLY DELICIOUS. AFTER WHATEVER ELSE I ATE TASTED GREAT. I ESPECIALLY LIKED SANGRIA (RED WINE WITH ORANGE THAT COMES WITH SOME ICE AND A PIECE OF ORANGE). IT HAD A DIFFERENT FLAVOR AT EACH URANT. AND, THERE WERE SO MANY BARS AROUND TOWN THAT FUNCTION AS CAFES DURING AY AND BARS AT NIGHT. THEY DISPLAY MANY DIFFERENT DISHES ON THE COUNTER, LIKE THE THAT SELLS READYMADE FOOD. PEOPLE PARTY THROUGH MIDNIGHT, I.E., SPANIARDS APPEAR JOY STAYING UP LATE.

W, ABOUT PARIS. IN PARIS, THERE D FROM ALL AROUND THE WORLD. VIETNAMESE FOOD THE FIRST TIME RIS. THERE ARE MANY JAPANESE URANTS AND RAMEN SHOPS, TOO. MANY TOURISTS. IT'S PROBABLY SE OF THE WORLD CUP, BUT I MANY FOREIGNERS SPREADING HEIR MAPS ON THE STREET ERS. IT BROUGHT A SMILE TO MY I HEARD THAT THE FRENCH N'T SPEAK ENGLISH, EVEN IF KNEW HOW, BUT IN REALITY, IT T THE CASE. WHAT WAS COMMON BETWEEN PARIS AND BARCELONA WAS THAT THE BREAD TASTED DELICIOUS. BUT OF COURSE, BREAD WAS ORIGINALLY MADE THERE (UNLIKE JAPAN, WHICH IMPORTED THE TECHNIQUE). I'M RUNNING OUT OF SPACE, SO THIS IS ALL FOR NOW.

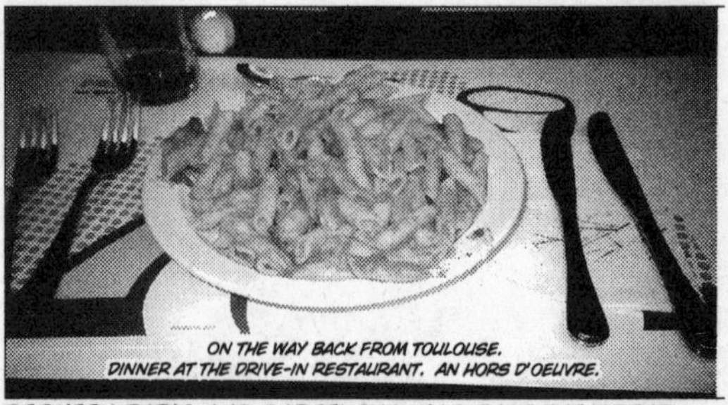

ON THE WAY BACK FROM TOULOUSE.
DINNER AT THE DRIVE-IN RESTAURANT. AN HORS D'OEUVRE.

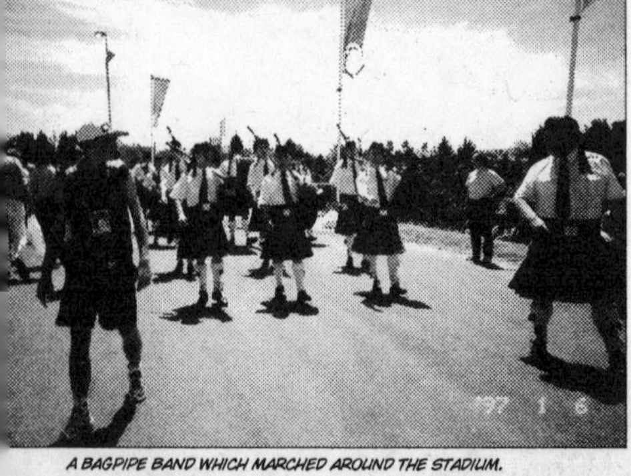

A BAGPIPE BAND WHICH MARCHED AROUND THE STADIUM.

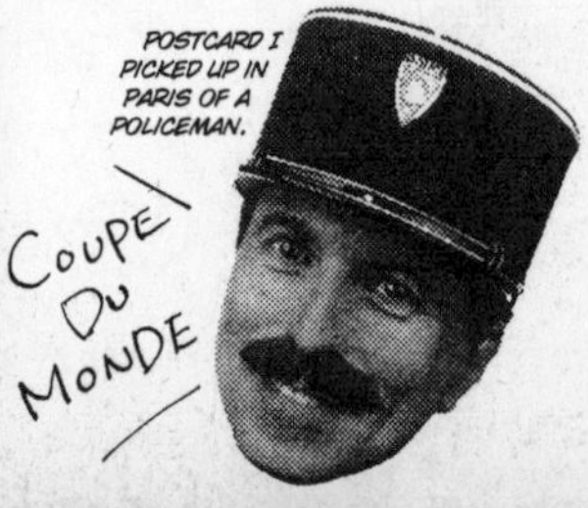
COUPE DU MONDE

POSTCARD I PICKED UP IN PARIS OF A POLICEMAN.

STAGE.12 THE LONG PASSAGEWAY TO THE FIELD

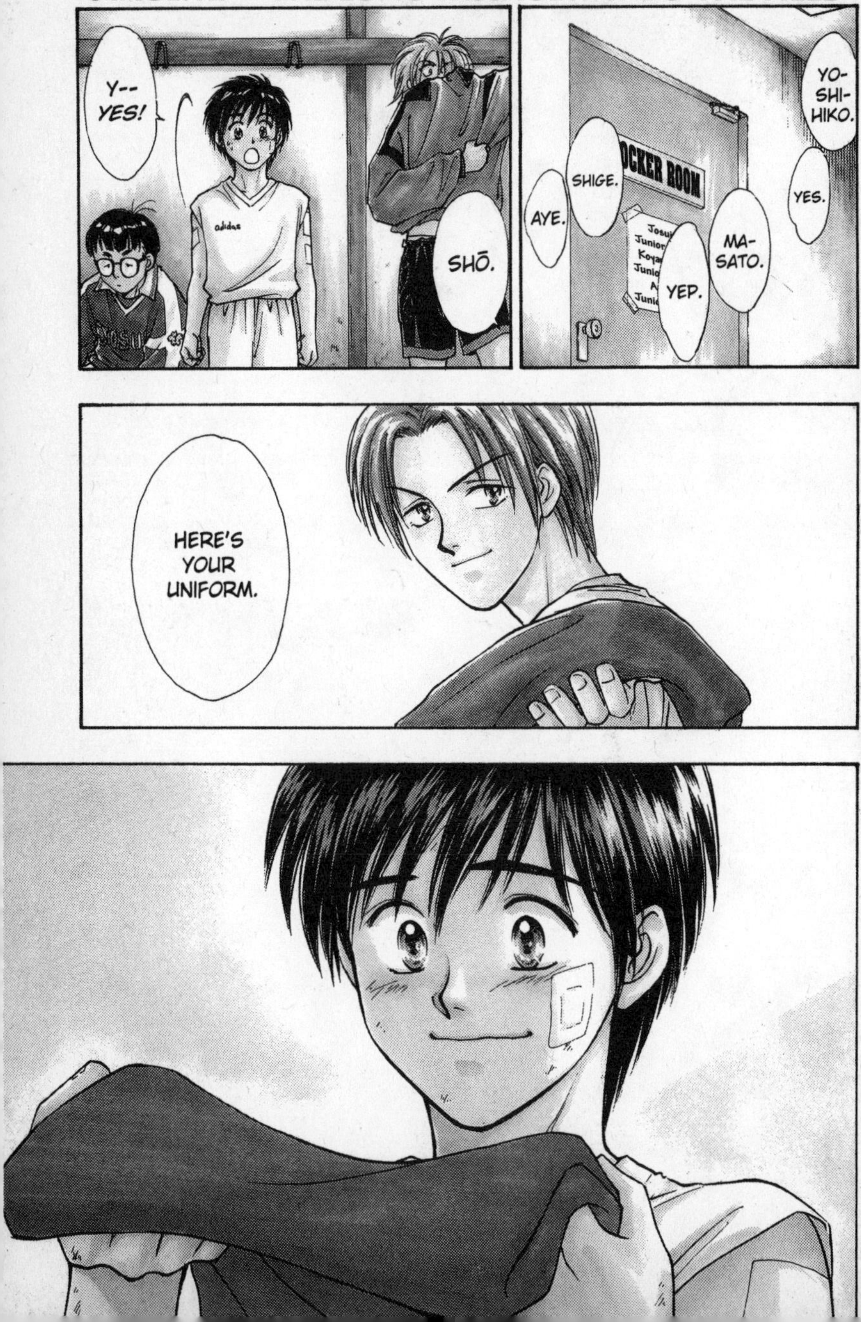
YO-SHI-HIKO.
YES.
MA-SATO.
YEP.
OCKER ROOM
SHIGE.
AYE.
SHŌ.
Y-- YES!
HERE'S YOUR UNIFORM.

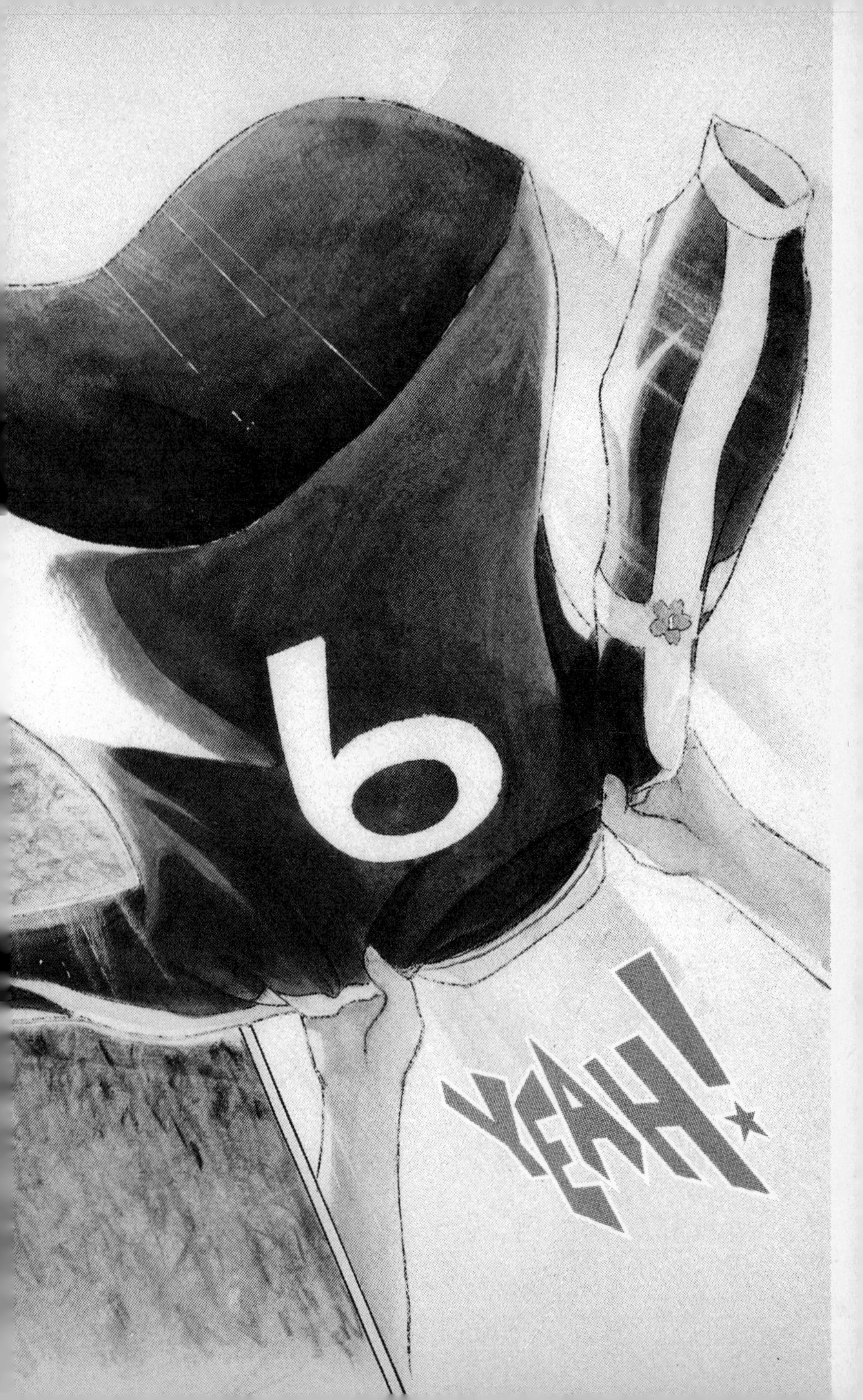
YEAH!★

STAGE.12

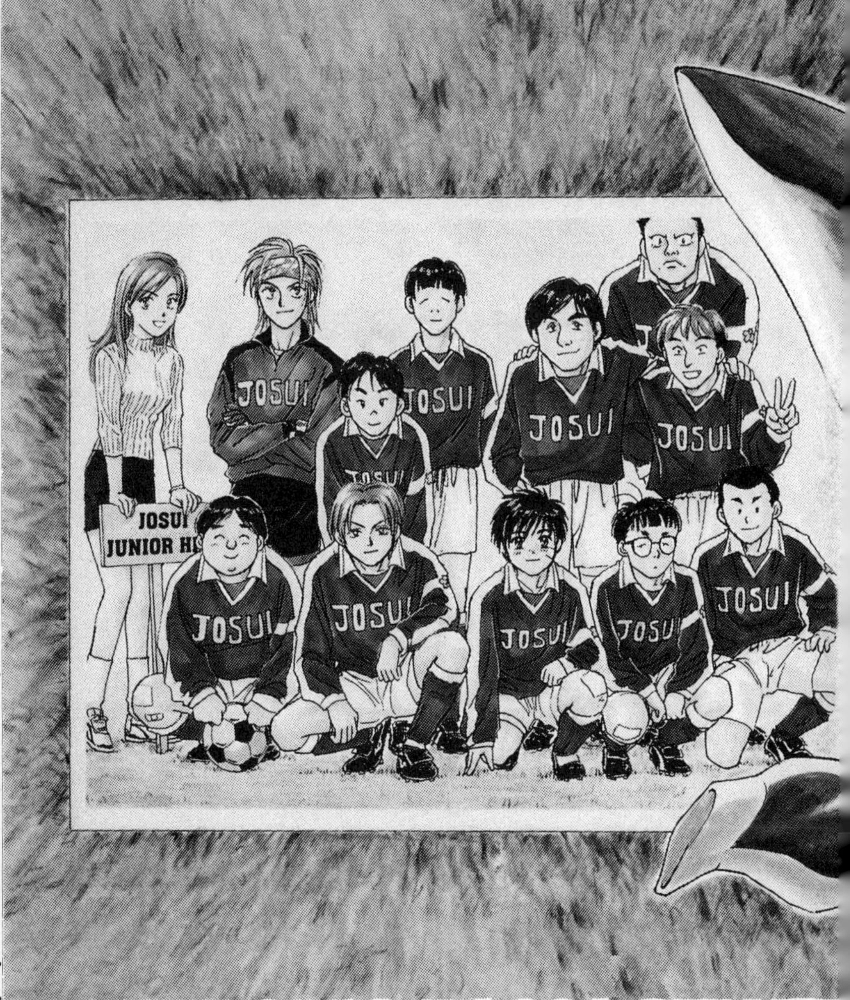

JOSUI
JUNIOR HI
JOSUI

THE LONG PASSAGEWA TO THE FIELD

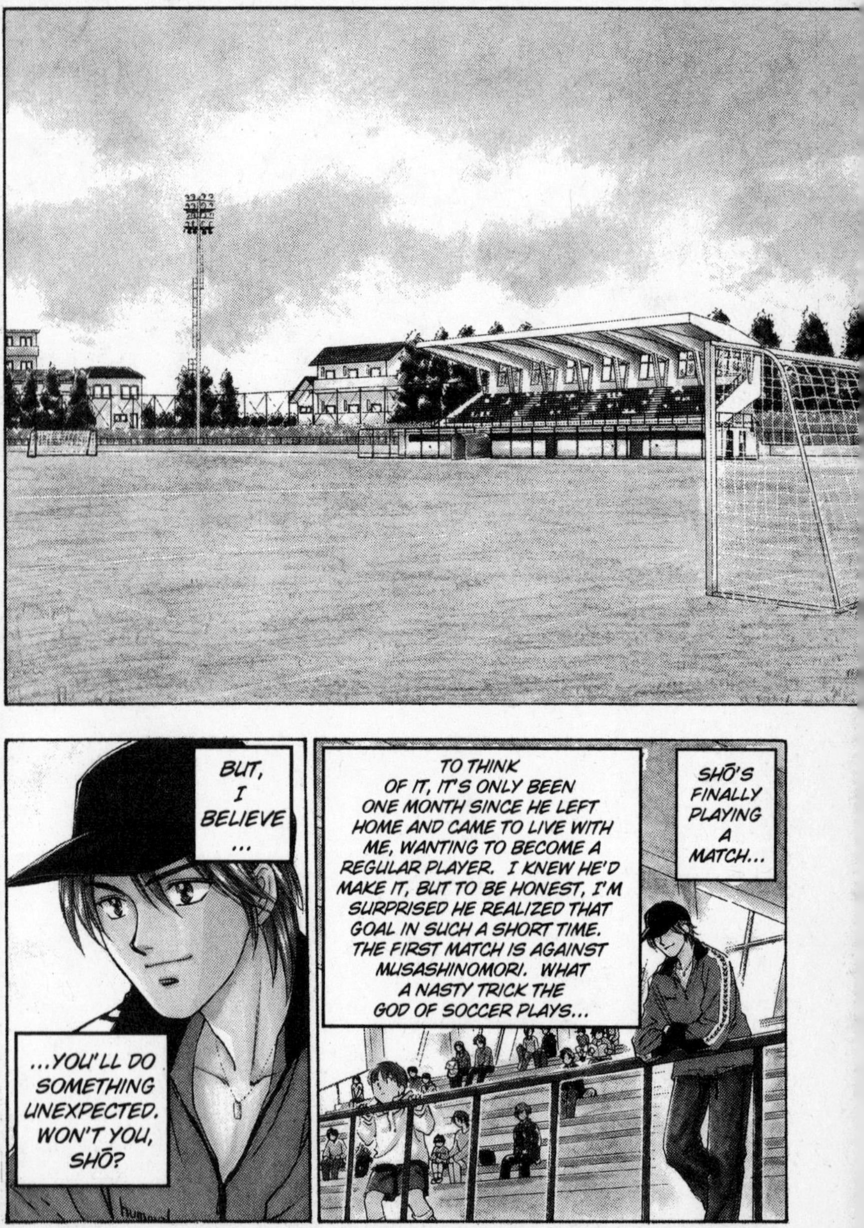
SHŌ'S FINALLY PLAYING A MATCH...
TO THINK OF IT, IT'S ONLY BEEN ONE MONTH SINCE HE LEFT HOME AND CAME TO LIVE WITH ME, WANTING TO BECOME A REGULAR PLAYER. I KNEW HE'D MAKE IT, BUT TO BE HONEST, I'M SURPRISED HE REALIZED THAT GOAL IN SUCH A SHORT TIME. THE FIRST MATCH IS AGAINST MUSASHINOMORI. WHAT A NASTY TRICK THE GOD OF SOCCER PLAYS...
BUT, I BELIEVE ...
...YOU'LL DO SOMETHING UNEXPECTED. WON'T YOU, SHŌ?

PLEASE EXCHANGE THE PLAYER'S NAME LIST.

Referee's Waiting Room

AS I EXPECTED...

!

ALTHOUGH HE SAID THE SUBSTITUTE TEAM COULD BEAT US, HE'S SENDING IN HIS REGULAR TEAM...

FORGET IT.

AS YOU EXPECTED?

SO PLEASE REMEMBER TO PLAY FAIR AND MEET JUNIOR HIGH STANDARDS.

ROSTER

(11) FW. Tatsumi	(3) MF. Shiger
(9) FW. Fujishiro	(4) DF. Takada
(10) MF. Mikami	(6) DF. Kasai
(8) MF. Kondō	(13) DF. Ōmori
(?)MF. Nakanishi	(2) DF. Negis

KREEE

FAM

DO YOU WANT TO HURT ME THAT MUCH, SOUICHIRO...?

WITH GOOD LUCK...

10

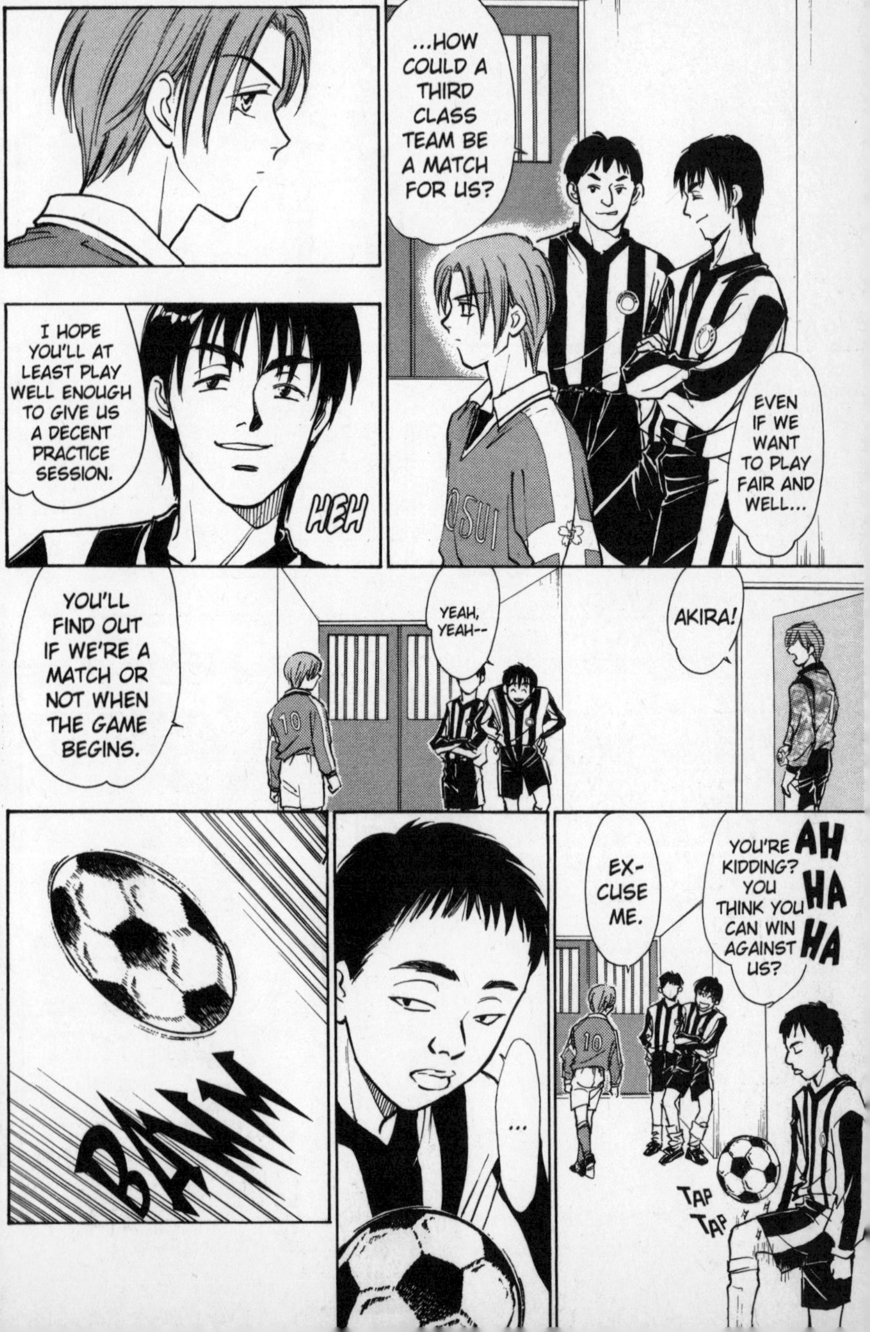
...HOW COULD A THIRD CLASS TEAM BE A MATCH FOR US?
EVEN IF WE WANT TO PLAY FAIR AND WELL...
I HOPE YOU'LL AT LEAST PLAY WELL ENOUGH TO GIVE US A DECENT PRACTICE SESSION.
HEH
YOU'LL FIND OUT IF WE'RE A MATCH OR NOT WHEN THE GAME BEGINS.
YEAH, YEAH--
AKIRA!
BAM
...
EX-CUSE ME.
YOU'RE KIDDING? YOU THINK YOU CAN WIN AGAINST US?
AH HA HA HA
TAP TAP

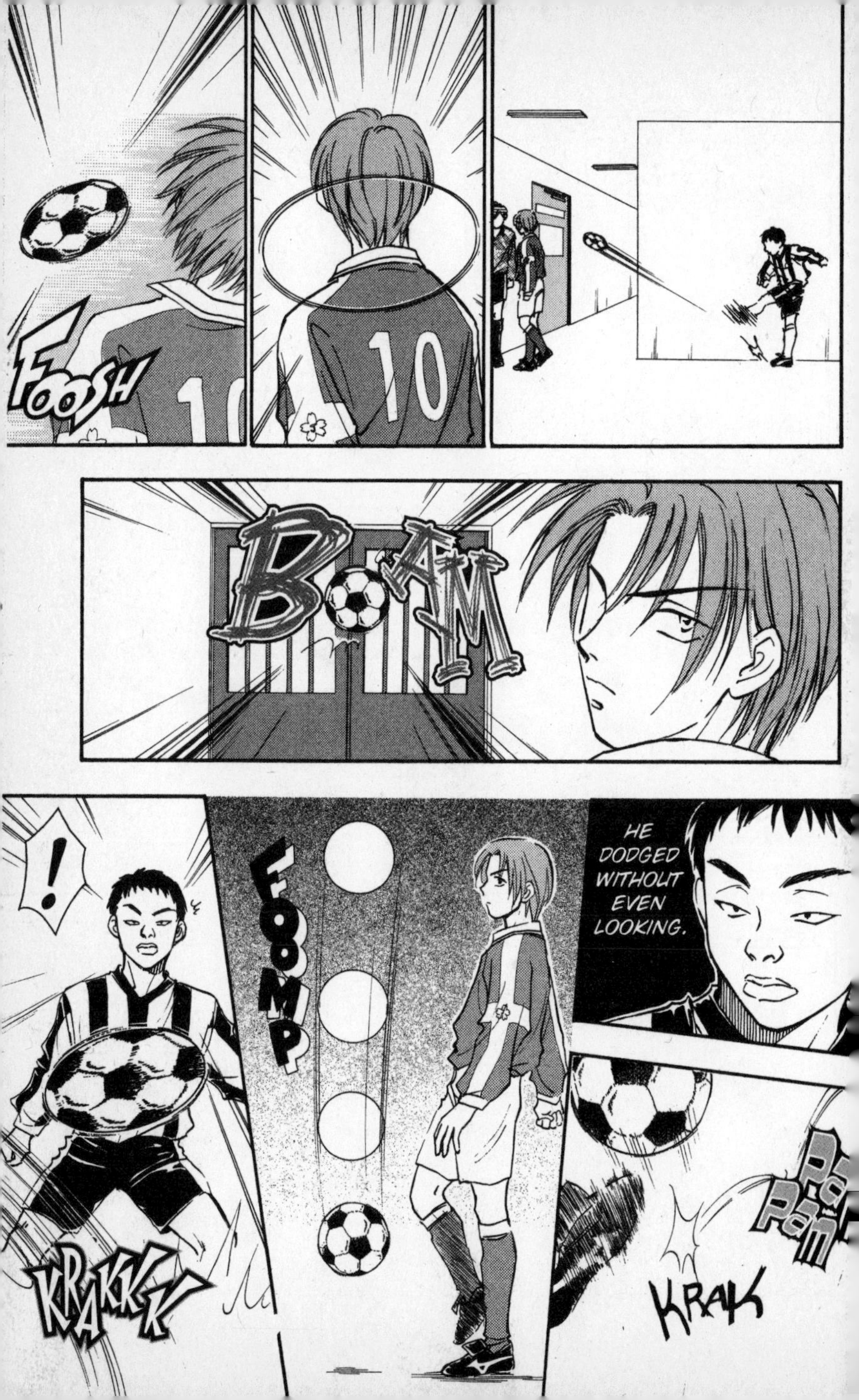
FOOSH
BOAM
HE DODGED WITHOUT EVEN LOOKING.
Pa Pam
KRAK
FOOMP
!
KRAKKK

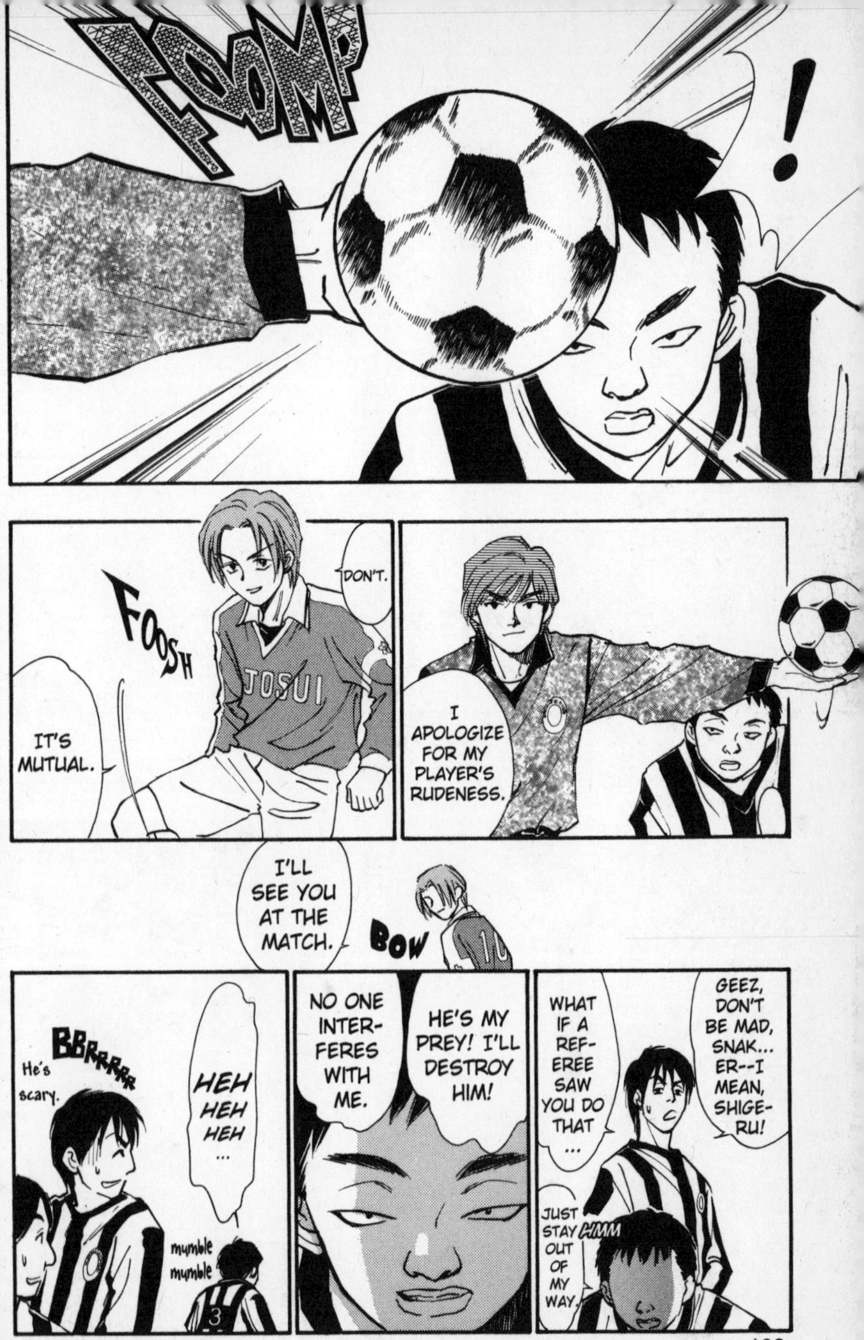
ZOOMP
!
I APOLOGIZE FOR MY PLAYER'S RUDENESS.
DON'T.
FOOSH
IT'S MUTUAL.
I'LL SEE YOU AT THE MATCH.
BOW
GEEZ, DON'T BE MAD, SNAK... ER--I MEAN, SHIGE-RU!
WHAT IF A REF-EREE SAW YOU DO THAT ...
HMM
JUST STAY OUT OF MY WAY.
HE'S MY PREY! I'LL DESTROY HIM!
NO ONE INTER-FERES WITH ME.
HEH HEH HEH ...
BBRRRRRR
He's scary.
mumble mumble

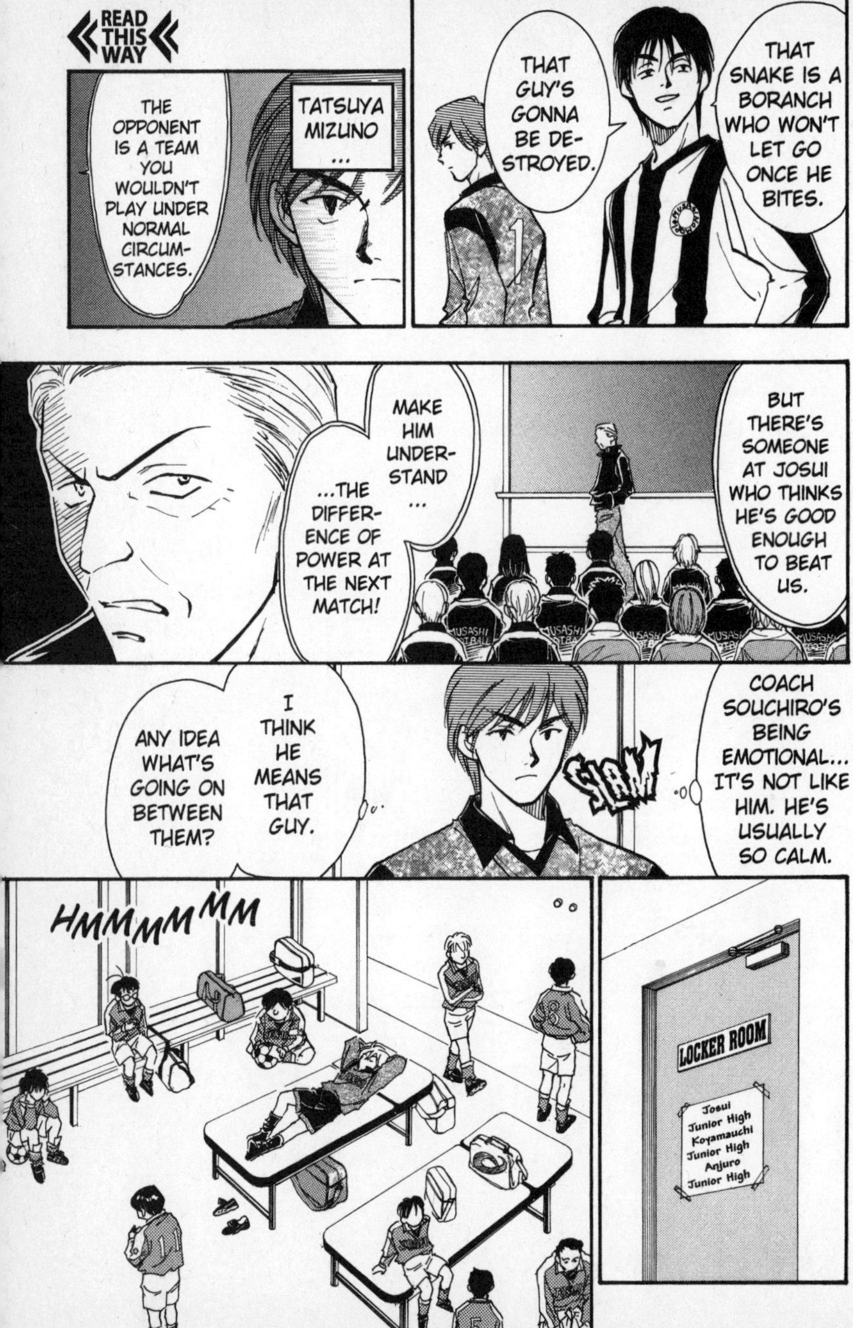
READ THIS WAY
THAT SNAKE IS A BORANCH WHO WON'T LET GO ONCE HE BITES.
THAT GUY'S GONNA BE DE-STROYED.
TATSUYA MIZUNO ...
THE OPPONENT IS A TEAM YOU WOULDN'T PLAY UNDER NORMAL CIRCUM-STANCES.
BUT THERE'S SOMEONE AT JOSUI WHO THINKS HE'S GOOD ENOUGH TO BEAT US.
MAKE HIM UNDER-STAND ...
...THE DIFFER-ENCE OF POWER AT THE NEXT MATCH!
COACH SOUCHIRO'S BEING EMOTIONAL... IT'S NOT LIKE HIM. HE'S USUALLY SO CALM.
SLAM
I THINK HE MEANS THAT GUY.
ANY IDEA WHAT'S GOING ON BETWEEN THEM?
LOCKER ROOM
Josui Junior High Koyamauchi Junior High Anjuro Junior High
HMMMMMMM

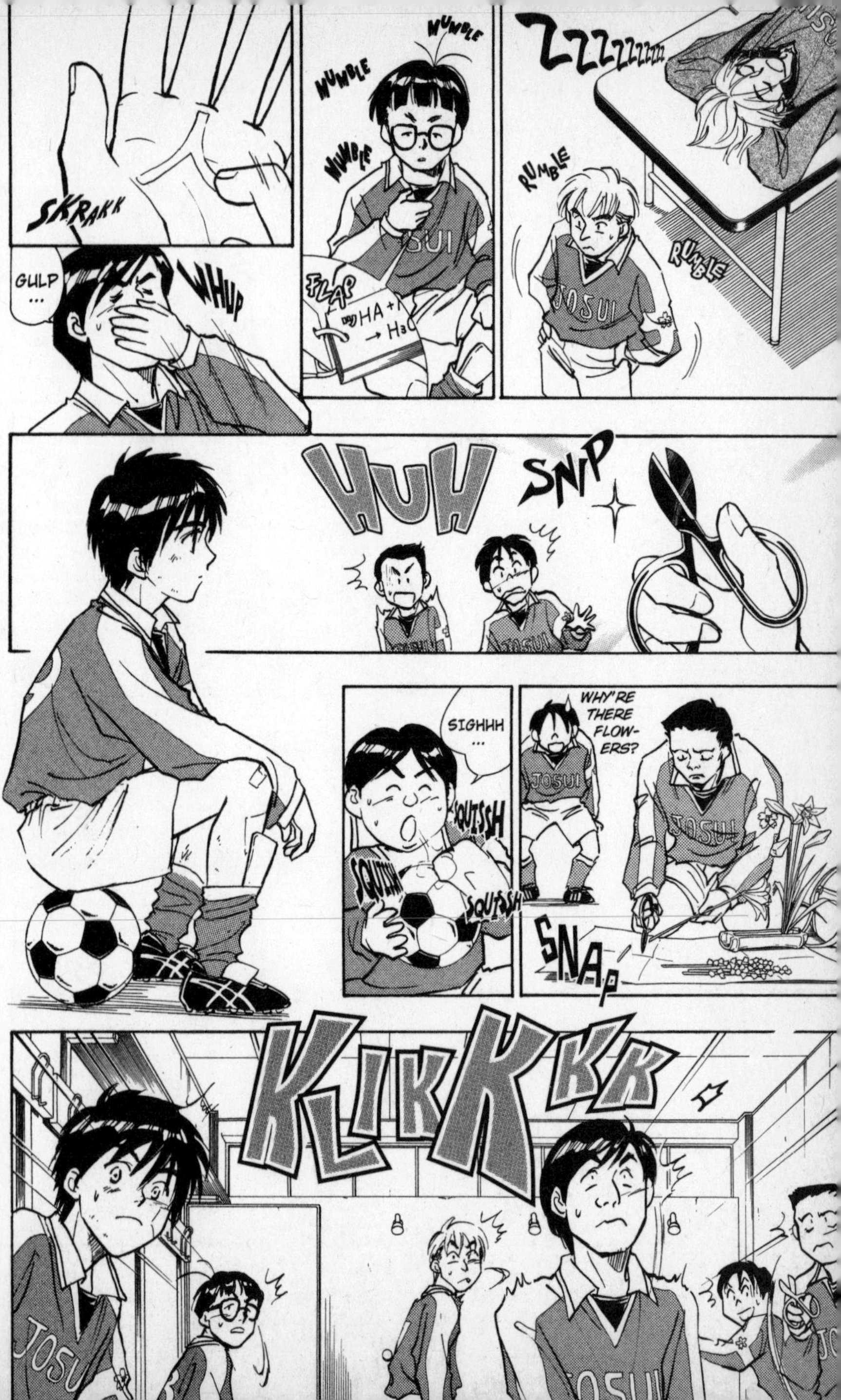

ZZZZZZZZZ
RUMBLE
RUMBLE
MUMBLE
MUMBLE
MUMBLE
FLAP
SKRAKK
WHUP
GULP ...
SNIP
HUH
SNAP
WHY'RE THERE FLOWERS?
SIGHHH ...
SQUISH
SQUISH
SQUISH
KLIKKKK

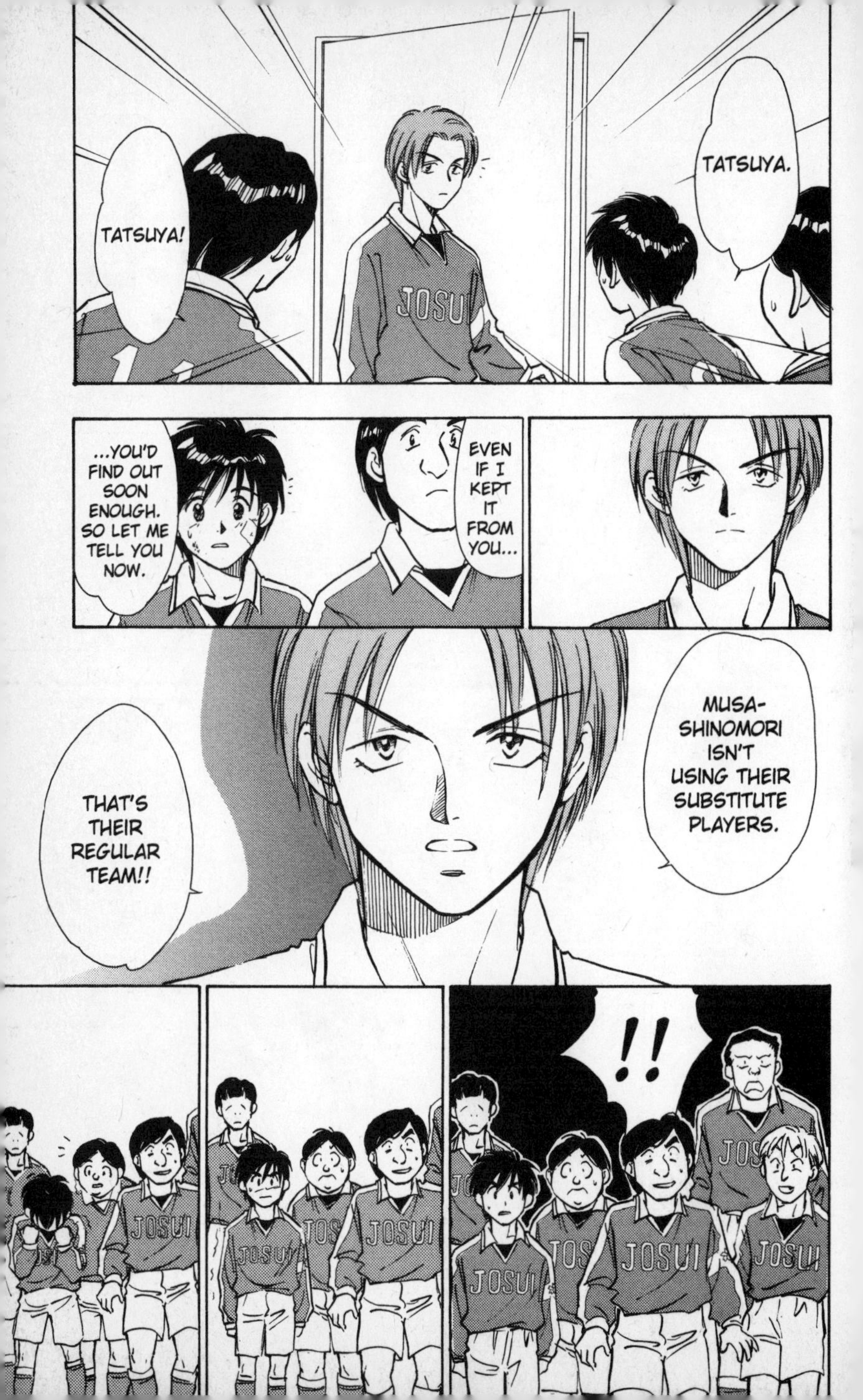
TATSUYA!
TATSUYA.
EVEN IF I KEPT IT FROM YOU...
...YOU'D FIND OUT SOON ENOUGH. SO LET ME TELL YOU NOW.
MUSA-SHINOMORI ISN'T USING THEIR SUBSTITUTE PLAYERS.
THAT'S THEIR REGULAR TEAM!!
!!

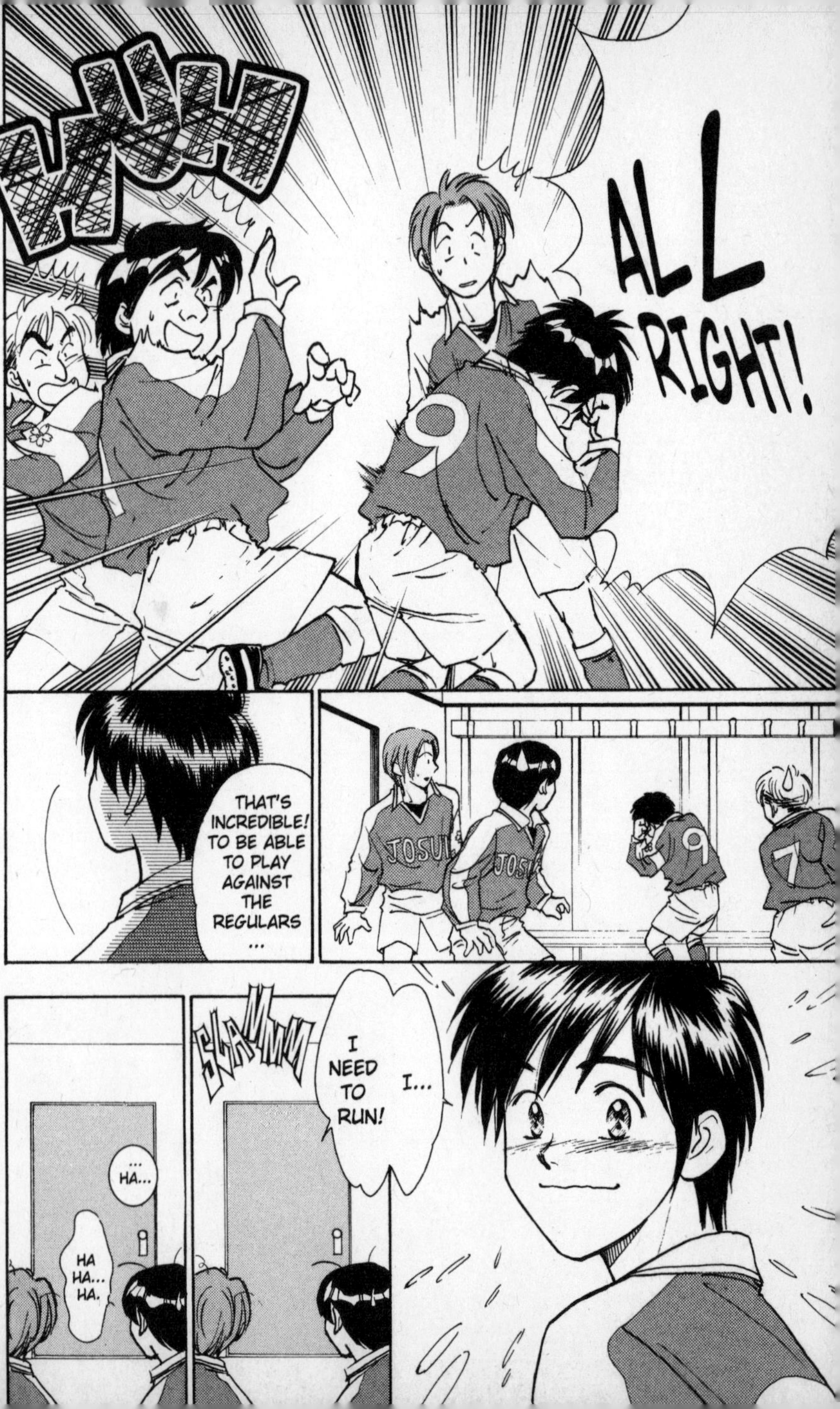
WUSH
ALL RIGHT!
THAT'S INCREDIBLE! TO BE ABLE TO PLAY AGAINST THE REGULARS ...
I...
I NEED TO RUN!
SLAMMM
... HA...
HA HA... HA.

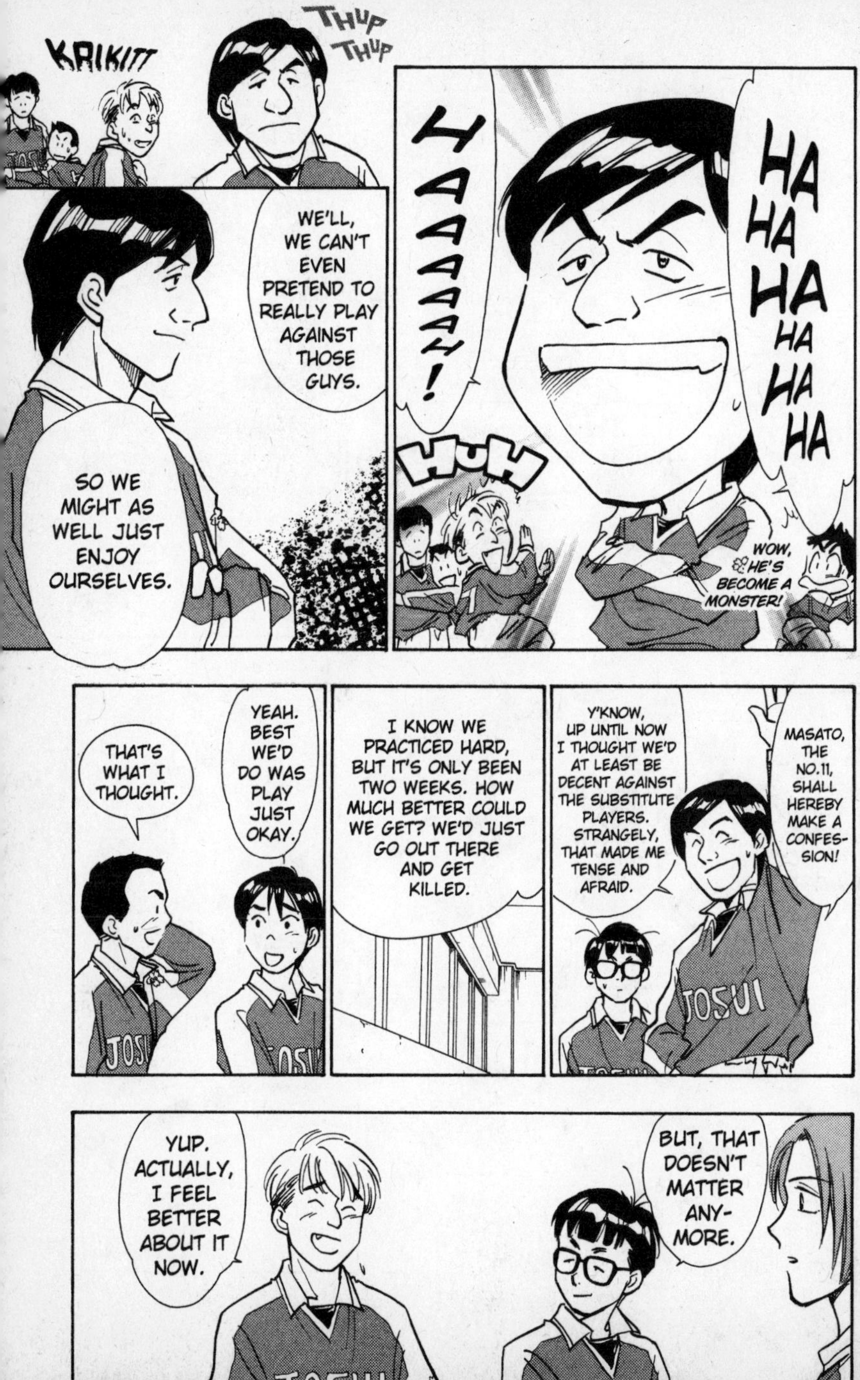
HA HA HA HA HA HA HA
HAAAAAAH!
HUH
WOW, HE'S BECOME A MONSTER!
WE'LL, WE CAN'T EVEN PRETEND TO REALLY PLAY AGAINST THOSE GUYS.
SO WE MIGHT AS WELL JUST ENJOY OURSELVES.
THUP THUP
KRIKITT
MASATO, THE NO.11, SHALL HEREBY MAKE A CONFES-SION!
Y'KNOW, UP UNTIL NOW I THOUGHT WE'D AT LEAST BE DECENT AGAINST THE SUBSTITUTE PLAYERS. STRANGELY, THAT MADE ME TENSE AND AFRAID.
I KNOW WE PRACTICED HARD, BUT IT'S ONLY BEEN TWO WEEKS. HOW MUCH BETTER COULD WE GET? WE'D JUST GO OUT THERE AND GET KILLED.
YEAH. BEST WE'D DO WAS PLAY JUST OKAY.
THAT'S WHAT I THOUGHT.
BUT, THAT DOESN'T MATTER ANY-MORE.
YUP. ACTUALLY, I FEEL BETTER ABOUT IT NOW.

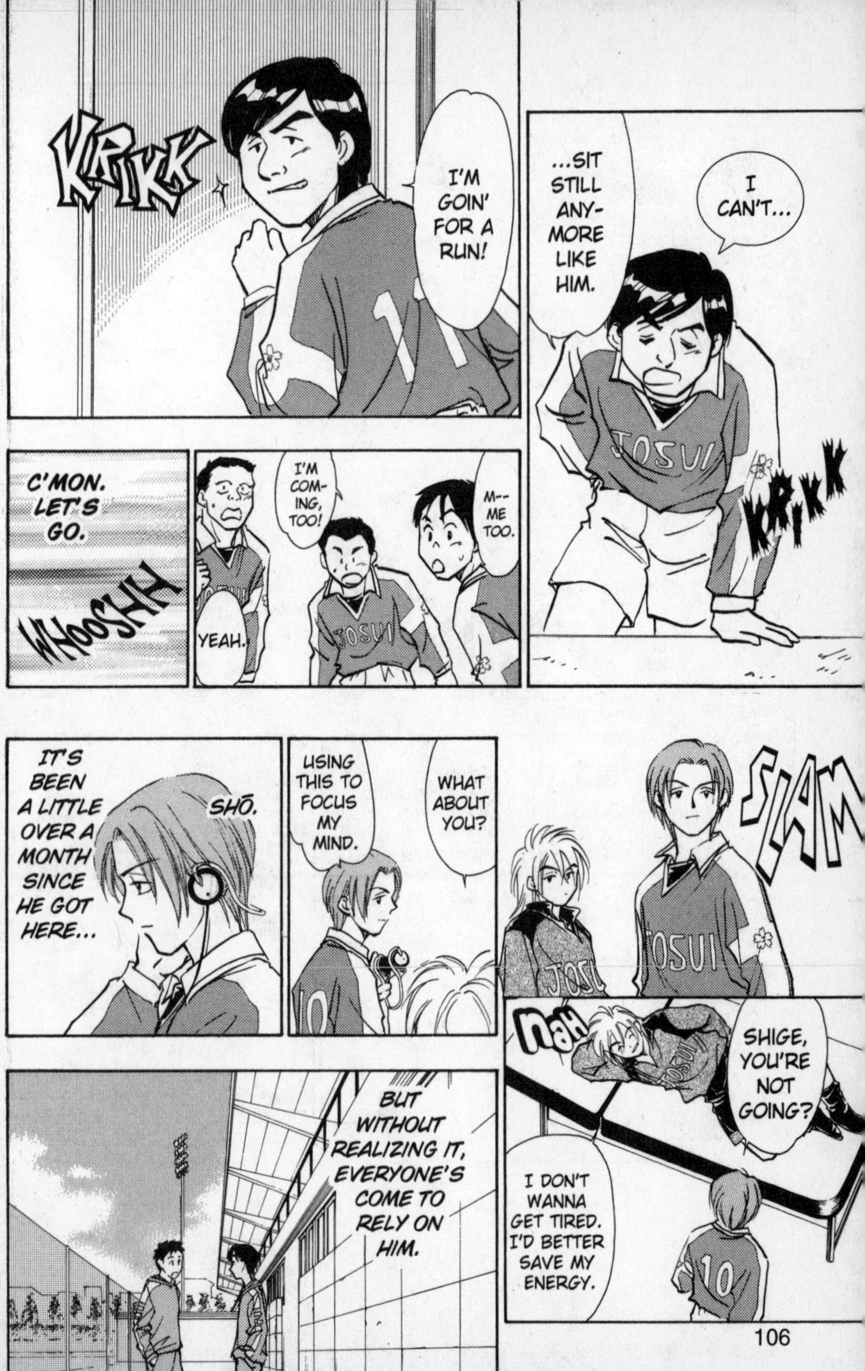
KRIKK
I'M GOIN' FOR A RUN!
I CAN'T...
...SIT STILL ANYMORE LIKE HIM.
KRIKK
C'MON. LET'S GO.
WHOOSHH
YEAH.
I'M COMING, TOO!
M-- ME TOO.
IT'S BEEN A LITTLE OVER A MONTH SINCE HE GOT HERE...
SHŌ.
USING THIS TO FOCUS MY MIND.
WHAT ABOUT YOU?
SLAM
nah
SHIGE, YOU'RE NOT GOING?
I DON'T WANNA GET TIRED. I'D BETTER SAVE MY ENERGY.
BUT WITHOUT REALIZING IT, EVERYONE'S COME TO RELY ON HIM.

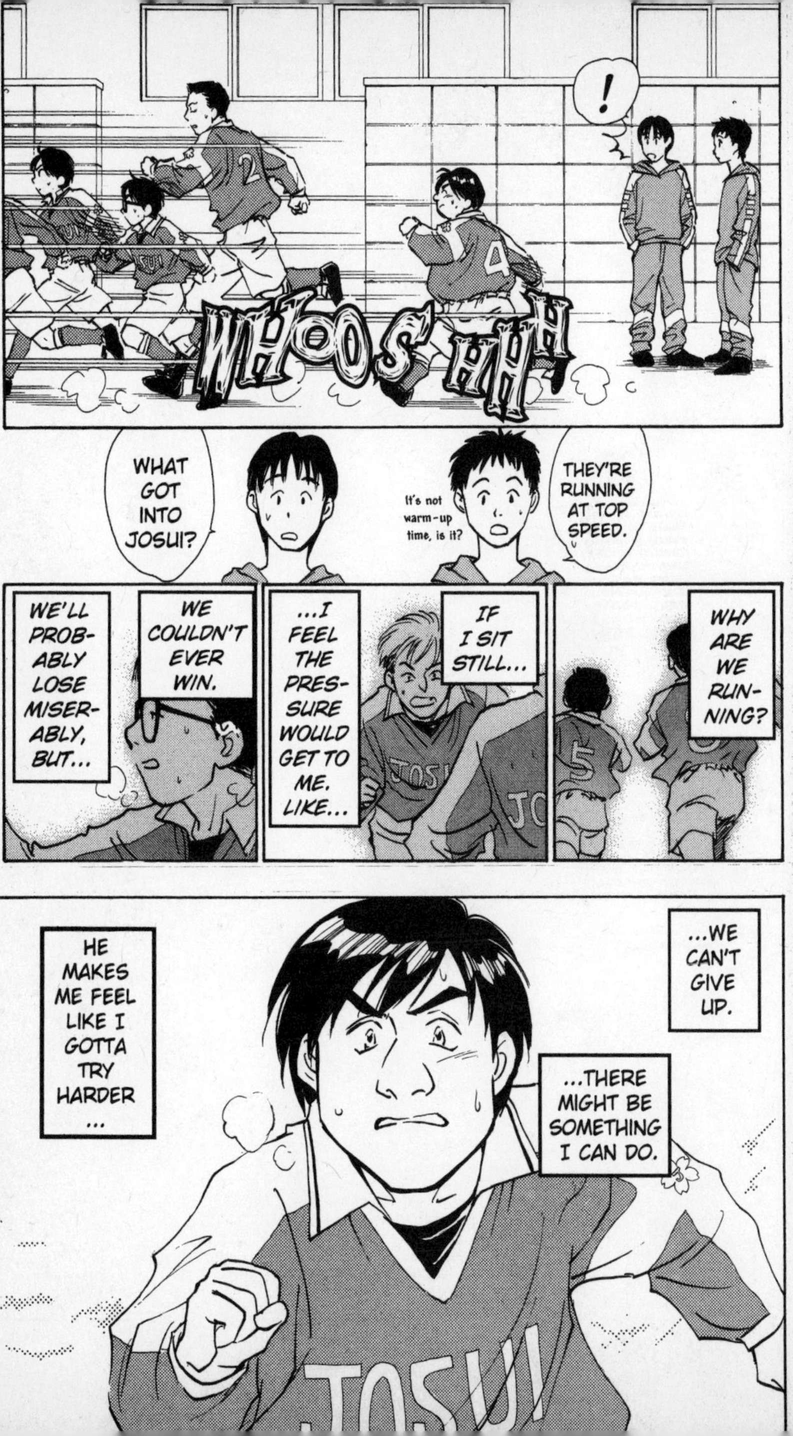
!
WHOOSHHH
THEY'RE RUNNING AT TOP SPEED.
It's not warm-up time, is it?
WHAT GOT INTO JOSUI?
WHY ARE WE RUNNING?
IF I SIT STILL...
...I FEEL THE PRESSURE WOULD GET TO ME. LIKE...
WE COULDN'T EVER WIN.
WE'LL PROBABLY LOSE MISERABLY, BUT...
...WE CAN'T GIVE UP.
...THERE MIGHT BE SOMETHING I CAN DO.
HE MAKES ME FEEL LIKE I GOTTA TRY HARDER...

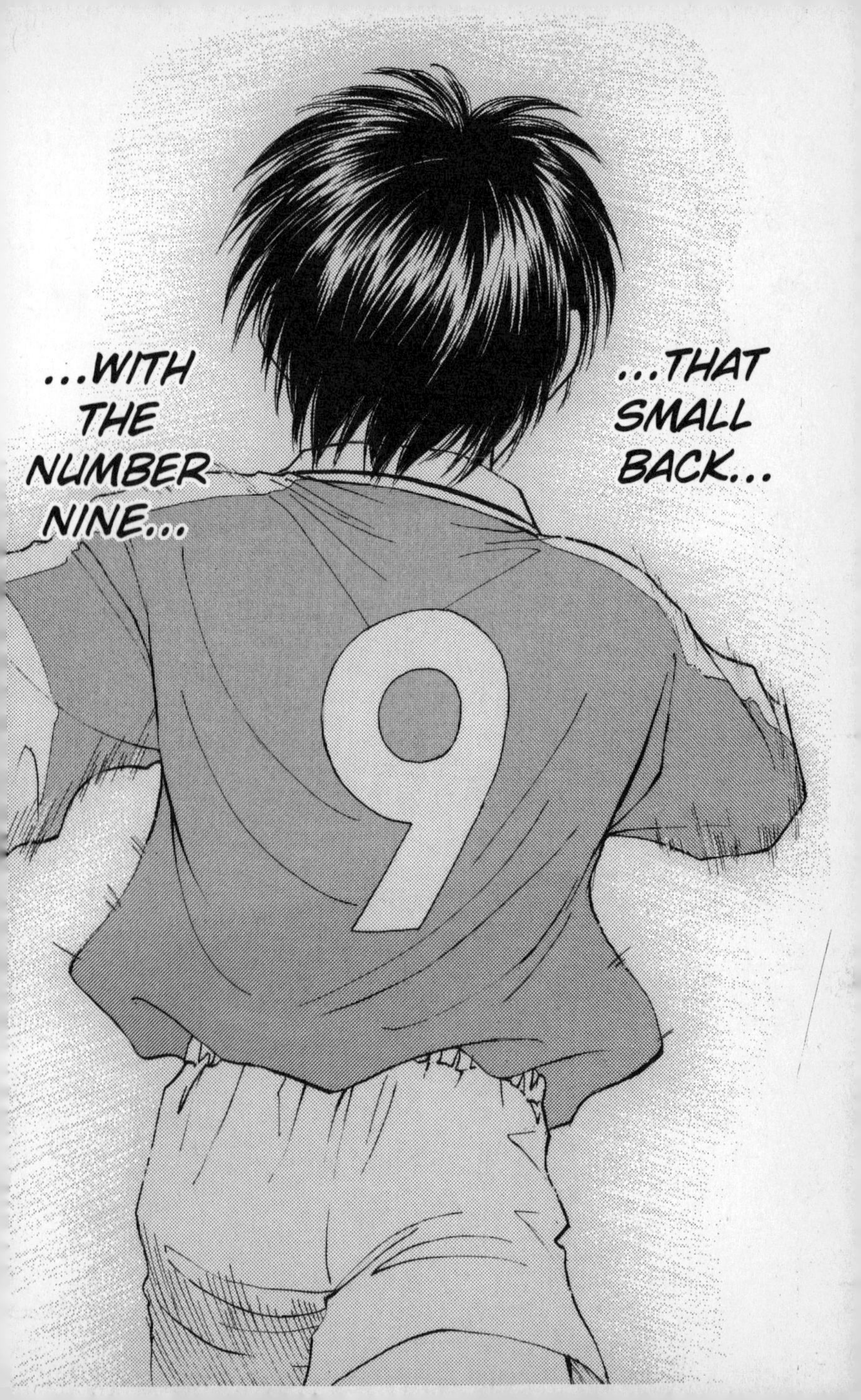
...THAT SMALL BACK...
...WITH THE NUMBER NINE...

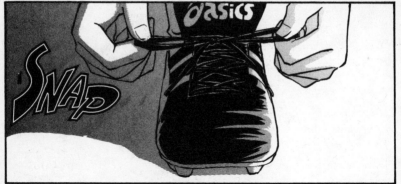

IT'S TIME TO GO TO THE FIELD.

KRIKK

EVERY-ONE...

SNAP

TAP

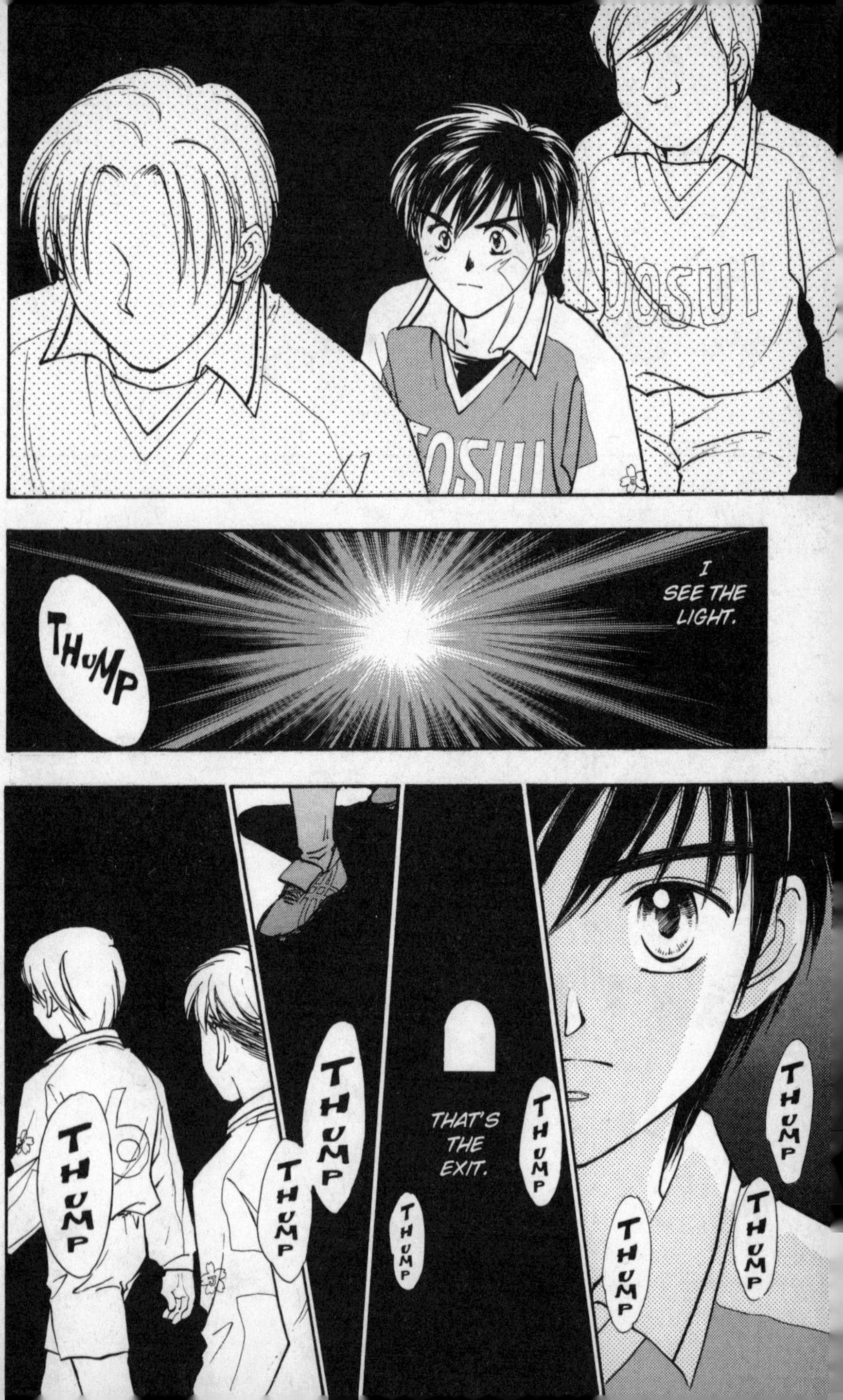
I SEE THE LIGHT.
THUMP
THUMP
THUMP
THUMP
THUMP
THAT'S THE EXIT.
THUMP
THUMP
THUMP
THUMP

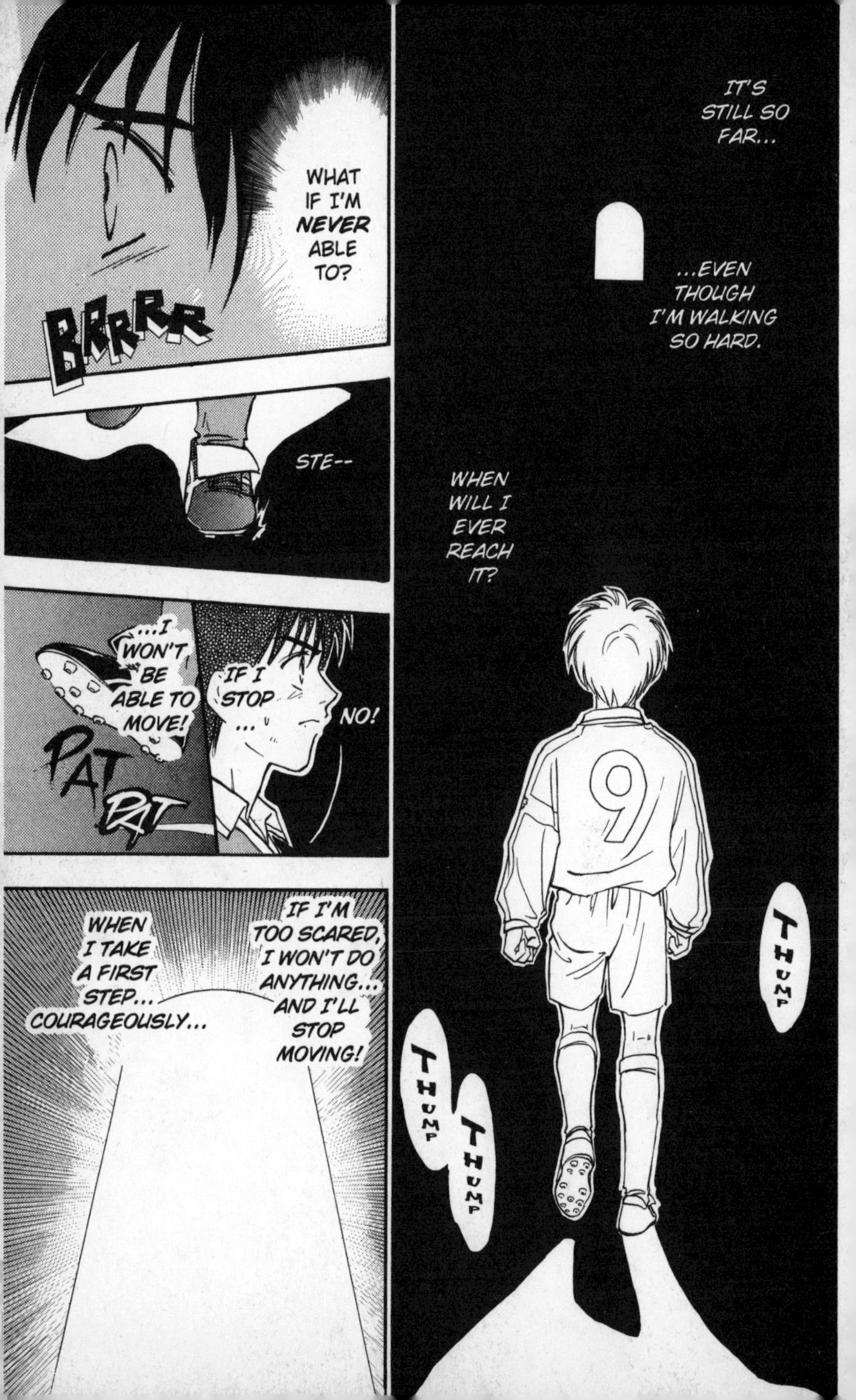

IT'S STILL SO FAR...
...EVEN THOUGH I'M WALKING SO HARD.
WHEN WILL I EVER REACH IT?
THUMP
THUMP
THUMP
WHAT IF I'M NEVER ABLE TO?
BRRRRR
STE--
NO!
IF I STOP...
...I WON'T BE ABLE TO MOVE!
PAT PAT
IF I'M TOO SCARED, I WON'T DO ANYTHING... AND I'LL STOP MOVING!
WHEN I TAKE A FIRST STEP... COURAGEOUSLY...

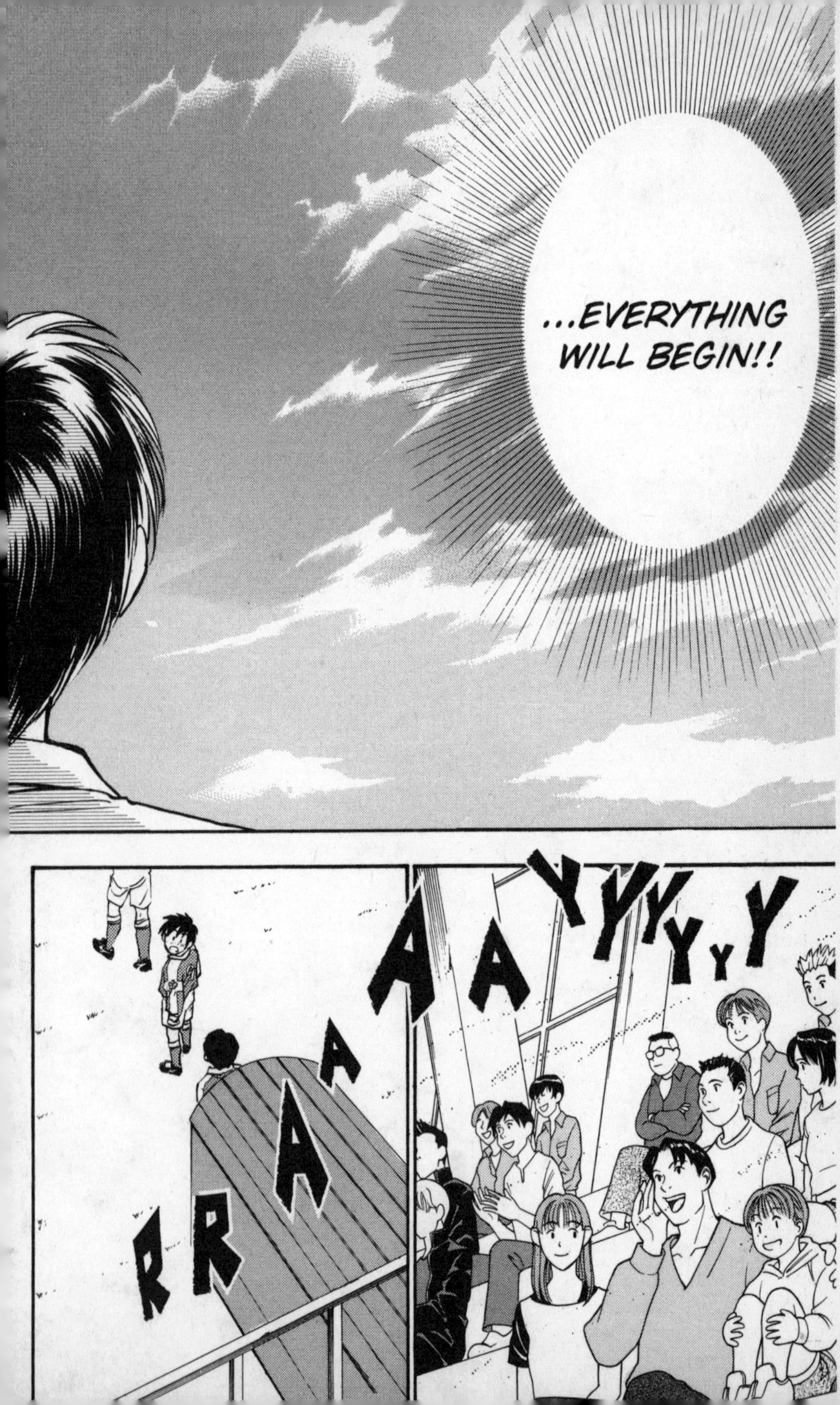
...EVERYTHING WILL BEGIN!!
RRAAAAAYYYYYYY

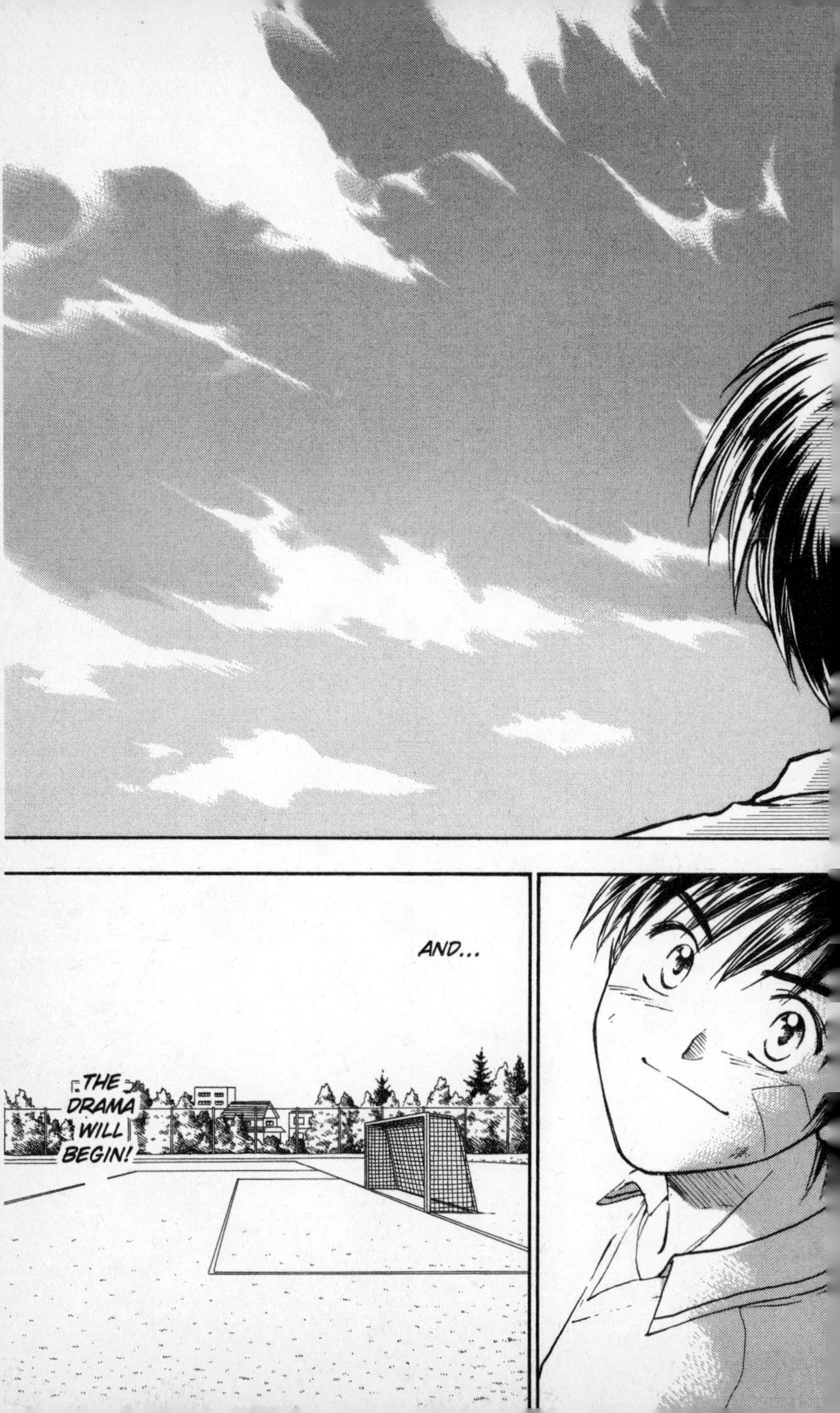
AND...
THE DRAMA WILL BEGIN!

Small Whistle! Theatre!!

CARTOON MASATO

Or, a
fisheye lens:
Masato Hiromatsu

Art: Assistant N

TATSU-BON'S HOLIDAY
GO GET IT.
RUFF!
PET PET
BOOM
PAT PAT PAT
TAP TAP TAP
GOOD BOY.
RUFF!
PET PET
WHISH

You'll find out what the dog looks like later in the story (perhaps).

PING
NIPPON・500

STAGE.13
ON YOUR MARKS

READ THIS WAY

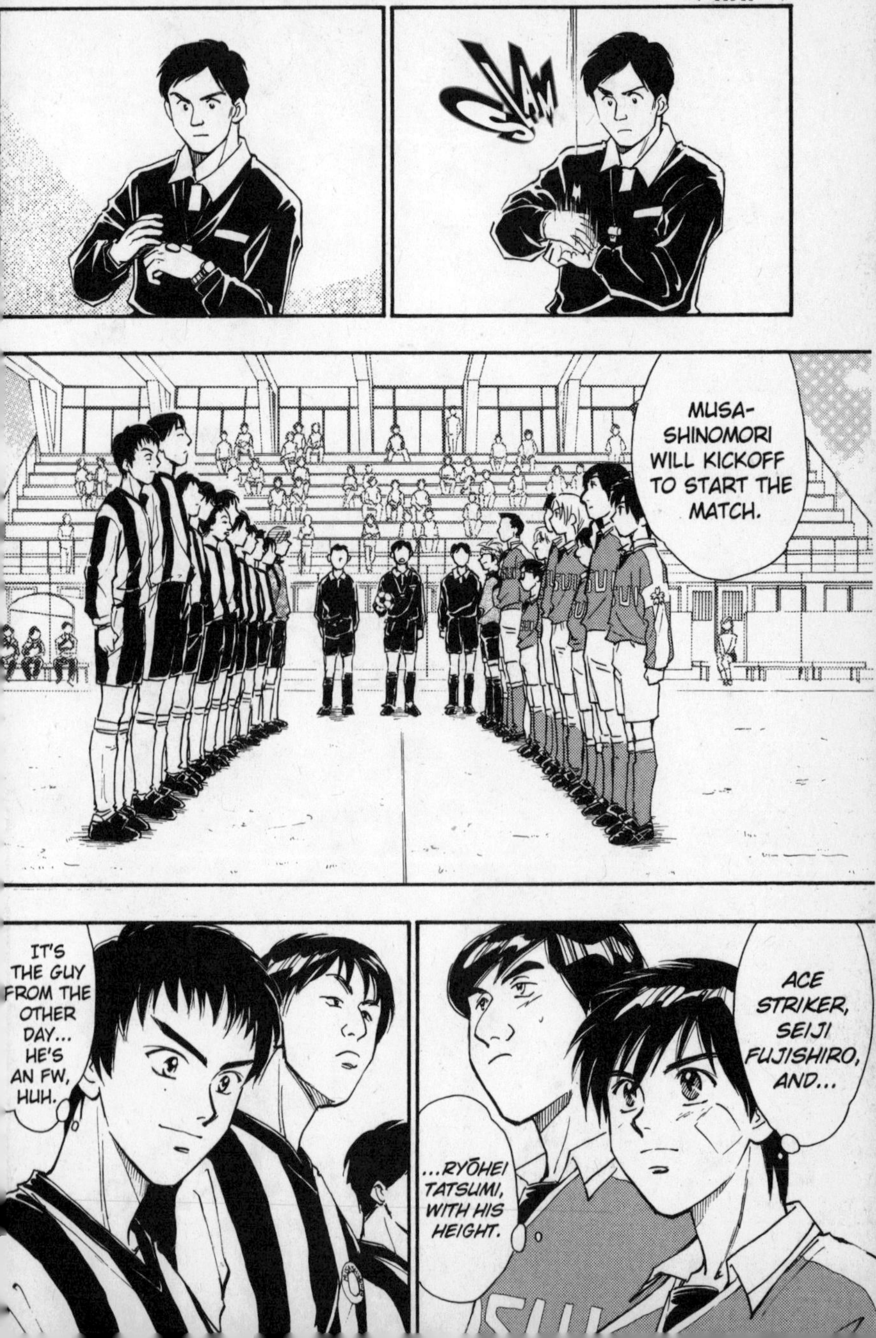
SLAM
MUSASHINOMORI WILL KICKOFF TO START THE MATCH.
ACE STRIKER, SEIJI FUJISHIRO, AND...
...RYŌHEI TATSUMI, WITH HIS HEIGHT.
IT'S THE GUY FROM THE OTHER DAY... HE'S AN FW, HUH.

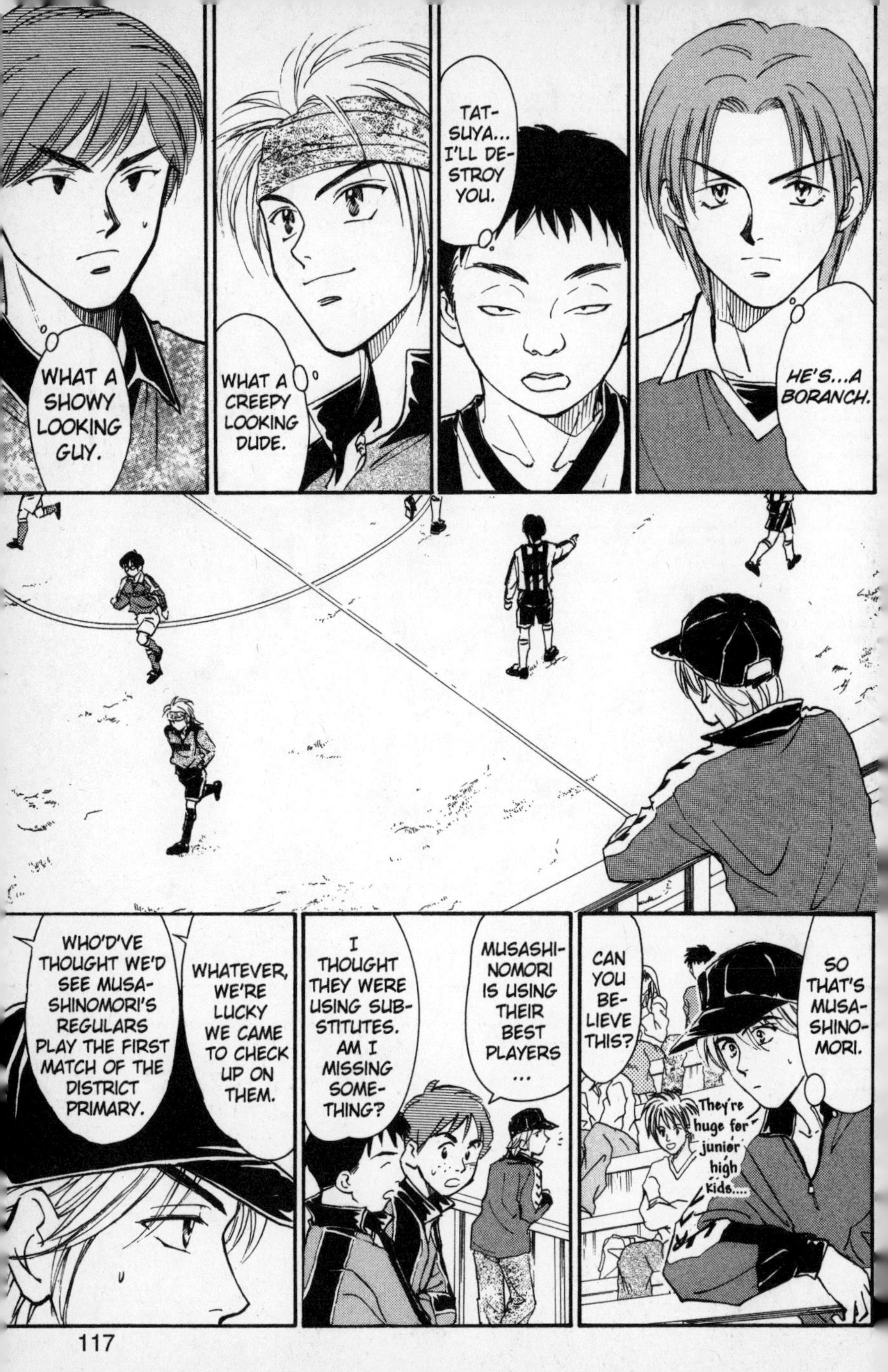
HE'S...A BORANCH.
TAT-SUYA... I'LL DE-STROY YOU.
WHAT A CREEPY LOOKING DUDE.
WHAT A SHOWY LOOKING GUY.
SO THAT'S MUSA-SHINO-MORI.
They're huge for junior high kids....
CAN YOU BE-LIEVE THIS?
MUSASHI-NOMORI IS USING THEIR BEST PLAYERS ...
I THOUGHT THEY WERE USING SUB-STITUTES. AM I MISSING SOME-THING?
WHATEVER, WE'RE LUCKY WE CAME TO CHECK UP ON THEM.
WHO'D'VE THOUGHT WE'D SEE MUSA-SHINOMORI'S REGULARS PLAY THE FIRST MATCH OF THE DISTRICT PRIMARY.

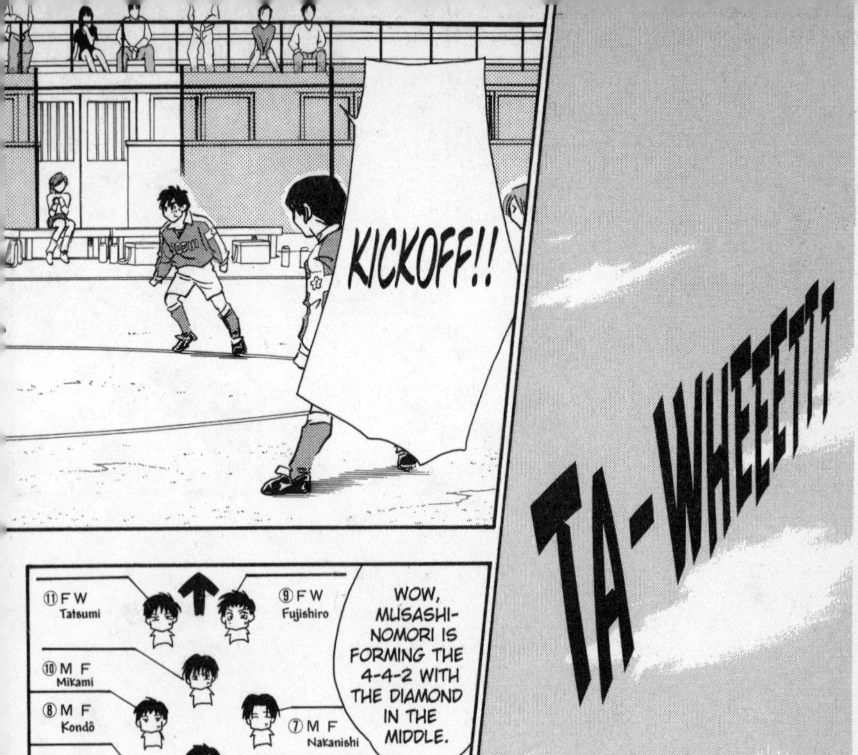
KICKOFF!!
TA-WHEEETTT
DO YOUR BEST, SHŌ!
WOW, MUSASHI-NOMORI IS FORMING THE 4-4-2 WITH THE DIAMOND IN THE MIDDLE.
⑪ F W Tatsumi
⑨ F W Fujishiro
⑩ M F Mikami
⑧ M F Kondô
⑦ M F Nakanishi
④ D F Takada
③ M F Shigeru
② D F Negishi
⑥ D F Kasai
⑬ D F Ômori
① G K Shibusawa
GOAL

② 4 — 4 — 2 System [Tres Boranch Formation]

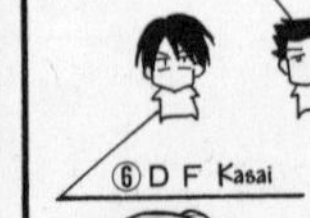
FW
MF
DF

TO ACHIEVE A SUPER DEFENSIVE MECHANISM, THIS FORMATION USES THREE BORANCHES TO WORK MAINLY ON DEFENSE. THE WORD "TRES" MEANS "THREE" IN PORTUGUESE. WHEN THERE IS A HUGE DISPARITY IN STRENGTH BETWEEN TEAMS, THIS STRATEGY IS USEFUL BECAUSE IT ENABLES THE TEAM TO SHOOT FROM THE COUNTER. JOSUI USED THIS SYSTEM AGAINST THEIR STRONG OPPONENT, MUSASHINOMORI.

③ 3 — 5 — 2 System

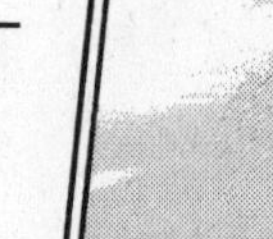
FW
MF
DF
Sweeper or Libero.

THIS IS A SYSTEM THAT IS USED TO PRESSURE THE STRONG FWS FOUND IN THE 4-4-2 SYSTEM. BASICALLY, TWO OUT OF THREE DFS ARE USED TO MAN-MARK (I.E., ONE-ON-ONE THOROUGH MAN-MARK AGAINST THE TWO FWS) AND THE LAST ONE BECOMES A SWEEPER (SPECIALIZES IN DF) OR A LIBERO (ONE WHO CAN FREELY CHOOSE TO JOIN THE OFFENSIVE). IN OTHER WORDS, THREE DFS WILL STOP THE OPPONENT'S TWO FWS. THE REPRESENTATIVE TEAM THAT USES THIS SYSTEM IS GERMAN.

4-4-2? DIAMOND? TRES BORANCH? WHAT THE HECK ARE THEY?
How are they different?
Near-sighted
GOAL
①G K Satô
②D F Hanazawa
③D F Koga
⑤D F Tanaka
④D F Hiroyoshi
⑥M F Toyama
⑦M F Morinaga
⑧M F Gomi
⑩M F Mizuno
⑪F W Masato
⑨F W Kazamatsuri
LOOKS LIKE JOSUI'S DOING TRES BORANCH TYPE 4-4-2. FORMATION:

TAT-CHAN'S ONE POINT LESSON

● "What is "FORMATION"?

THE FORMATION WAS ORIGINALLY ESTABLISHED FOR THE GAME OF SOCCER IN THE MID 19TH CENTURY WITH THE UNBELIEVABLE STYLE OF ONE DF AND NINE FWS. IN THE 1960S, THE 4-4-2 SYSTEM WITH FOUR DFS, FOUR MFS AND TWO FWS WAS FINALLY BORN. IN THE 1980S, 3-5-2 SYSTEM WITH THREE DFS, FIVE MFS AND TWO FWS WAS BORN TO COUNTER THE 4-4-2 SYSTEM. CURRENTLY, THESE TWO ARE THE SYSTEMS MAINLY USED BY THE TEAMS.

① 4 — 4 — 2 System [Diamond Formatio

FW
MF
DF
One Boranch only

FOUR DFS ARE LINED UP HO
TALLY TO DEFEND THE ZONE.
THE MIDDLE OFFENSIVE, THIS
FORMATION USES ONLY ONE B
RECENTLY, HOWEVER, THE BO
FORMATION WITH TWO BORAN
BECOME MORE POPULAR. THE
SENTATIVE TEAM THAT IS KNO
USE THIS SYSTEM IS BRAZIL.

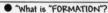

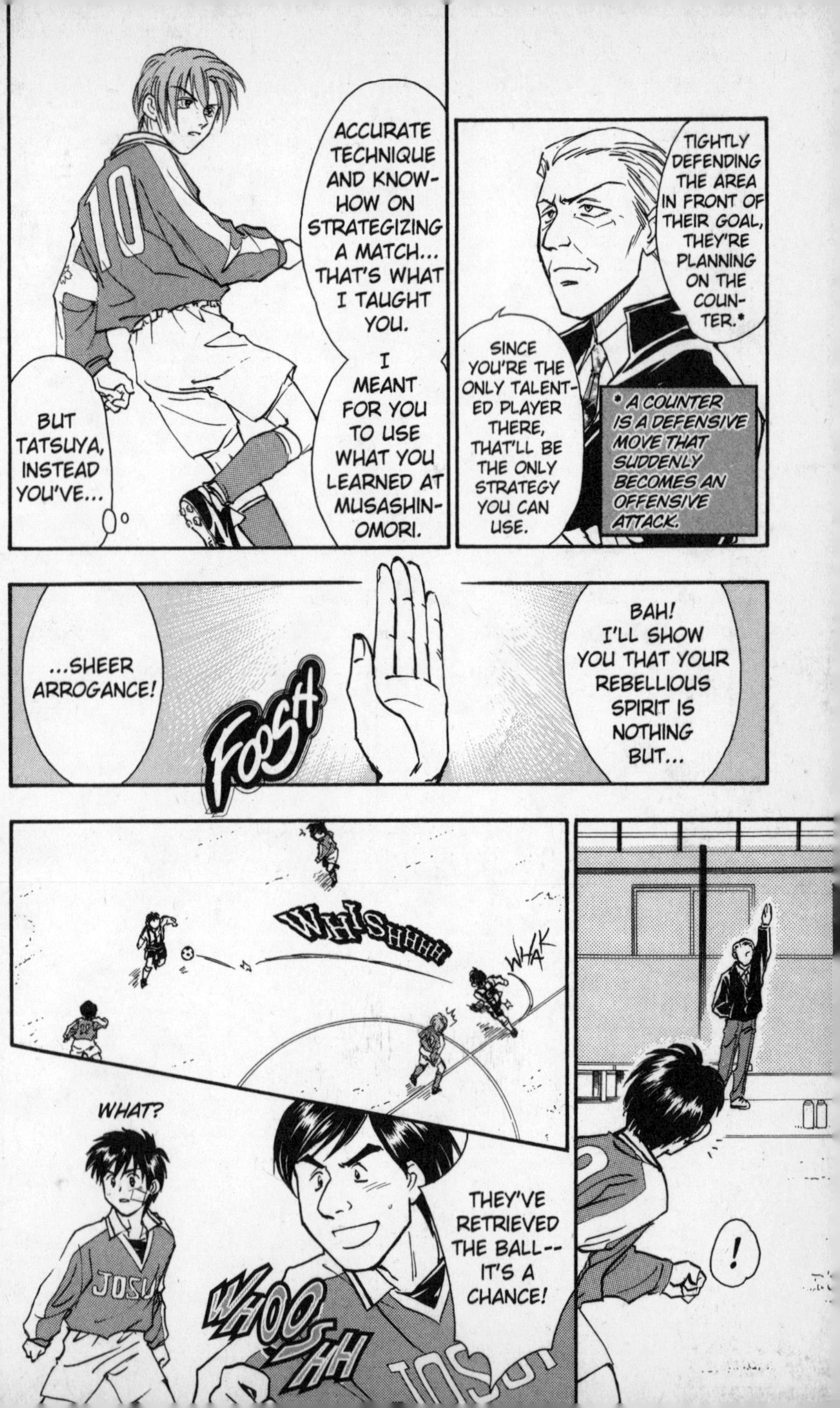
TIGHTLY DEFENDING THE AREA IN FRONT OF THEIR GOAL, THEY'RE PLANNING ON THE COUNTER.*
SINCE YOU'RE THE ONLY TALENTED PLAYER THERE, THAT'LL BE THE ONLY STRATEGY YOU CAN USE.
* A COUNTER IS A DEFENSIVE MOVE THAT SUDDENLY BECOMES AN OFFENSIVE ATTACK.
ACCURATE TECHNIQUE AND KNOW-HOW ON STRATEGIZING A MATCH... THAT'S WHAT I TAUGHT YOU.
I MEANT FOR YOU TO USE WHAT YOU LEARNED AT MUSASHINOMORI.
BUT TATSUYA, INSTEAD YOU'VE...
BAH! I'LL SHOW YOU THAT YOUR REBELLIOUS SPIRIT IS NOTHING BUT...
...SHEER ARROGANCE!
FOSH
!
WHISHHHH
WHAK
WHAT?
THEY'VE RETRIEVED THE BALL-- IT'S A CHANCE!
WHOOSHH

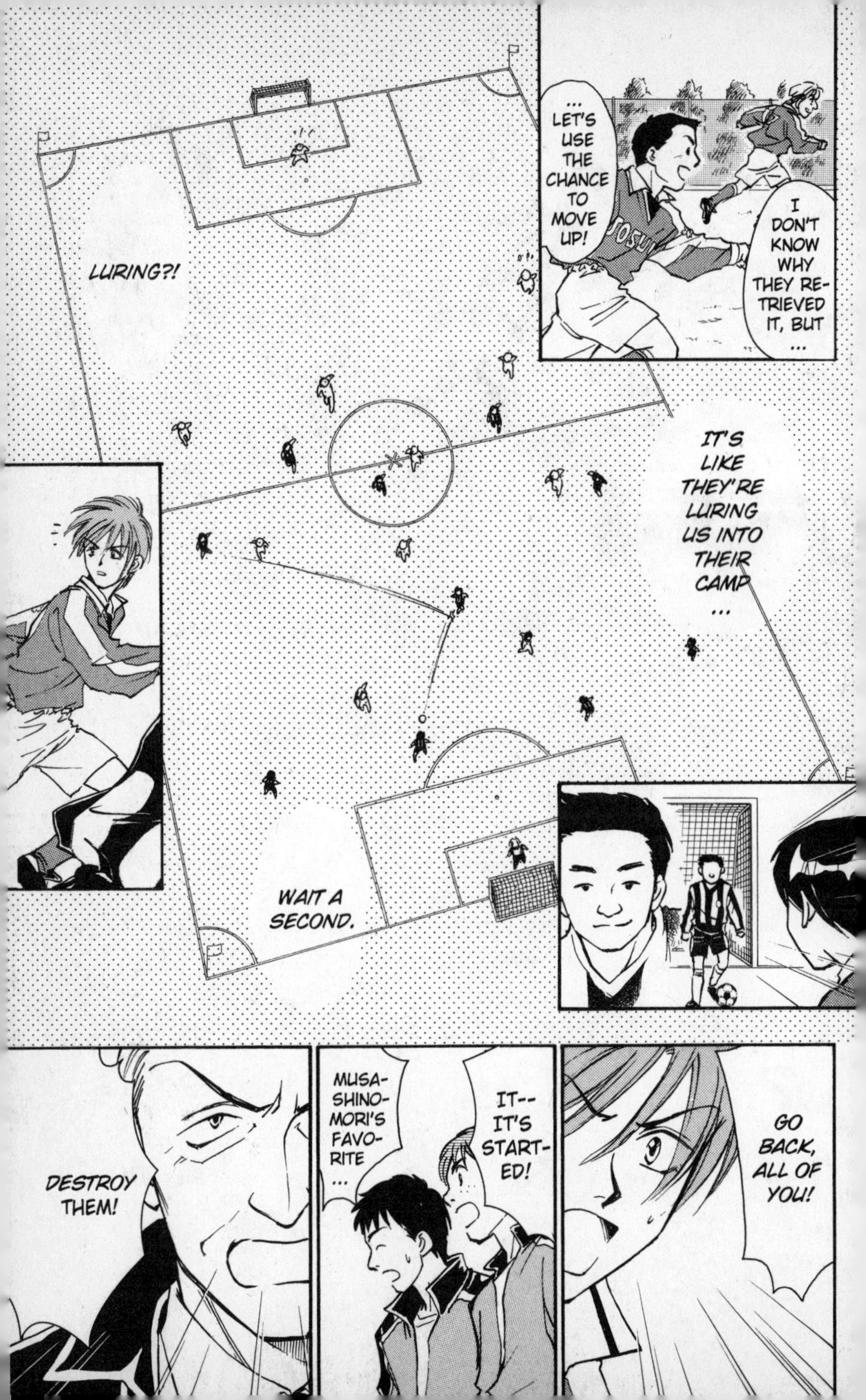
I DON'T KNOW WHY THEY RE-TRIEVED IT, BUT ...
... LET'S USE THE CHANCE TO MOVE UP!
LURING?!
IT'S LIKE THEY'RE LURING US INTO THEIR CAMP ...
WAIT A SECOND.
GO BACK, ALL OF YOU!
IT-- IT'S START-ED!
MUSA-SHINO-MORI'S FAVO-RITE ...
DESTROY THEM!

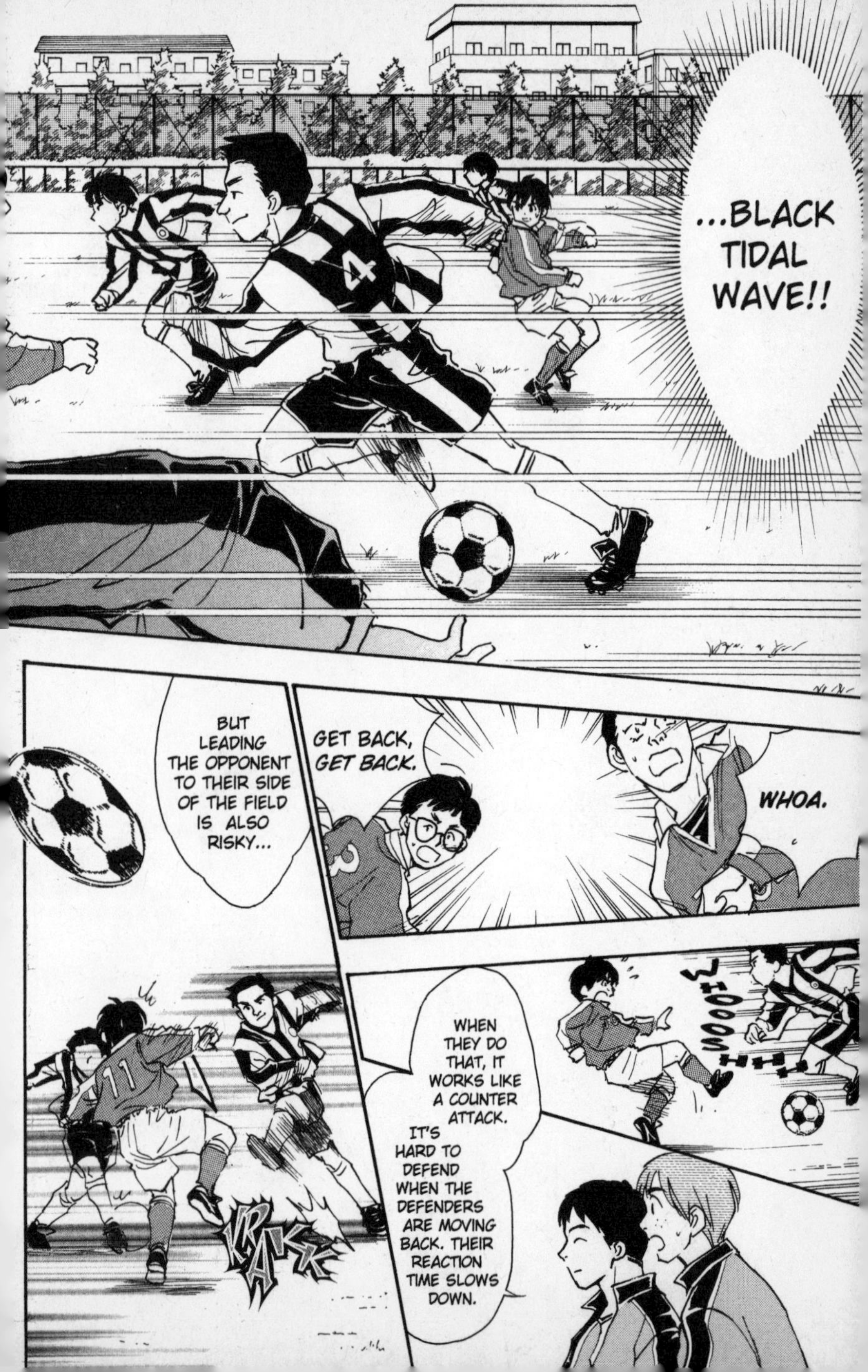

...BLACK TIDAL WAVE!!
BUT LEADING THE OPPONENT TO THEIR SIDE OF THE FIELD IS ALSO RISKY...
GET BACK, *GET BACK.*
WHOA.
KRAKK
WHOOOSHHH
WHEN THEY DO THAT, IT WORKS LIKE A COUNTER ATTACK.
IT'S HARD TO DEFEND WHEN THE DEFENDERS ARE MOVING BACK. THEIR REACTION TIME SLOWS DOWN.

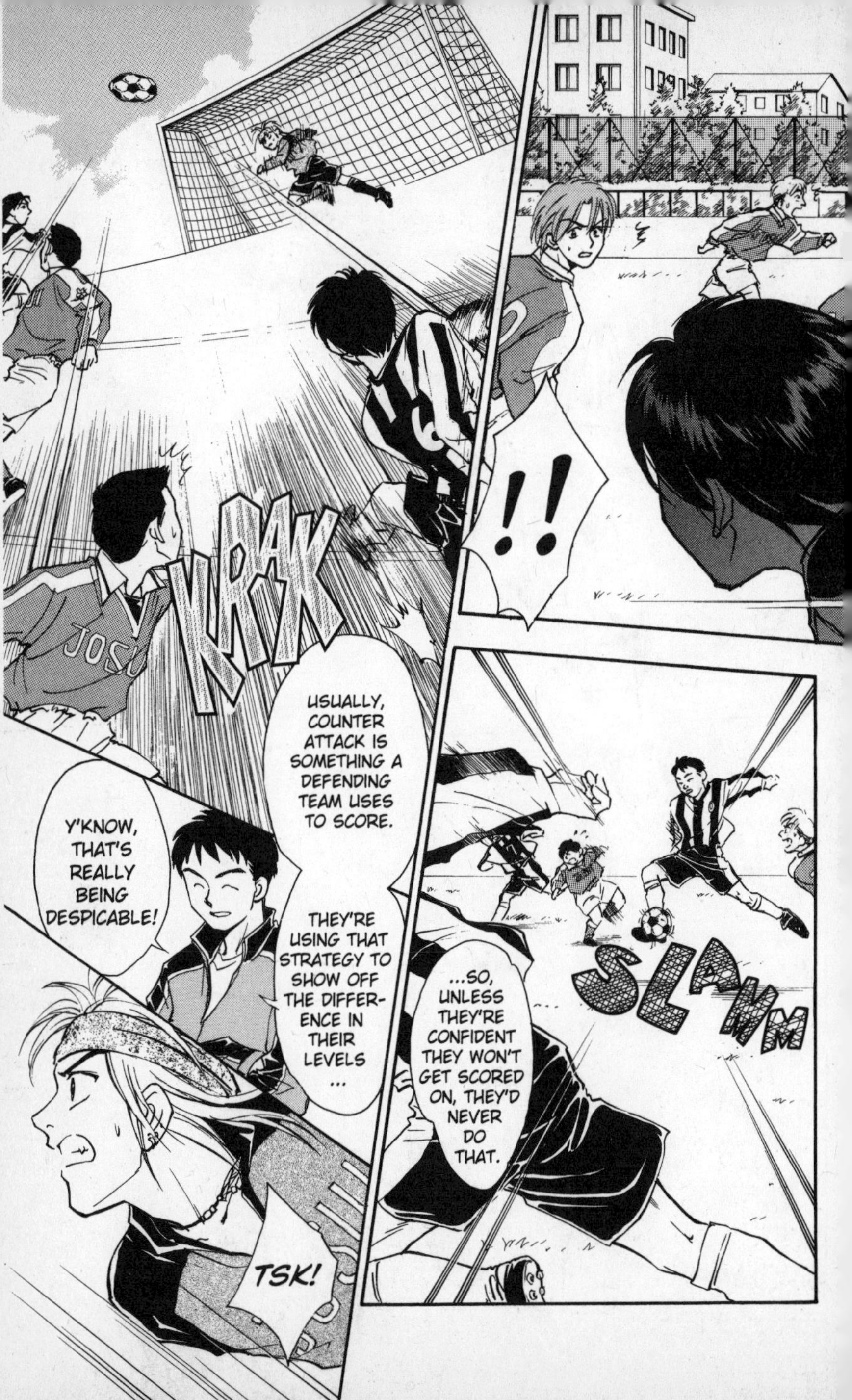
KRAAK
!!
Y'KNOW, THAT'S REALLY BEING DESPICABLE!
USUALLY, COUNTER ATTACK IS SOMETHING A DEFENDING TEAM USES TO SCORE.
THEY'RE USING THAT STRATEGY TO SHOW OFF THE DIFFER-ENCE IN THEIR LEVELS ...
SLAMM
...SO, UNLESS THEY'RE CONFIDENT THEY WON'T GET SCORED ON, THEY'D NEVER DO THAT.
TSK!

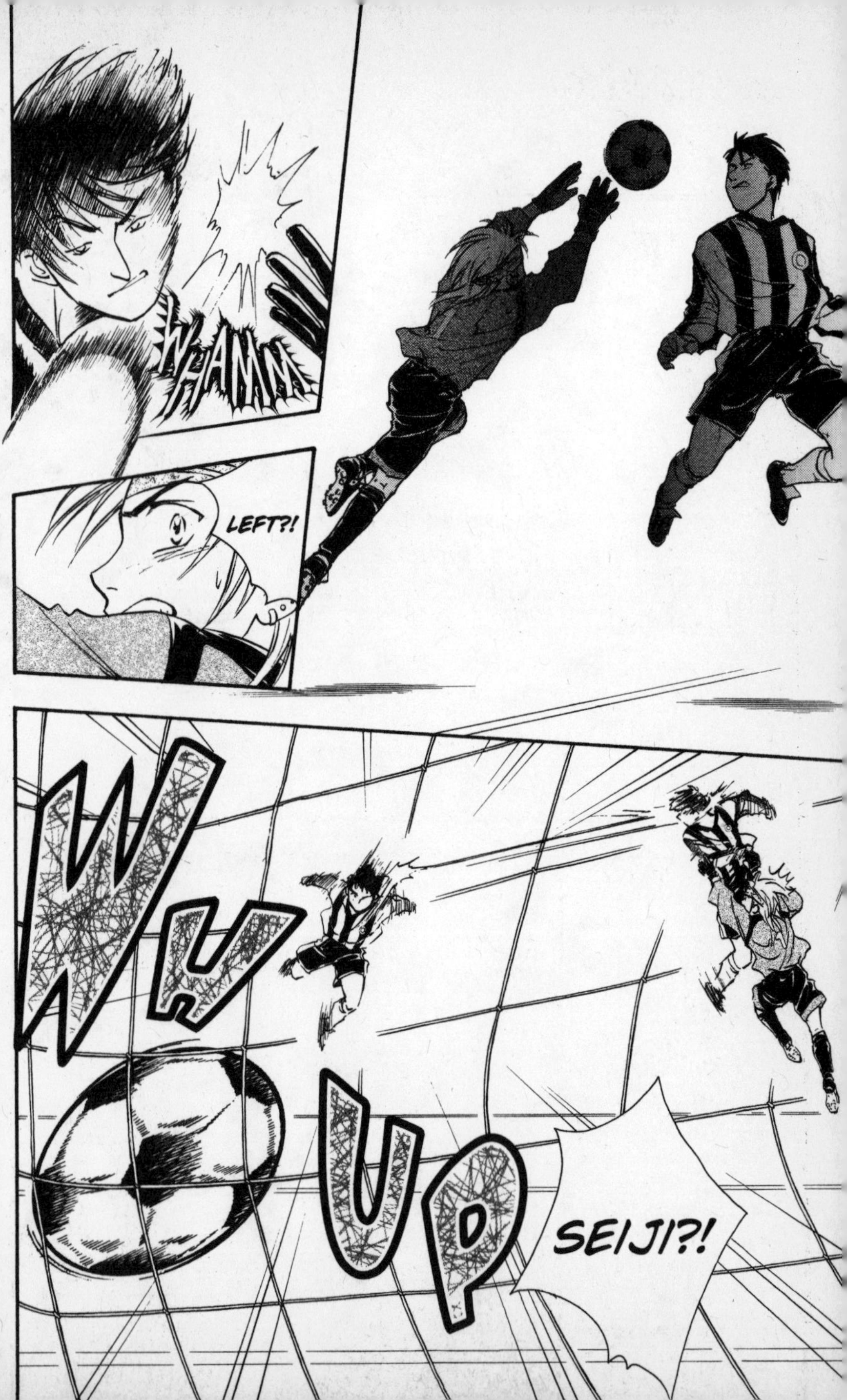
WHAMM
LEFT?!
WHUP
SEIJI?!

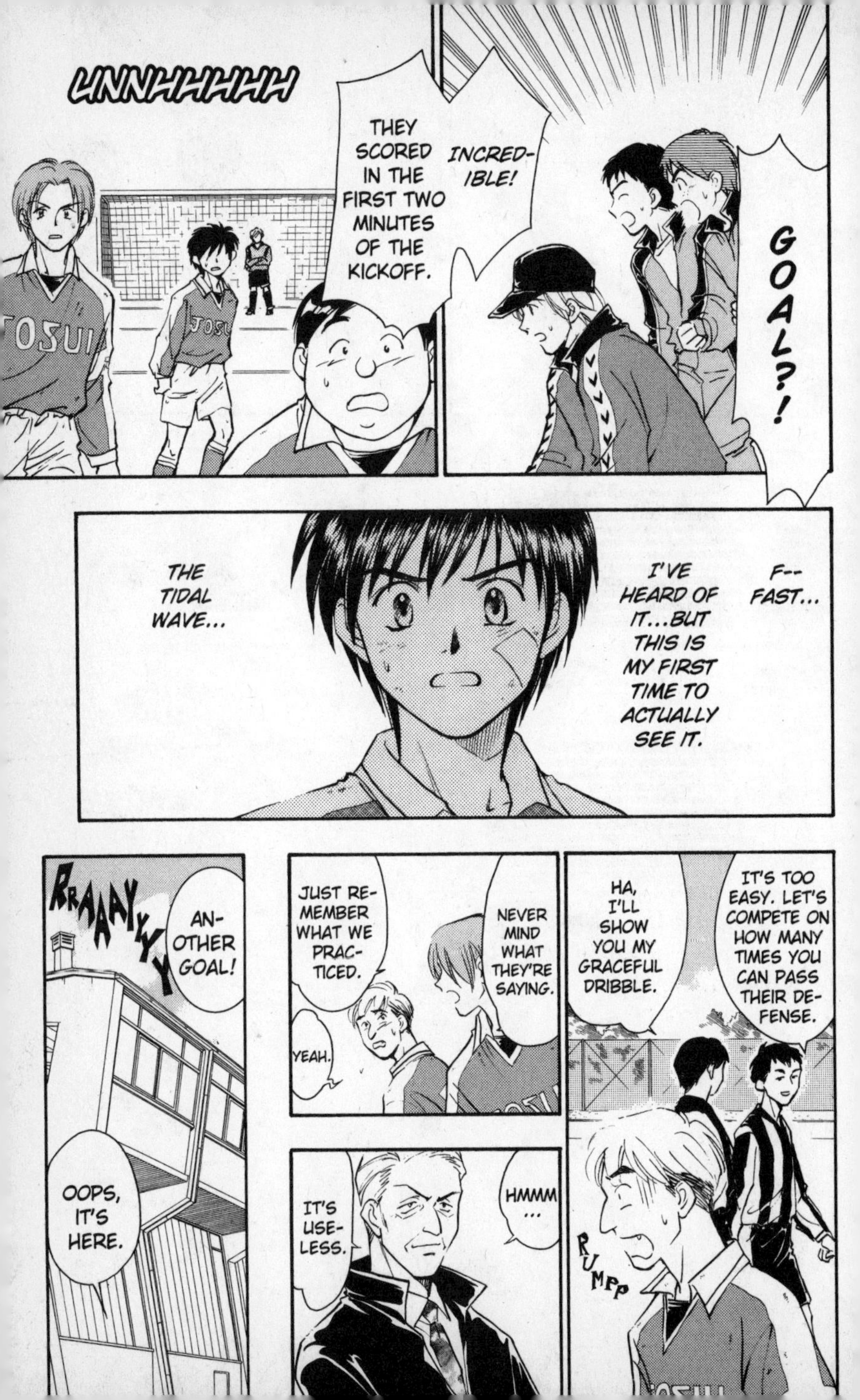
UNNHHHHHH
THEY SCORED IN THE FIRST TWO MINUTES OF THE KICKOFF.
INCRED-IBLE!
GOAL?!
THE TIDAL WAVE...
I'VE HEARD OF IT...BUT THIS IS MY FIRST TIME TO ACTUALLY SEE IT.
F-- FAST...
RRAAAYYYY
AN-OTHER GOAL!
OOPS, IT'S HERE.
JUST RE-MEMBER WHAT WE PRAC-TICED.
YEAH.
NEVER MIND WHAT THEY'RE SAYING.
HA, I'LL SHOW YOU MY GRACEFUL DRIBBLE.
IT'S TOO EASY. LET'S COMPETE ON HOW MANY TIMES YOU CAN PASS THEIR DE-FENSE.
IT'S USE-LESS.
HMMMM ...
RUMPP

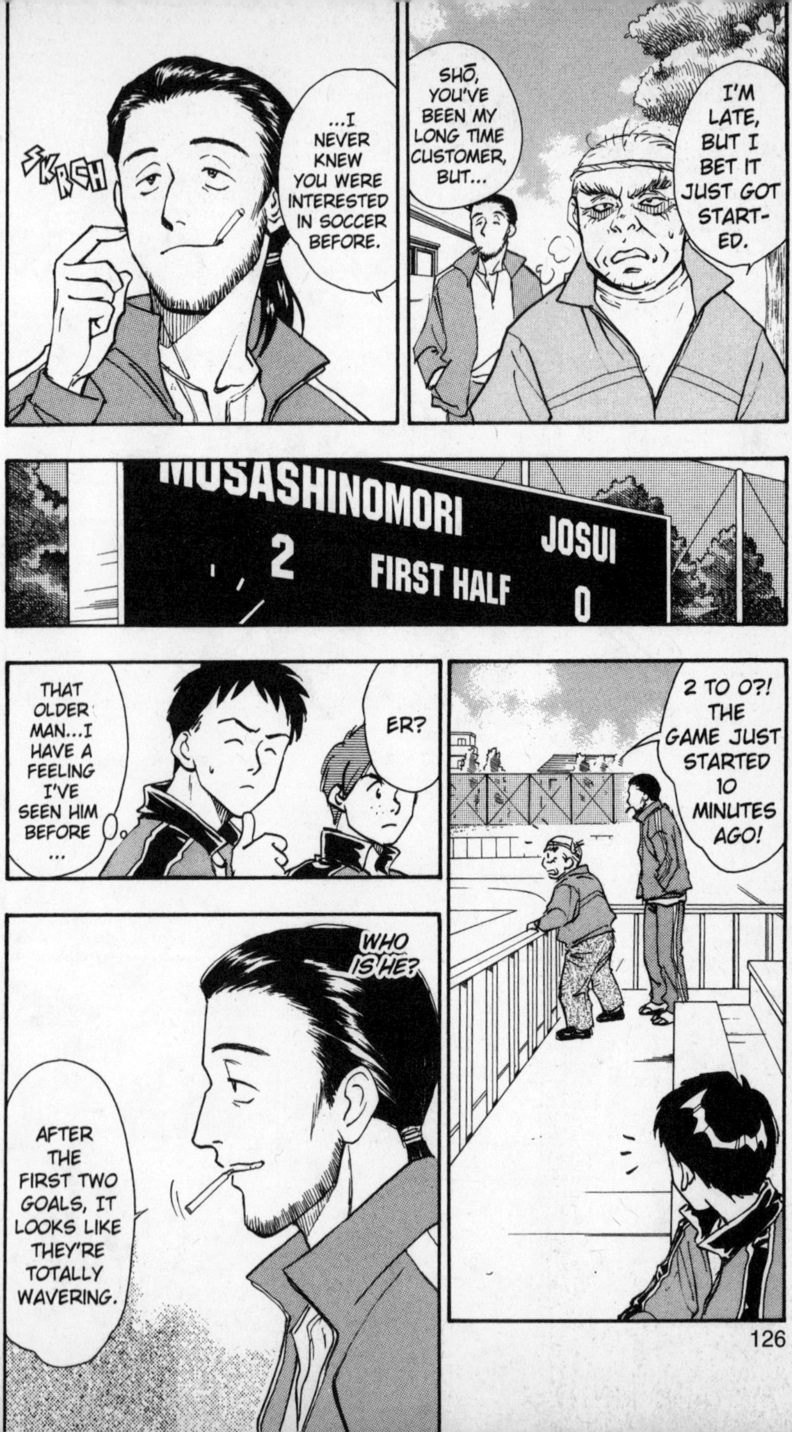
I'M LATE, BUT I BET IT JUST GOT START-ED.
SHŌ, YOU'VE BEEN MY LONG TIME CUSTOMER, BUT...
...I NEVER KNEW YOU WERE INTERESTED IN SOCCER BEFORE.
SKRCH
MUSASHINOMORI
JOSUI
2
FIRST HALF
0
2 TO 0?! THE GAME JUST STARTED 10 MINUTES AGO!
ER?
THAT OLDER MAN...I HAVE A FEELING I'VE SEEN HIM BEFORE...
WHO IS HE?
AFTER THE FIRST TWO GOALS, IT LOOKS LIKE THEY'RE TOTALLY WAVERING.

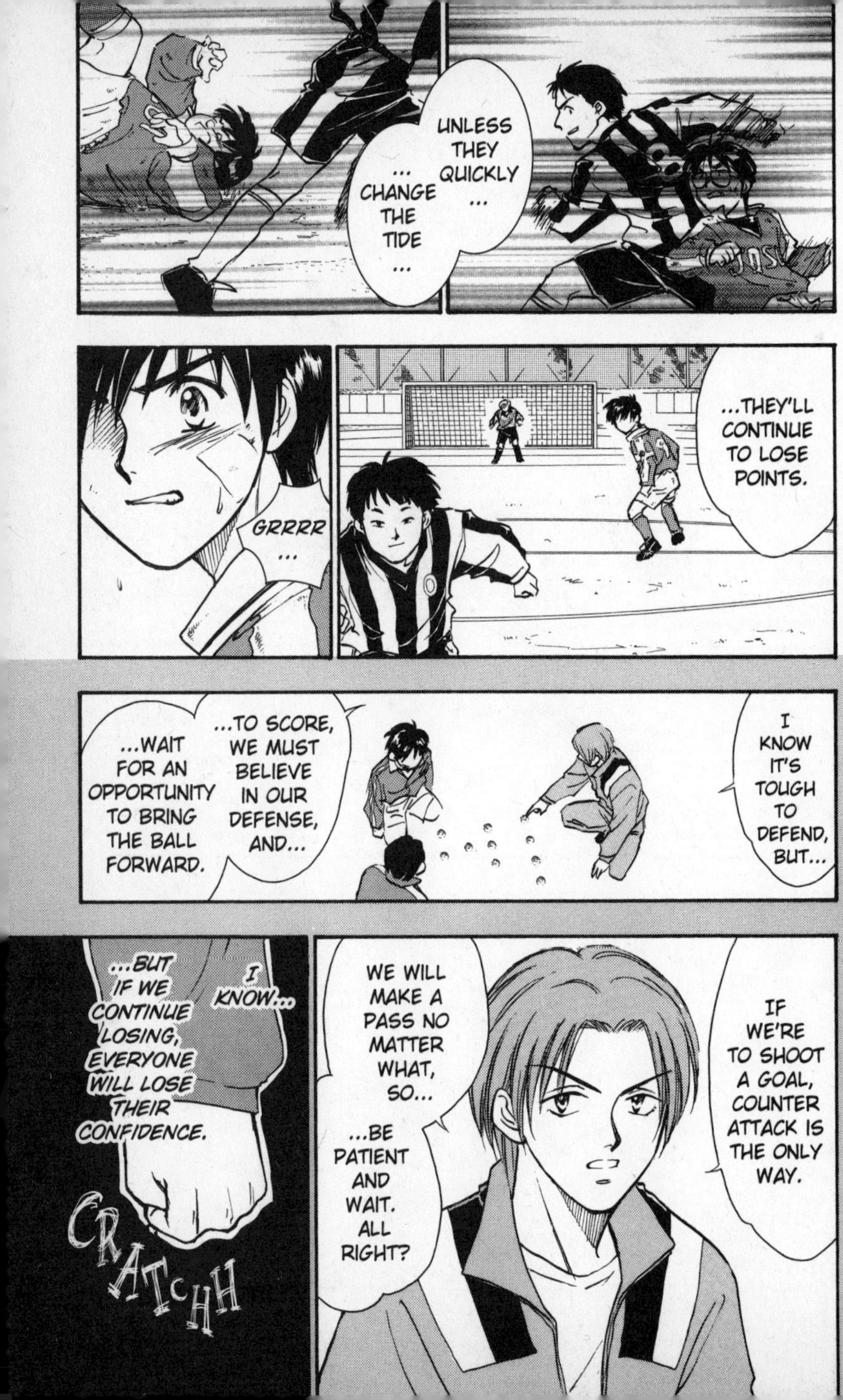
UNLESS THEY QUICKLY ...
... CHANGE THE TIDE ...
...THEY'LL CONTINUE TO LOSE POINTS.
GRRRR ...
I KNOW IT'S TOUGH TO DEFEND, BUT...
...TO SCORE, WE MUST BELIEVE IN OUR DEFENSE, AND...
...WAIT FOR AN OPPORTUNITY TO BRING THE BALL FORWARD.
IF WE'RE TO SHOOT A GOAL, COUNTER ATTACK IS THE ONLY WAY.
WE WILL MAKE A PASS NO MATTER WHAT, SO...
...BE PATIENT AND WAIT. ALL RIGHT?
I KNOW...
...BUT IF WE CONTINUE LOSING, EVERYONE WILL LOSE THEIR CONFIDENCE.
CRATCHH

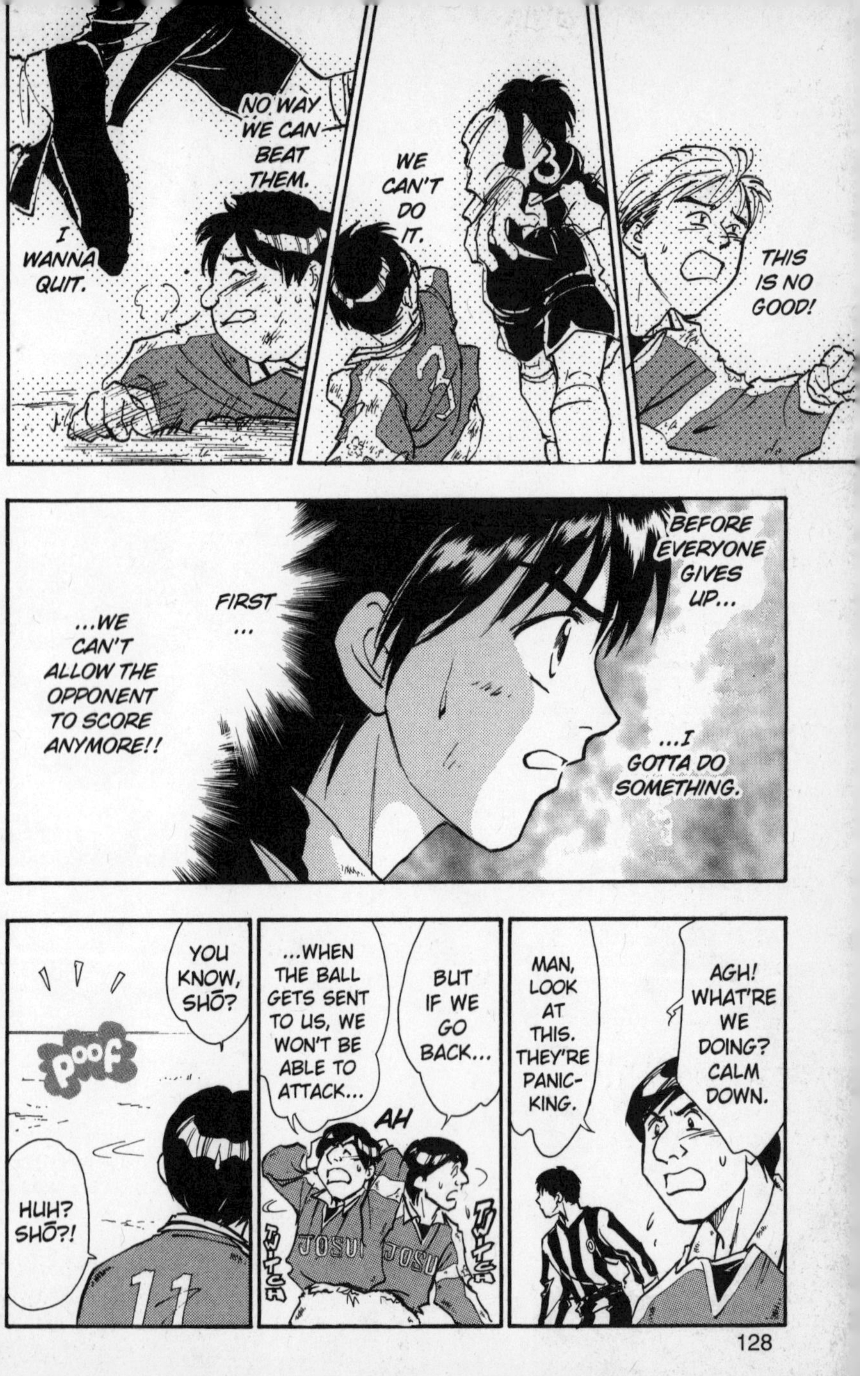
THIS IS NO GOOD!
WE CAN'T DO IT.
NO WAY WE CAN BEAT THEM.
I WANNA QUIT.
BEFORE EVERYONE GIVES UP...
...I GOTTA DO SOMETHING.
FIRST...
...WE CAN'T ALLOW THE OPPONENT TO SCORE ANYMORE!!
AGH! WHAT'RE WE DOING? CALM DOWN.
MAN, LOOK AT THIS. THEY'RE PANIC-KING.
BUT IF WE GO BACK...
...WHEN THE BALL GETS SENT TO US, WE WON'T BE ABLE TO ATTACK...
AH
TWITCH
TWITCH
YOU KNOW, SHŌ?
POOF
HUH? SHŌ?!

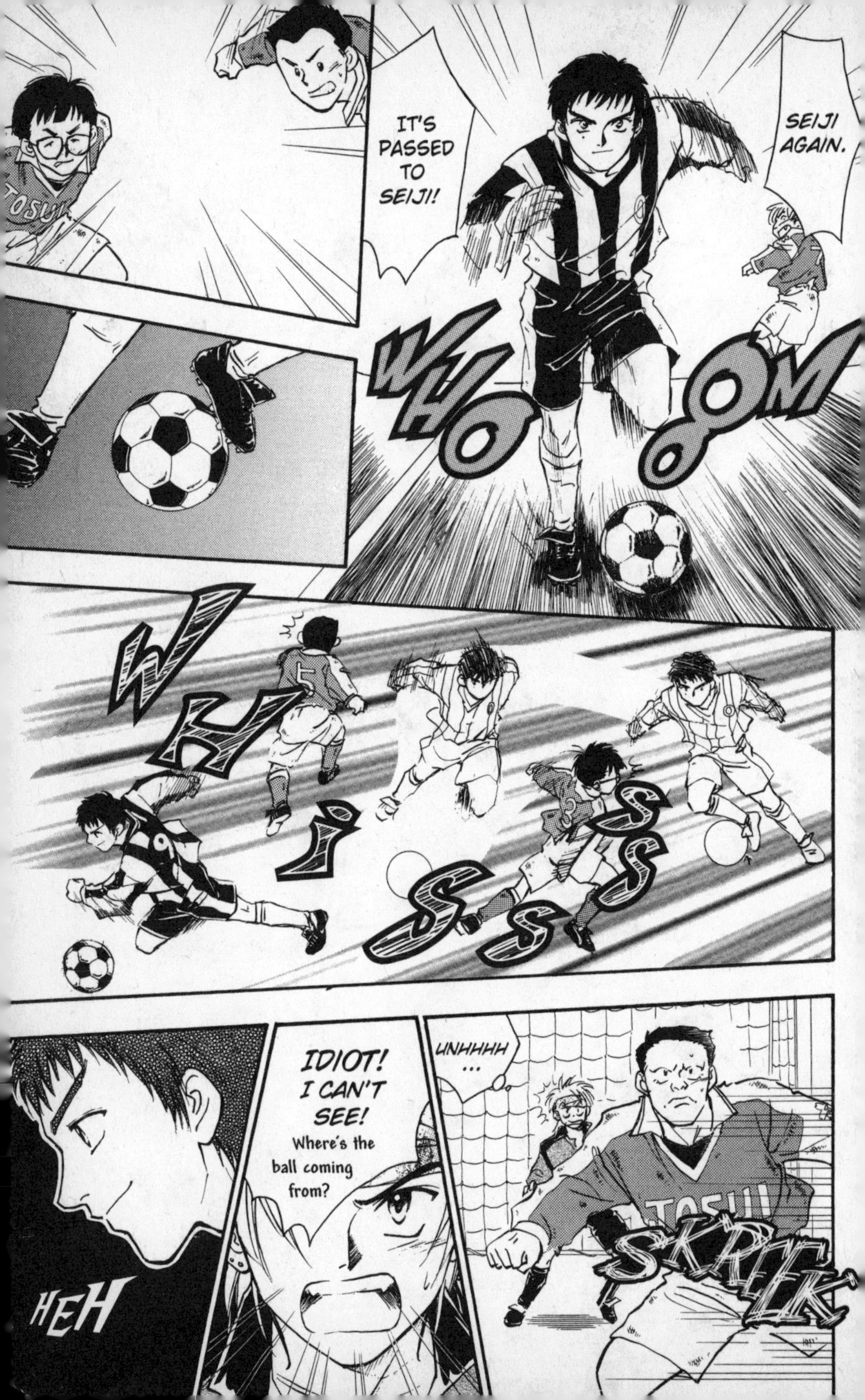
IT'S PASSED TO SEIJI!
SEIJI AGAIN.
WHOOOM
WHISSSSS
HEH
IDIOT! I CAN'T SEE!
Where's the ball coming from?
UNHHHH ...
SKREEK

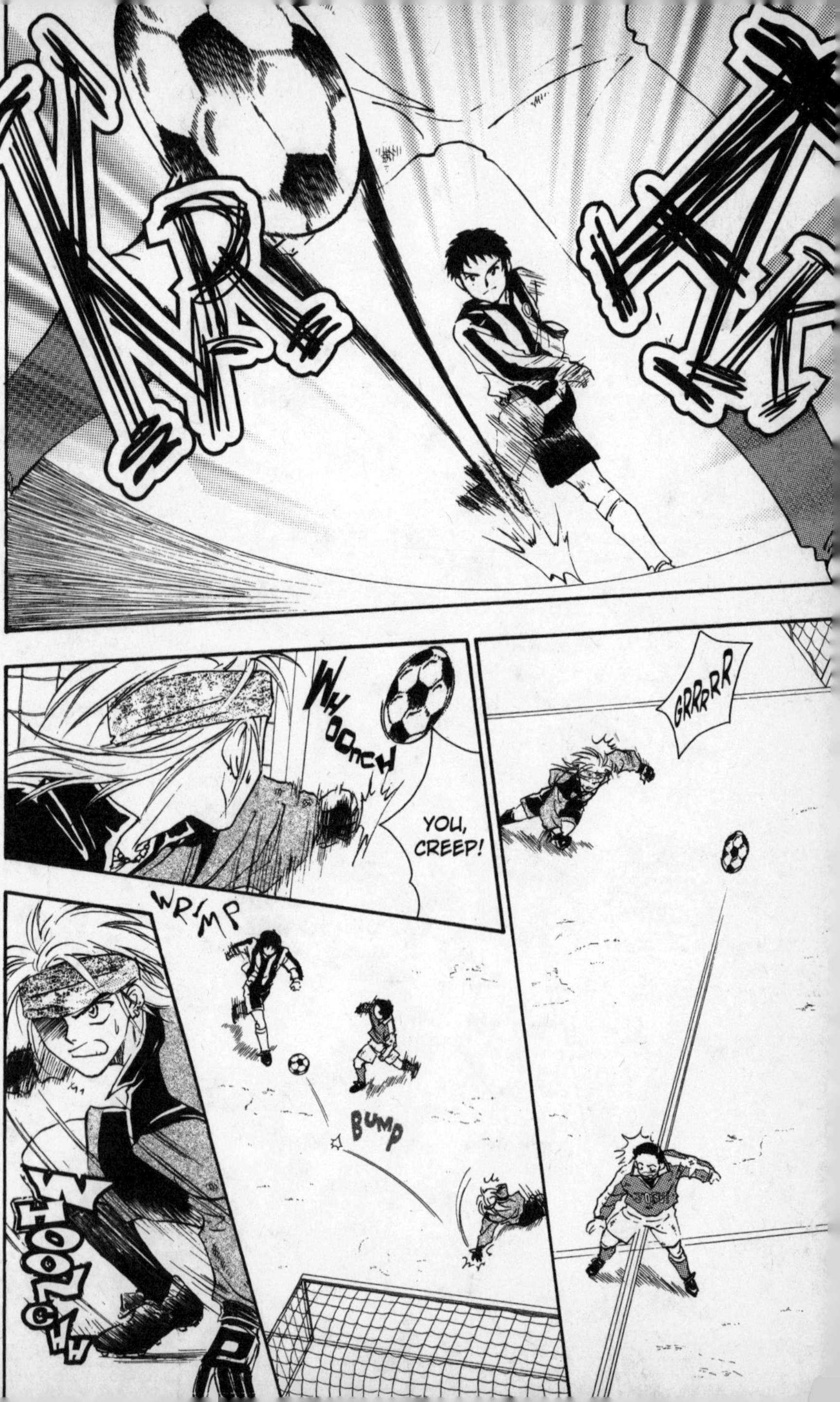
KRA
AK
WHOONCH
YOU, CREEP!
GRRRRR
WRIMP
BUMP
WHOOZCHH

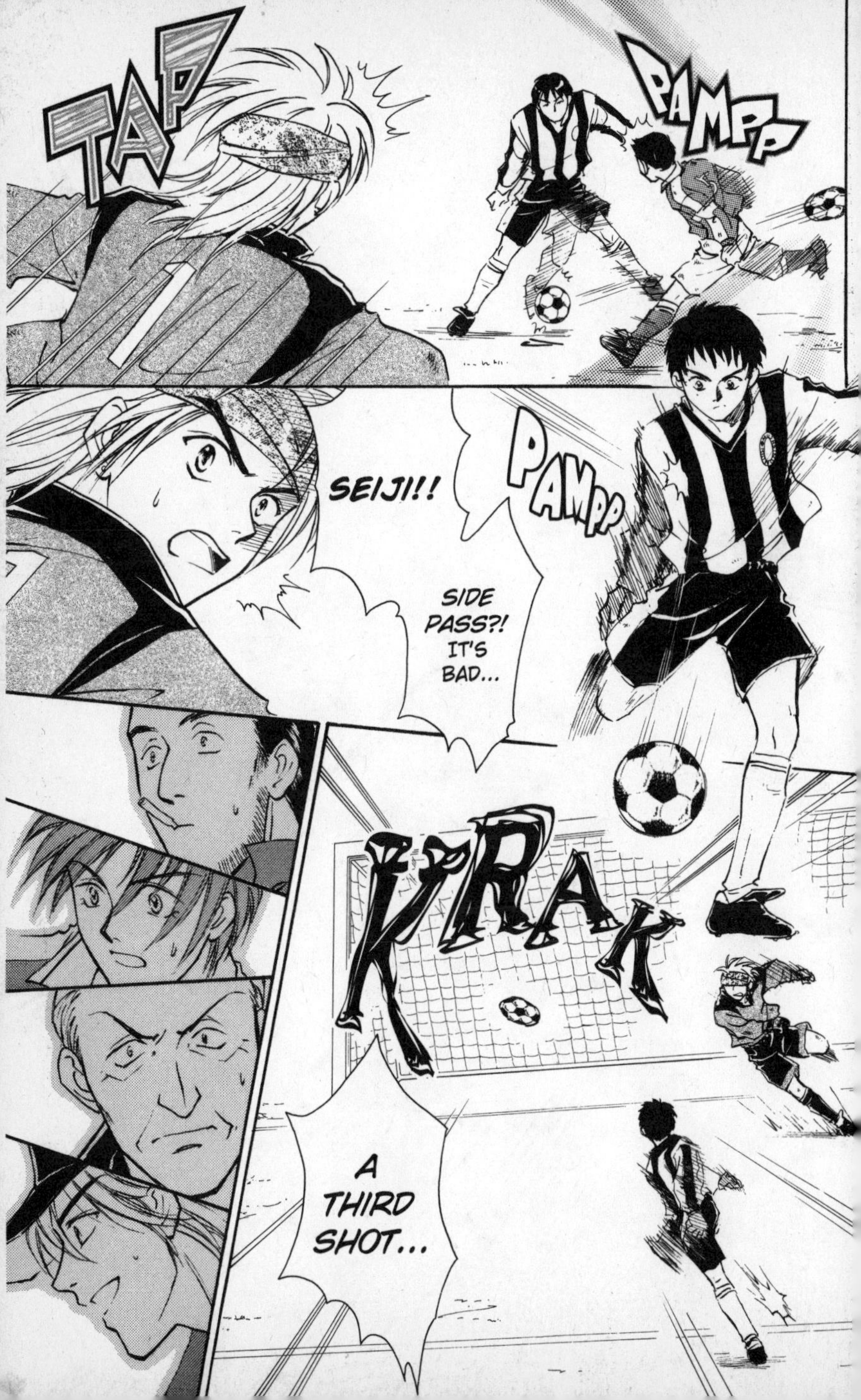
PAMPP
TAP
PAMPP
SEIJI!!
SIDE PASS?! IT'S BAD...
KRAK
A THIRD SHOT...

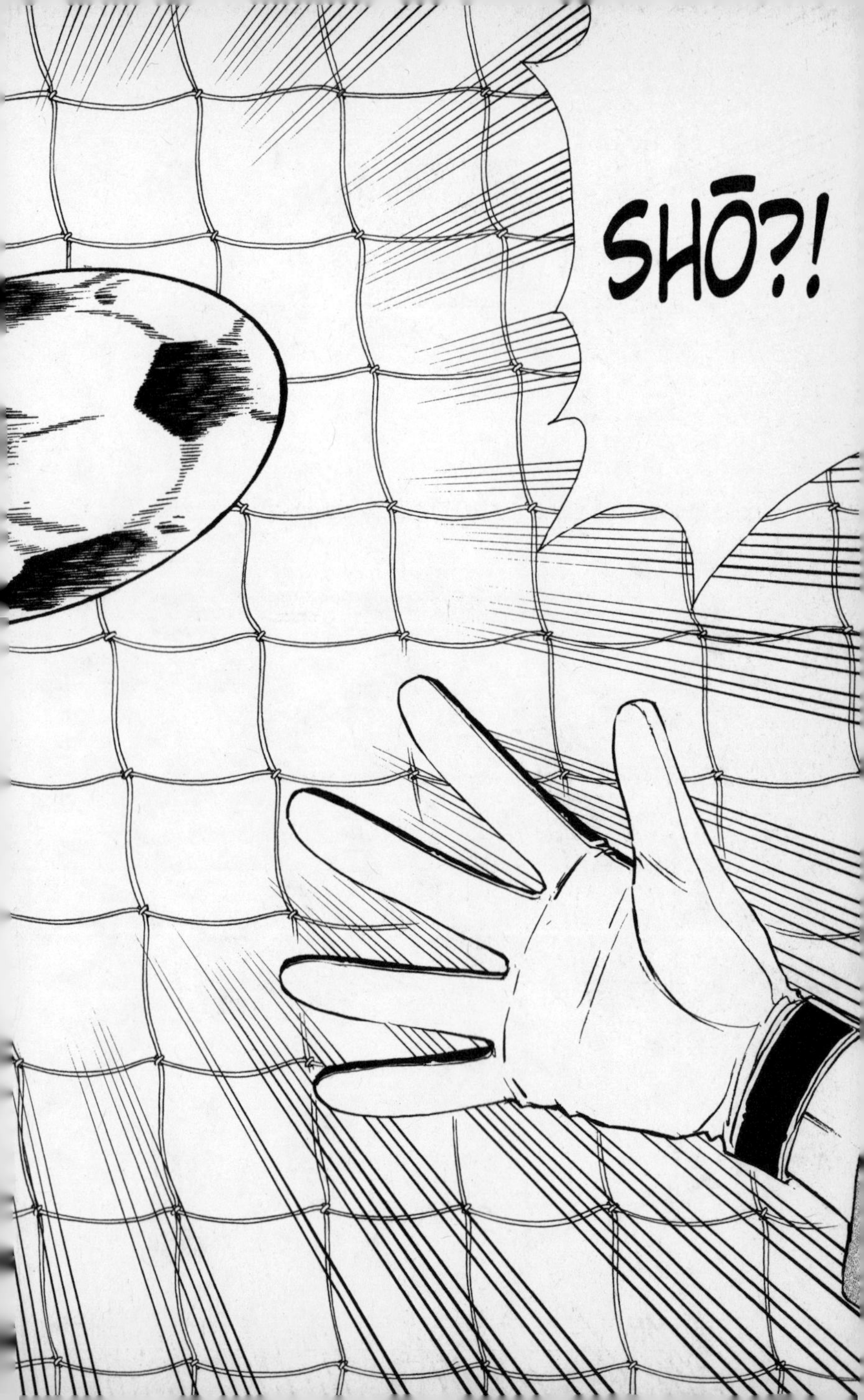
SHŌ?!

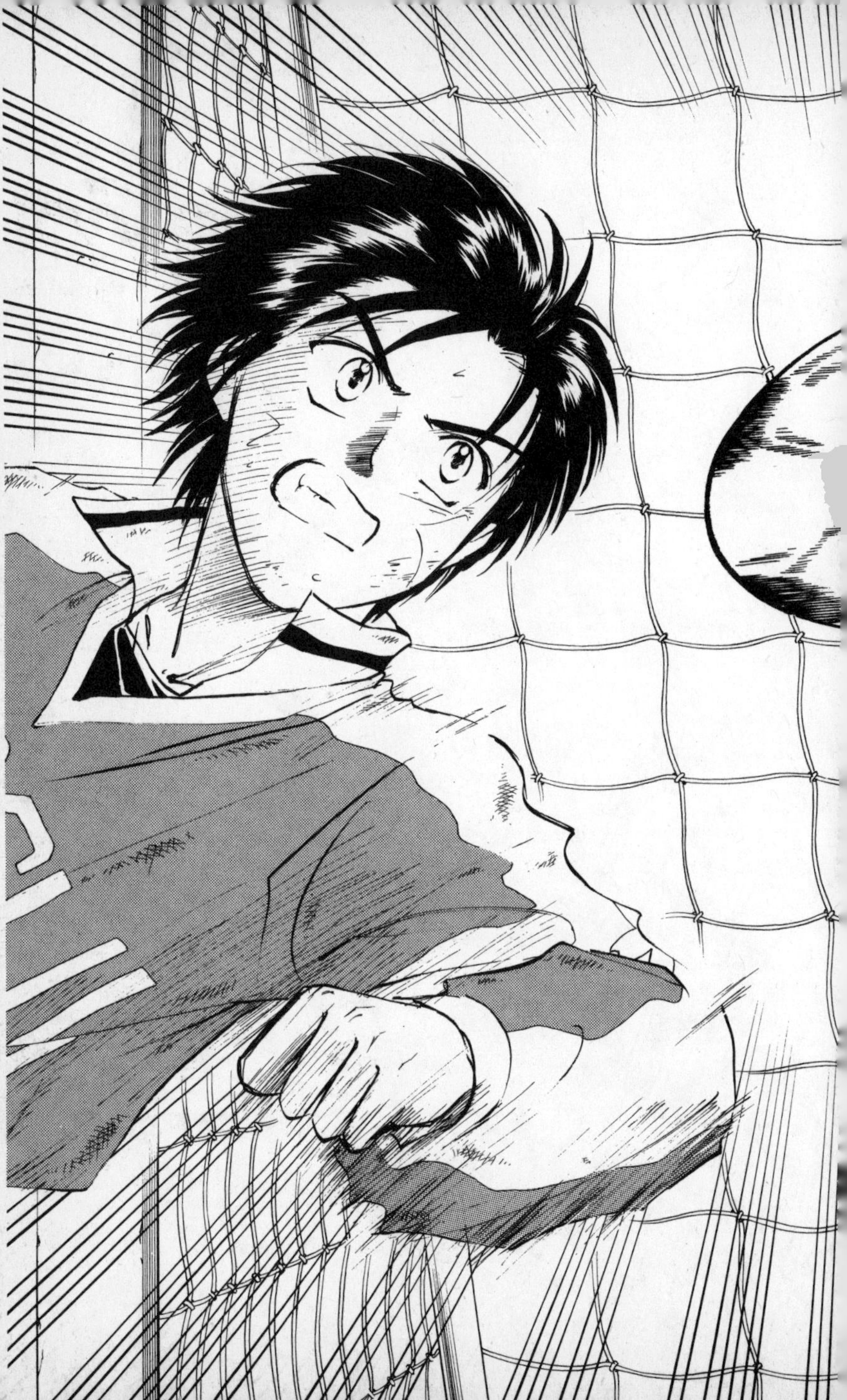

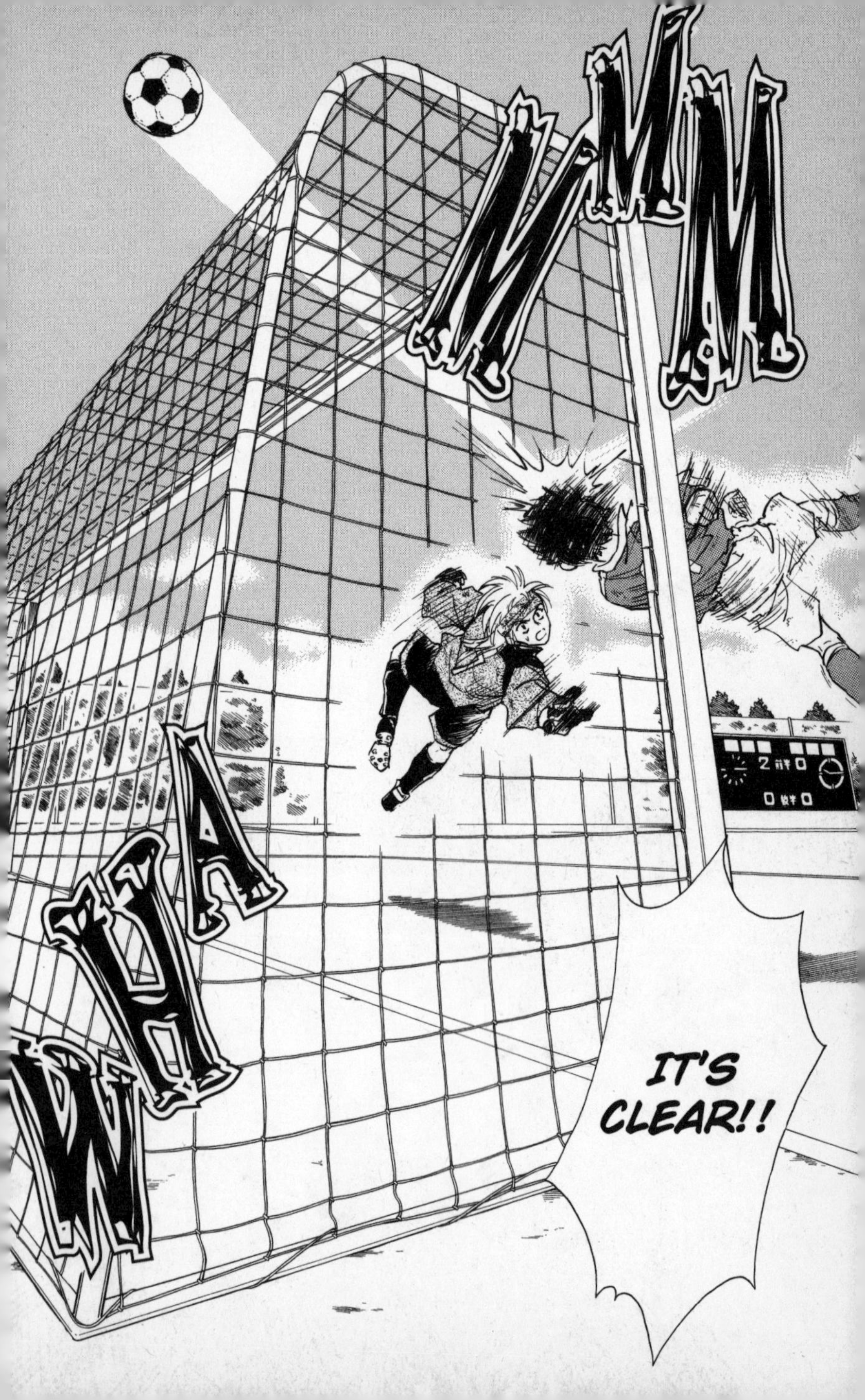
WHAMMM
IT'S CLEAR!!

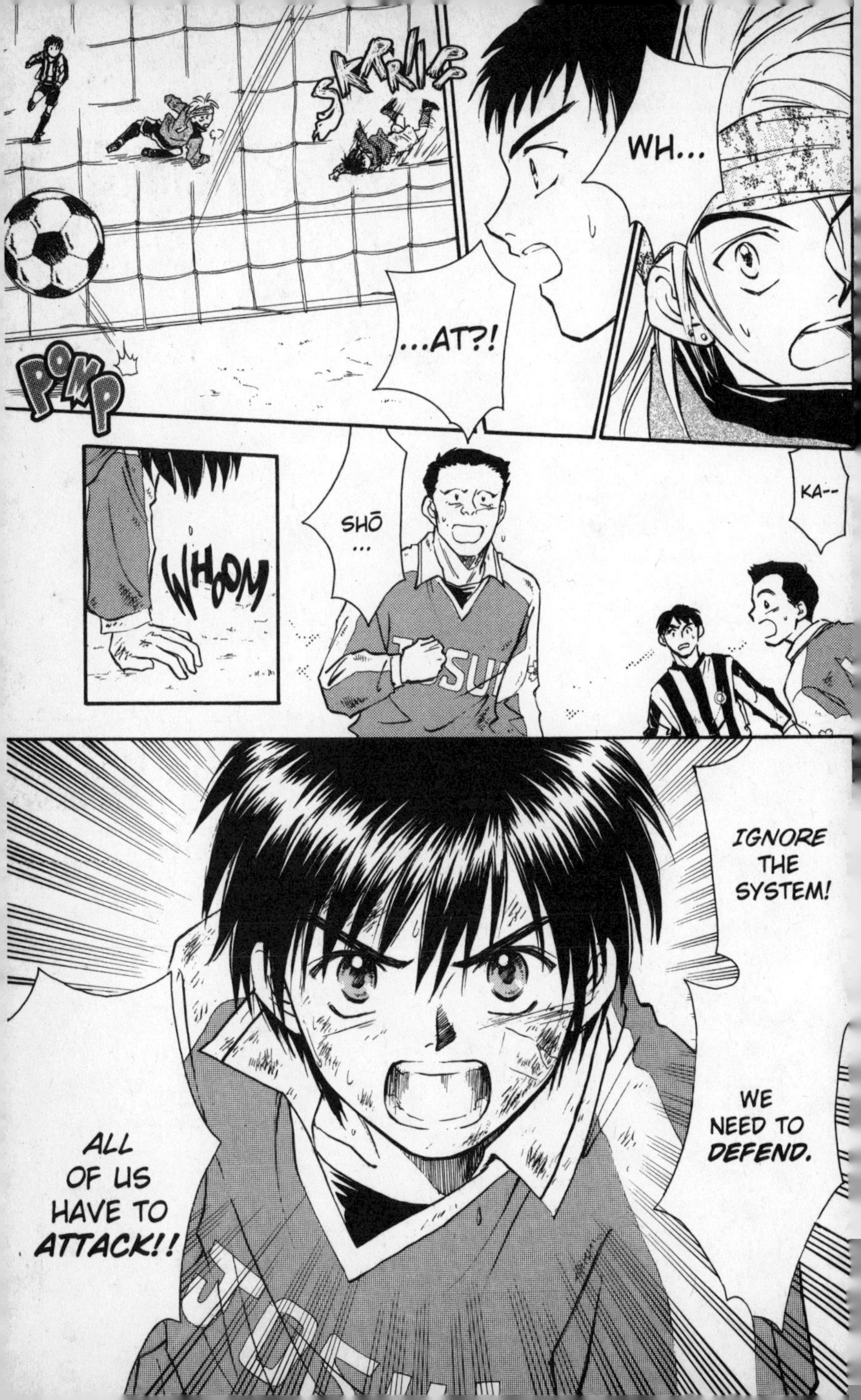
WH...
...AT?!
SKRRIIG
POMP
KA--
SHŌ ...
WHOOM
IGNORE THE SYSTEM!
WE NEED TO DEFEND.
ALL OF US HAVE TO ATTACK!!

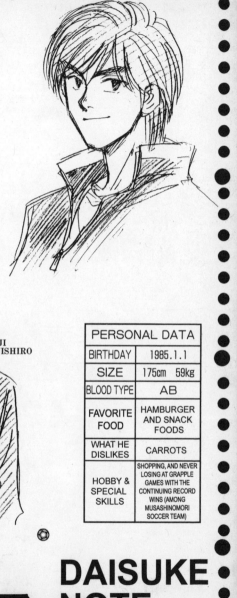

KATSURŌ SHIBUSAWA

PERSONAL DATA	
BIRTHDAY	1983.7.29
SIZE	183cm 65kg
BLOOD TYPE	A
FAVORITE FOOD	MACKEREL COOKED IN MISO SAUCE, RICE CAKE WITH SWEET BEANS
WHAT HE DISLIKES	REPTILES
HOBBY & SPECIAL SKILLS	WATCHING F1, COOKING

SEIJI FUJISHIRO

PERSONAL DATA	
BIRTHDAY	1985.1.1
SIZE	175cm 59kg
BLOOD TYPE	AB
FAVORITE FOOD	HAMBURGER AND SNACK FOODS
WHAT HE DISLIKES	CARROTS
HOBBY & SPECIAL SKILLS	SHOPPING, AND NEVER LOSING AT GRAPPLE GAMES WITH THE CONTINUING RECORD WINS (AMONG MUSASHINOMORI SOCCER TEAM)

DAISUKE NOTE

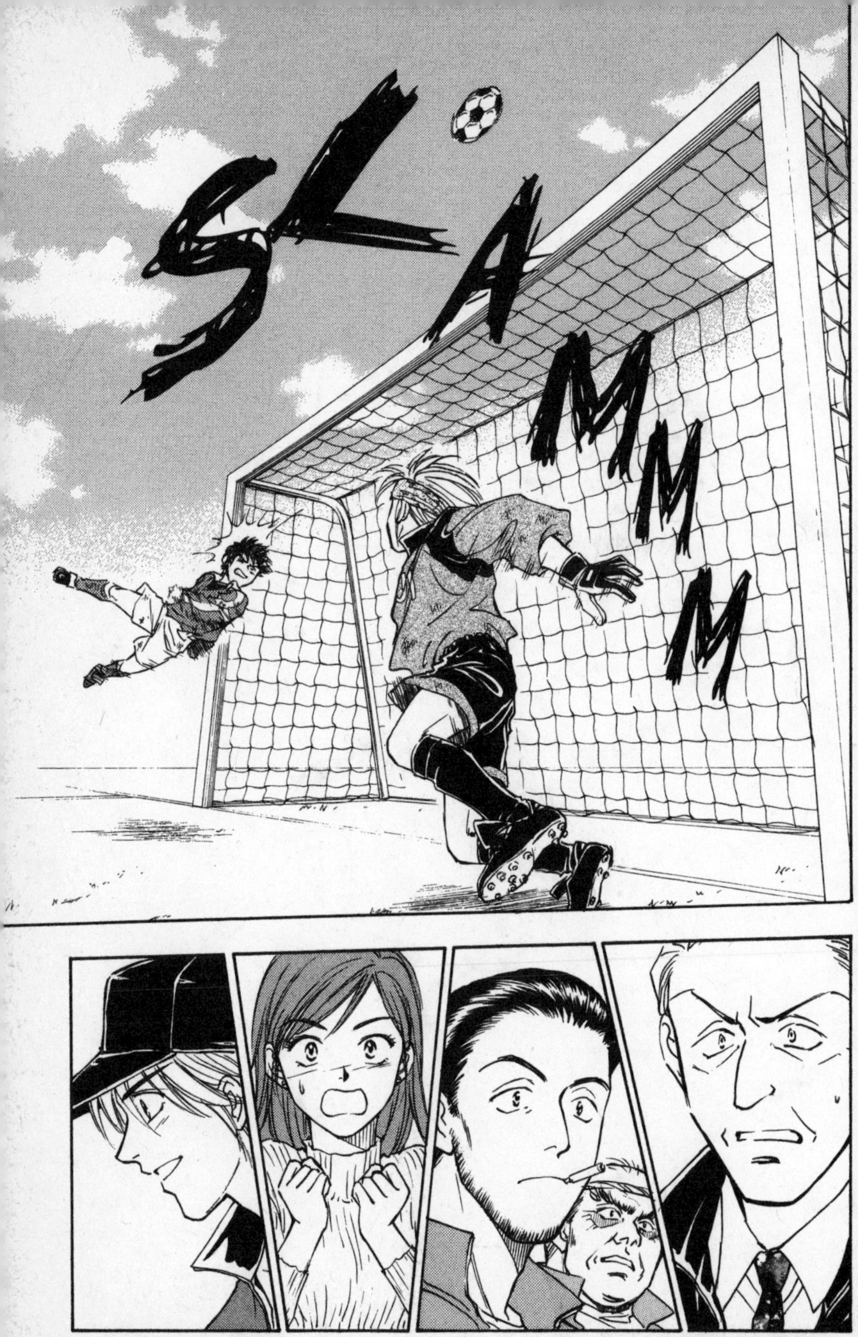
SLAMMMM

STAGE.14 I AM HERE

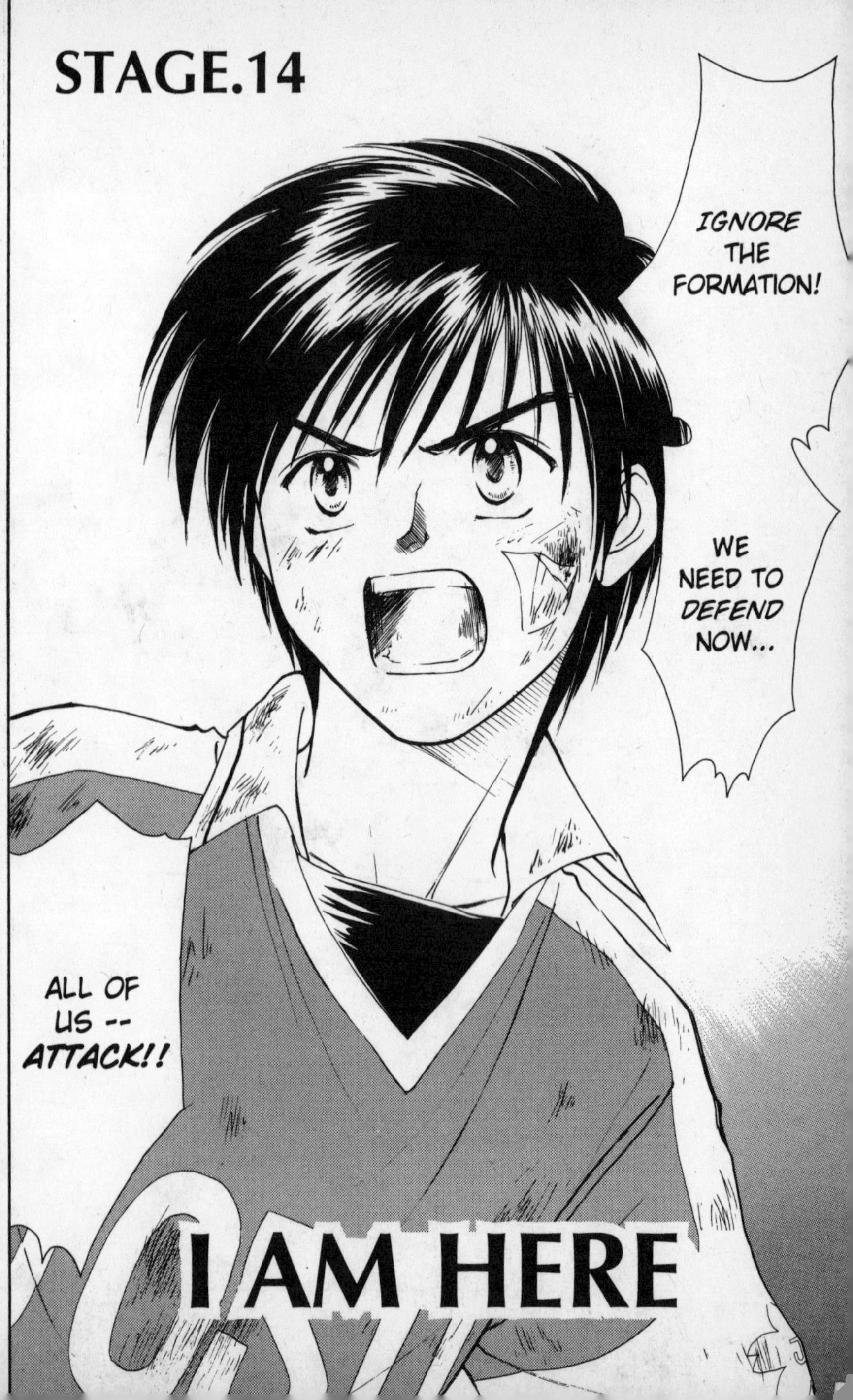
STAGE.14
IGNORE THE FORMATION!
WE NEED TO DEFEND NOW...
ALL OF US -- ATTACK!!
I AM HERE

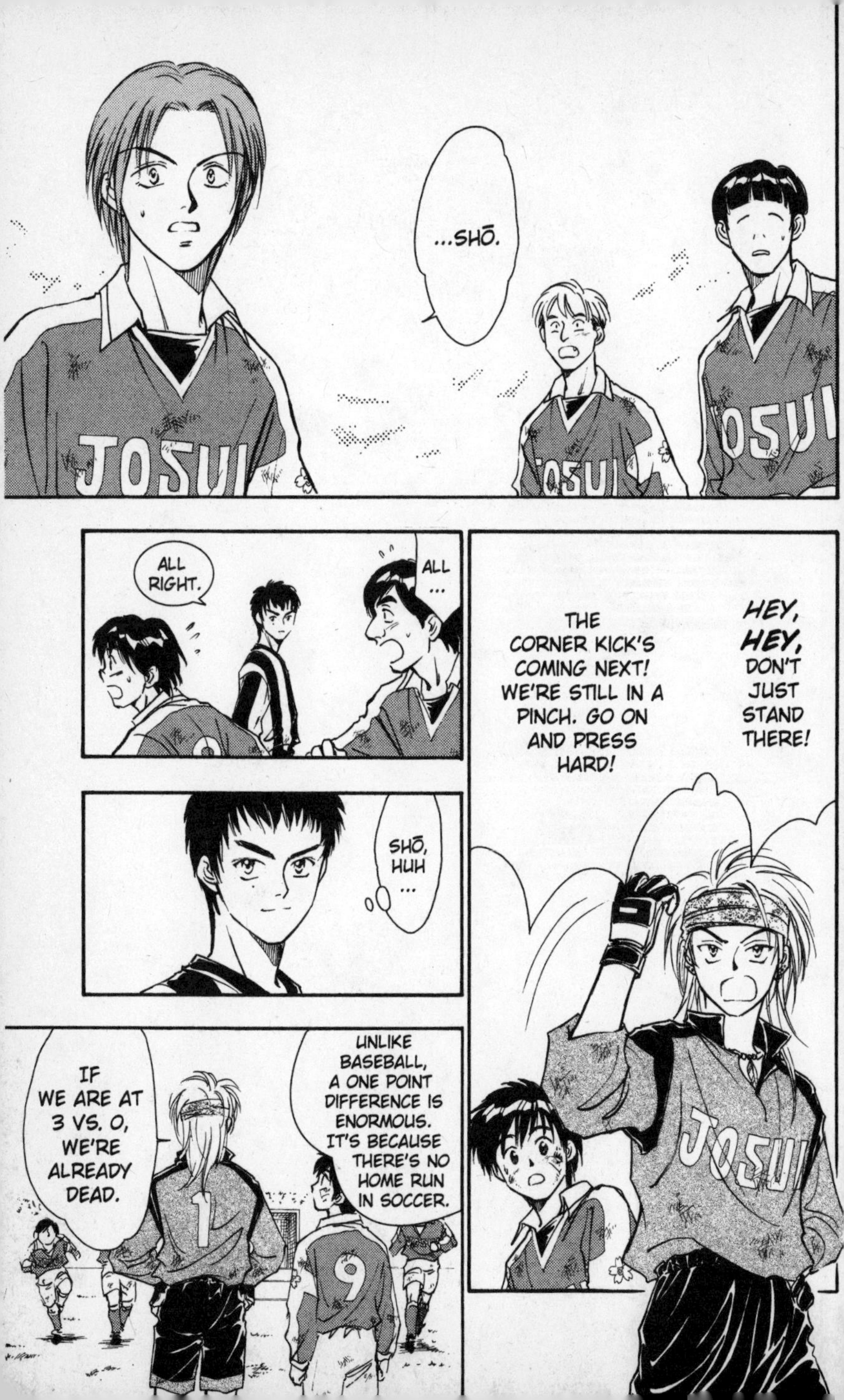
...SHŌ.
HEY, HEY, DON'T JUST STAND THERE!
THE CORNER KICK'S COMING NEXT! WE'RE STILL IN A PINCH. GO ON AND PRESS HARD!
ALL ...
ALL RIGHT.
SHŌ, HUH ...
UNLIKE BASEBALL, A ONE POINT DIFFERENCE IS ENORMOUS. IT'S BECAUSE THERE'S NO HOME RUN IN SOCCER.
IF WE ARE AT 3 VS. 0, WE'RE ALREADY DEAD.

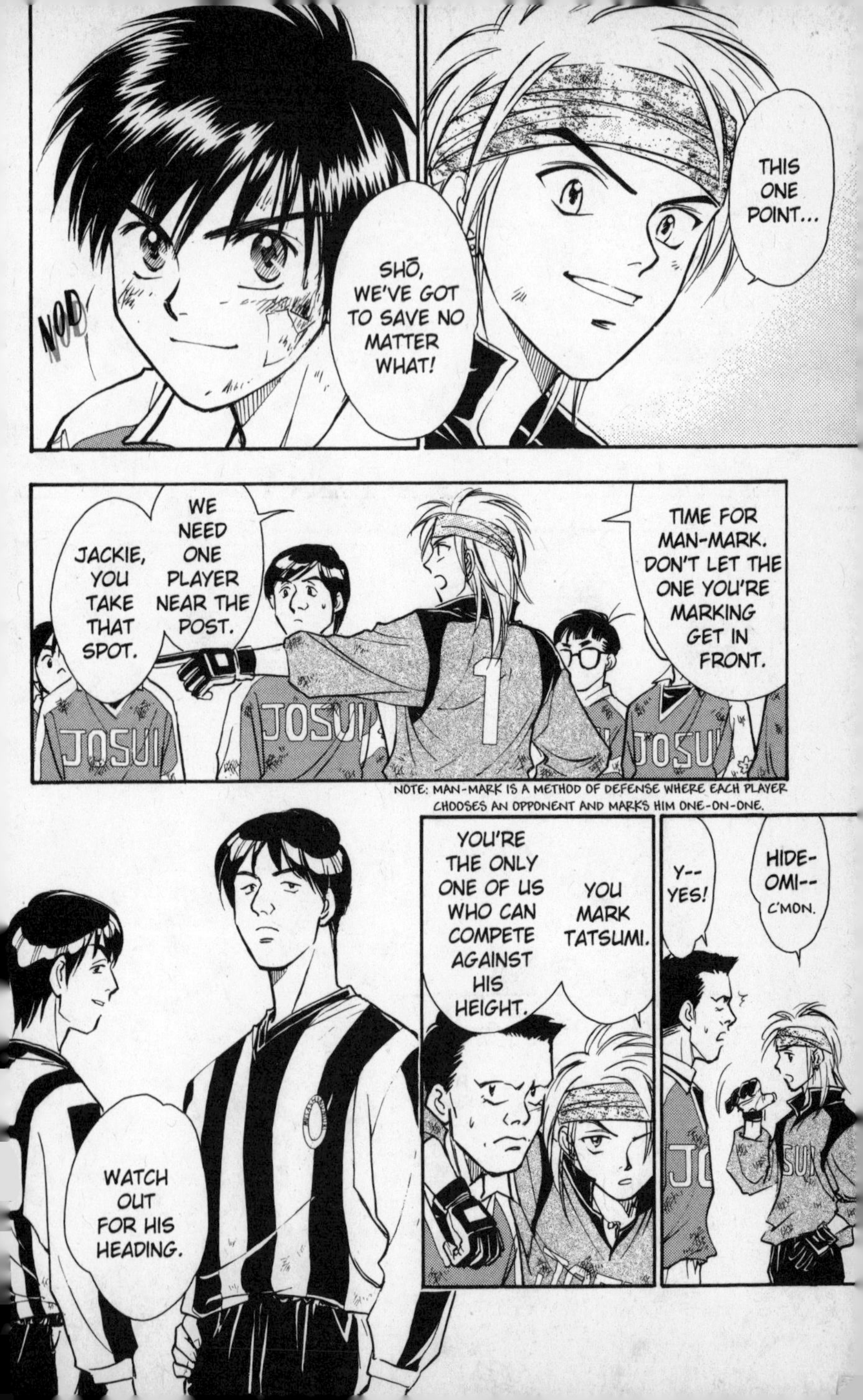
THIS ONE POINT...
SHŌ, WE'VE GOT TO SAVE NO MATTER WHAT!
NOD
TIME FOR MAN-MARK. DON'T LET THE ONE YOU'RE MARKING GET IN FRONT.
WE NEED ONE PLAYER NEAR THE POST.
JACKIE, YOU TAKE THAT SPOT.
JOSUI
NOTE: MAN-MARK IS A METHOD OF DEFENSE WHERE EACH PLAYER CHOOSES AN OPPONENT AND MARKS HIM ONE-ON-ONE.
HIDE-OMI-- C'MON.
Y-- YES!
YOU MARK TATSUMI.
YOU'RE THE ONLY ONE OF US WHO CAN COMPETE AGAINST HIS HEIGHT.
WATCH OUT FOR HIS HEADING.

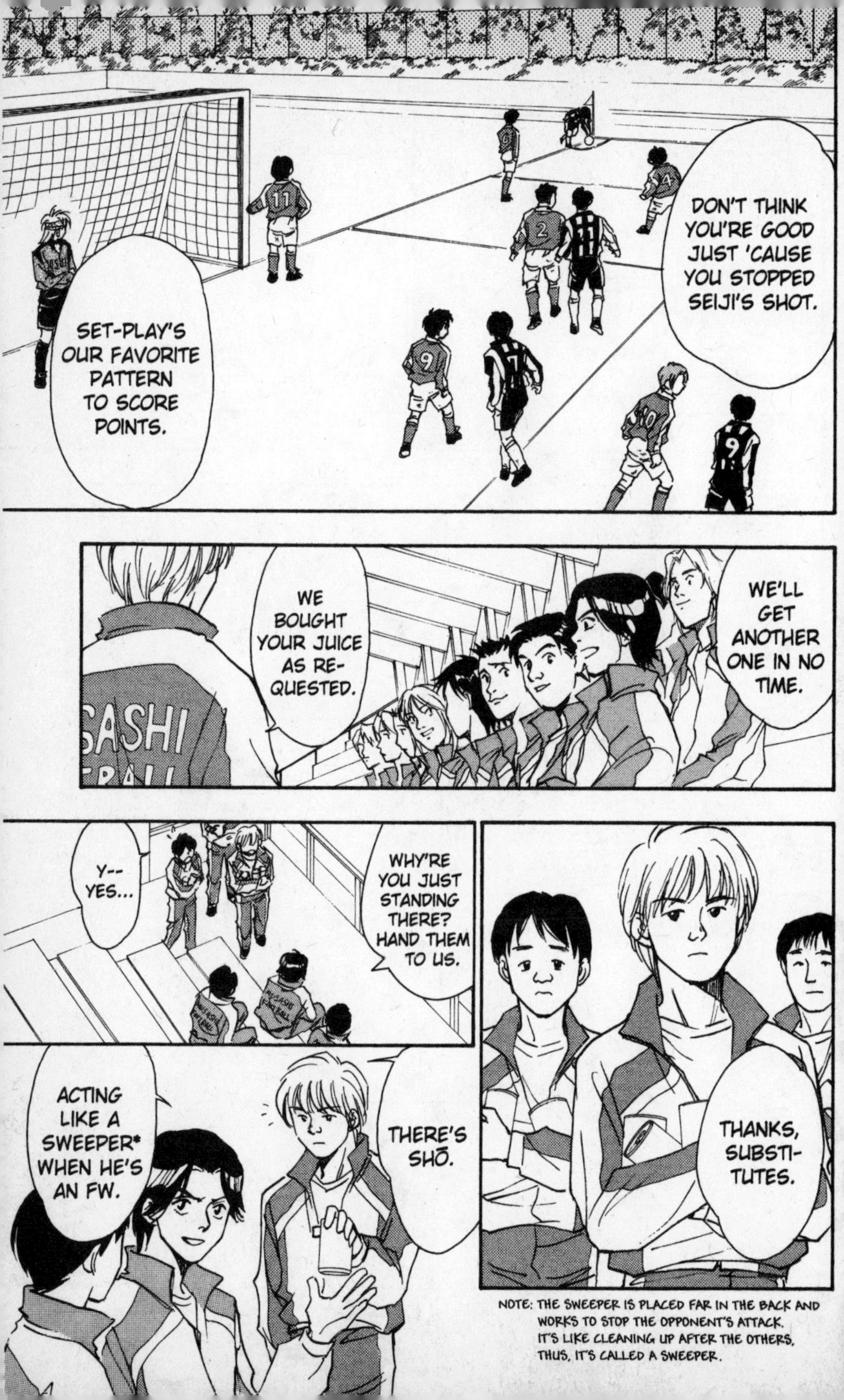
SET-PLAY'S OUR FAVORITE PATTERN TO SCORE POINTS.
DON'T THINK YOU'RE GOOD JUST 'CAUSE YOU STOPPED SEIJI'S SHOT.
WE BOUGHT YOUR JUICE AS RE-QUESTED.
WE'LL GET ANOTHER ONE IN NO TIME.
Y-- YES...
WHY'RE YOU JUST STANDING THERE? HAND THEM TO US.
ACTING LIKE A SWEEPER* WHEN HE'S AN FW.
THERE'S SHŌ.
THANKS, SUBSTI-TUTES.

NOTE: THE SWEEPER IS PLACED FAR IN THE BACK AND WORKS TO STOP THE OPPONENT'S ATTACK. IT'S LIKE CLEANING UP AFTER THE OTHERS. THUS, IT'S CALLED A SWEEPER.

READ THIS WAY

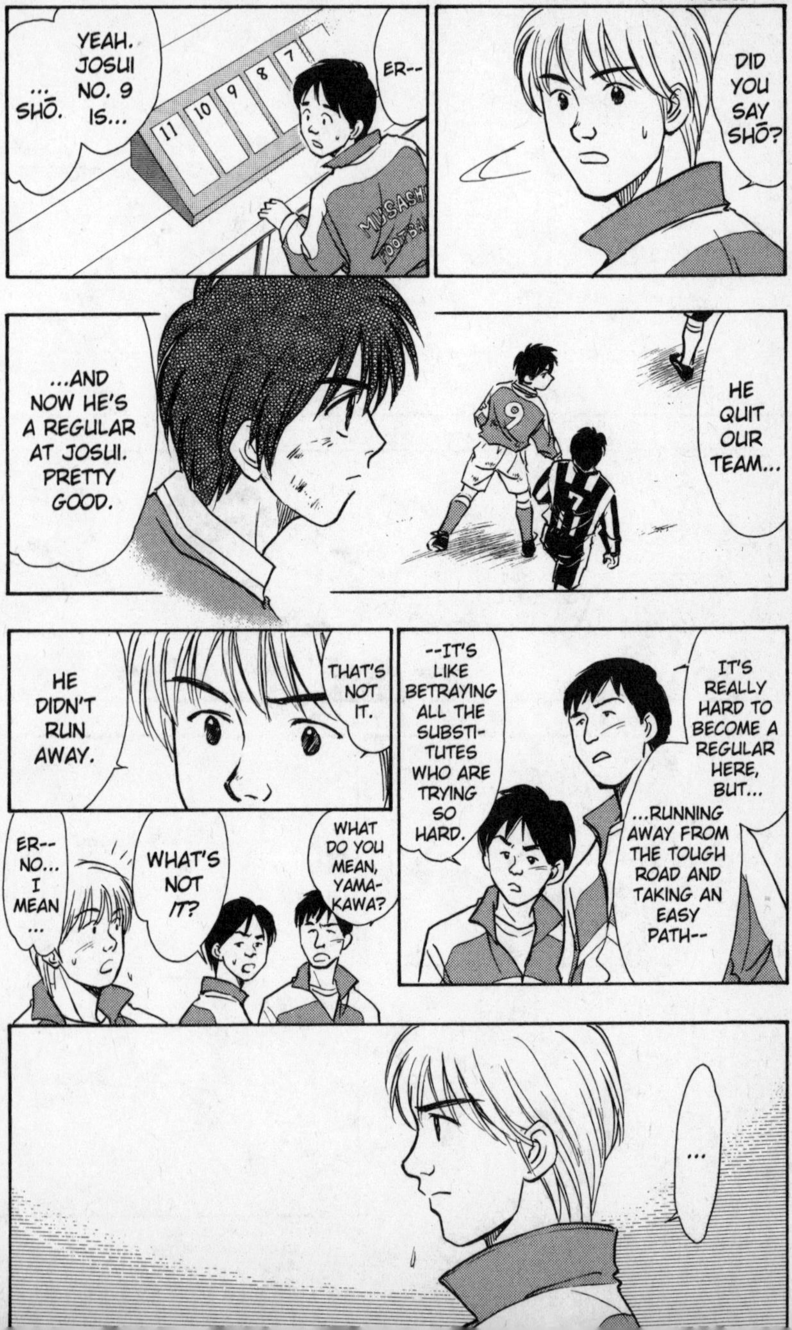
DID YOU SAY SHŌ?
ER--
YEAH. JOSUI NO. 9 IS...
... SHŌ.
HE QUIT OUR TEAM...
...AND NOW HE'S A REGULAR AT JOSUI. PRETTY GOOD.
IT'S REALLY HARD TO BECOME A REGULAR HERE, BUT...
...RUNNING AWAY FROM THE TOUGH ROAD AND TAKING AN EASY PATH--
--IT'S LIKE BETRAYING ALL THE SUBSTI-TUTES WHO ARE TRYING SO HARD.
THAT'S NOT IT.
HE DIDN'T RUN AWAY.
WHAT DO YOU MEAN, YAMA-KAWA?
WHAT'S NOT IT?
ER-- NO... I MEAN ...
...

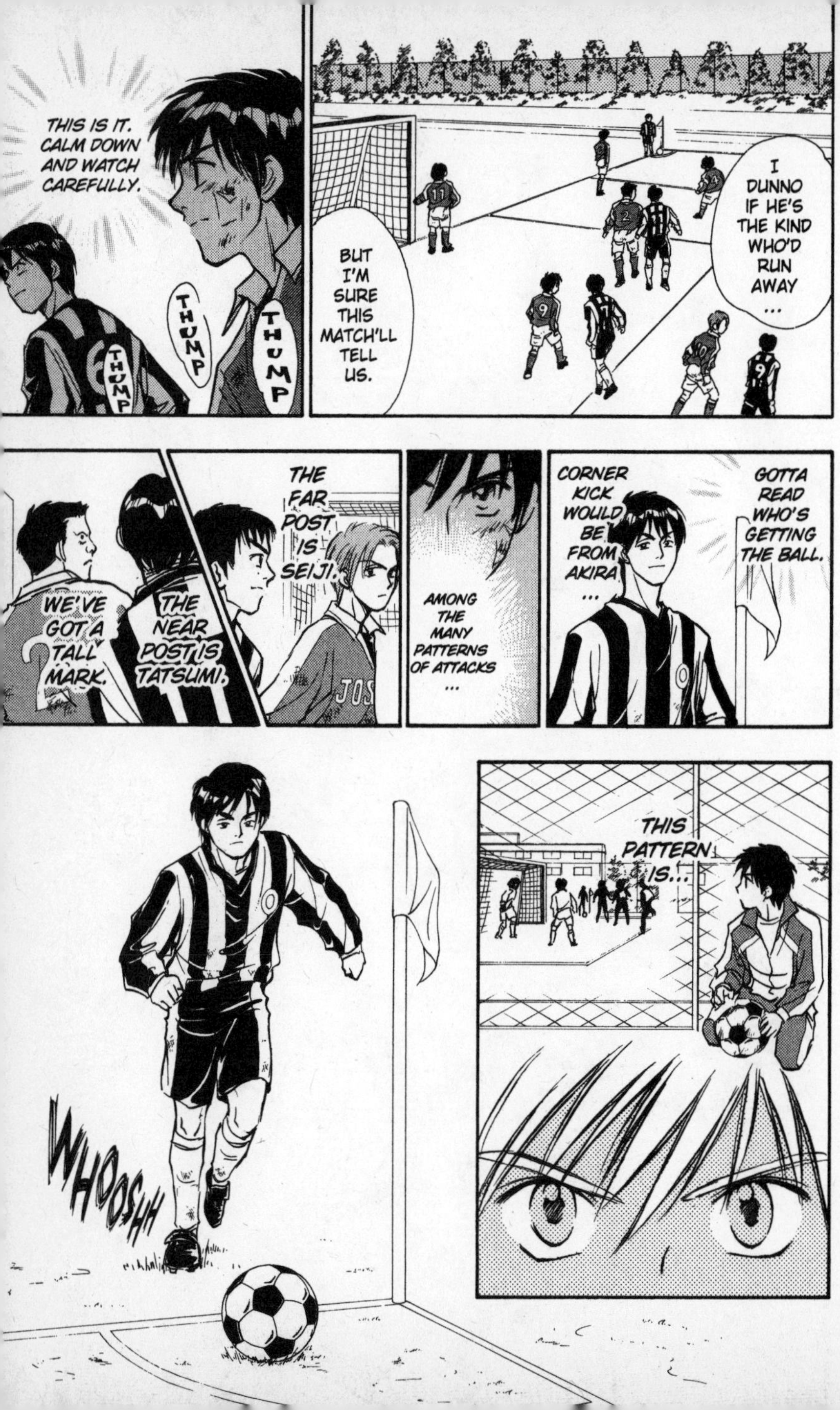
I DUNNO IF HE'S THE KIND WHO'D RUN AWAY ...
BUT I'M SURE THIS MATCH'LL TELL US.
THIS IS IT. CALM DOWN AND WATCH CAREFULLY.
THUMP
THUMP
THUMP
CORNER KICK WOULD BE FROM AKIRA ...
GOTTA READ WHO'S GETTING THE BALL.
AMONG THE MANY PATTERNS OF ATTACKS ...
THE FAR POST IS SEIJI.
THE NEAR POST IS TATSUMI.
WE'VE GOT A TALL MARK.
THIS PATTERN IS...
WHOOSH

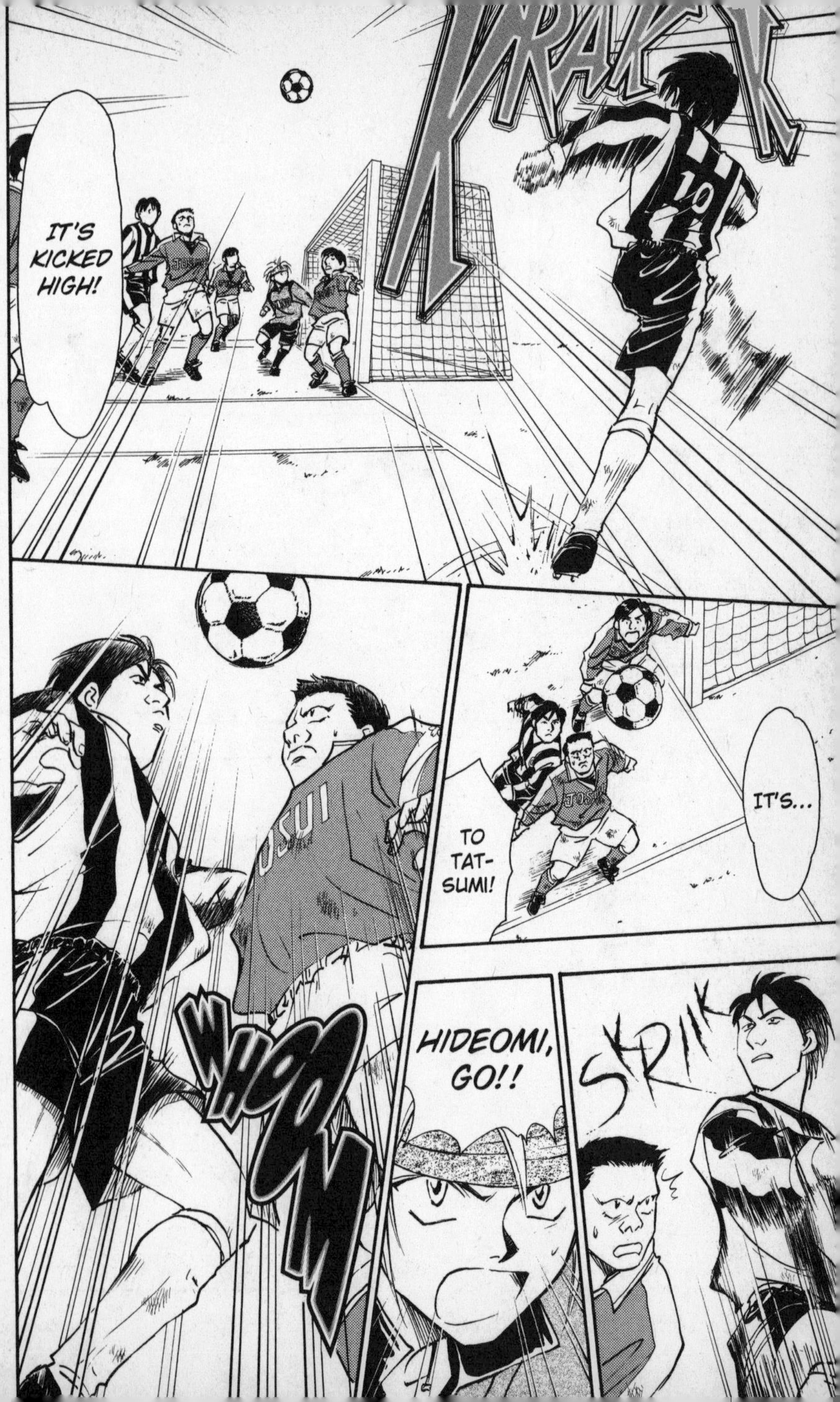
IT'S KICKED HIGH!
IT'S...
TO TAT-SUMI!
HIDEOMI, GO!!

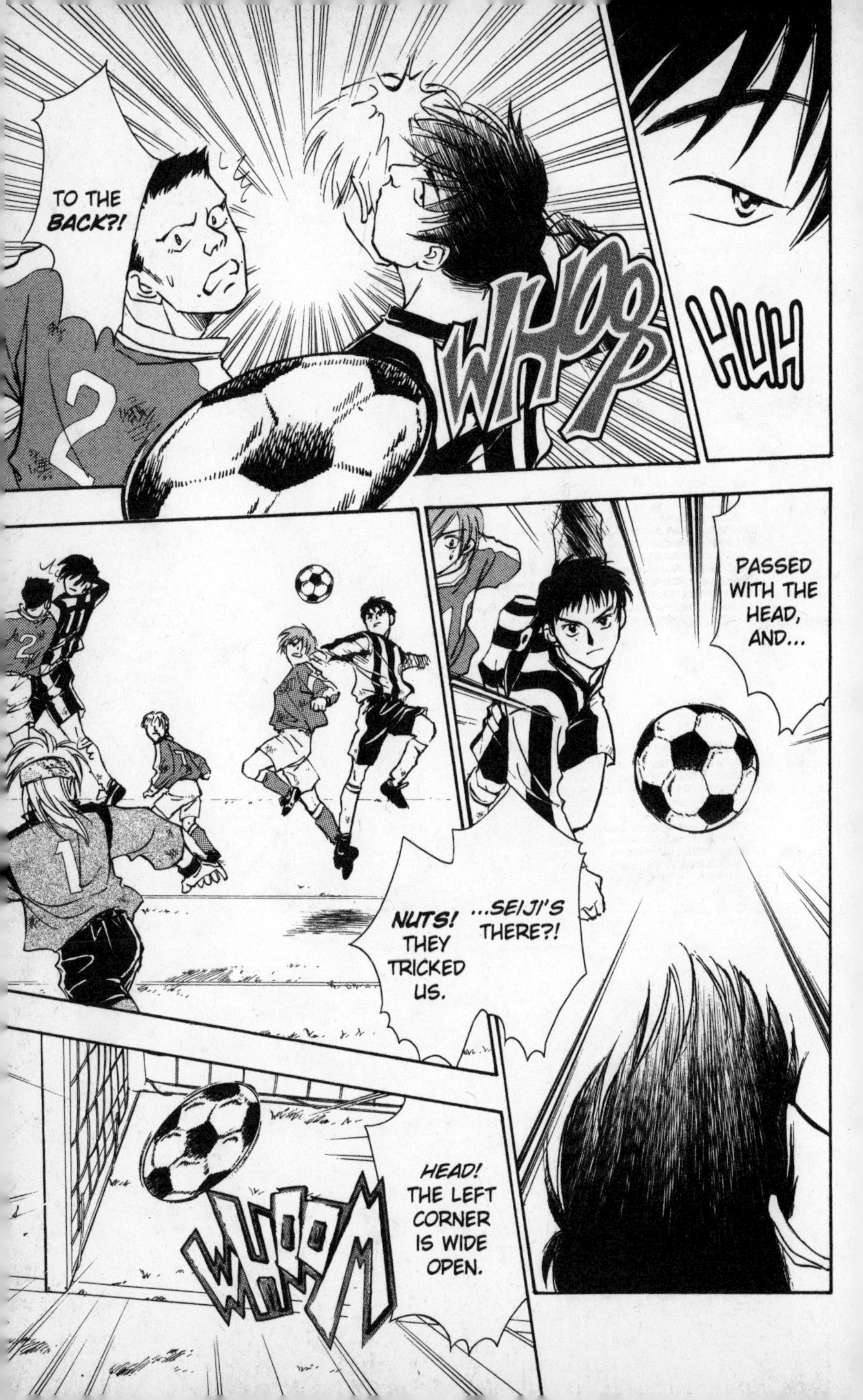
HUH
WHOP
TO THE BACK?!
PASSED WITH THE HEAD, AND...
...SEIJI'S THERE?!
NUTS! THEY TRICKED US.
HEAD! THE LEFT CORNER IS WIDE OPEN.
WHOOM

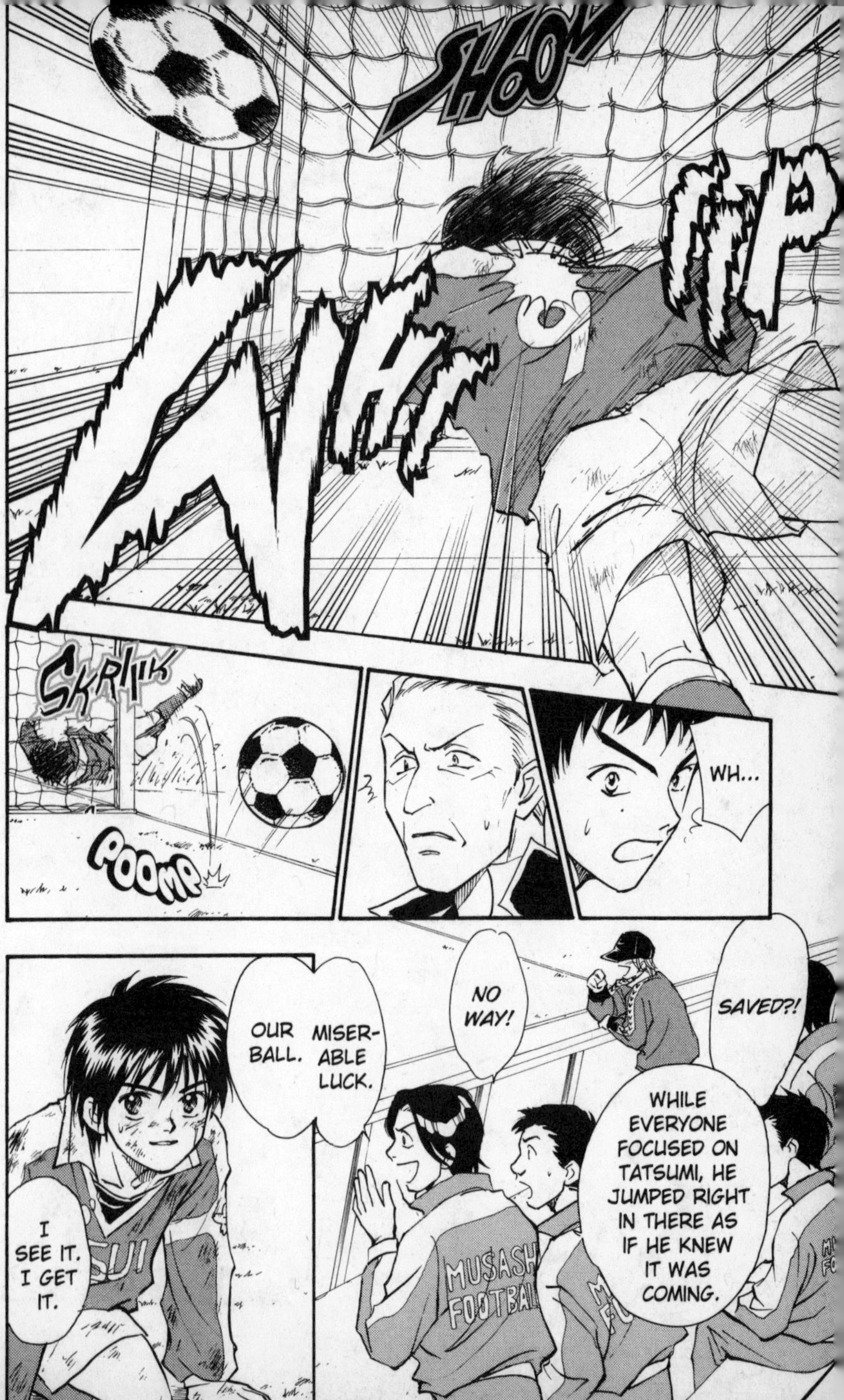
SHOOM
POOMP
WH...
SAVED?!
NO WAY!
WHILE EVERYONE FOCUSED ON TATSUMI, HE JUMPED RIGHT IN THERE AS IF HE KNEW IT WAS COMING.
MISER-ABLE LUCK.
OUR BALL.
I SEE IT. I GET IT.
MUSASH FOOTBALL

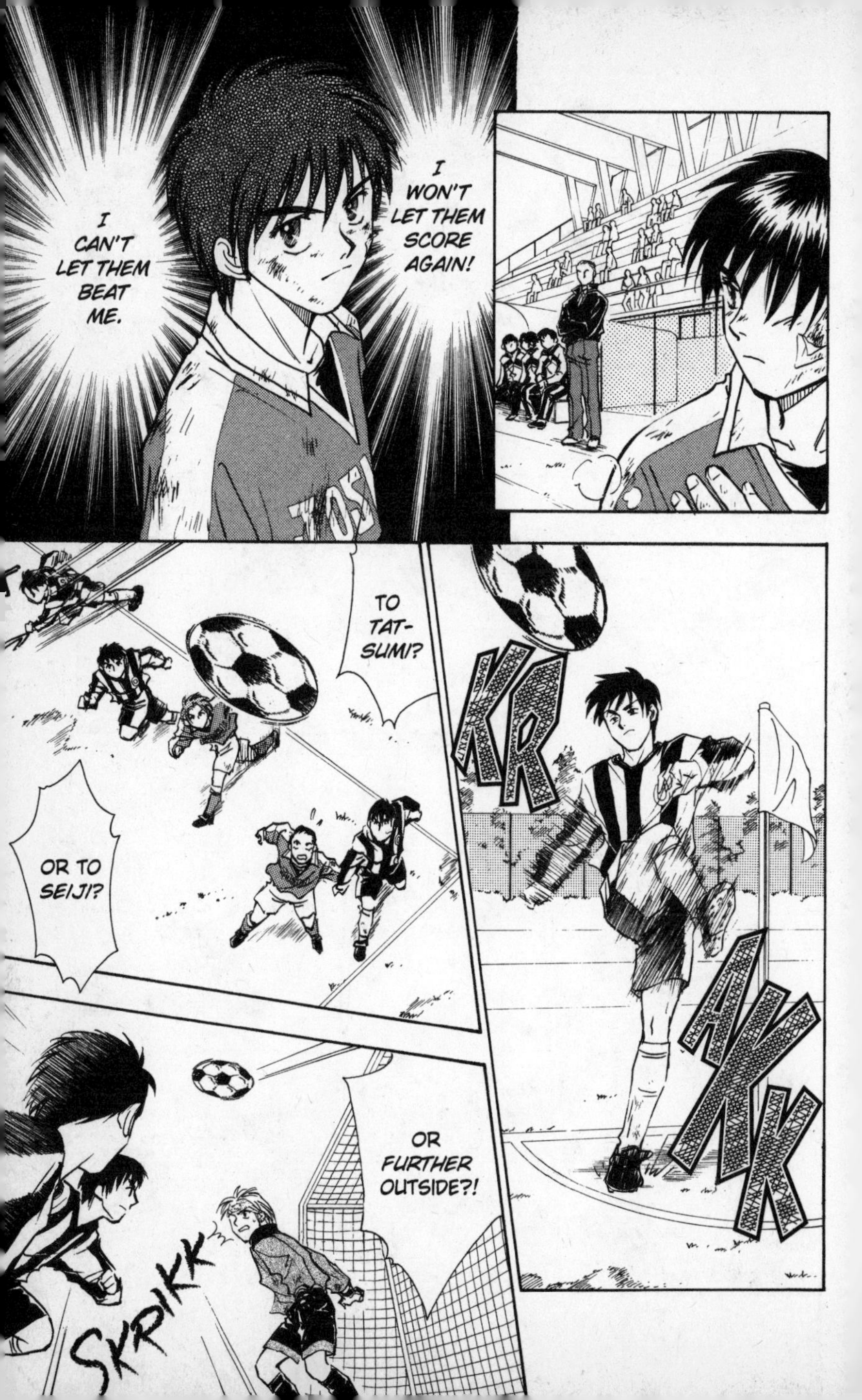
I WON'T LET THEM SCORE AGAIN!
I CAN'T LET THEM BEAT ME.
KRAKK
TO TAT-SUMI?
OR TO SEIJI?
OR FURTHER OUTSIDE?!
SKRIKK

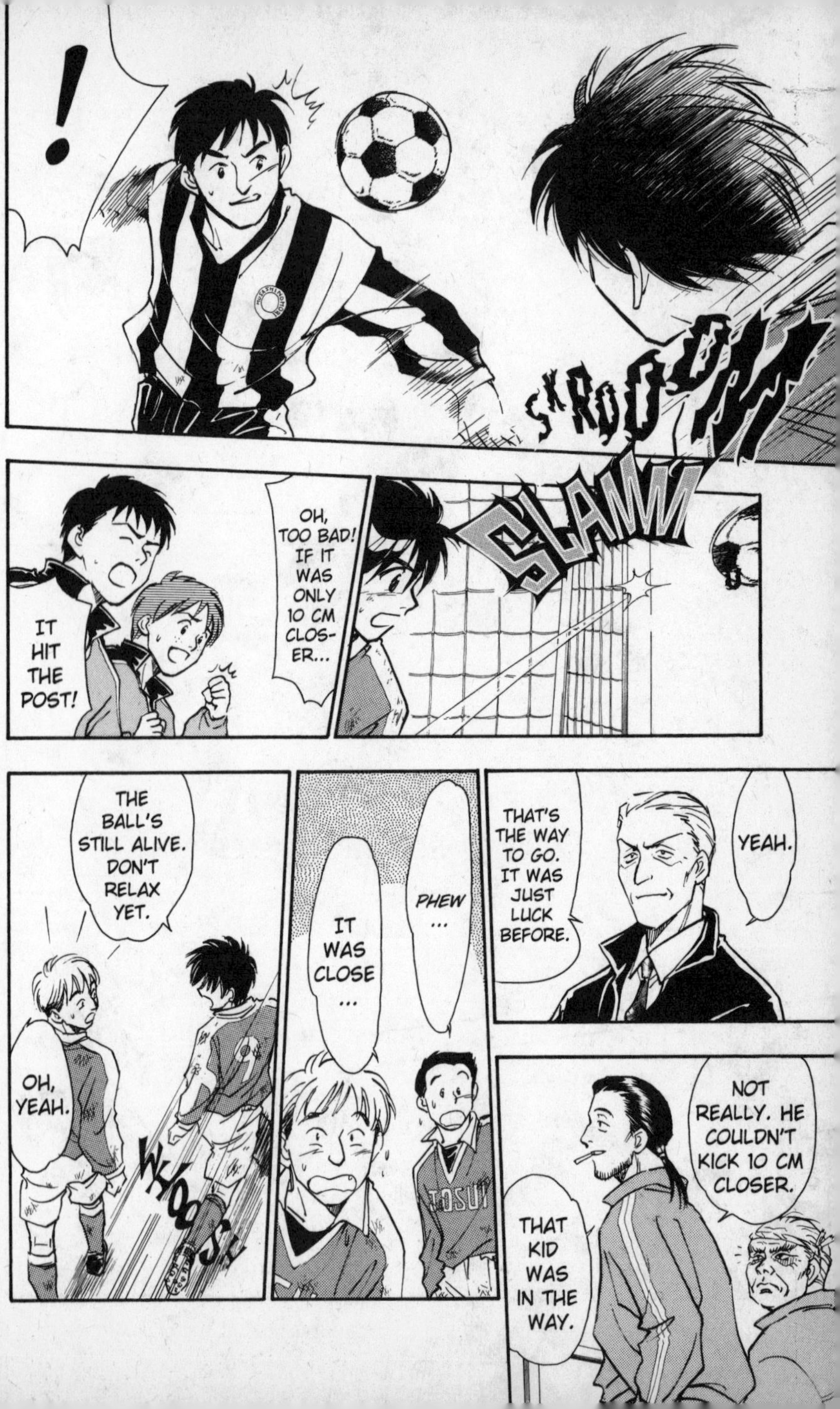
!
SKROOOM
SLAM
IT HIT THE POST!
OH, TOO BAD! IF IT WAS ONLY 10 CM CLOSER...
THE BALL'S STILL ALIVE. DON'T RELAX YET.
OH, YEAH.
WHOOSH
PHEW...
IT WAS CLOSE...
THAT'S THE WAY TO GO. IT WAS JUST LUCK BEFORE.
YEAH.
NOT REALLY. HE COULDN'T KICK 10 CM CLOSER.
THAT KID WAS IN THE WAY.

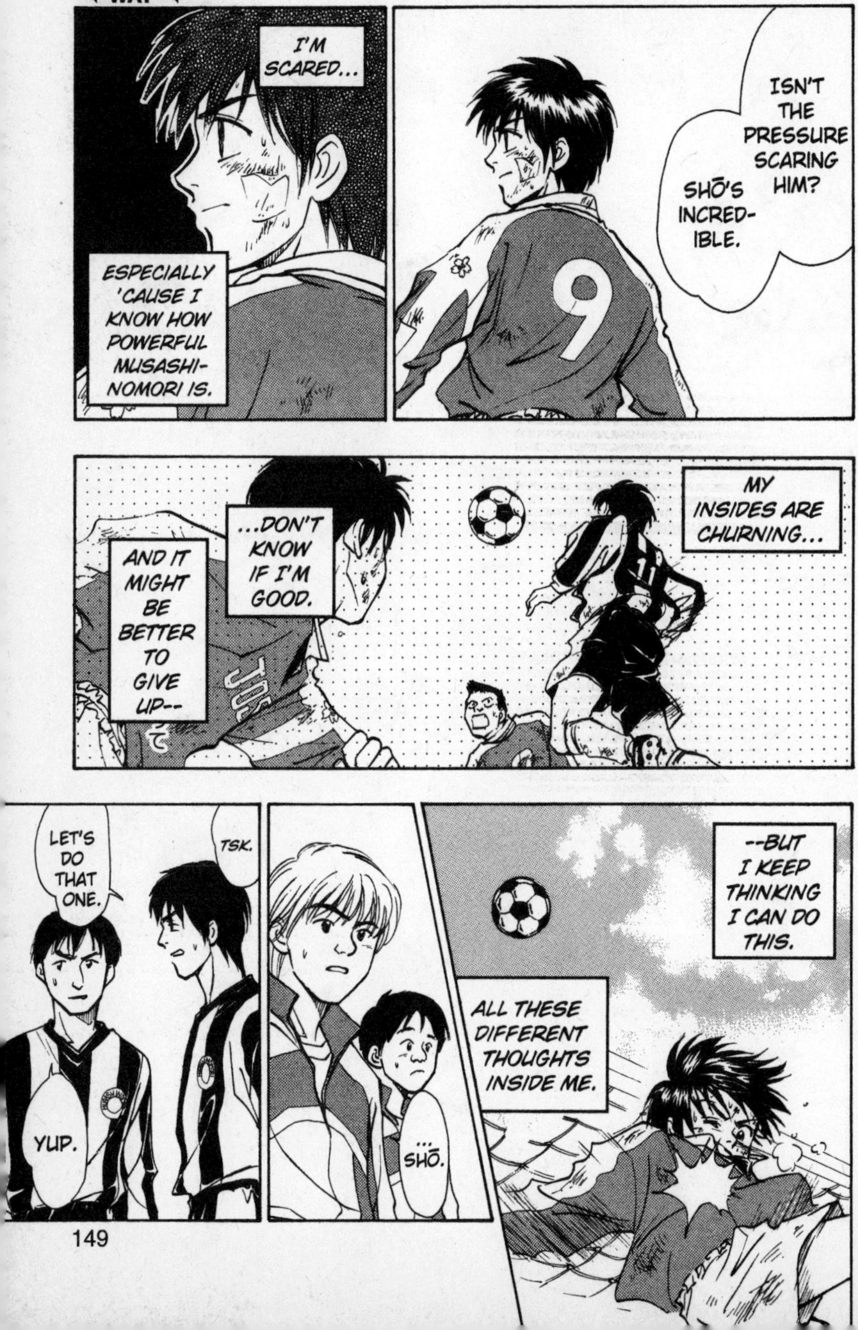
ISN'T THE PRESSURE SCARING HIM?
SHŌ'S INCREDIBLE.
I'M SCARED...
ESPECIALLY 'CAUSE I KNOW HOW POWERFUL MUSASHINOMORI IS.
MY INSIDES ARE CHURNING...
...DON'T KNOW IF I'M GOOD.
AND IT MIGHT BE BETTER TO GIVE UP--
--BUT I KEEP THINKING I CAN DO THIS.
ALL THESE DIFFERENT THOUGHTS INSIDE ME.
...SHŌ.
TSK.
LET'S DO THAT ONE.
YUP.

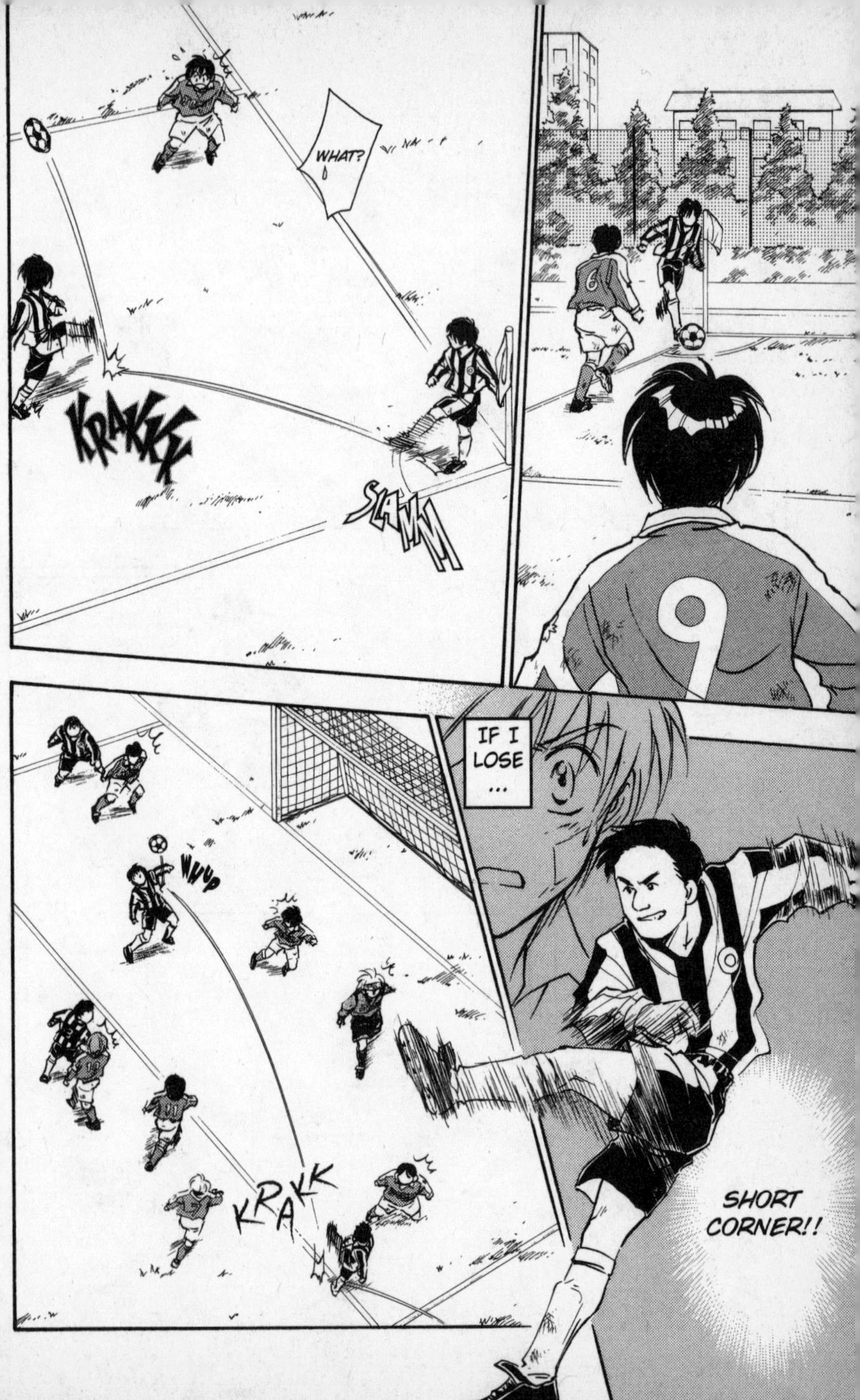
WHAT?
KRAKKK
SLAMM
IF I LOSE ...
SHORT CORNER!!
WHUP
KRAKK

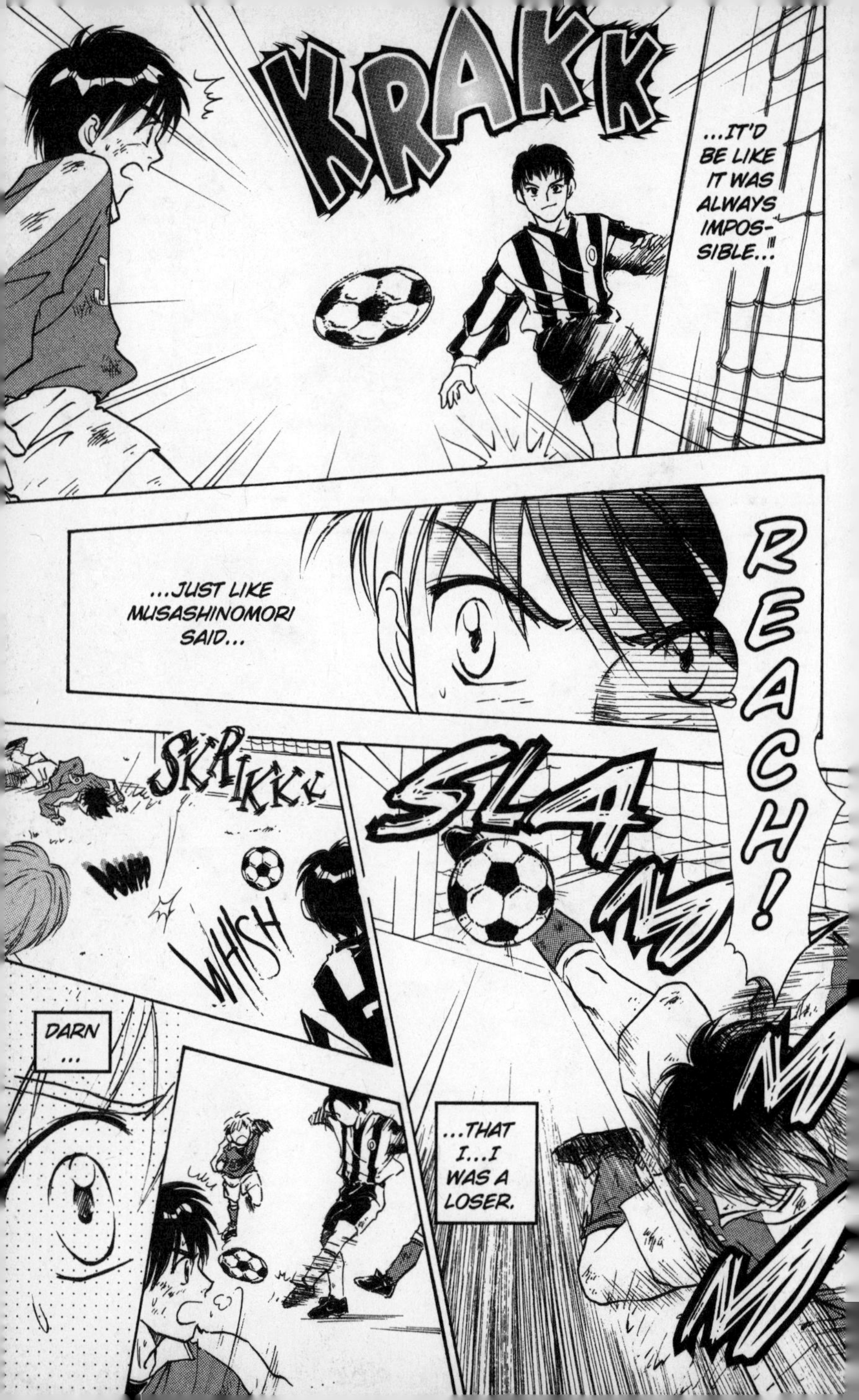
KRAKK
...IT'D BE LIKE IT WAS ALWAYS IMPOS-SIBLE...!
REACH!
...JUST LIKE MUSASHINOMORI SAID...
SLAM
SKRIKKK
WHISH
...THAT I...I WAS A LOSER.
DARN ...

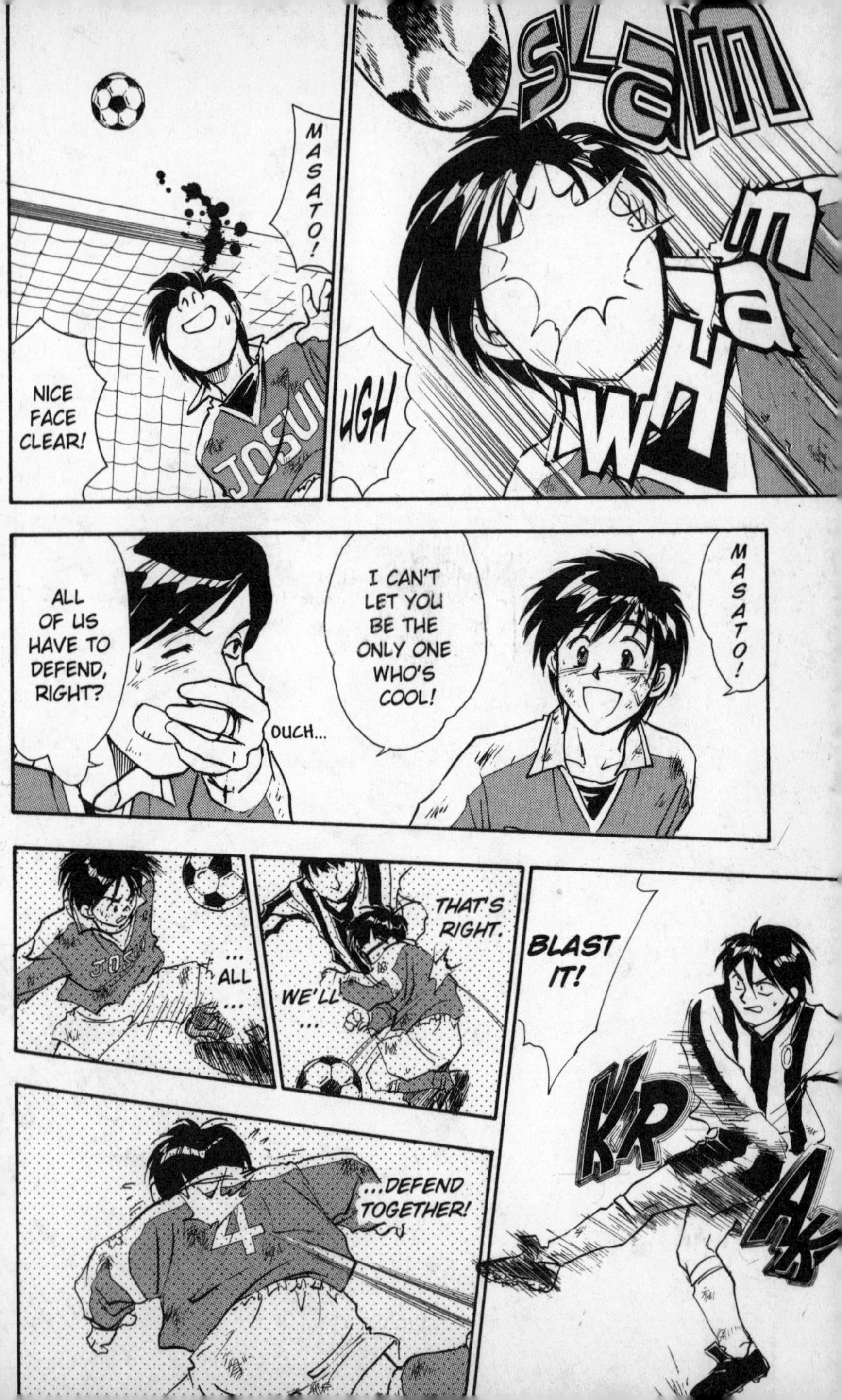
SLAM
WHAM
UGH
MASATO!
NICE FACE CLEAR!
MASATO!
I CAN'T LET YOU BE THE ONLY ONE WHO'S COOL!
OUCH...
ALL OF US HAVE TO DEFEND, RIGHT?
BLAST IT!
KRAK
THAT'S RIGHT.
WE'LL...
...ALL...
...DEFEND TOGETHER!

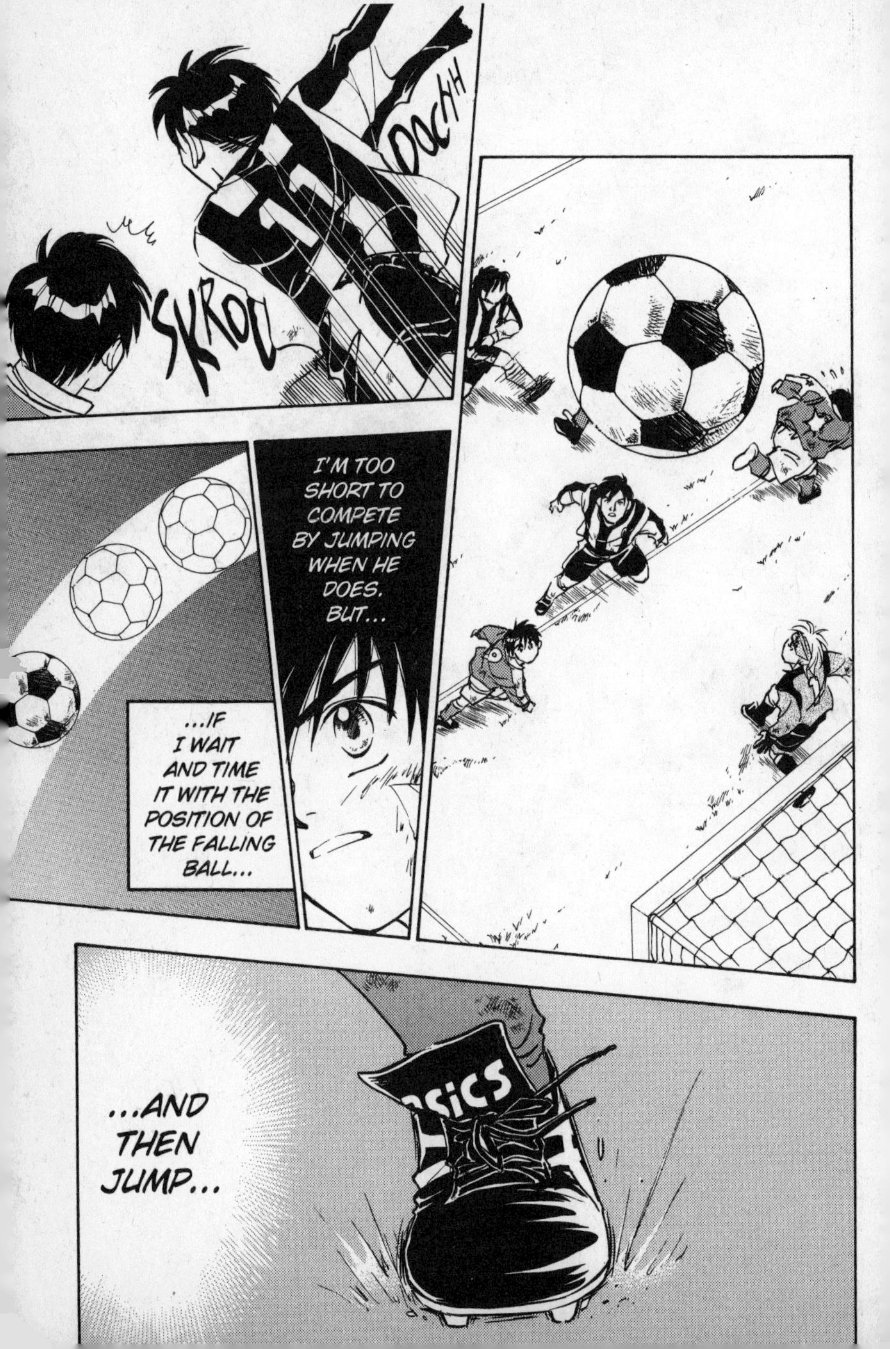
DOCHH
SKROU
I'M TOO SHORT TO COMPETE BY JUMPING WHEN HE DOES. BUT...
...IF I WAIT AND TIME IT WITH THE POSITION OF THE FALLING BALL...
...AND THEN JUMP...
asics

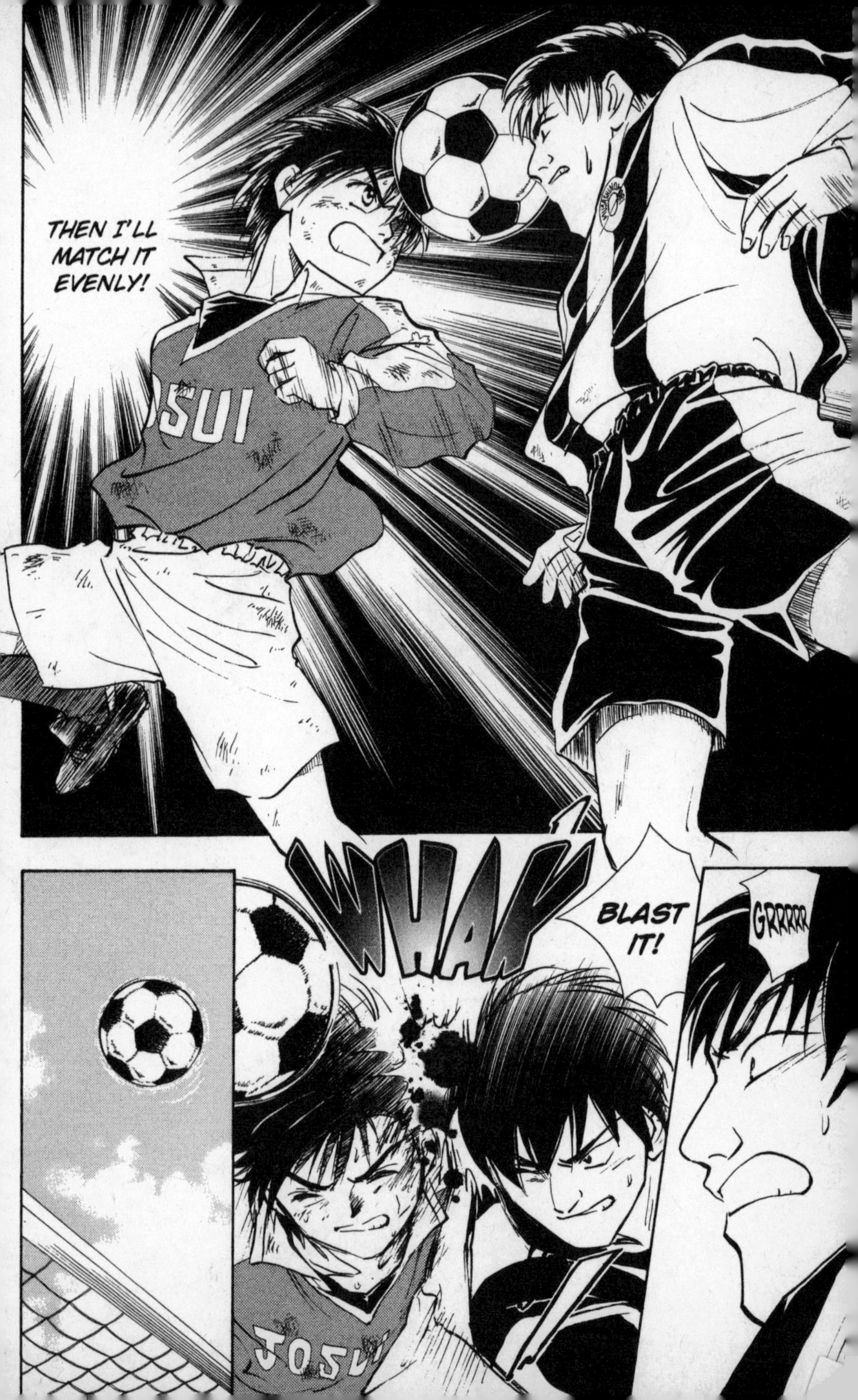
THEN I'LL MATCH IT EVENLY!
WHAK
BLAST IT!
GRRRRR

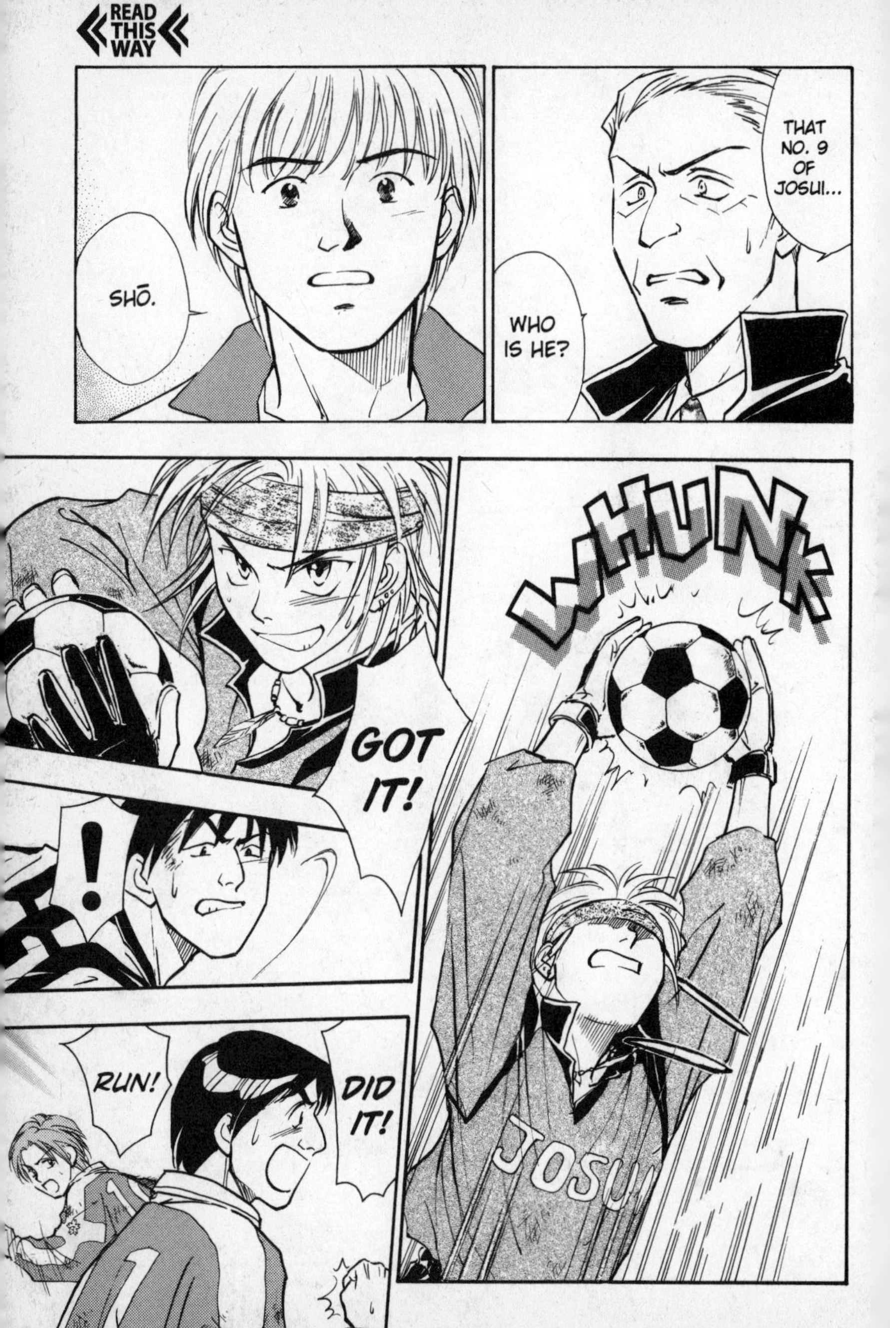
READ THIS WAY
THAT NO. 9 OF JOSUI...
WHO IS HE?
SHŌ.
WHUNK
GOT IT!
!
DID IT!
RUN!
JOSU

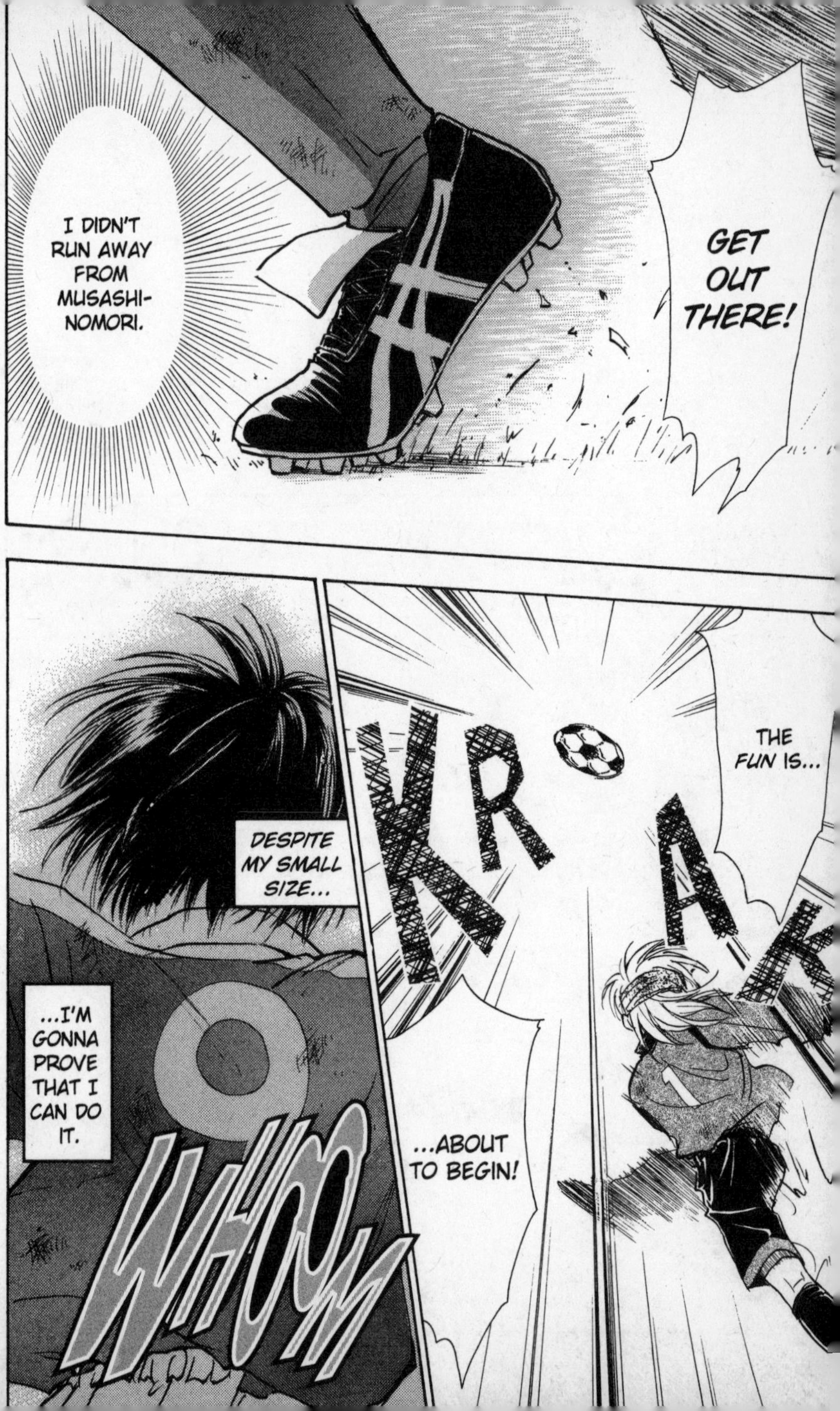
GET OUT THERE!
I DIDN'T RUN AWAY FROM MUSASHI-NOMORI.
THE FUN IS...
KRAAK
...ABOUT TO BEGIN!
DESPITE MY SMALL SIZE...
...I'M GONNA PROVE THAT I CAN DO IT.
WHOOM

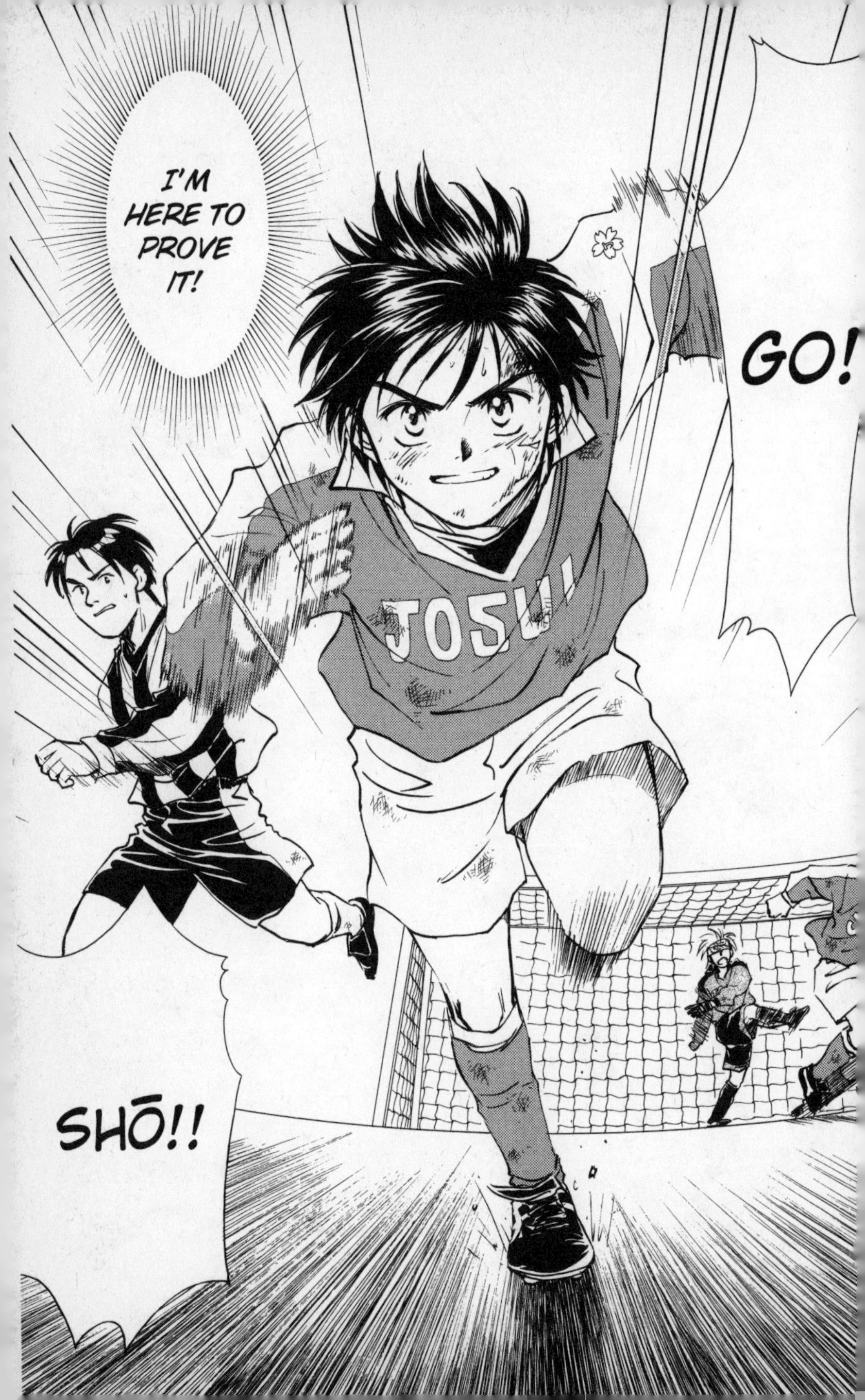
GO!
I'M HERE TO PROVE IT!
SHŌ!!

HIS FAVORITE SPIKE IS [ASICS]

AMONG THE JAPANESE REPRESENTATIVES, THE PLAYER NAOKI S■MA (KASHIMA ANTLERS) AND THE PLAYER DAISUKE ICHIKAWA, USE THE SAME MAKE. THE PLAYER YOSHIKATSU KAWAGUCHI ALSO USES THE SAME MAKE BUT HE USES KAWAGUCHI MODEL WITH A DIFFERENT MARK.

WE CARE

PART. 1
EPISODE OF SHOES

DRAWING THE UNIFORM AND THE LIKE FOR A MATCH IS A LOT OF WORK. THE VARIATION ALONE (BECAUSE THERE ARE 22 FOR BOTH TEAMS AND THEN THERE ARE OUTFIELD BLEACHERS) REALLY KILLS ME. BUT, MY ASSISTANTS, WHOSE JOB IT IS TO FINISH MY DRAWINGS, PROBABLY GET THE BRUNT OF IT. DESPITE KNOWING HOW MUCH TROUBLE IT IS, I STILL CAN'T HELP BUT CARE, SO HERE'S THE PAGE THAT FURTHER INCREASES THE BURDEN ON MY ASSISTANTS. THIS IS A VERY ROUGH DRAWING, SO YOU MIGHT WONDER WHAT THE HECK, BUT PLEASE SHUT YOUR EYES AND OVERLOOK IT.

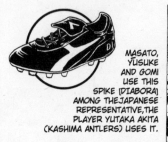

MASATO, YŪSUKE AND GOMI USE THIS SPIKE [DIABORA] AMONG THE JAPANESE REPRESENTATIVE, THE PLAYER YUTAKA AKITA (KASHIMA ANTLERS) USES IT.

TATSUYA FAVORS TATSUYA (BY THE WAY, I DIDN'T CHOOSE THIS AS A SILLY JOKE). AMONG THE JAPANESE REPRESENTATIVE, THE PLAYER HIROAKI MORISHIMA (SELESSO ŌSAKA) AND THE PLAYER NORIO OMURA (YOKOHAMA MARINERS) FAVOR THIS.

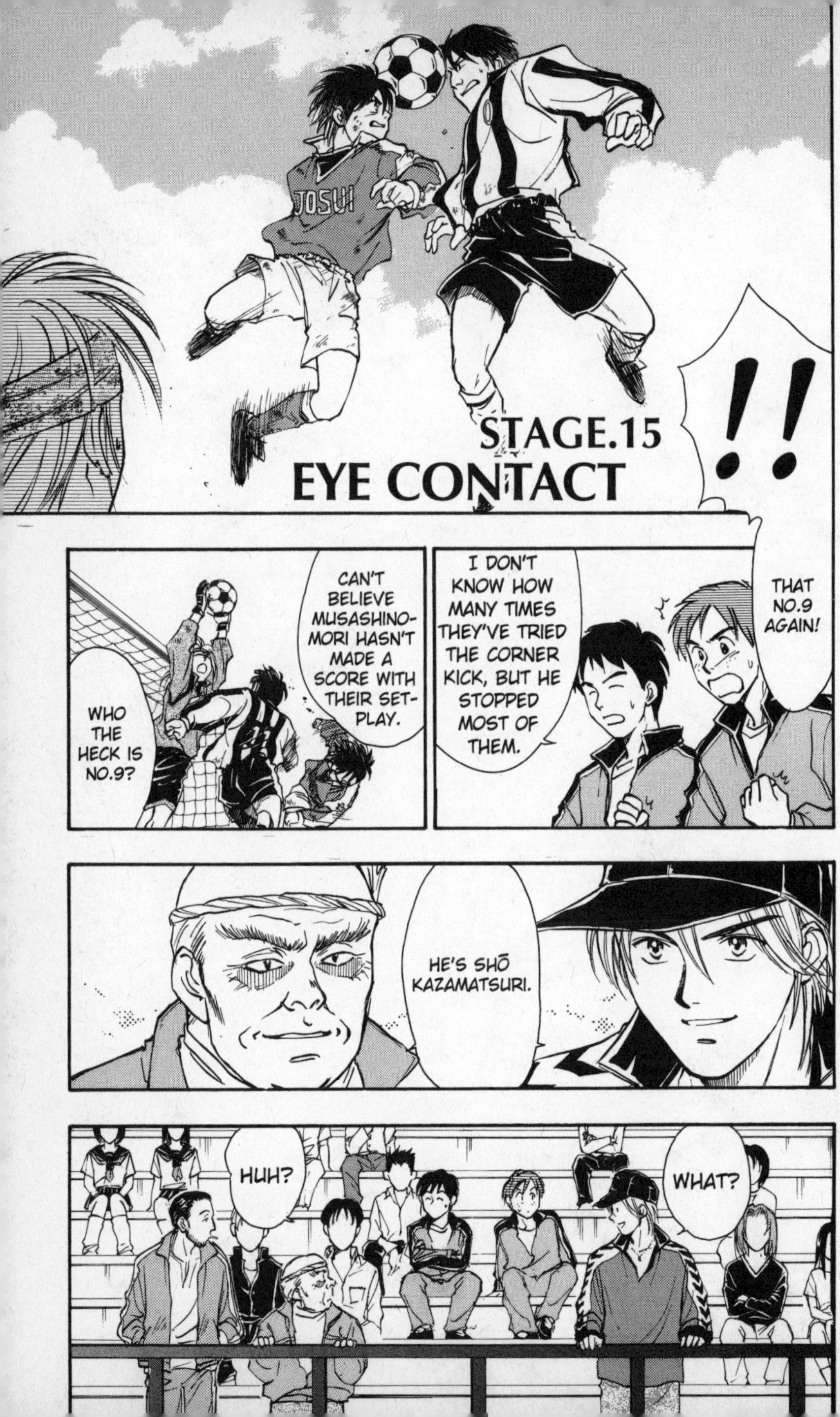

STAGE.15
EYE CONTACT
!!
JOSUI
THAT NO.9 AGAIN!
I DON'T KNOW HOW MANY TIMES THEY'VE TRIED THE CORNER KICK, BUT HE STOPPED MOST OF THEM.
CAN'T BELIEVE MUSASHINO-MORI HASN'T MADE A SCORE WITH THEIR SET-PLAY.
WHO THE HECK IS NO.9?
HE'S SHŌ KAZAMATSURI.
WHAT?
HUH?

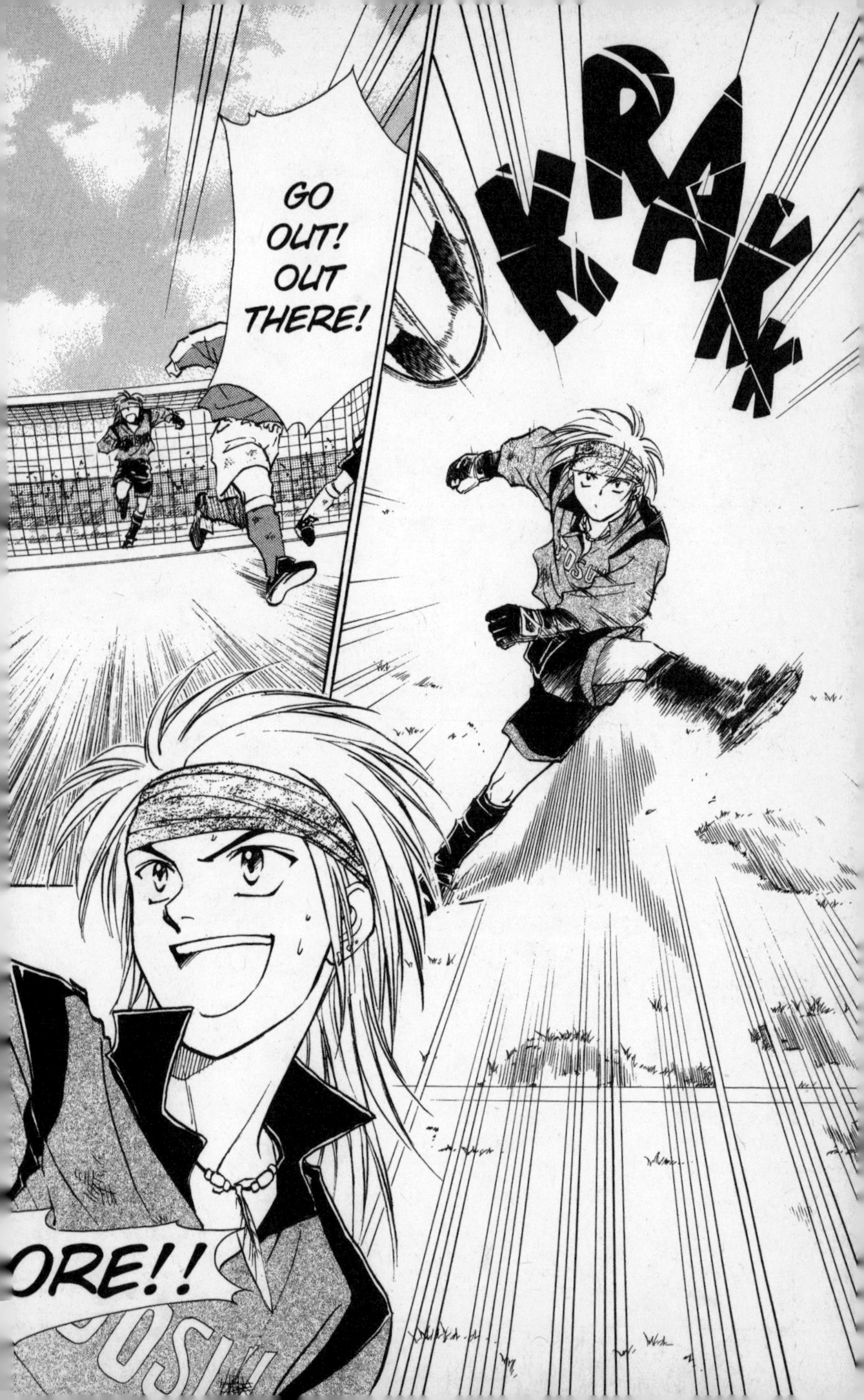
GO OUT! OUT THERE!
KRAKK
ORE!!

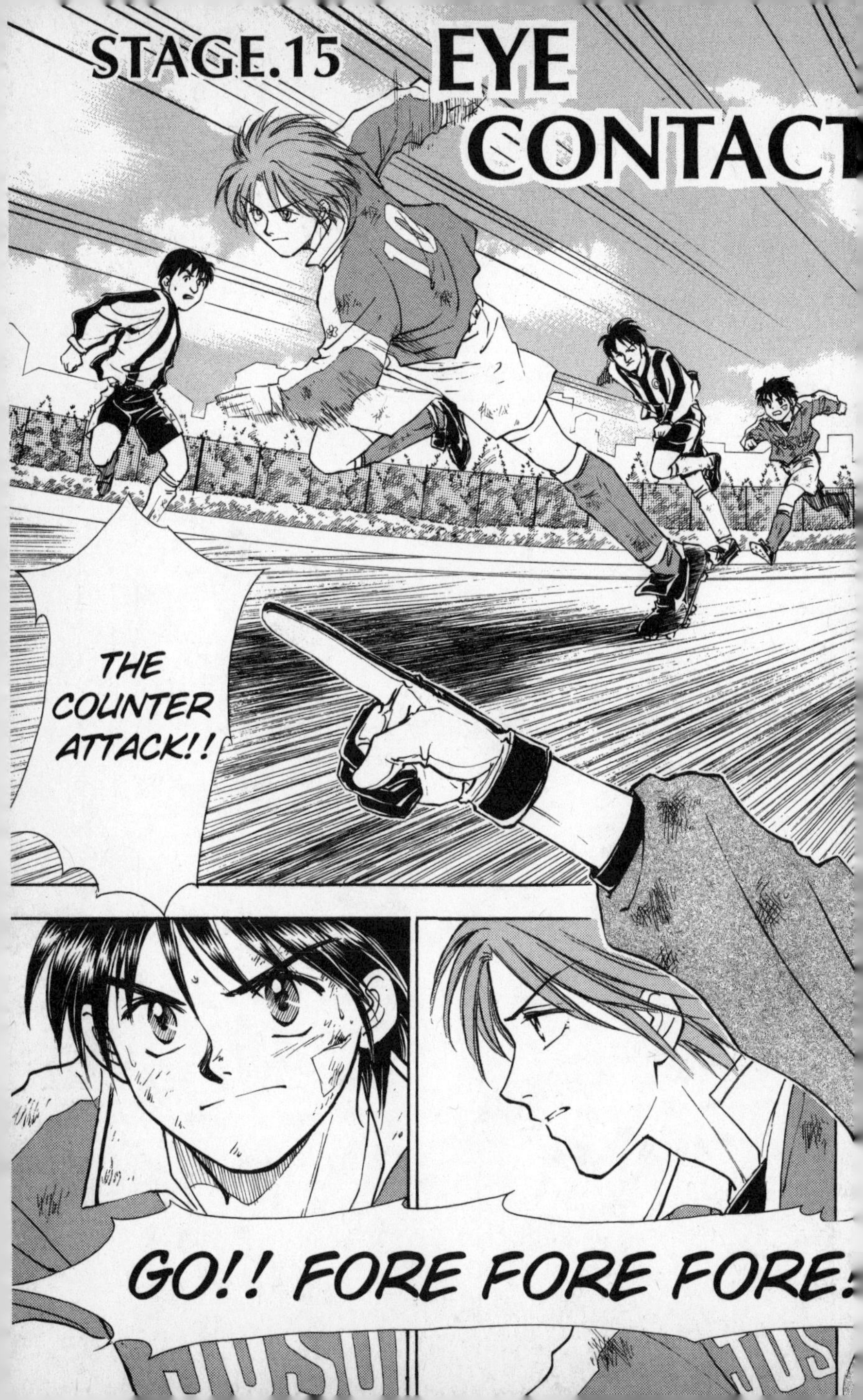
STAGE.15
EYE CONTACT
THE COUNTER ATTACK!!
GO!! FORE FORE FORE

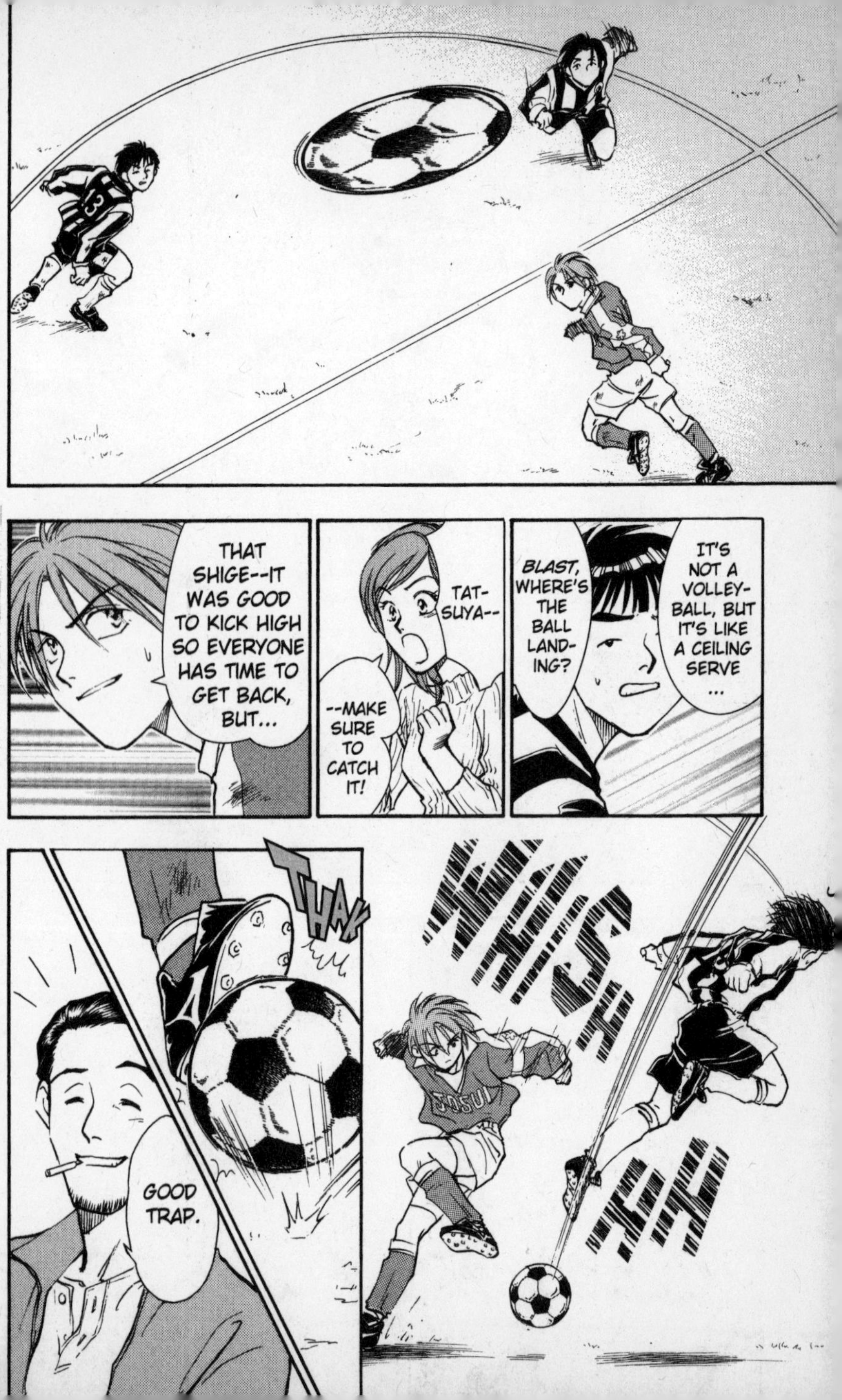
IT'S NOT A VOLLEY-BALL, BUT IT'S LIKE A CEILING SERVE ...
BLAST, WHERE'S THE BALL LAND-ING?
TAT-SUYA--
--MAKE SURE TO CATCH IT!
THAT SHIGE--IT WAS GOOD TO KICK HIGH SO EVERYONE HAS TIME TO GET BACK, BUT...
WHISH
HHH
THAK
GOOD TRAP.

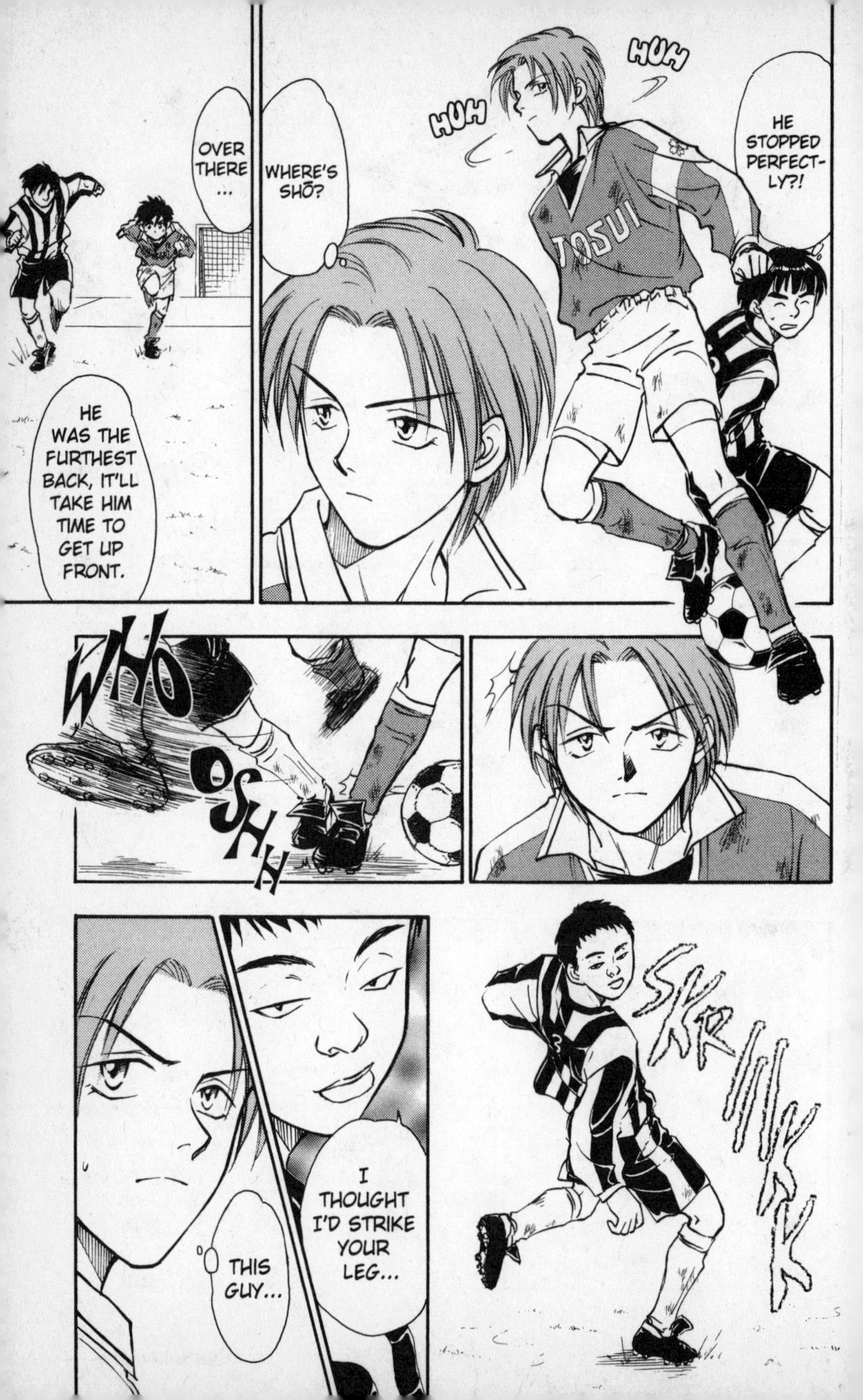
HUH
HUH
HE STOPPED PERFECT-LY?!
WHERE'S SHŌ?
OVER THERE...
HE WAS THE FURTHEST BACK, IT'LL TAKE HIM TIME TO GET UP FRONT.
WHOOSHH
SKRINK
I THOUGHT I'D STRIKE YOUR LEG...
THIS GUY...

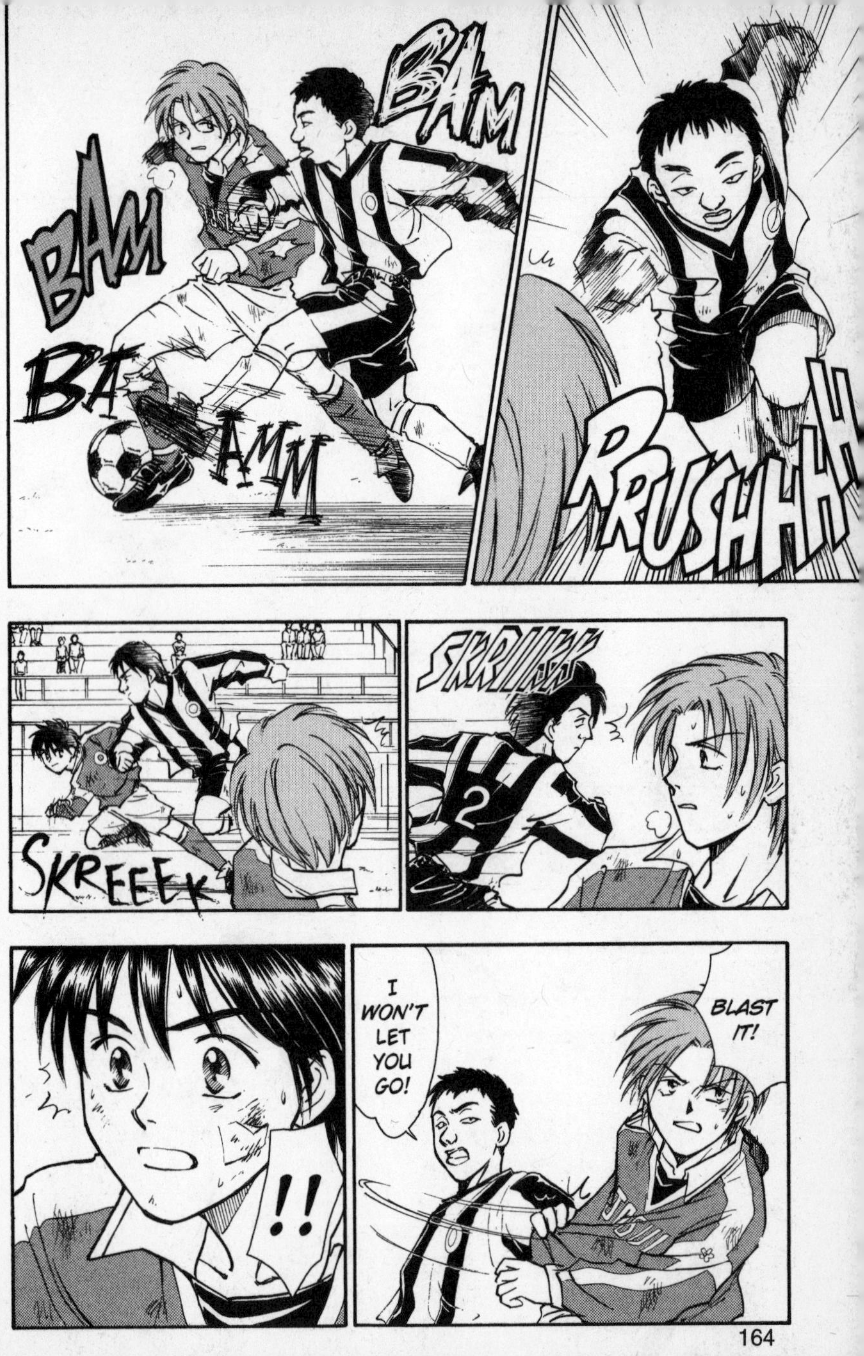
RUSHHH
BAM
BAM
BA
AMM
SKREEEK
BLAST IT!
I WON'T LET YOU GO!
!!

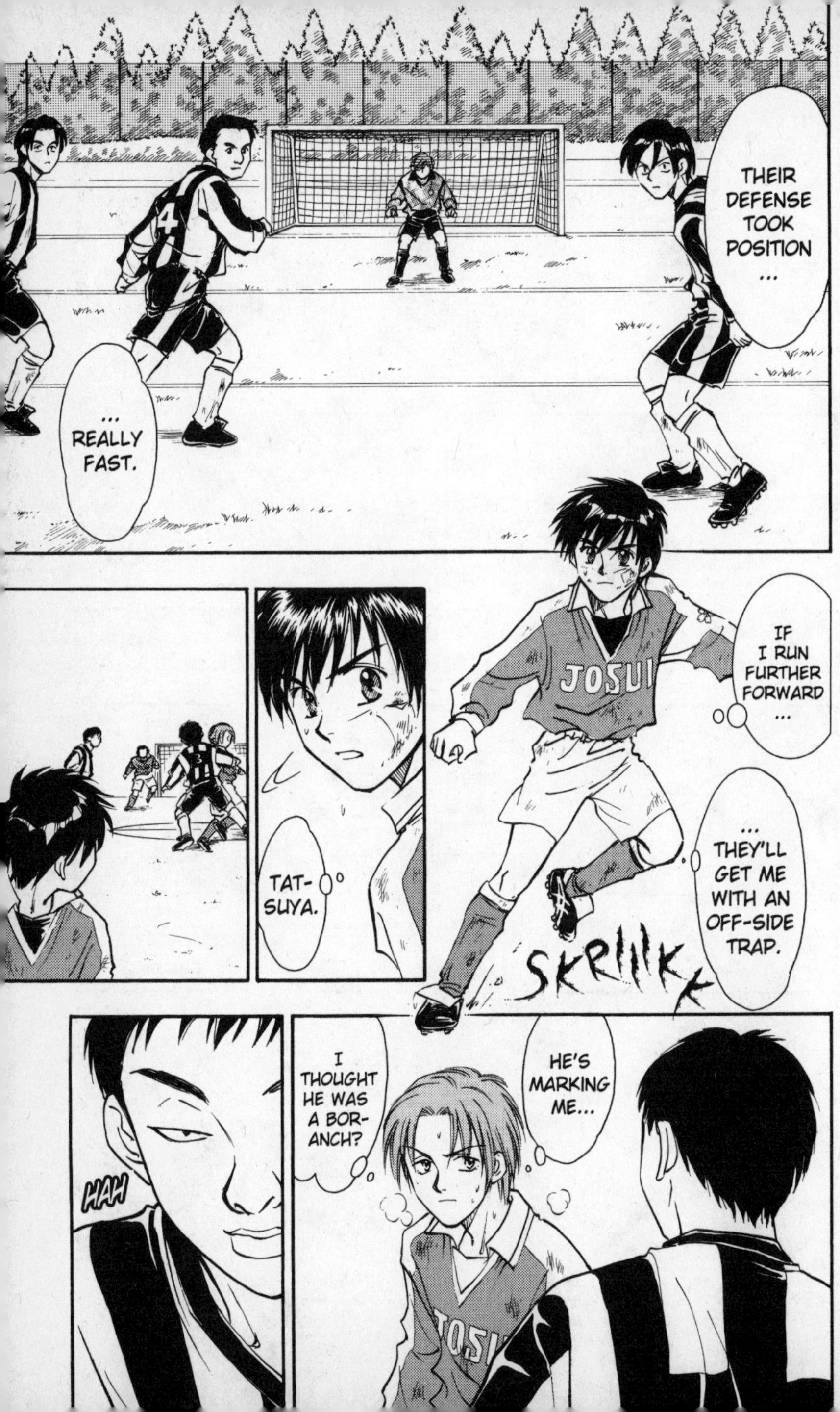
THEIR DEFENSE TOOK POSITION ...
... REALLY FAST.
IF I RUN FURTHER FORWARD ...
... THEY'LL GET ME WITH AN OFF-SIDE TRAP.
SKRIIIK
TAT-SUYA.
HE'S MARKING ME...
I THOUGHT HE WAS A BOR-ANCH?
HAH

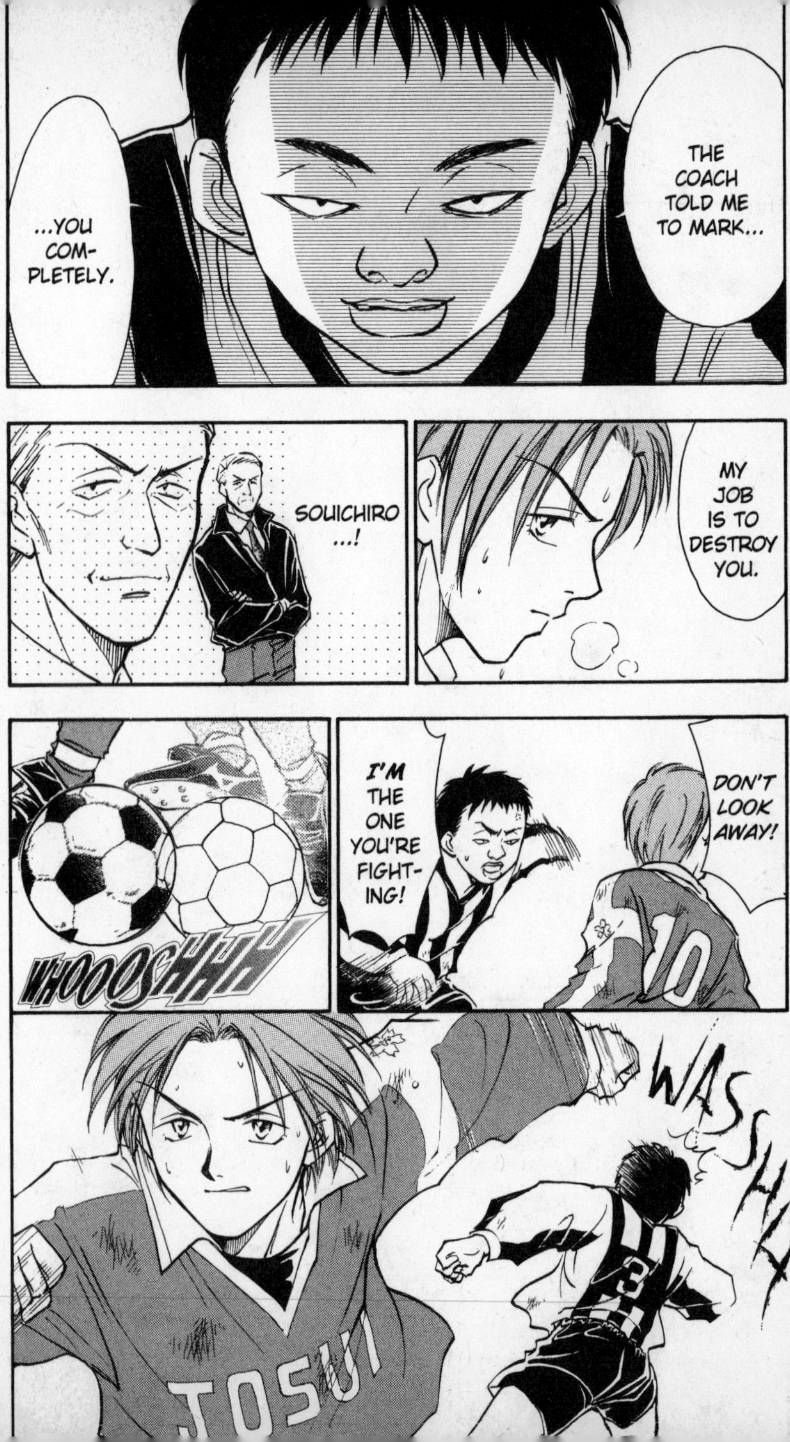
THE COACH TOLD ME TO MARK...
...YOU COMPLETELY.
MY JOB IS TO DESTROY YOU.
SOUICHIRO ...!
DON'T LOOK AWAY!
I'M THE ONE YOU'RE FIGHTING!
WHOOOSCHHH
WASSHH
JOSUI

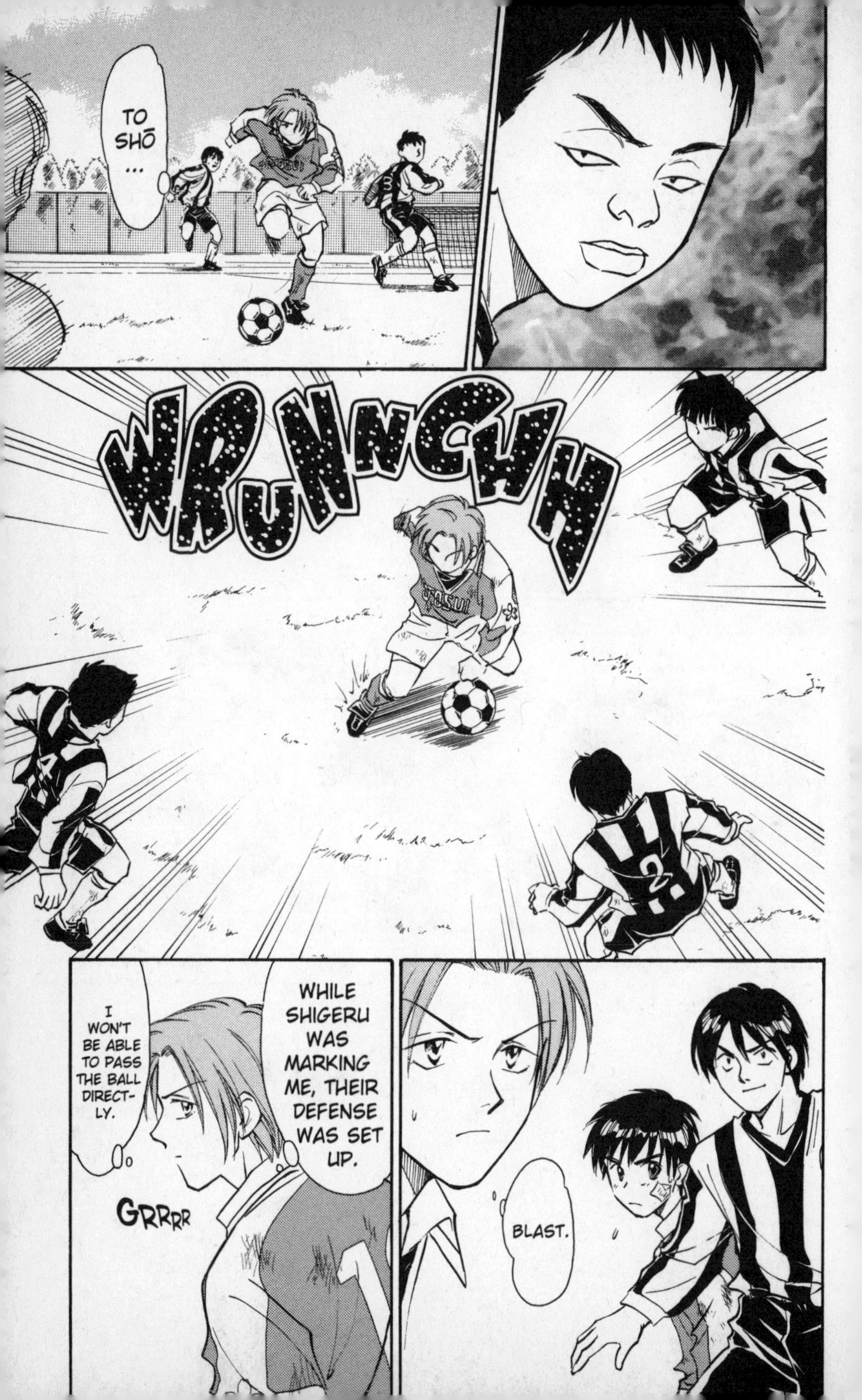
TO SHŌ ...
WRUNNCWH
BLAST.
WHILE SHIGERU WAS MARKING ME, THEIR DEFENSE WAS SET UP.
I WON'T BE ABLE TO PASS THE BALL DIRECTLY.
GRRRR

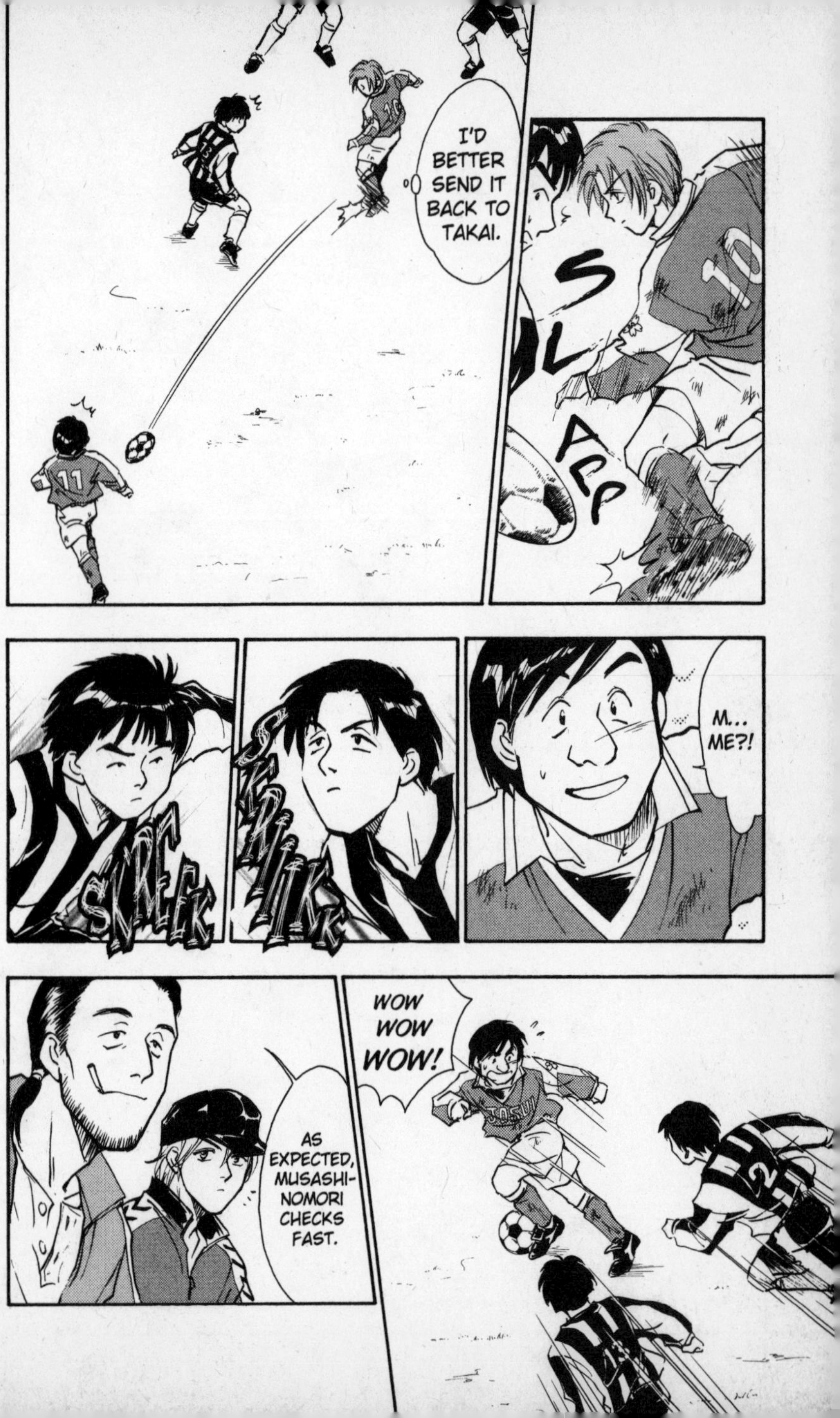
I'D BETTER SEND IT BACK TO TAKAI.
SLAPP
SKREEK
M... ME?!
AS EXPECTED, MUSASHINOMORI CHECKS FAST.
WOW WOW WOW!

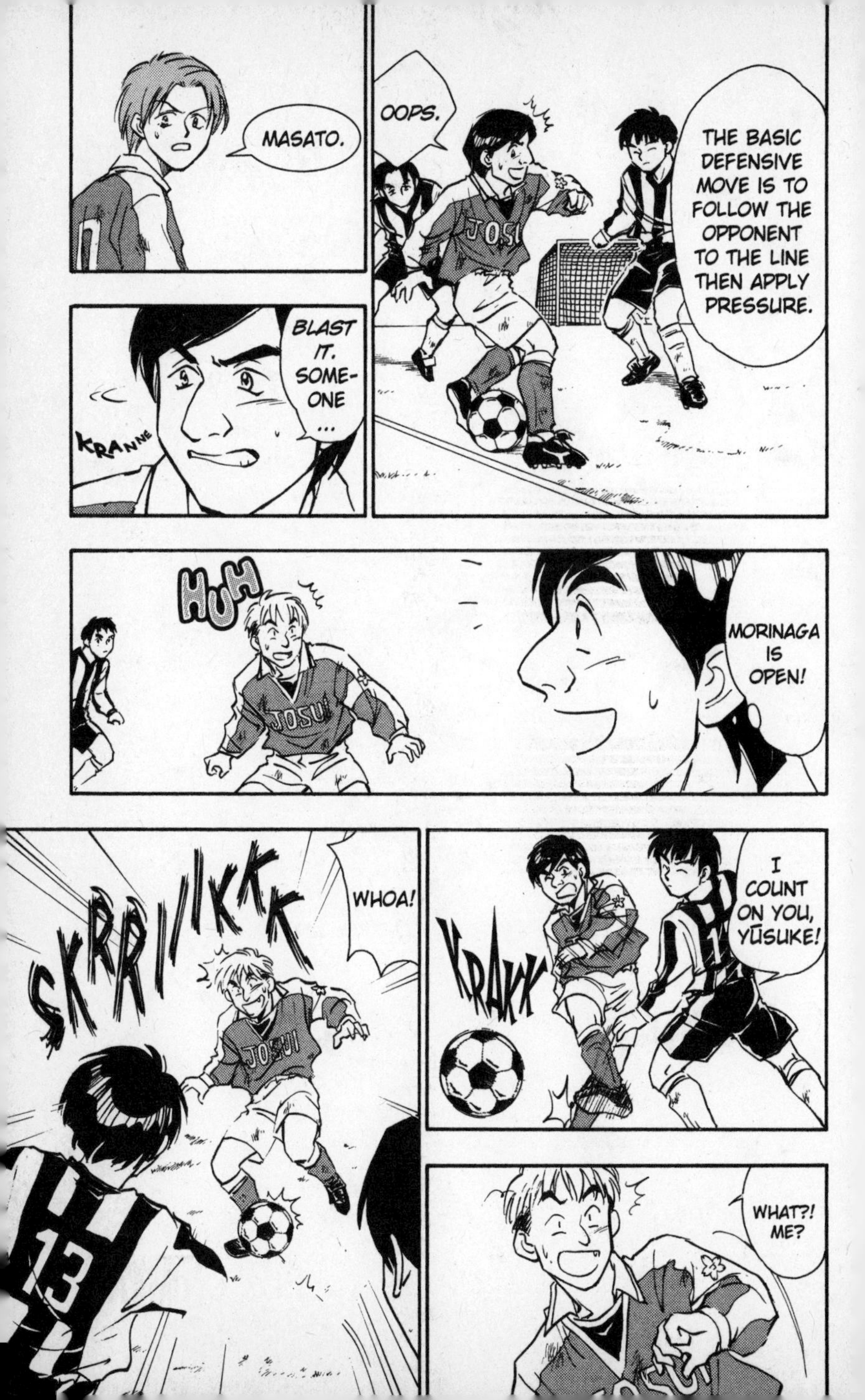
MASATO.
OOPS.
THE BASIC DEFENSIVE MOVE IS TO FOLLOW THE OPPONENT TO THE LINE THEN APPLY PRESSURE.
BLAST IT. SOME-ONE ...
KRANNE
HUH
MORINAGA IS OPEN!
SKRRIIKKK
WHOA!
KRAKK
I COUNT ON YOU, YŪSUKE!
WHAT?! ME?

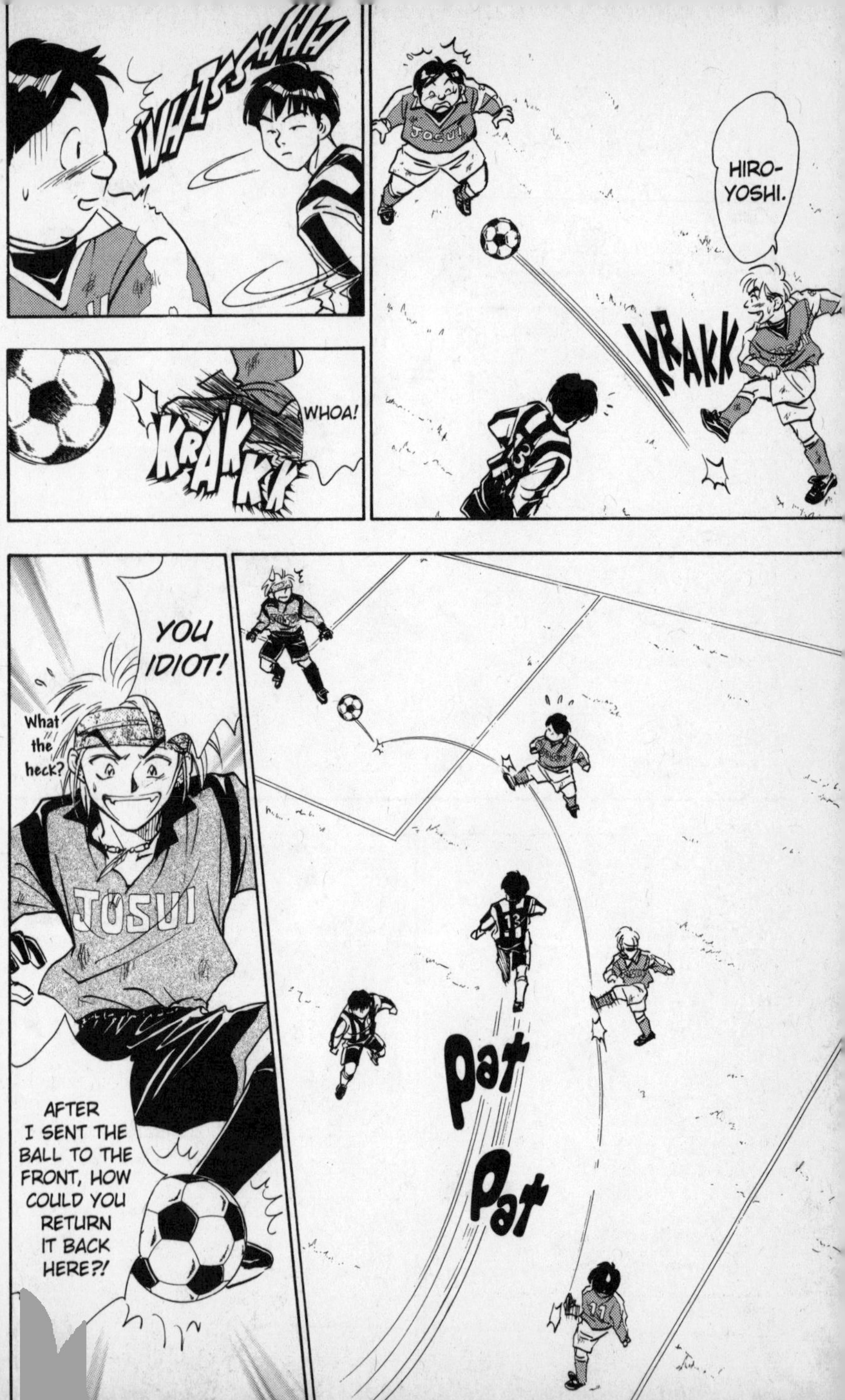
HIRO-
YOSHI.
KRAKK
WHISSHH
KRAKKK
WHOA!
Pat
Pat
YOU IDIOT!
What the heck?
AFTER I SENT THE BALL TO THE FRONT, HOW COULD YOU RETURN IT BACK HERE?!

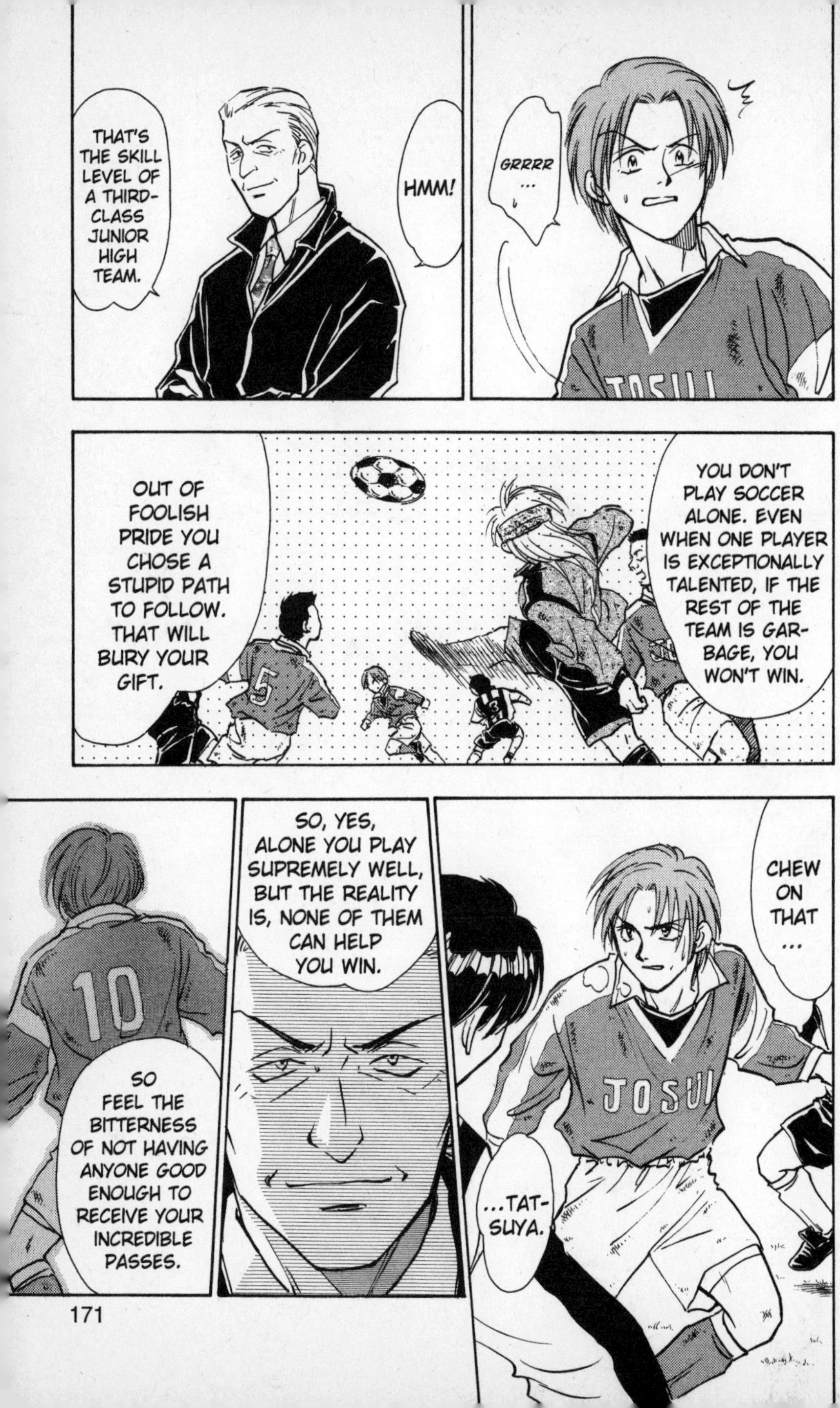
THAT'S THE SKILL LEVEL OF A THIRD-CLASS JUNIOR HIGH TEAM.
HMM!
GRRRR ...
OUT OF FOOLISH PRIDE YOU CHOSE A STUPID PATH TO FOLLOW. THAT WILL BURY YOUR GIFT.
YOU DON'T PLAY SOCCER ALONE. EVEN WHEN ONE PLAYER IS EXCEPTIONALLY TALENTED, IF THE REST OF THE TEAM IS GAR-BAGE, YOU WON'T WIN.
SO, YES, ALONE YOU PLAY SUPREMELY WELL, BUT THE REALITY IS, NONE OF THEM CAN HELP YOU WIN.
SO FEEL THE BITTERNESS OF NOT HAVING ANYONE GOOD ENOUGH TO RECEIVE YOUR INCREDIBLE PASSES.
CHEW ON THAT ...
...TAT-SUYA.
JOSUI

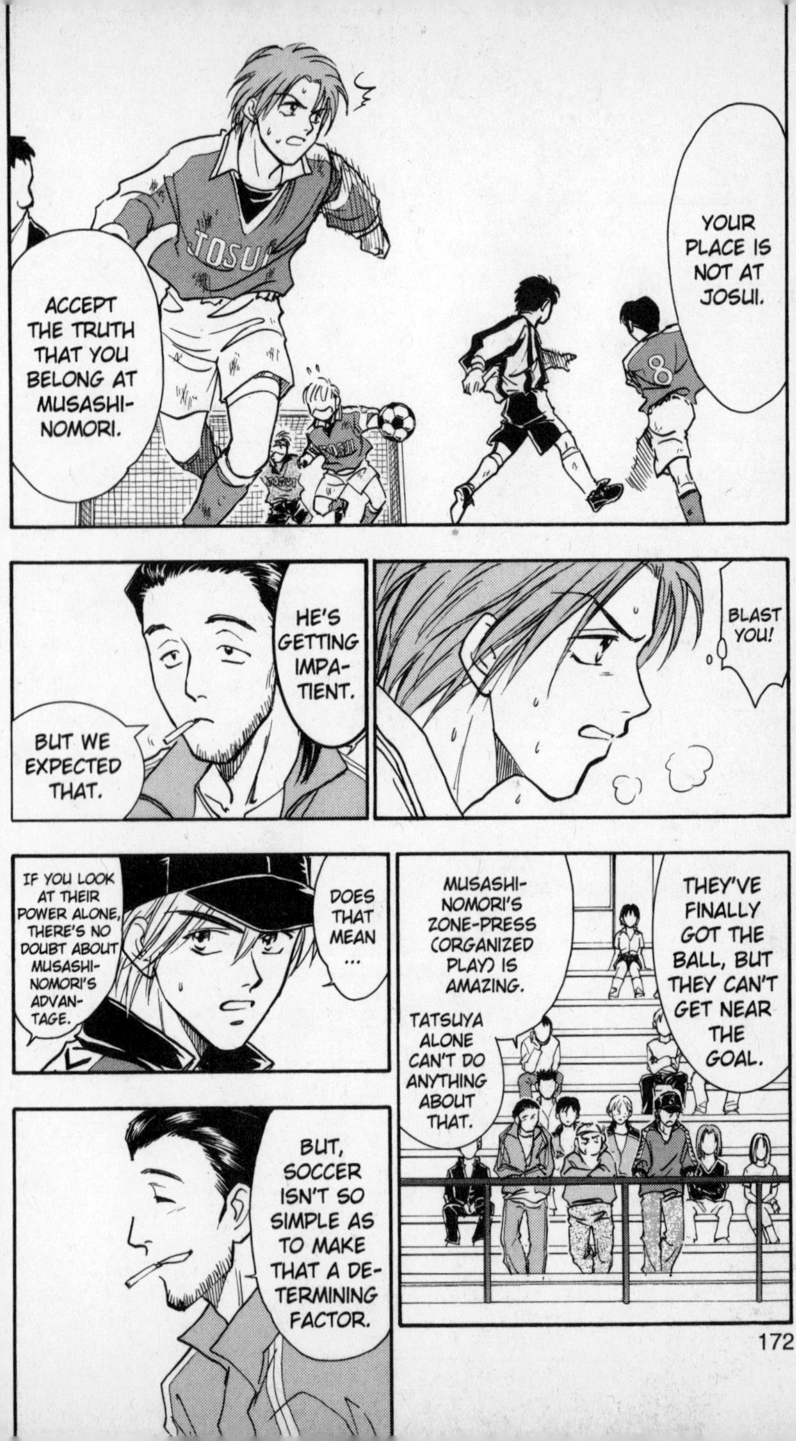

ACCEPT THE TRUTH THAT YOU BELONG AT MUSASHI-NOMORI.
YOUR PLACE IS NOT AT JOSUI.
JOSUI
HE'S GETTING IMPA-TIENT.
BUT WE EXPECTED THAT.
BLAST YOU!
IF YOU LOOK AT THEIR POWER ALONE, THERE'S NO DOUBT ABOUT MUSASHI-NOMORI'S ADVAN-TAGE.
DOES THAT MEAN ...
MUSASHI-NOMORI'S ZONE-PRESS (ORGANIZED PLAY) IS AMAZING.
THEY'VE FINALLY GOT THE BALL, BUT THEY CAN'T GET NEAR THE GOAL.
TATSUYA ALONE CAN'T DO ANYTHING ABOUT THAT.
BUT, SOCCER ISN'T SO SIMPLE AS TO MAKE THAT A DE-TERMINING FACTOR.

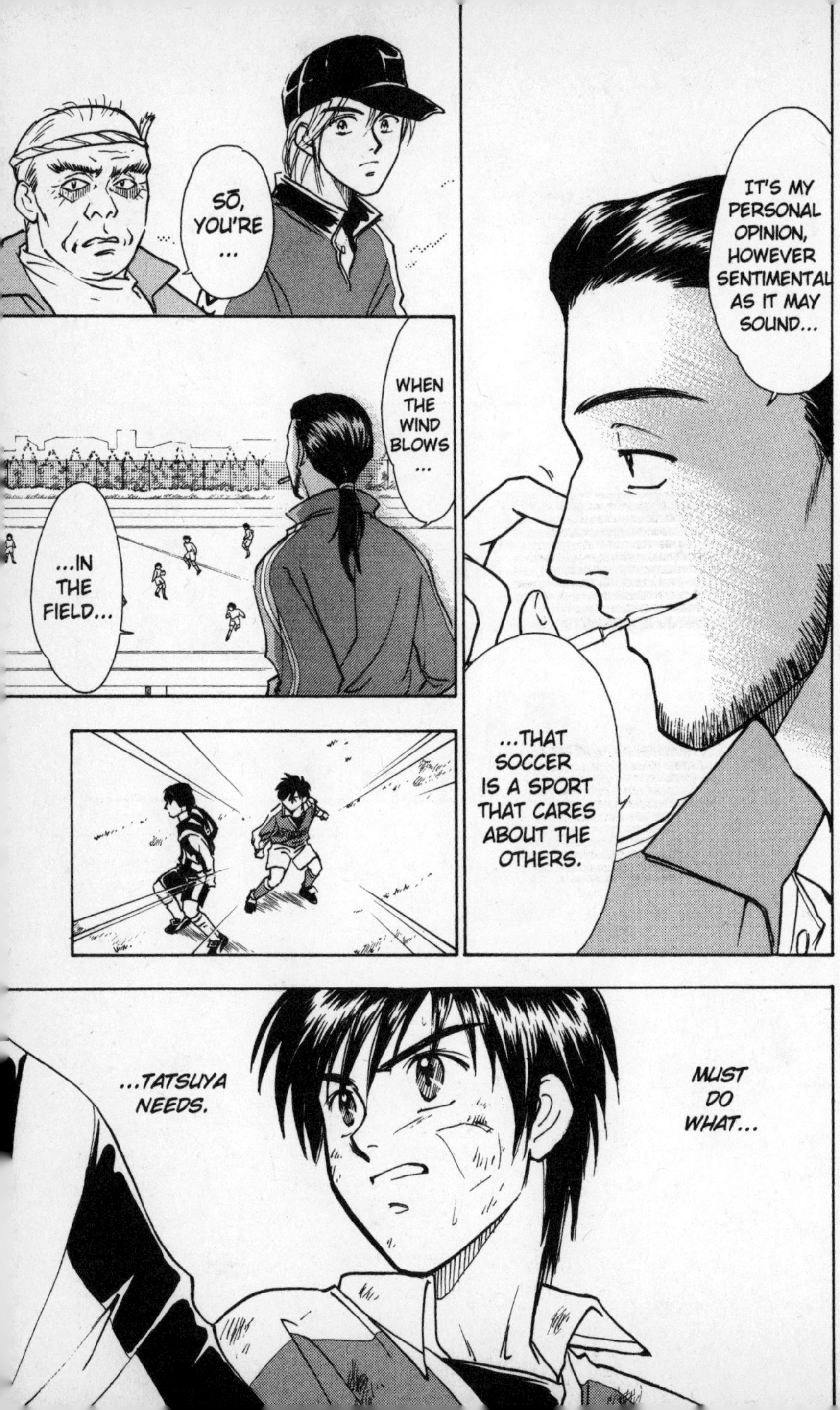
IT'S MY PERSONAL OPINION, HOWEVER SENTIMENTAL AS IT MAY SOUND...
...THAT SOCCER IS A SPORT THAT CARES ABOUT THE OTHERS.
SŌ, YOU'RE ...
WHEN THE WIND BLOWS ...
...IN THE FIELD...
MUST DO WHAT...
...TATSUYA NEEDS.

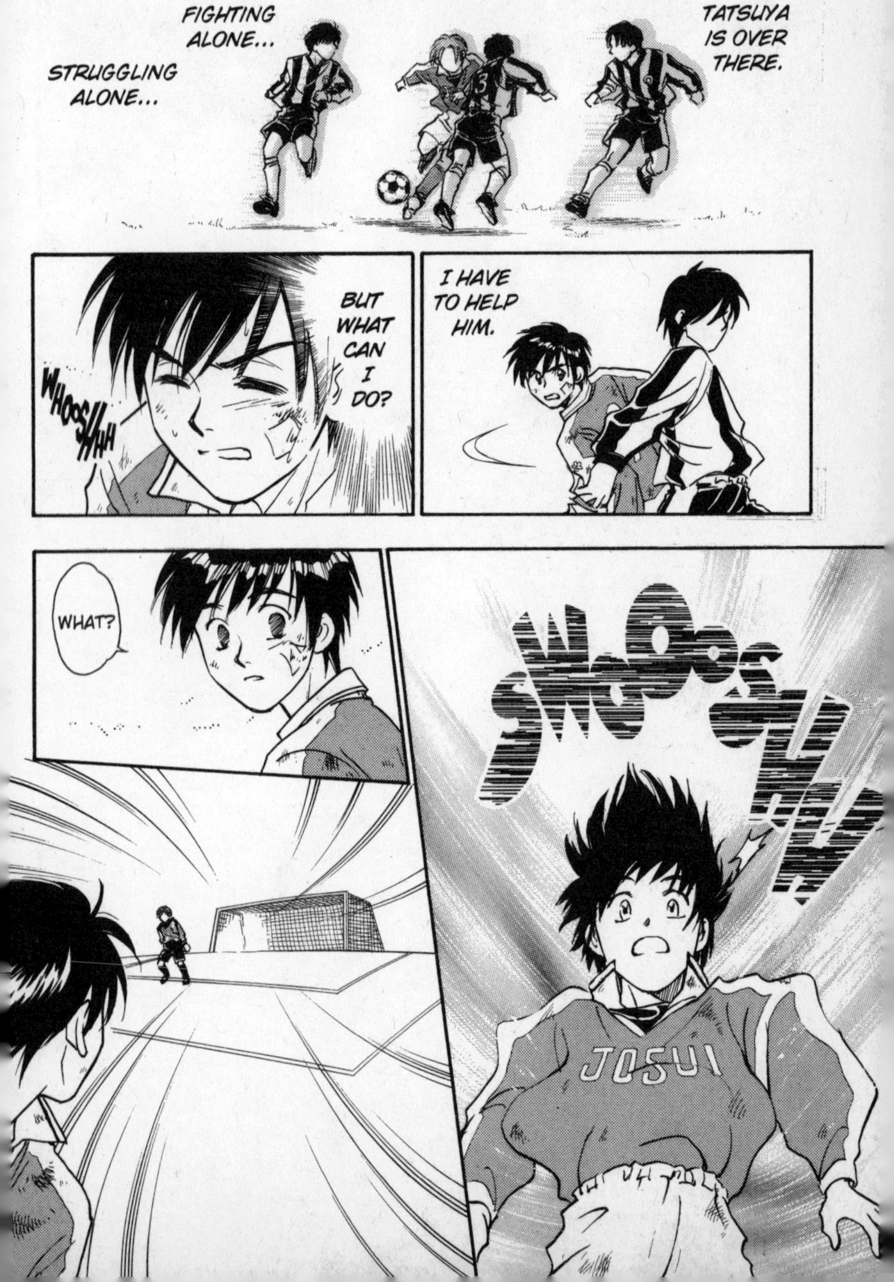

TATSUYA IS OVER THERE.
FIGHTING ALONE...
STRUGGLING ALONE...
I HAVE TO HELP HIM.
BUT WHAT CAN I DO?
WHOOSHHH
WHAT?
SWOOOSH
JOSUI

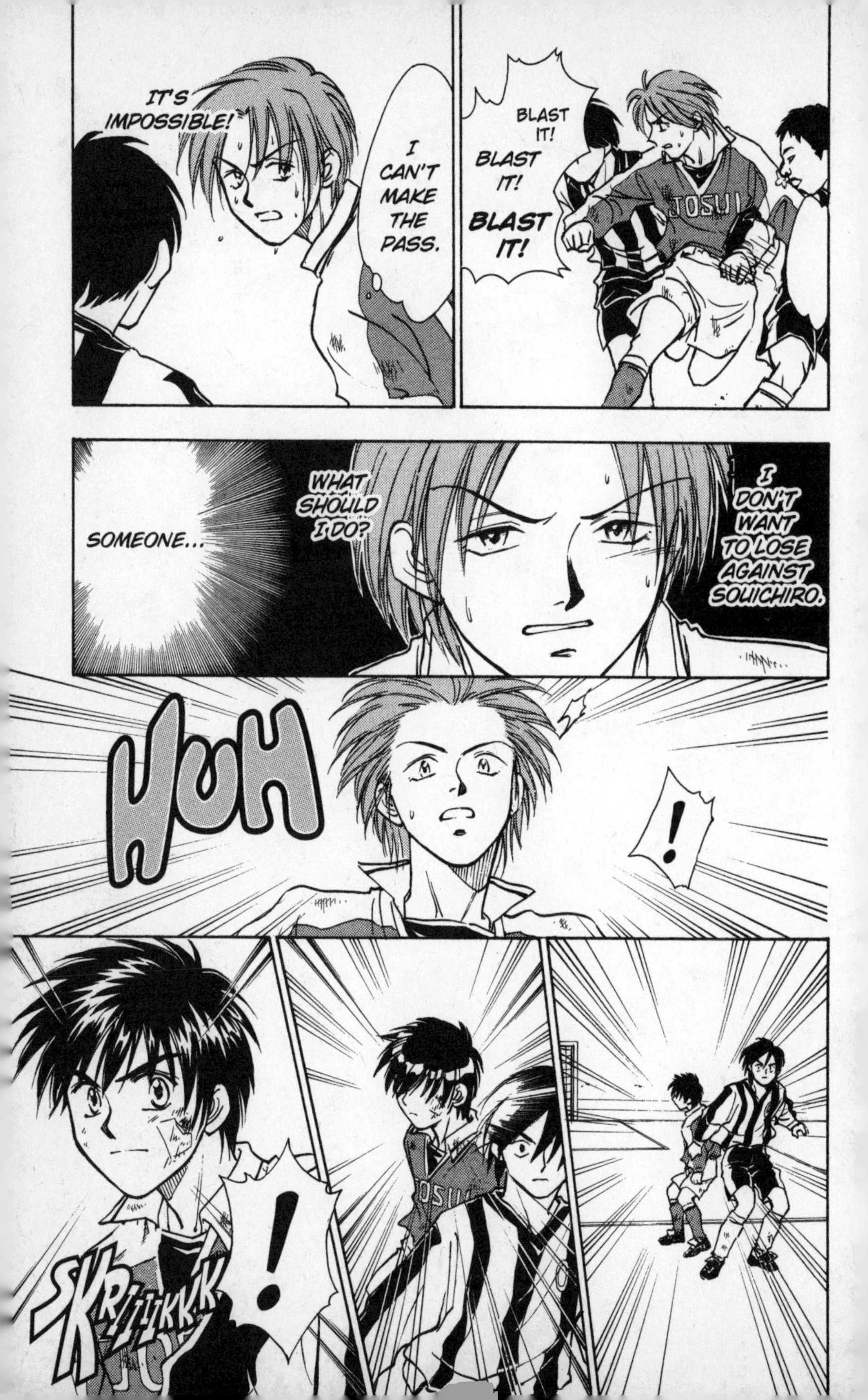
BLAST IT! BLAST IT! BLAST IT!
IT'S IMPOSSIBLE!
I CAN'T MAKE THE PASS.
I DON'T WANT TO LOSE AGAINST SOUICHIRO.
WHAT SHOULD I DO?
SOMEONE...
!
HUH
!
SKRIIIKKK

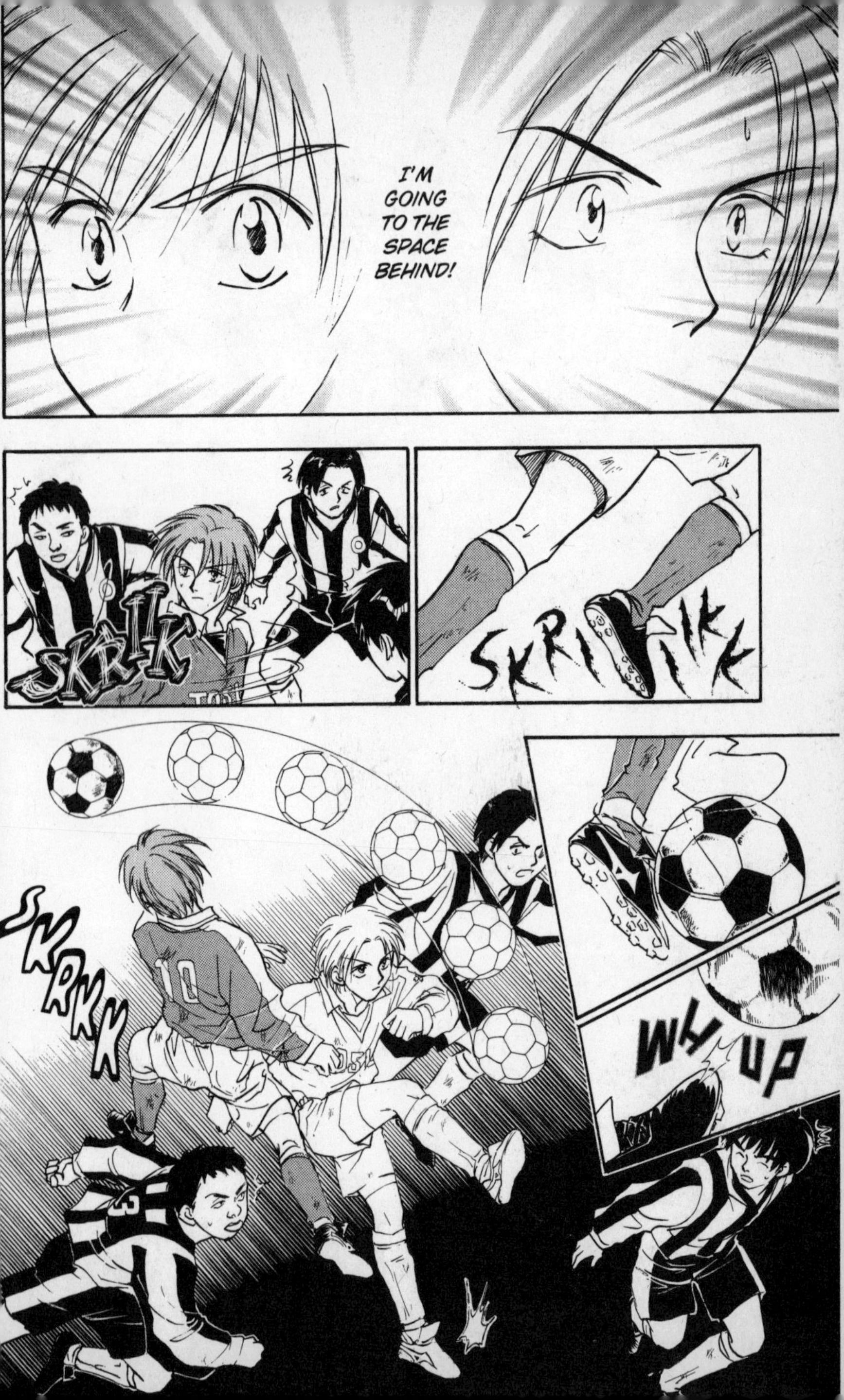
I'M GOING TO THE SPACE BEHIND!
SKRIK
SKRIIKK
SKRKK
WHUP

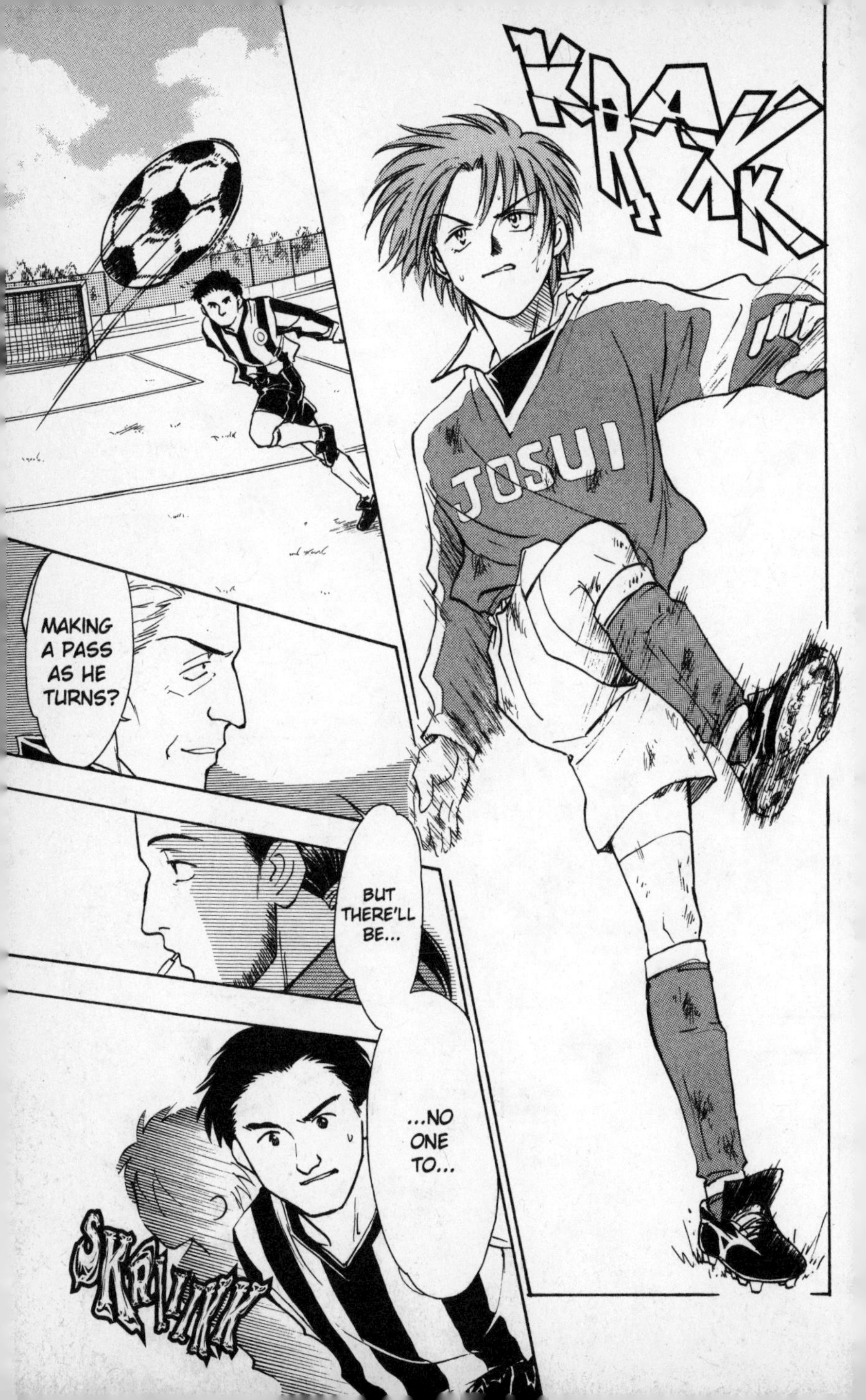
KRAAK
MAKING A PASS AS HE TURNS?
BUT THERE'LL BE...
...NO ONE TO...

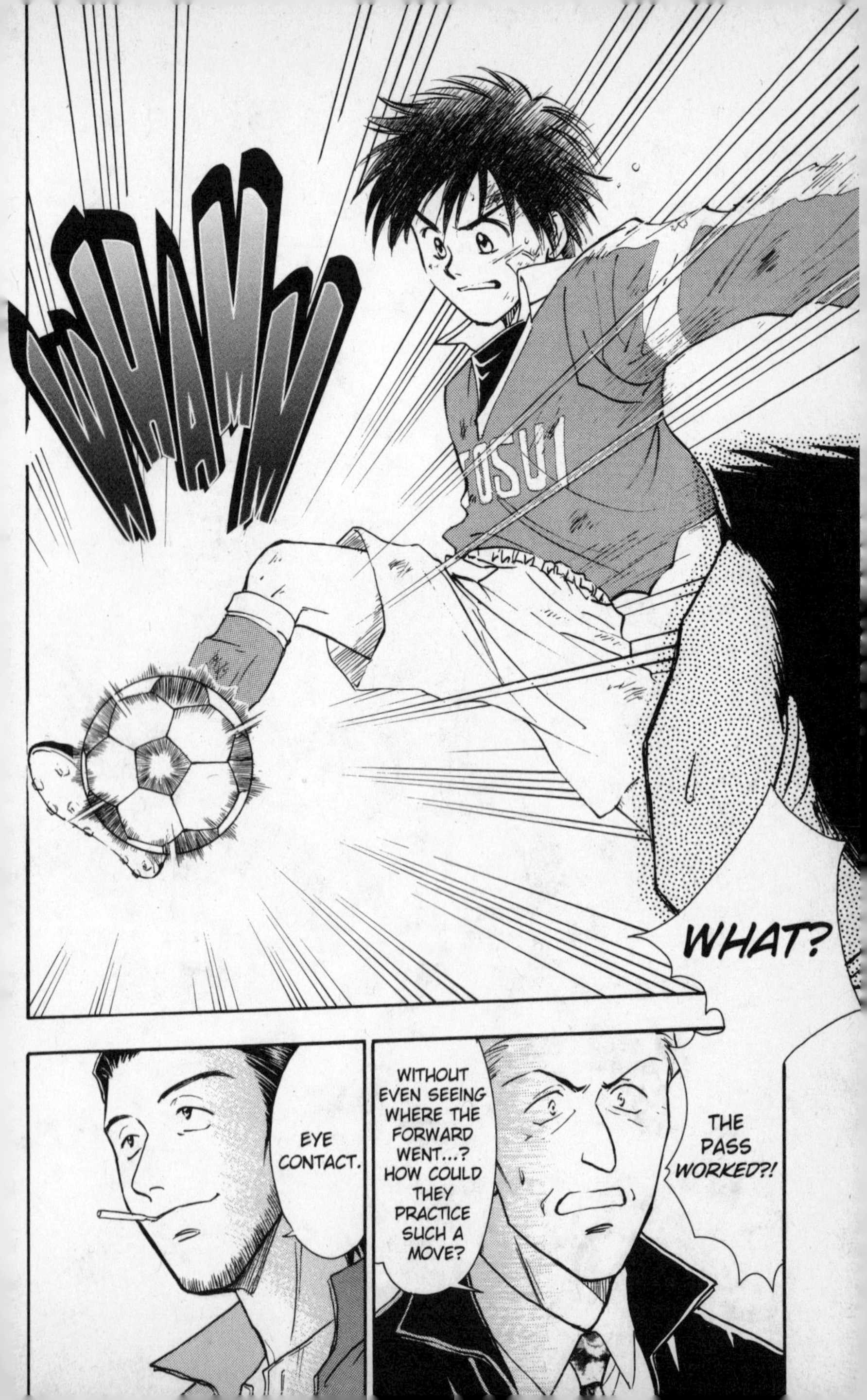
WHAMM
WHAT?
THE PASS WORKED?!
WITHOUT EVEN SEEING WHERE THE FORWARD WENT...? HOW COULD THEY PRACTICE SUCH A MOVE?
EYE CONTACT.

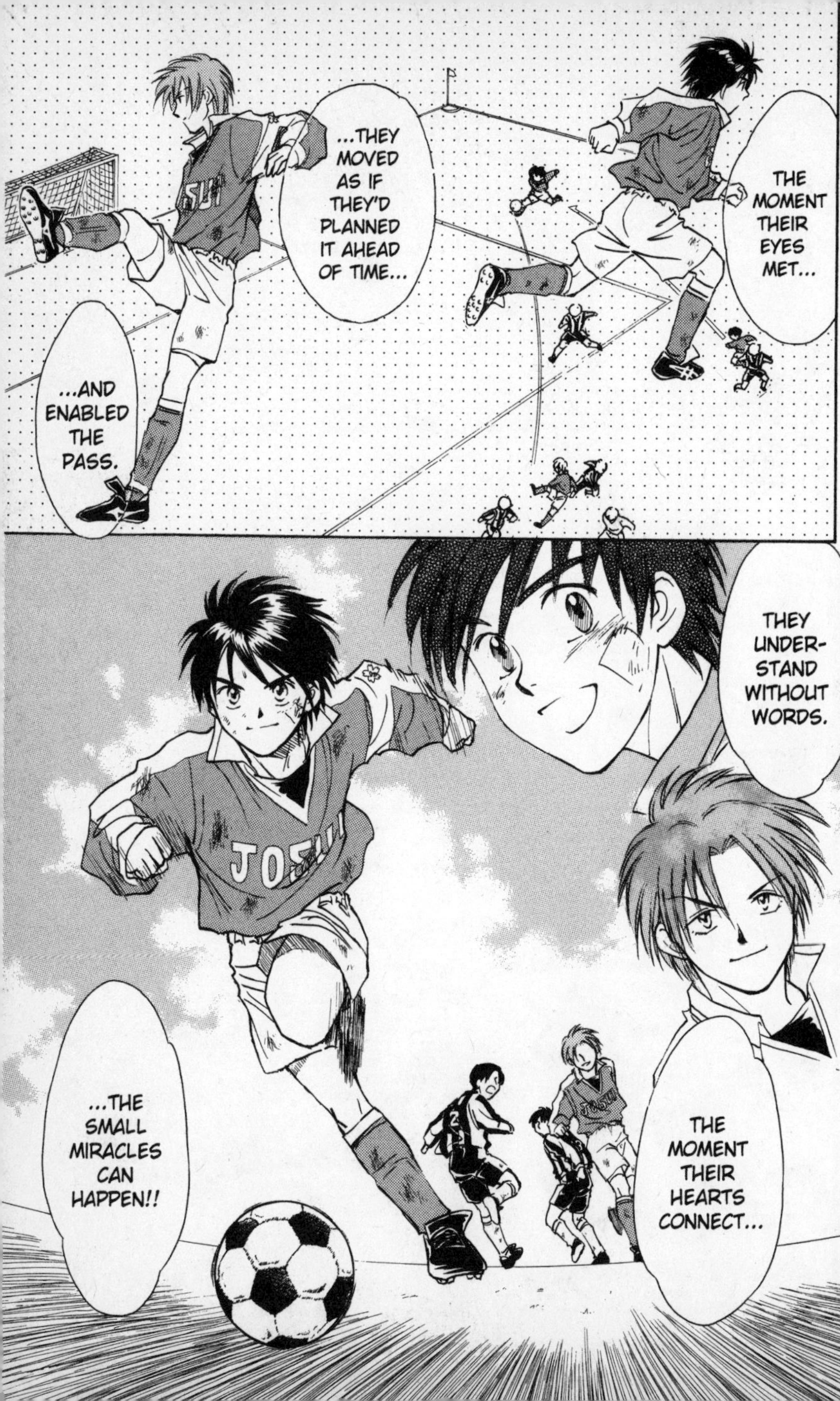
THE MOMENT THEIR EYES MET...
...THEY MOVED AS IF THEY'D PLANNED IT AHEAD OF TIME...
...AND ENABLED THE PASS.
THEY UNDER-STAND WITHOUT WORDS.
THE MOMENT THEIR HEARTS CONNECT...
...THE SMALL MIRACLES CAN HAPPEN!!

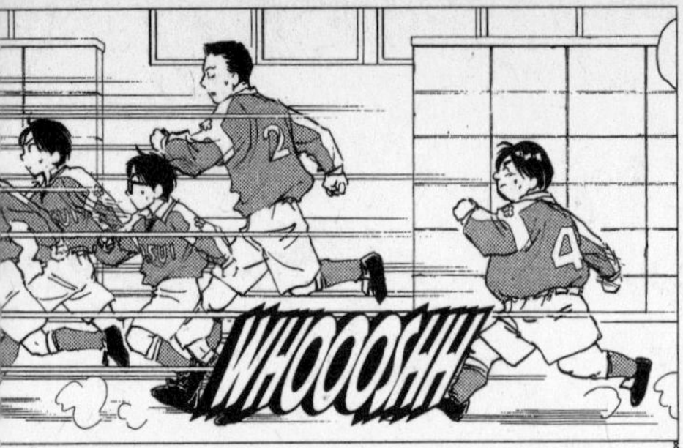
WHOOOSH

WE CARE

EPISODE OF SHOES PART.2

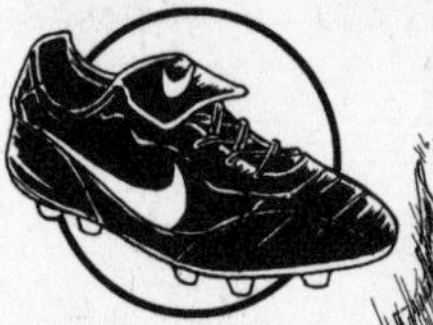

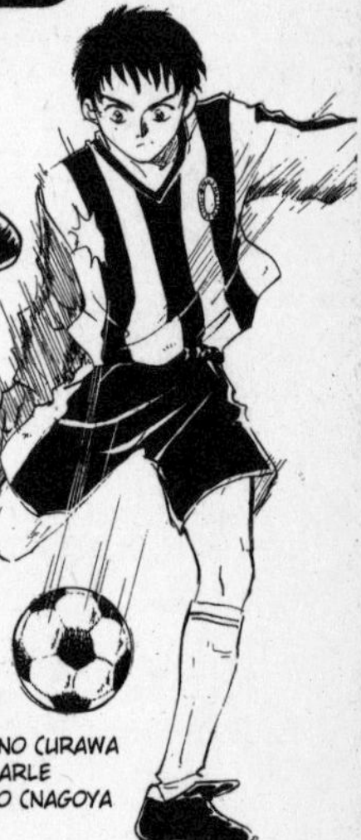

THE ONES WHO FAVOR [*ADIDAS*] ARE, HANAZAWA, TANAKA AND TOYAMA. AMONG THE JAPANESE REPRESENTATIVE, THE PLAYER TOSHIHIDE SAITŌ (SHIMIZU ESPAL) AND THE PLAYER HIROSHI NANAMI (JUBIRO IWATA) USE THE MAKE. (I HEAR THE MODEL USED BY FAMOUS PLAYER NANAMI IS ESPECIALLY POPULAR.)

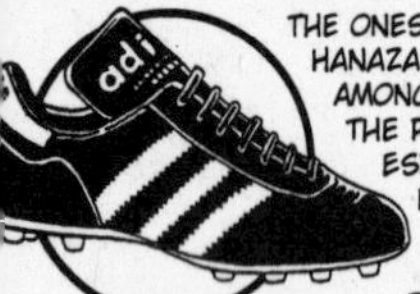

RECENTLY, [*NIKE*] IS GETTING BIG. BESIDES FUJISHIRO, AKIRA, CHIKAMORI, NAKANISHI AND TAKADA USE THE BRAND. THERE ARE MANY PLAYERS AMONG JAPANESE REPRESENTATIVES WHO USE THE SAME. THE PLAYER SHŌJI JŌ USES BLUE NIKE, THE PLAYER MASAMI IHARA (BOTH YOKOHAMA MARINOS). NICE FIGHT USED TO BE WORN BY THE PLAYER EISUKE NAKANISHI (JEFF ICHIHARA). OTHERS WHO USE NIKE ARE THE PLAYER AKIRA NARAHASHI (KASHIMA ANTLERS), THE PLAYER TERUYOSHI ITŌ (SHIMIZU ESPALS), THE PLAYER SHINJI ONO (URAWA LEZZU), THE PLAYER WAGNER ROBESU (BELMARLE HIRATSUKA), AND THE PLAYER TAKASHI HIRANO (NAGOYA GRANDPASS).

TALKING ABOUT SOCCER SHOES, WHEN I WAS A GRADE SCHOOL STUDENT, WE USED [*PUMA*]. THIS MAKE IS USED BY JOSUI'S PLAYER, KOGA, AND MUSASHINOMORI'S PLAYERS, SHIBUSAWA, NEGISHI, SHIGERU, KAWAI, TATSUMI, ŌMORI. AMONG THE JAPANESE REPRESENTATIVES, THE PLAYER MASASHI NAKAYAMA, WHO MADE THE VERY FIRST GOAL AT THE WORLD CUP, AND THE PLAYER TOSHIHIRO HATTORI (BOTH JUBIRO IWATA) USE THE MAKE.

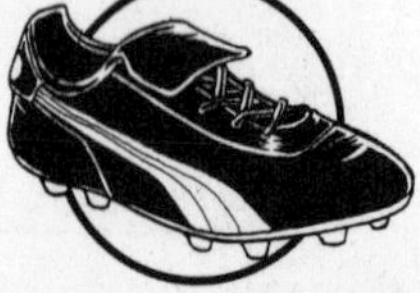

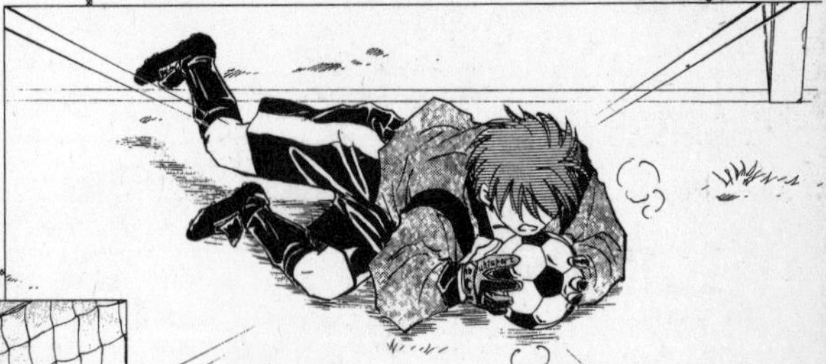

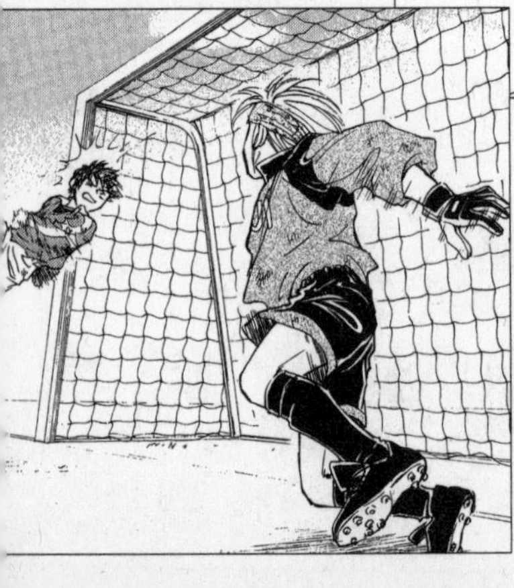

SHIGE USES [*LOTTO*]. I BELIEVE IT'S AN ITALIAN MAKE. IF YOU KNOW ANY JAPANESE PLAYER WHO USES IT, PLEASE LET ME KNOW.

THIS SUBJECT MATTER IS A PART OF THE MANGA YOU'RE READING, BUT WHEN YOU ACTUALLY WATCH A REAL SOCCER GAME, YOU MIGHT WANT TO PAY ATTENTION TO THESE TYPE OF DETAILS. YOU MIGHT FIND IT INTERESTING.

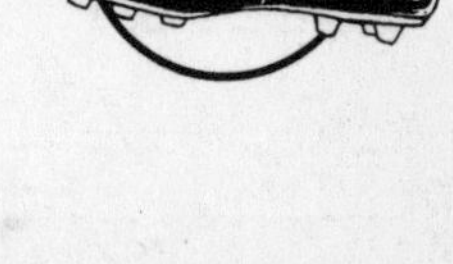

THANKS FOR THE ADVICE REGARDING THE SHOES AND WHO WEARS THEM, K-KUN.

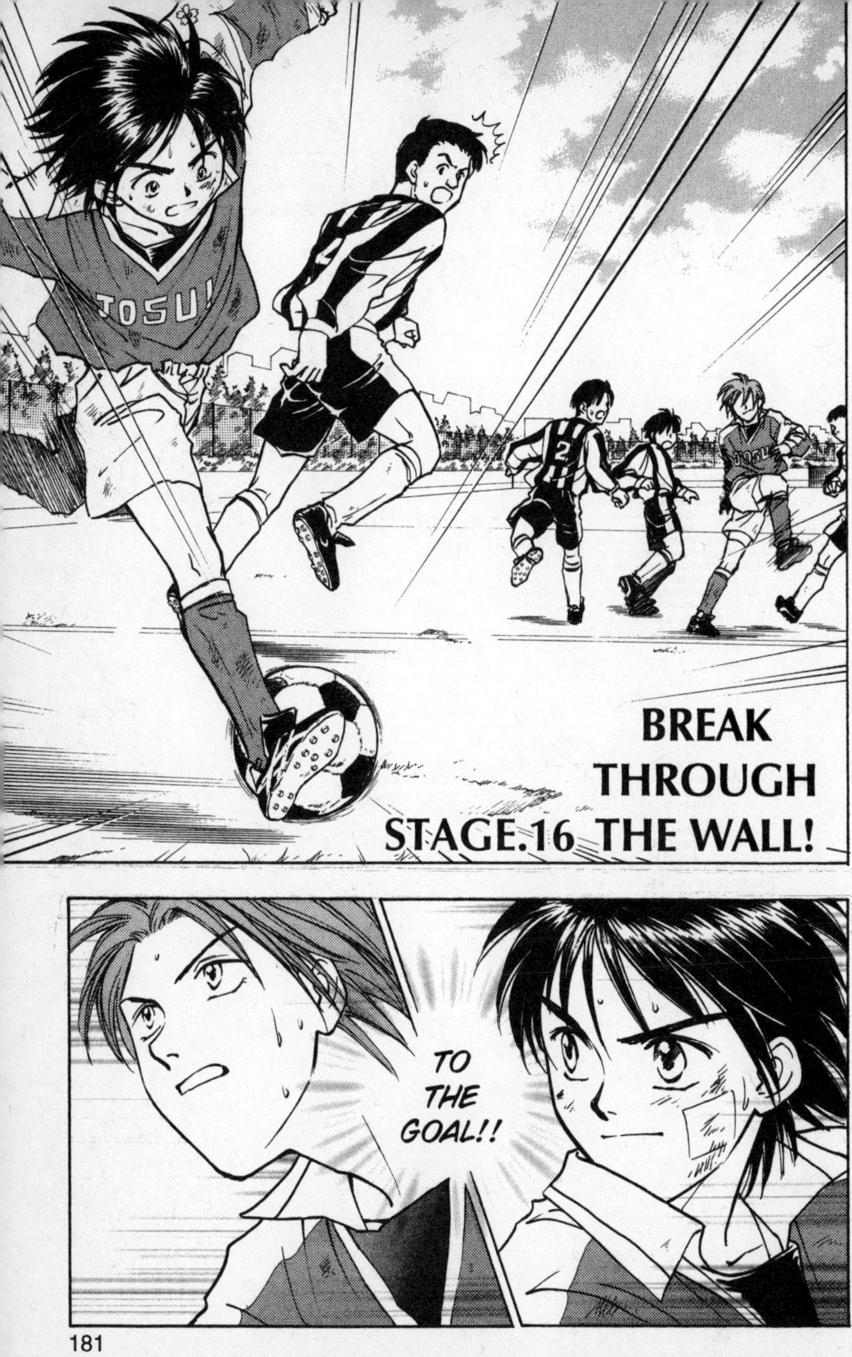
BREAK THROUGH THE WALL!
STAGE.16
TO THE GOAL!!

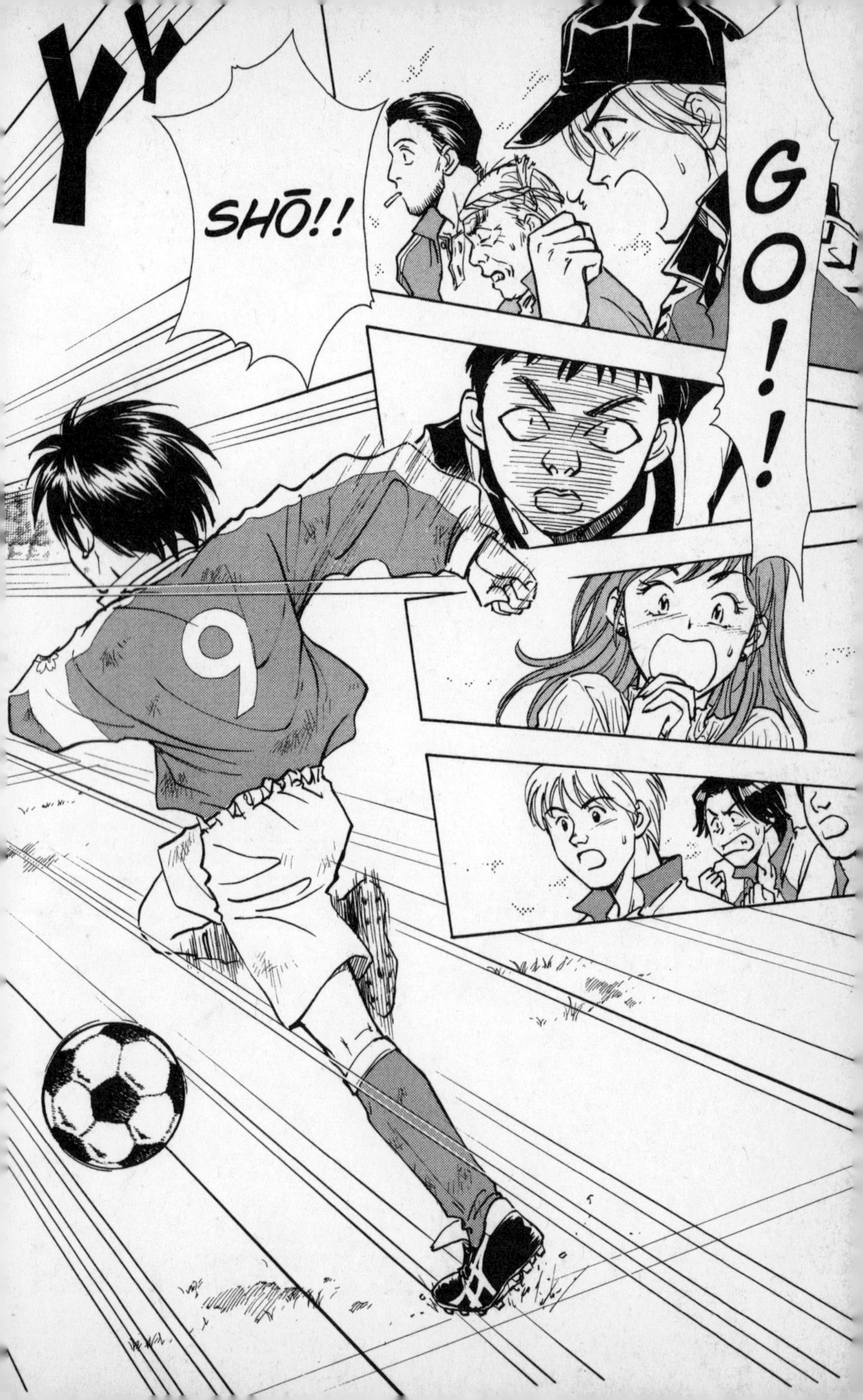
SHŌ!!
GO!!

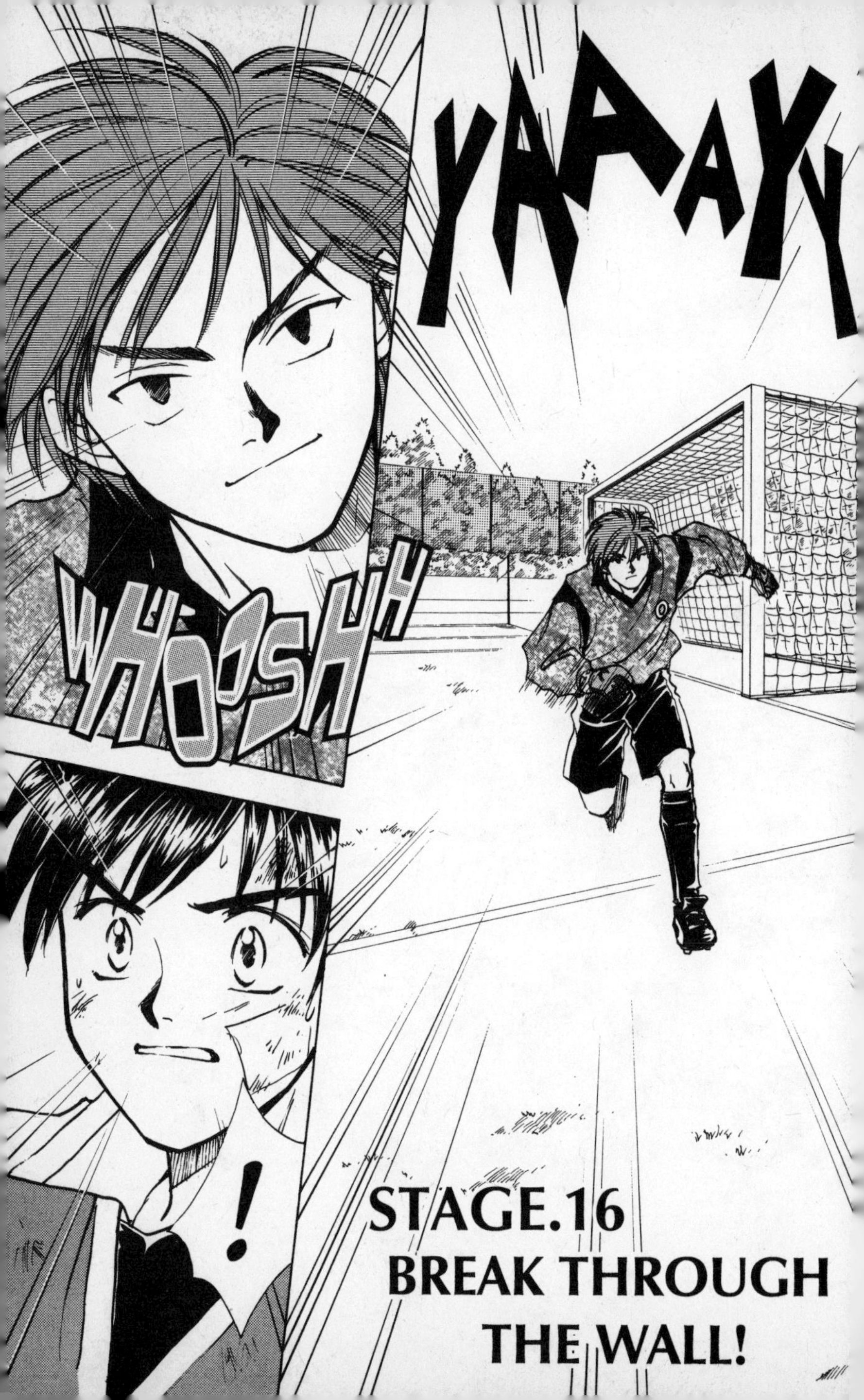
WHOOSH
!
STAGE.16
BREAK THROUGH
THE WALL!

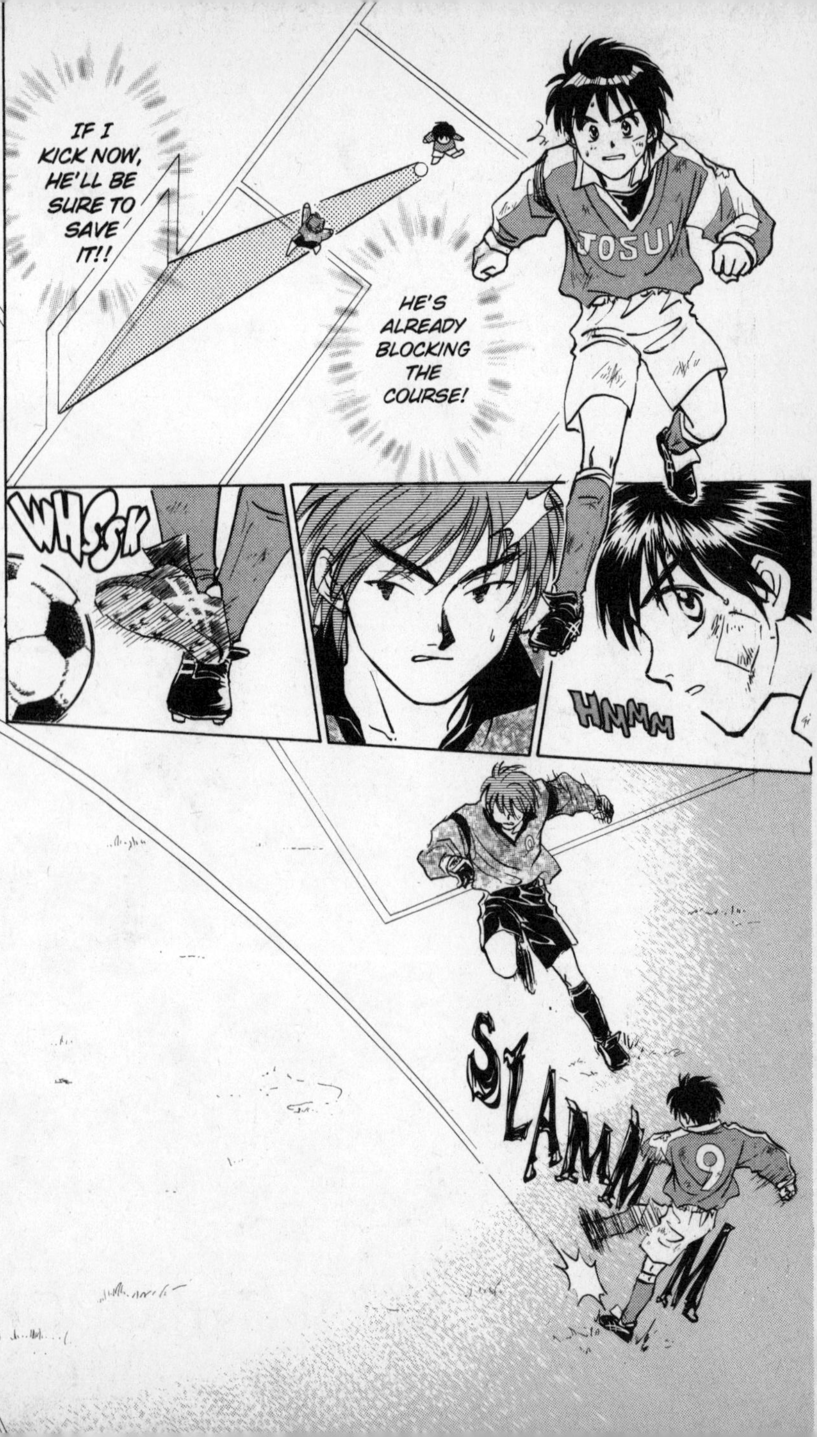
HE'S ALREADY BLOCKING THE COURSE!
IF I KICK NOW, HE'LL BE SURE TO SAVE IT!!
JOSUI
HMMM
WHSSK
SLAMMM
9

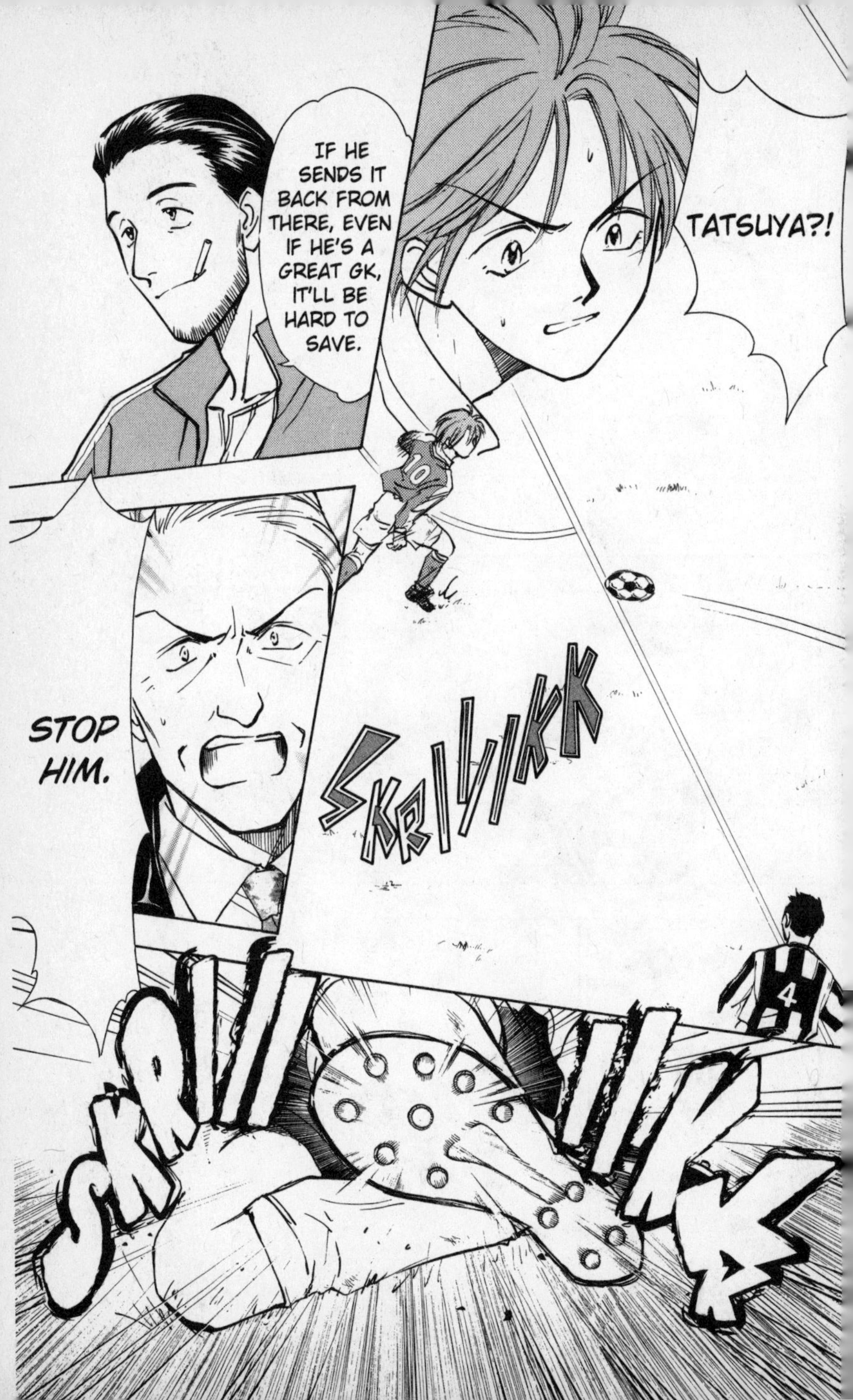

TATSUYA?!
IF HE SENDS IT BACK FROM THERE, EVEN IF HE'S A GREAT GK, IT'LL BE HARD TO SAVE.
STOP HIM.

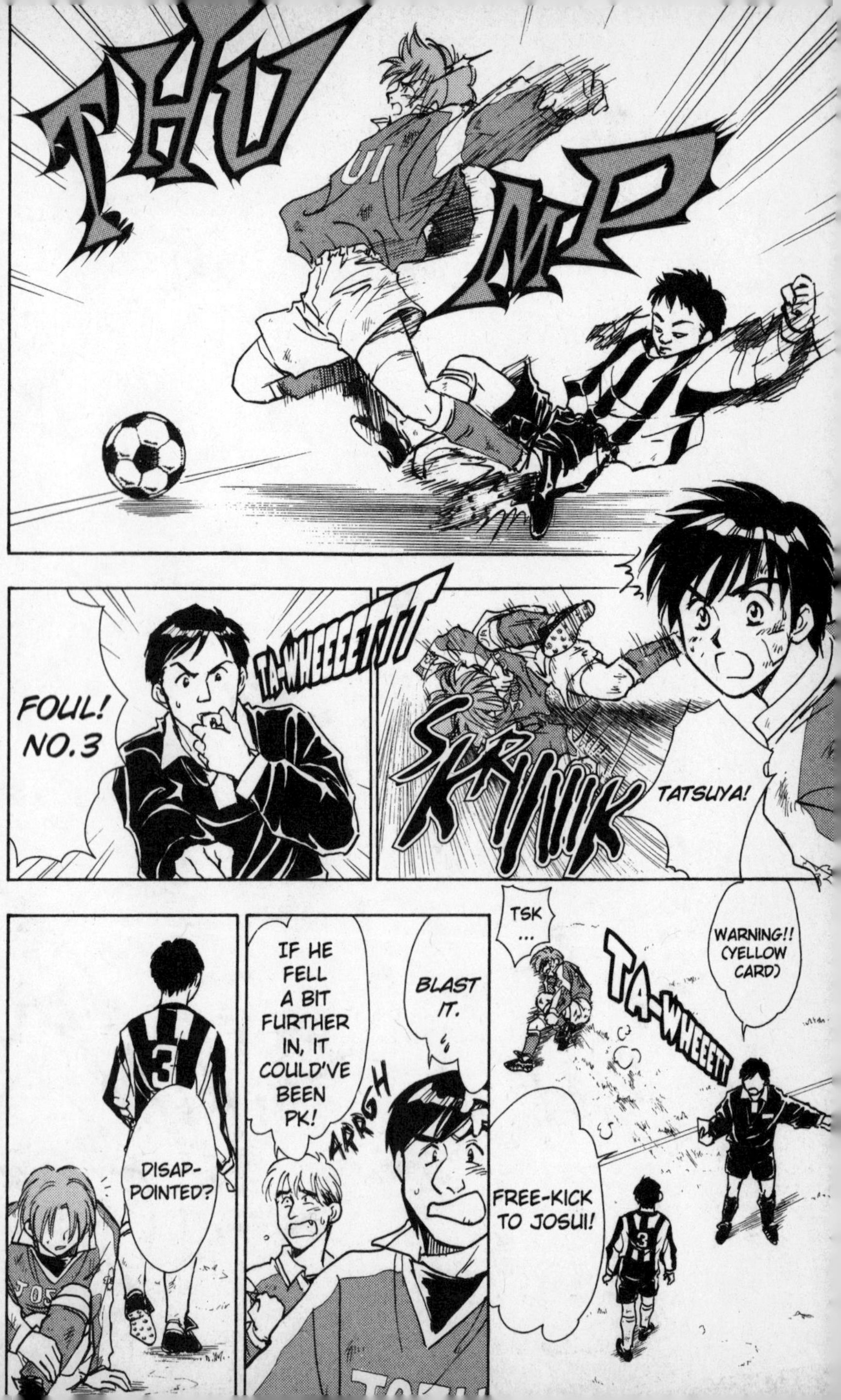
FOUL! NO.3
TATSUYA!
DISAP-POINTED?
IF HE FELL A BIT FURTHER IN, IT COULD'VE BEEN PK!
BLAST IT.
ARRGH
TSK ...
WARNING!! (YELLOW CARD)
FREE-KICK TO JOSUI!

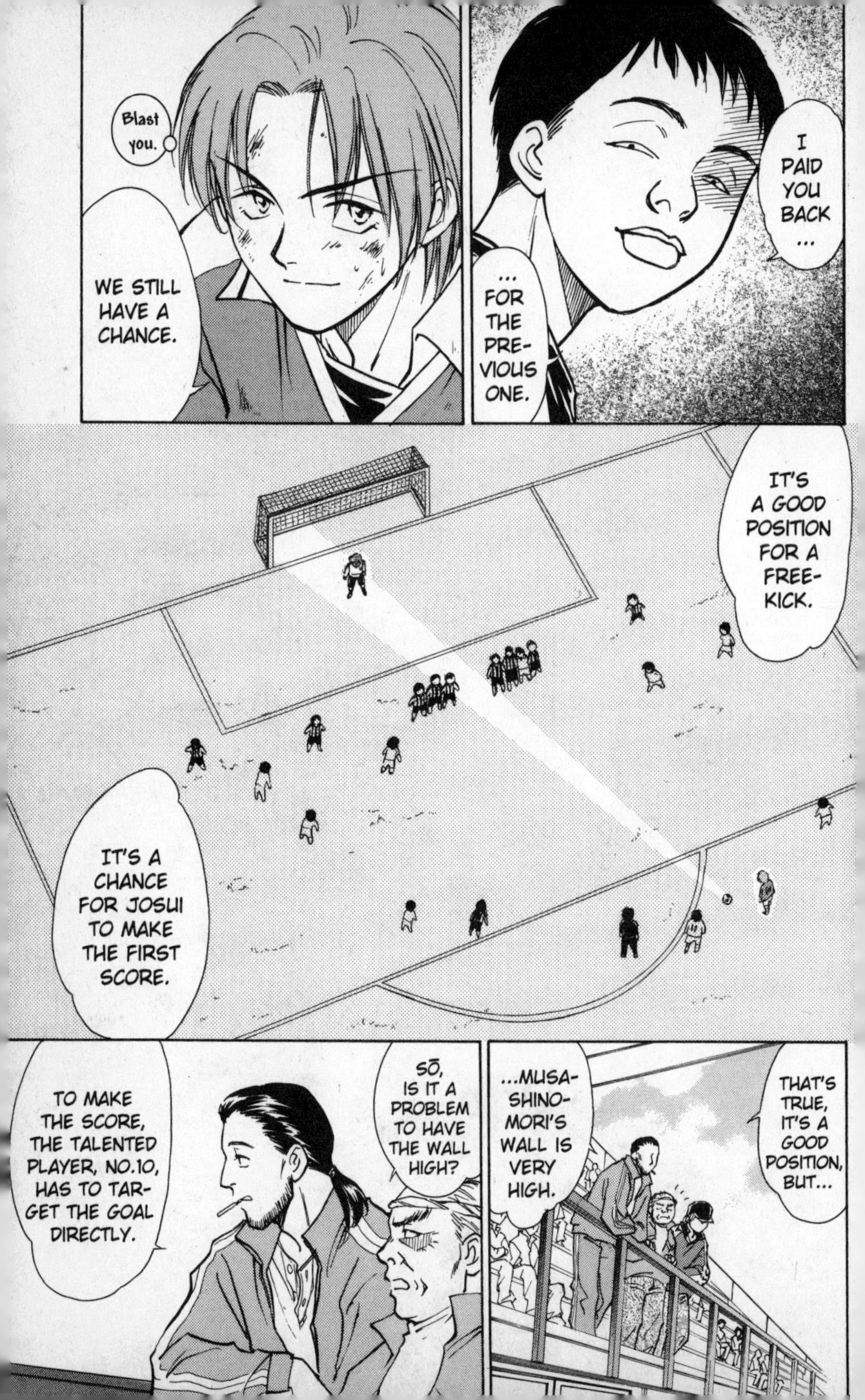
I PAID YOU BACK ...
... FOR THE PREVIOUS ONE.
Blast you.
WE STILL HAVE A CHANCE.
IT'S A GOOD POSITION FOR A FREE-KICK.
IT'S A CHANCE FOR JOSUI TO MAKE THE FIRST SCORE.
THAT'S TRUE, IT'S A GOOD POSITION, BUT...
...MUSASHINOMORI'S WALL IS VERY HIGH.
SŌ, IS IT A PROBLEM TO HAVE THE WALL HIGH?
TO MAKE THE SCORE, THE TALENTED PLAYER, NO.10, HAS TO TARGET THE GOAL DIRECTLY.

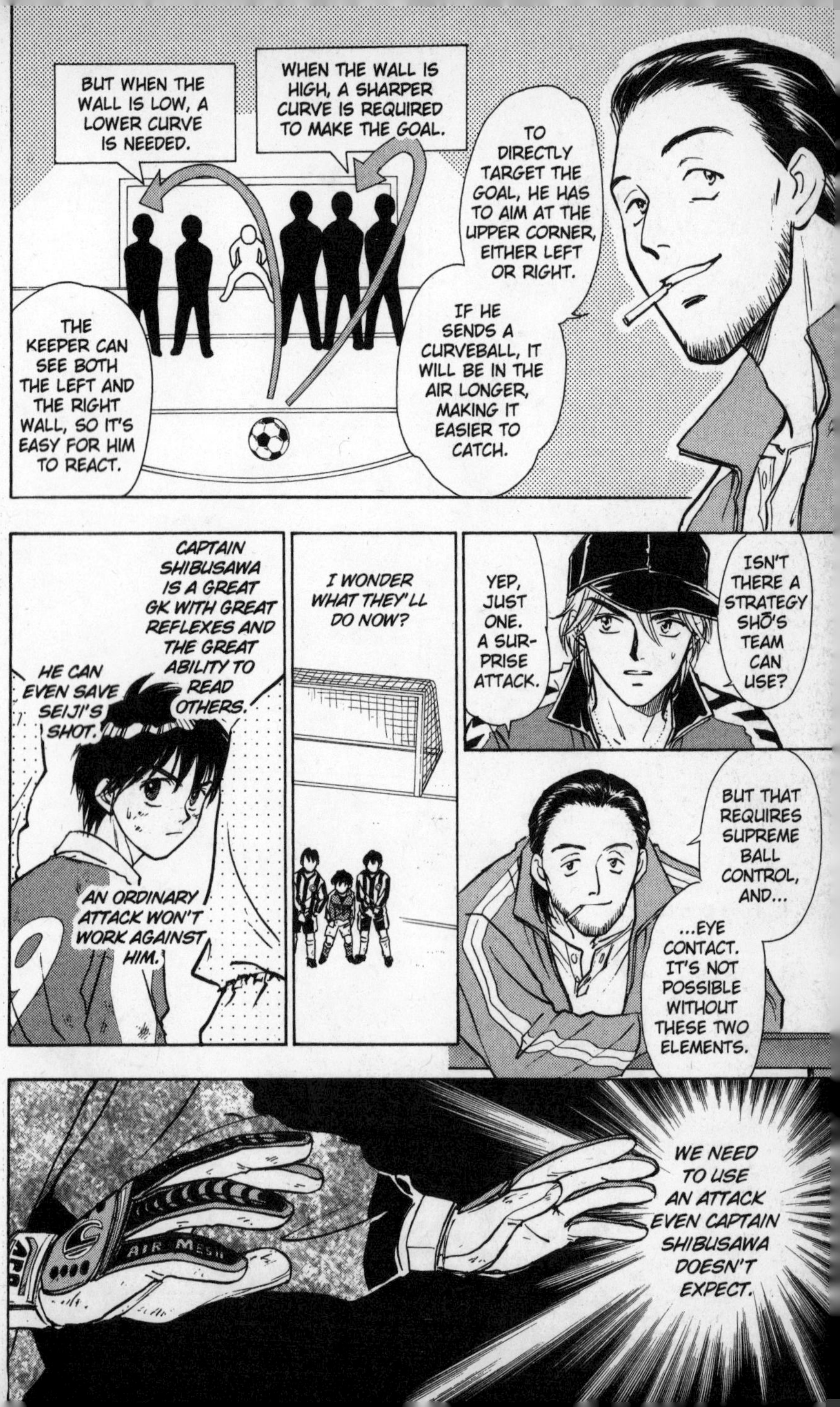
TO DIRECTLY TARGET THE GOAL, HE HAS TO AIM AT THE UPPER CORNER, EITHER LEFT OR RIGHT.
IF HE SENDS A CURVEBALL, IT WILL BE IN THE AIR LONGER, MAKING IT EASIER TO CATCH.
WHEN THE WALL IS HIGH, A SHARPER CURVE IS REQUIRED TO MAKE THE GOAL.
BUT WHEN THE WALL IS LOW, A LOWER CURVE IS NEEDED.
THE KEEPER CAN SEE BOTH THE LEFT AND THE RIGHT WALL, SO IT'S EASY FOR HIM TO REACT.
ISN'T THERE A STRATEGY SHŌ'S TEAM CAN USE?
YEP, JUST ONE. A SUR-PRISE ATTACK.
BUT THAT REQUIRES SUPREME BALL CONTROL, AND...
...EYE CONTACT. IT'S NOT POSSIBLE WITHOUT THESE TWO ELEMENTS.
I WONDER WHAT THEY'LL DO NOW?
CAPTAIN SHIBUSAWA IS A GREAT GK WITH GREAT REFLEXES AND THE GREAT ABILITY TO READ OTHERS.
HE CAN EVEN SAVE SEIJI'S SHOT.
AN ORDINARY ATTACK WON'T WORK AGAINST HIM.
WE NEED TO USE AN ATTACK EVEN CAPTAIN SHIBUSAWA DOESN'T EXPECT.
AIR MESH

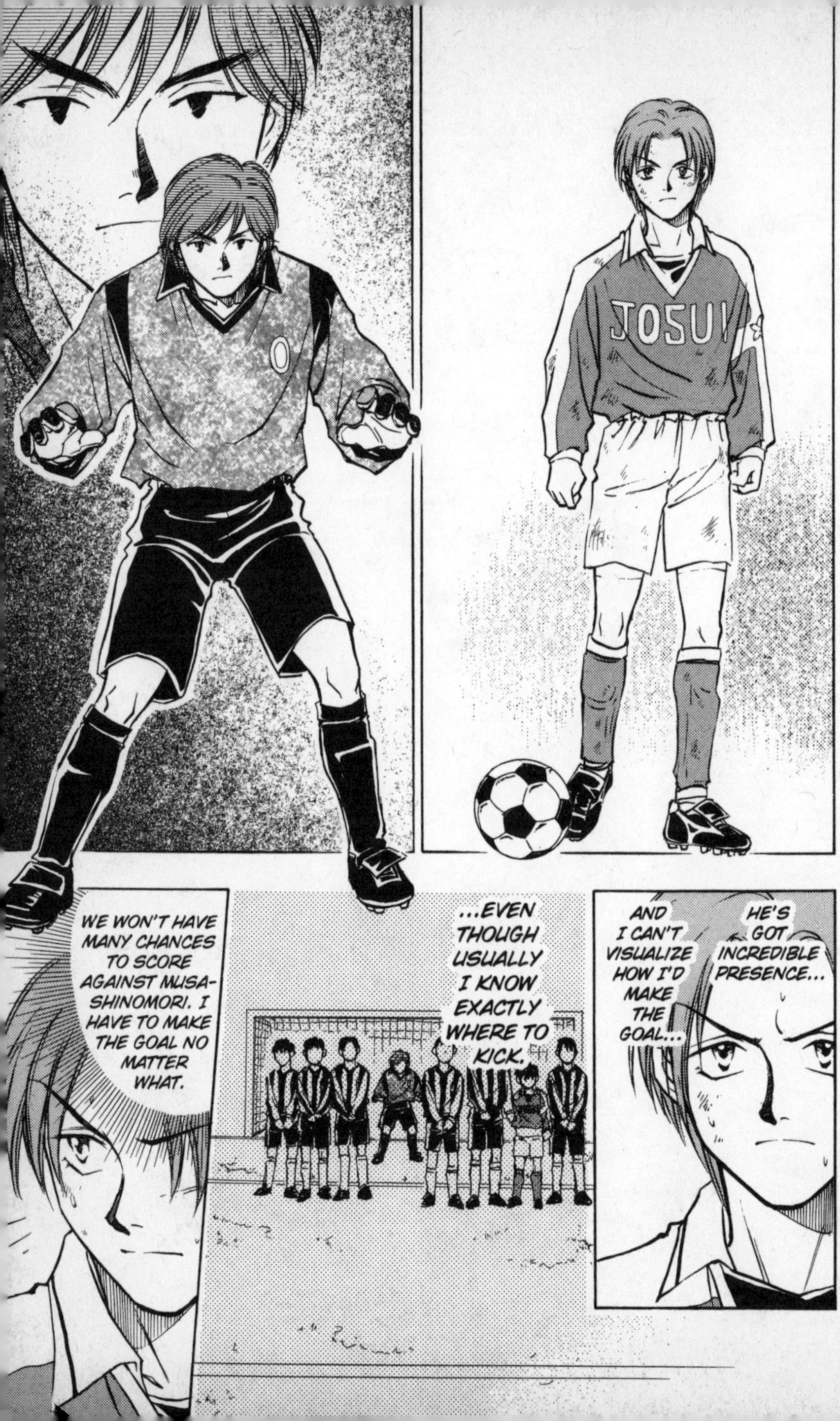
JOSUI
HE'S GOT INCREDIBLE PRESENCE...
AND I CAN'T VISUALIZE HOW I'D MAKE THE GOAL...
...EVEN THOUGH USUALLY I KNOW EXACTLY WHERE TO KICK.
WE WON'T HAVE MANY CHANCES TO SCORE AGAINST MUSA-SHINOMORI. I HAVE TO MAKE THE GOAL NO MATTER WHAT.

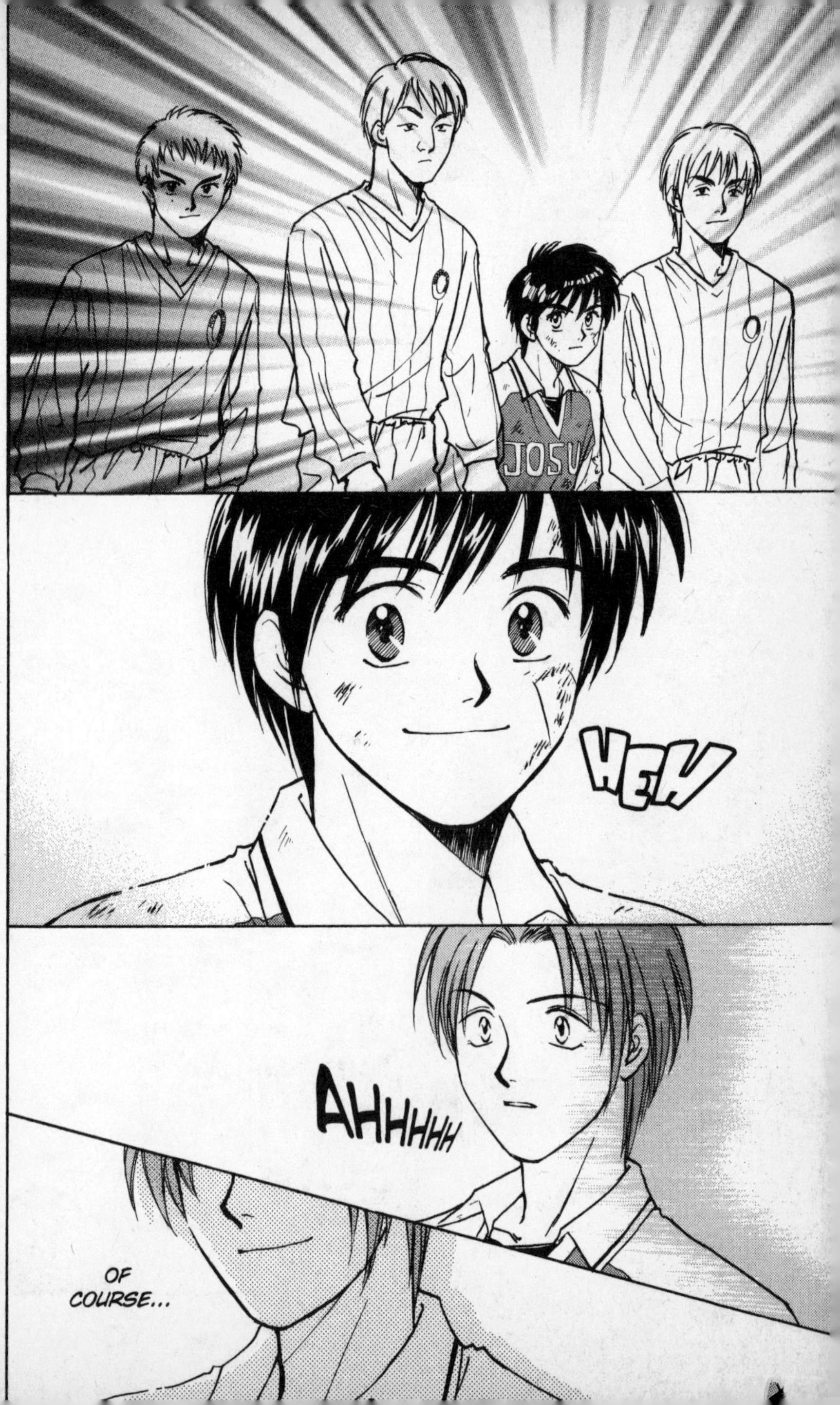
JOSU
HEH
AHHHHH
OF COURSE...

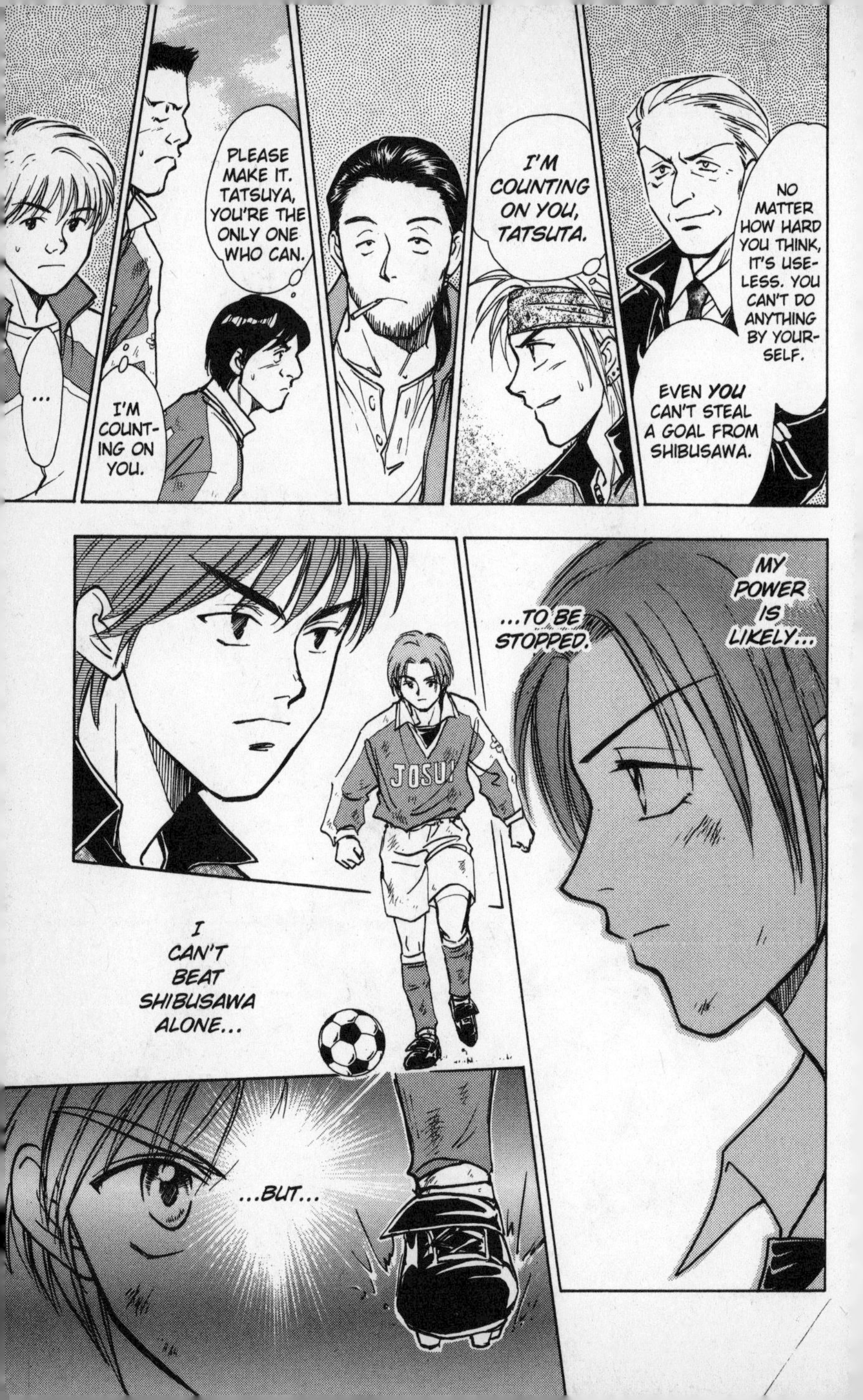
NO MATTER HOW HARD YOU THINK, IT'S USELESS. YOU CAN'T DO ANYTHING BY YOURSELF.
EVEN YOU CAN'T STEAL A GOAL FROM SHIBUSAWA.
I'M COUNTING ON YOU, TATSUTA.
PLEASE MAKE IT. TATSUYA, YOU'RE THE ONLY ONE WHO CAN.
I'M COUNTING ON YOU.
...
MY POWER IS LIKELY...
...TO BE STOPPED.
I CAN'T BEAT SHIBUSAWA ALONE...
...BUT...

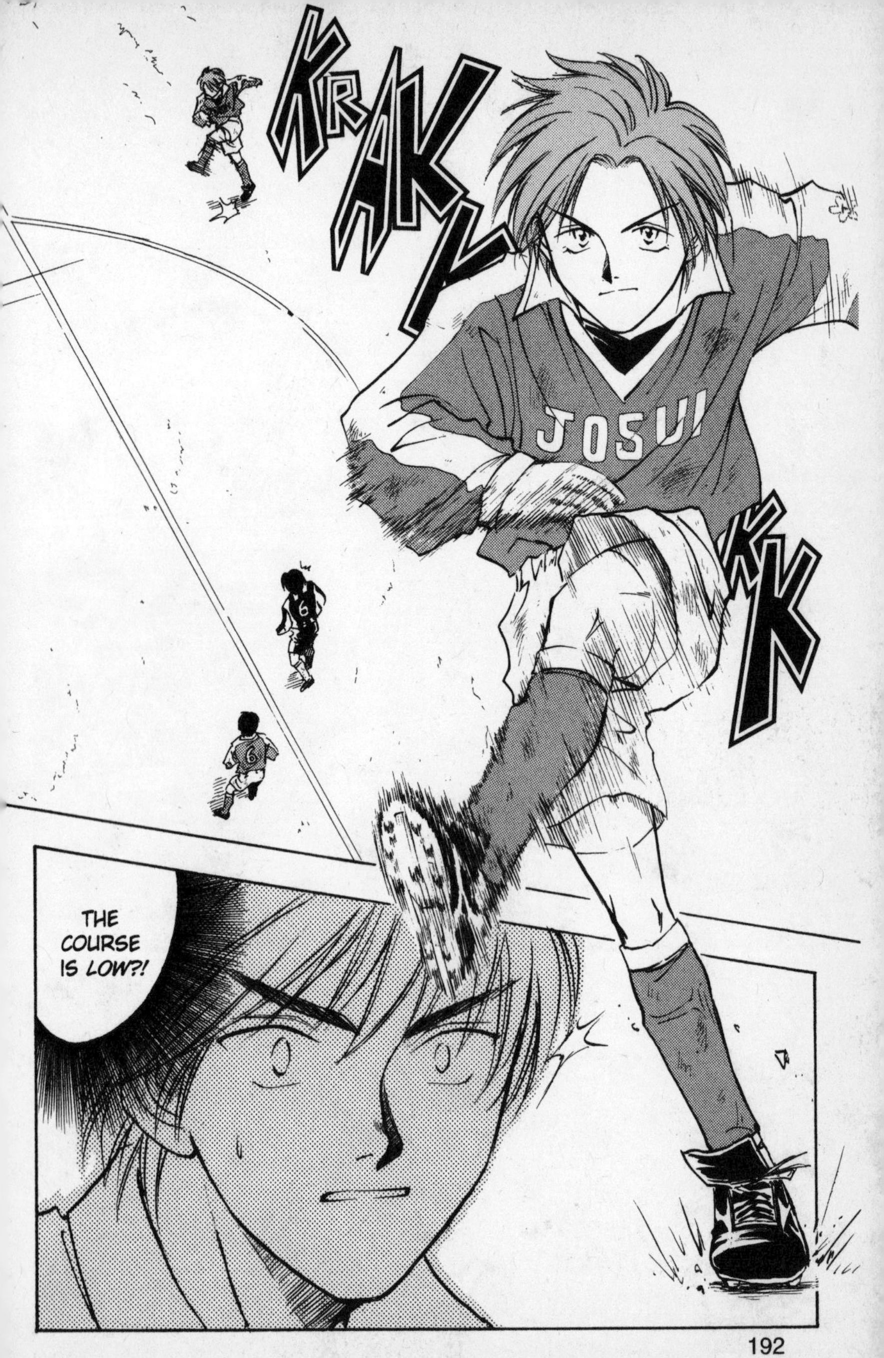
KRAAK
KK
THE COURSE IS LOW?!

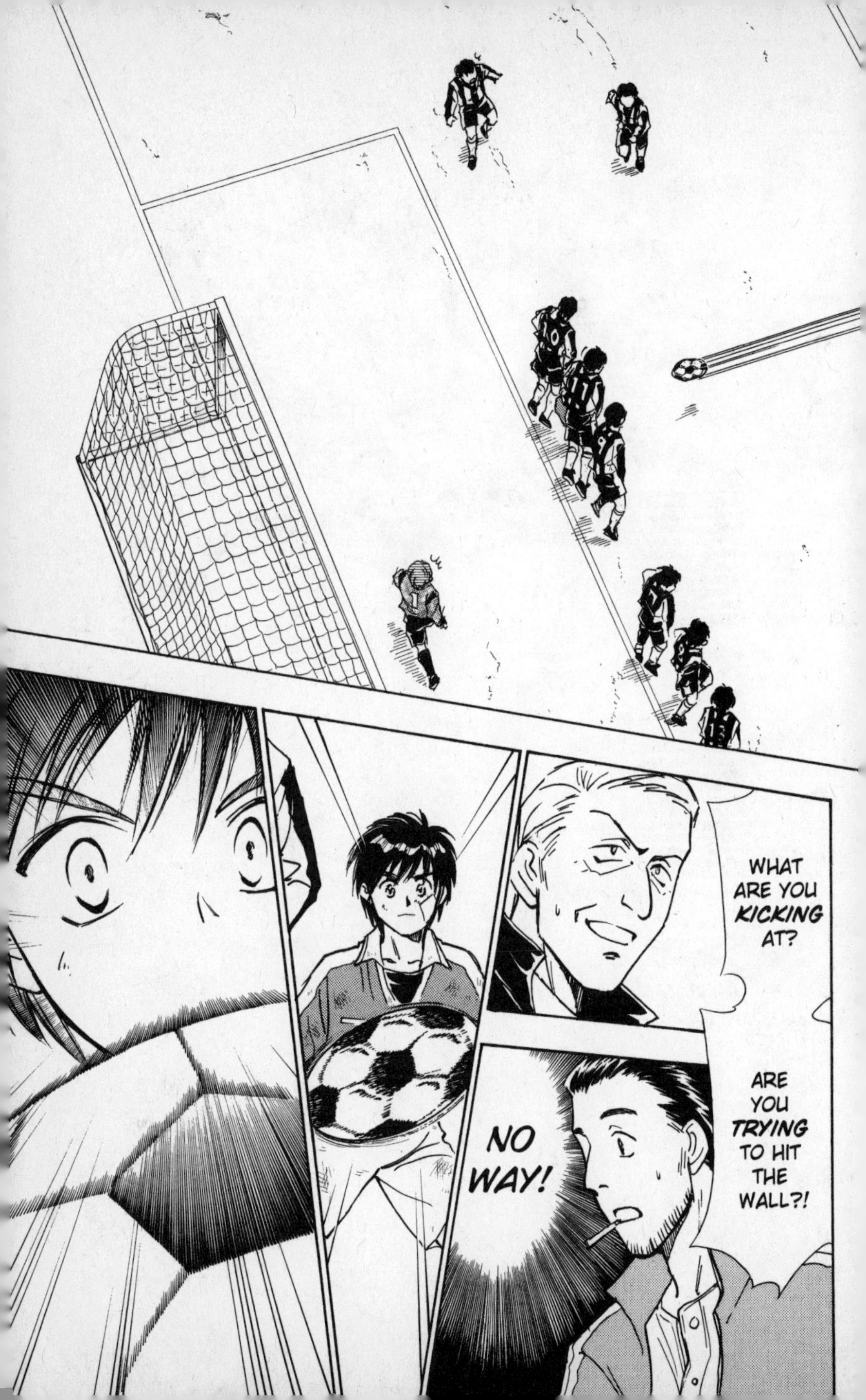
WHAT ARE YOU *KICKING* AT?
ARE YOU *TRYING* TO HIT THE WALL?!
NO WAY!

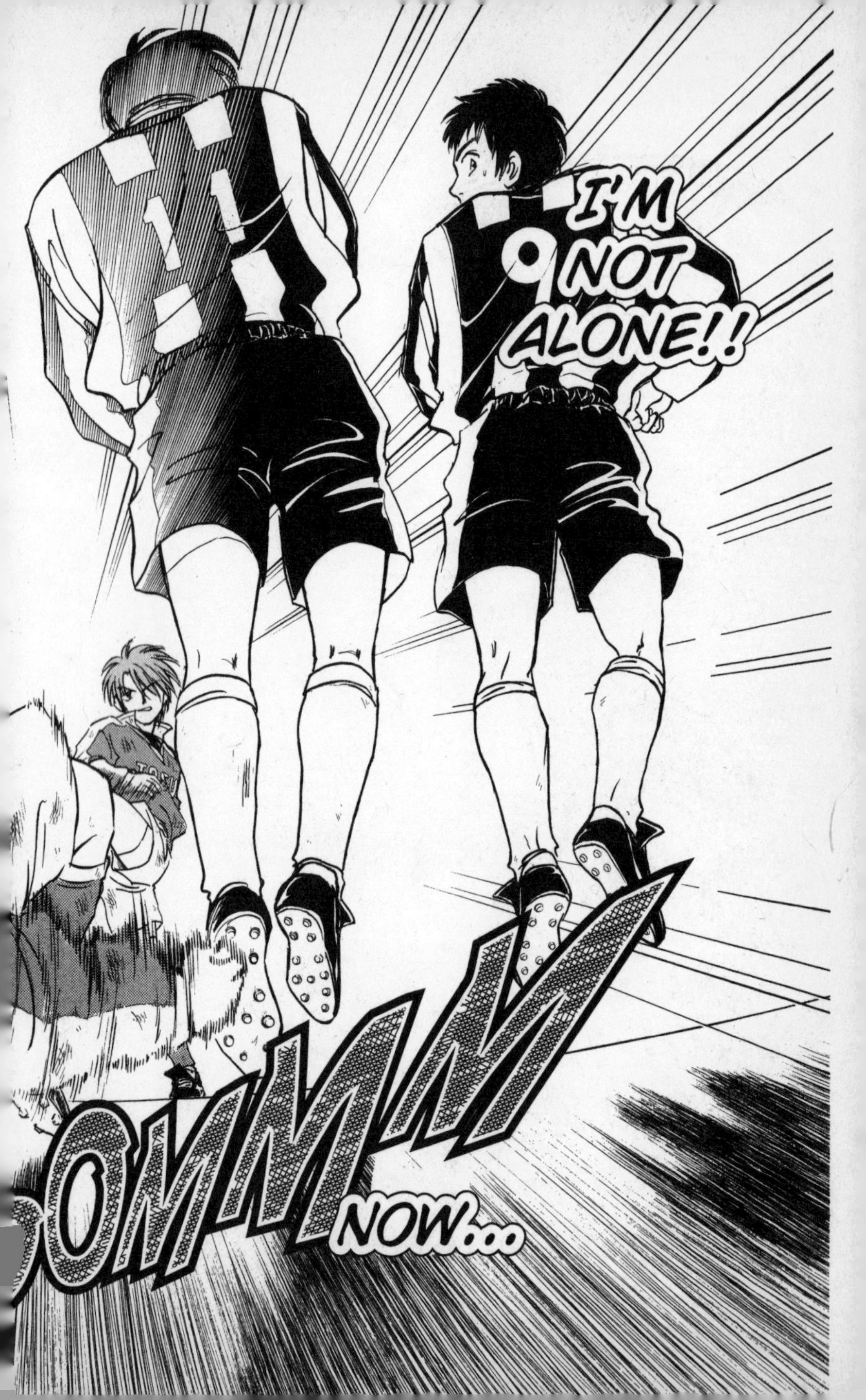
I'M NOT ALONE!!
OMMM
NOW...

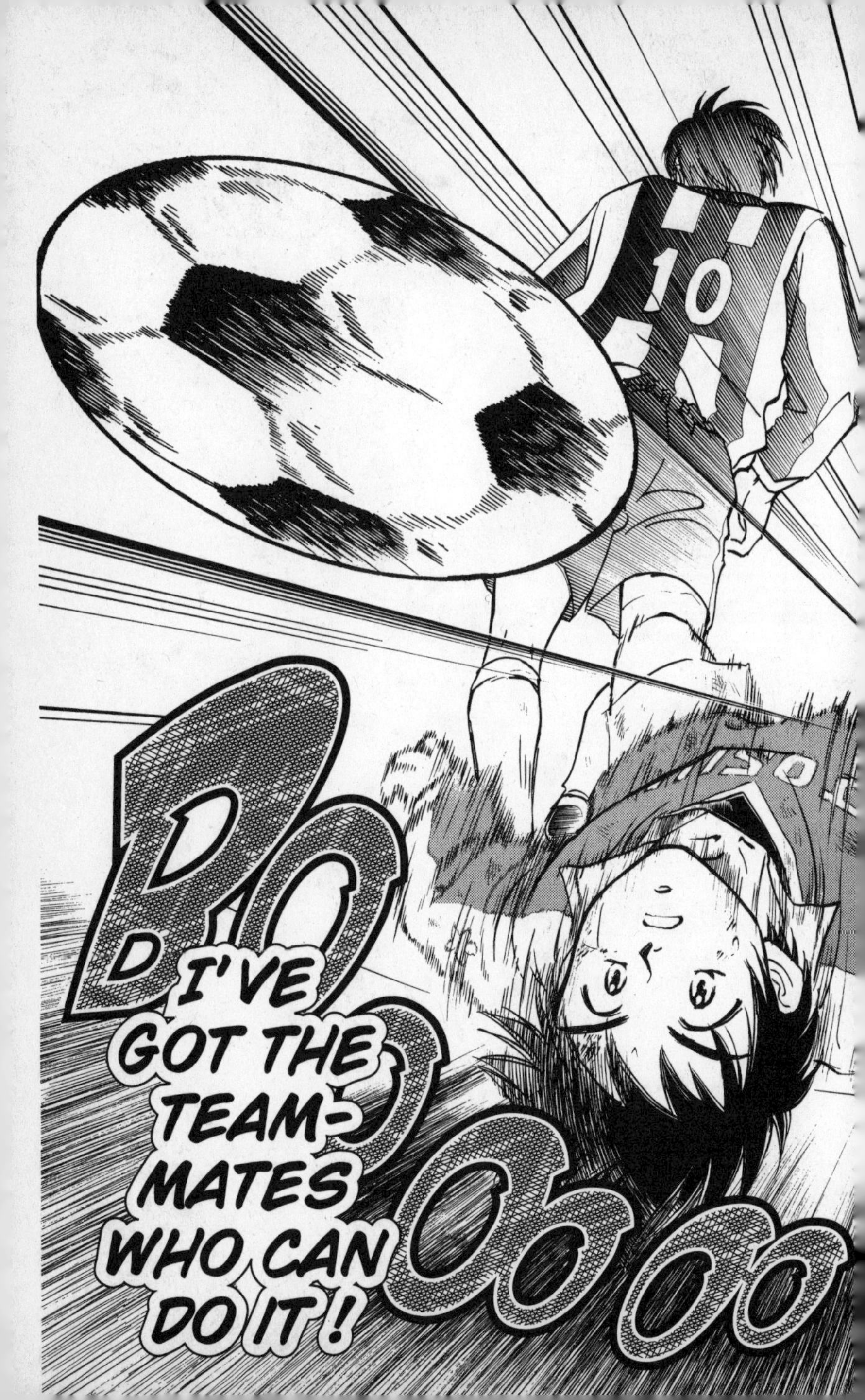
I'VE GOT THE TEAM-MATES WHO CAN DO IT!

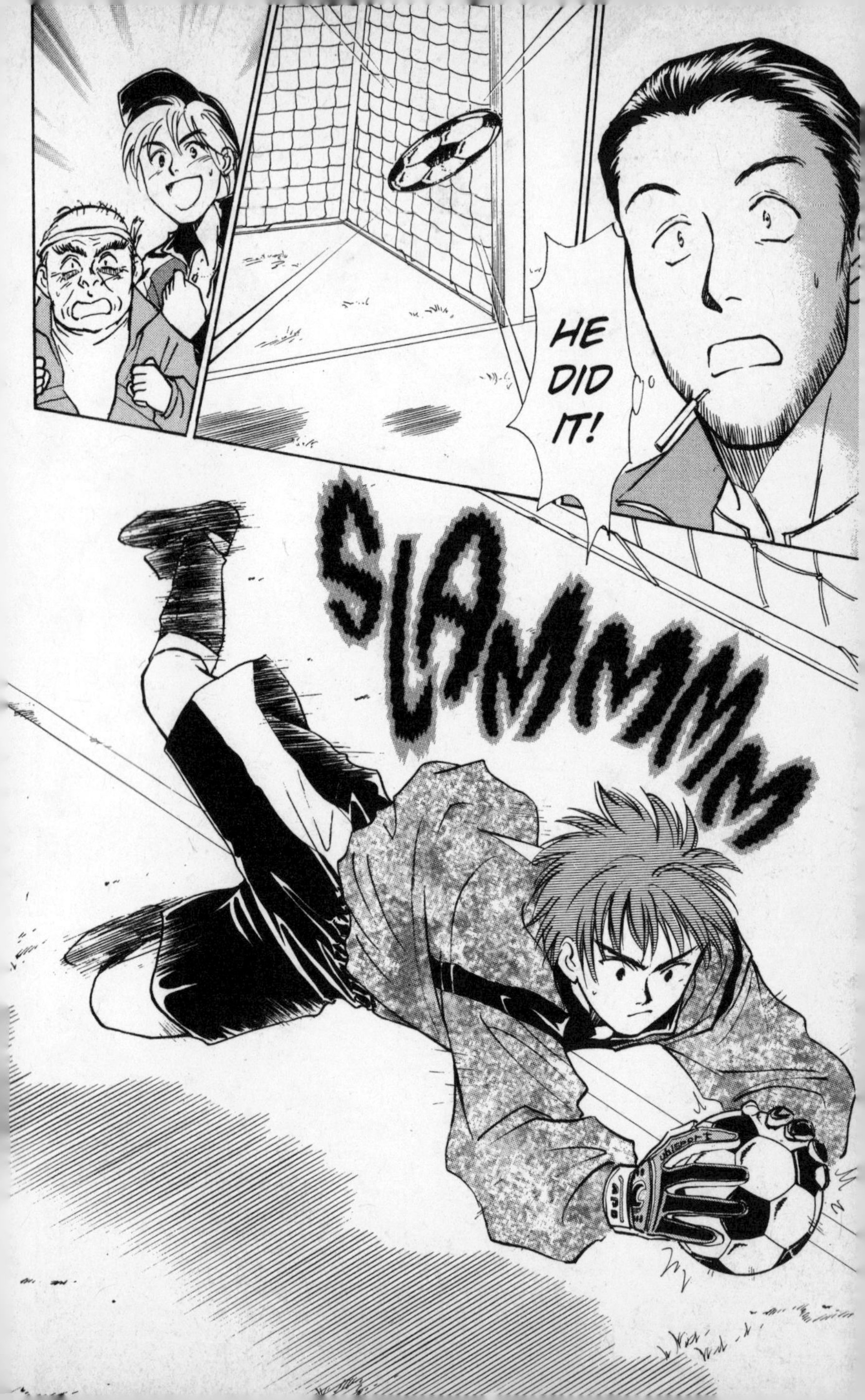
HE DID IT!
SLAMMM

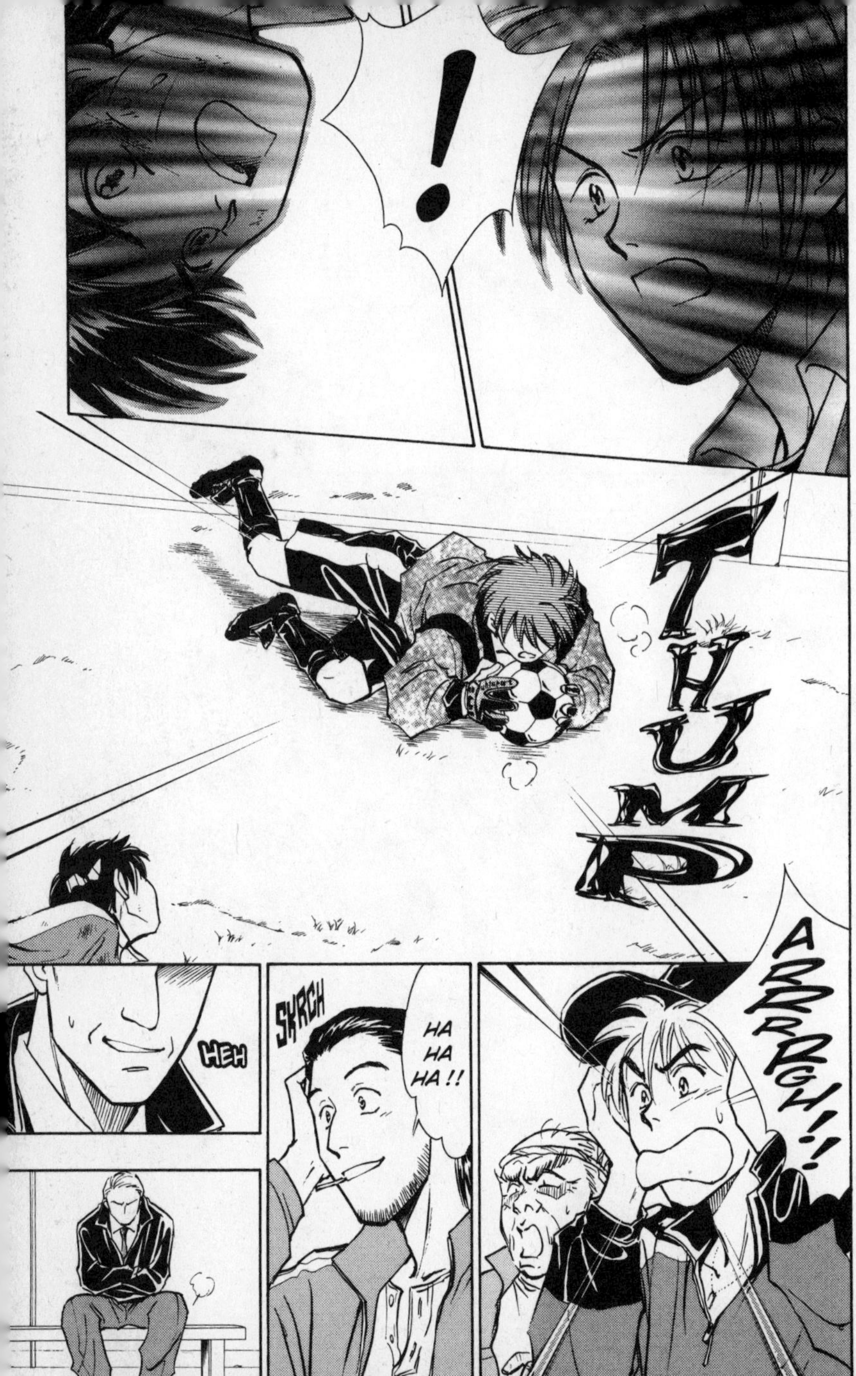
!
THUMP
ARRRRGH!!!
HA HA HA!!
SKRCH
HEH

FIC
HIG

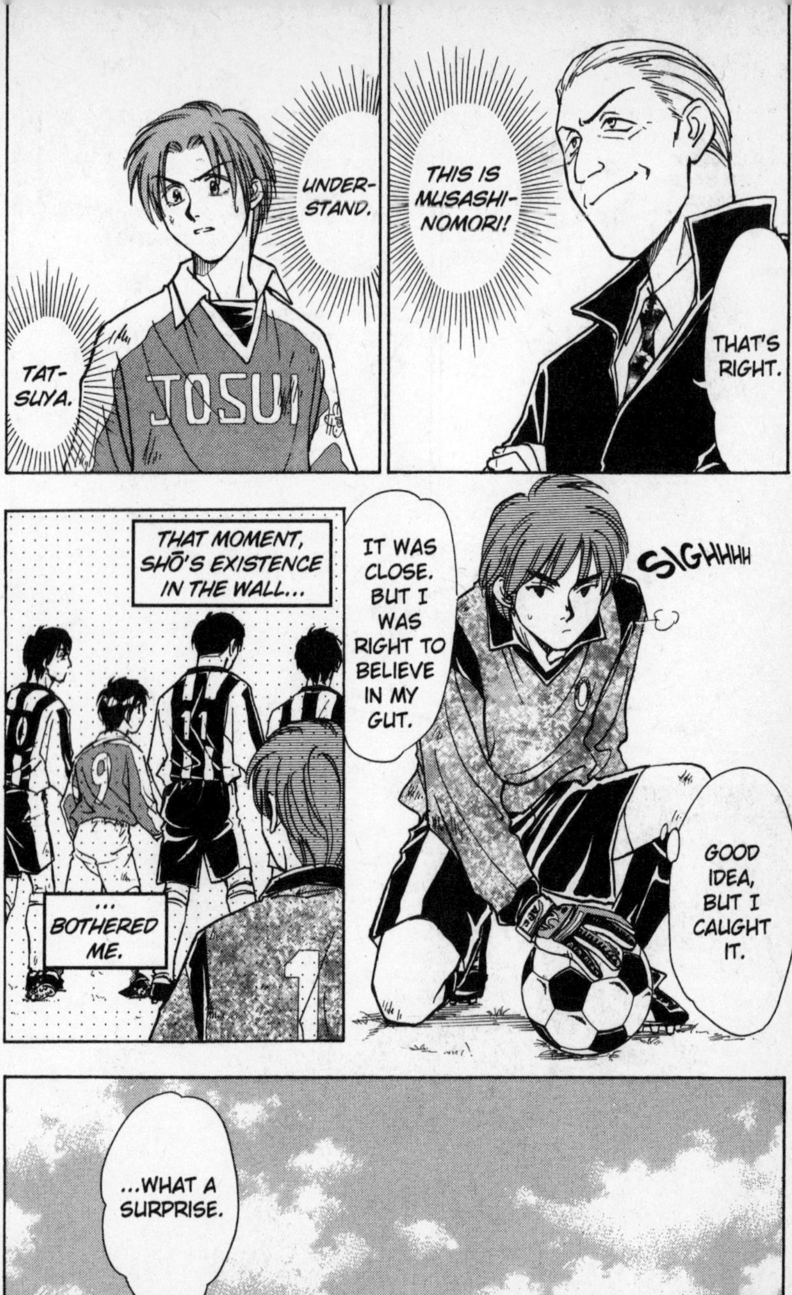
THIS IS MUSASHI-NOMORI!
THAT'S RIGHT.
UNDER-STAND.
TAT-SUYA.
IT WAS CLOSE. BUT I WAS RIGHT TO BELIEVE IN MY GUT.
SIGHHHH
GOOD IDEA, BUT I CAUGHT IT.
THAT MOMENT, SHŌ'S EXISTENCE IN THE WALL...
... BOTHERED ME.
...WHAT A SURPRISE.